DAVID LIVINGSTONE.

H. M. STANLEY.

The Life and African Explorations of Dr. David Livingstone

The Life and African Explorations of Dr. David Livingstone

Comprising All His Extensive Travels and Discoveries
As Detailed in
His Diary, Reports, and Letters
Including His Famous
Last Journals

WITH MAPS AND NUMEROUS ILLUSTRATIONS

Cooper Square Press

First Cooper Square Press edition 2002

This Cooper Square Press paperback edition of *The Life and African Explorations of David Livingstone* is an unabridged republication of the edition first published in St. Louis, Missouri, in 1874, with the addition of one textual emendation and the reduction of one photo map. The original edition was paginated incorrectly so that it appears that pages 451–52 are omitted.

Published by Cooper Square Press
A Member of the Rowman & Littlefield Publishing Group
200 Park Avenue South, Suite 1109
New York, New York 10003-1503
www.coopersquarepress.com

Distributed by National Book Network

Library of Congress Cataloging-in-Publication Data

Livingstone, David, 1813-1873.
    The life and African explorations of Dr. David Livingstone : comprising all his extensive travels and discoveries : as detailed in his diary, reports, and letters, including his famous last journals : with maps and numerous illustrations.—1st Cooper Square Press ed.
        p. cm.
Originally published: St. Louis : Valley Pub., 1874.
ISBN 0-8154-1208-8 (pbk. : alk. paper)
        1. Livingstone, David, 1813-1873. 2. Explorers—Africa, Southern—Biography. 3. Explorers—Africa, Central—Biography. 4. Explorers—Scotland—Biography. 5. Africa Southern—Discovery and exploration. 6. Africa, Central—Discovery and exploration. I. Title.

DT1110.L58 A3 2002
916.704'23'092—dc21
[B]   2002025657

PREFACE.

The recent success of the unique expedition of the New-York
" Herald " newspaper in search of Dr. Livingstone, the most distinguished of African missionaries, and modern travellers, has given
renewed interest to a continent which has been well described as
"the division of the world which is the most interesting, and about
which we know the least." To supply the popular demand for information in regard to Africa, the explorations of Dr. Livingstone,
the " Herald " expedition, and subjects most intimately connected
therewith, the following volume has been prepared. It will be seen
that Dr. Livingstone himself, and Mr. Stanley, the conductor of the
" Herald " expedition, have been largely quoted in the compila-
tion of the work. No one has written of Africa more intelligently,
graphically, or fully, than Dr. Livingstone, and none so recently
as Mr. Stanley. They are, of course, the principal authorities for
this volume, as they are the best that can be had, but the researches of others have been used whenever necessary to add interest to the subject, and to make this book as nearly a complete
account of all that is now known of Africa as possible. As such,
it is now given to the public in the confident belief that it will
supply a want generally felt, and which has often been expressed
by the journals of our own and other countries, and other recognized representatives of public opinion.

No book of travels is more interesting than the great work of
Dr. Livingstone, and none, we think, which contains so much
information valuable to the reading world. There we have a narrative in which are finely blended accounts of missionary labors,
scientific researches, explorations among strange people, wonderful
animals, a country to which attaches the deepest interest; and all
told in the most attractive manner. In Mr. Stanley's dispatches,

letters, and more formal narrations, we have among the best examples of the astonishing development and enterprise of the modern press, as aided by the magnetic telegraph. Much that is most excellent in what these men have said of Africa on the spot will be found, and in their own language, in this volume. Thus it may be seen how ancient and modern customs and habits, and a continent of the old and the new world clasp hands across the gulf of time and space, through the marvelous means of the lightning and the press.

Whilst no pains and research have been spared in the preparation of the book, it has been entrusted to one familiar with the subject and able to place before the public in the least practicable space, all that is most valuable and interesting connected therewith. It is confidently believed, therefore, that no book of so much interesting matter, at so cheap a price as this has been published. The greatest pains have been taken also in its mechanical execution. We feel justified, therefore, in commending it to the public as a complete hand-book of information in regard to one of the most interesting topics to which mankind are now giving attention, and religion, literature, and science their best labors and studies.

ILLUSTRATIONS.

CONTENTS.

CHAPTER I.

INTRODUCTORY.

CHAPTER II.

BIOGRAPHICAL SKETCH OF LIVINGSTONE.

CHAPTER III.

MISSIONARY LIFE IN SOUTHERN AFRICA.

CONTENTS.

CHAPTER IV.

LIVINGSTONE'S FIRST AND SECOND JOURNEYS INTO THE INTERIOR.

CHAPTER V.

FROM CAPE TOWN TO LOANDA.

CHAPTER VI.

ACROSS THE CONTINENT.

CHAPTER VII.

DR. LIVINGSTONE IN ENGLAND.

CONTENTS.

CHAPTER VIII.

LIVINGSTONE'S SECOND (AND PRESENT) EXPEDITION TO AFRICA.

CHAPTER IX.

THE HERALD EXPEDITION OF SEARCH.

CHAPTER X.

HENRY M. STANLEY.

CHAPTER XI.

MR. STANLEY IN AFRICA.

CONTENTS.

CHAPTER XII.

THE MEETING OF LIVINGSTONE AND STANLEY.

CHAPTER XIII.

LIVINGSTONE AND STANLEY IN AFRICA.

CHAPTER XIV.

LIVINGSTONE AND STANLEY IN AFRICA.

[CONTINUED.]

CHAPTER XV.

DR. LIVINGSTONE STILL IN AFRICA.

CONTENTS.

CHAPTER XVI.

INTELLIGENCE OF THE SUCCESS OF THE HERALD ENTERPRISE.

CHAPTER XVII.

MR. STANLEY'S RECEPTION IN EUROPE.

CHAPTER XVIII.

THE SLAVE TRADE OF EAST AFRICA.

CHAPTER XIX.

THE ANIMAL KINGDOM OF AFRICA.

CONTENTS.

CHAPTER XX.

AFRICAN TREES AND VEGETATION.

CHAPTER XXI.
THE DESERT OF SAHARA.

CHAPTER XXII.
GEOLOGY OF AFRICA—ANTIQUITY OF MAN.

CHAPTER XXIII.
THE RESULTS OF THE EXPLORATIONS IN AFRICA.

CONTENTS.

CHAPTER XXIV.

THE LAST JOURNEY, AND THE DEATH OF DR. LIVINGSTONE.

CHAPTER XXV.

THE CORPSE BORNE TO ENGLAND AND LAID IN WESTMINSTER ABBEY.

CHAPTER XXVI.

CHAPTER XXVII.

LIVINGSTONE'S LAST JOURNAL.

CHAPTER XXVIII.

RESTING AT UNYANYEMBE.

CONTENTS.

CHAPTER XXIX.
THE START FROM UNYANYEMBE.

A PARTY OF BAGANDA—BOYS' PLAYTHINGS IN AFRICA—REFLEC-
TIONS—ARRIVAL OF THE MEN—FERVENT THANKFULNESS—AN
END OF THE WEARY WAITING—JACOB WAINWRIGHT TAKES SER-
VICE UNDER THE DOCTOR—PREPARATIONS FOR THE JOURNEY—
FLAGGING AND ILLNESS—GREAT HEAT—APPROACHES LAKE TAN-
GANYIKA—THE BORDERS OF FIPA—CAPES AND ISLANDS OF
LAKE TANGANYIKA—MOUNTAIN CLIMBING—LARGE BAY...........

CHAPTER XXX.
THE MARCH TOWARDS BANGWEOLO.

FALSE GUIDES—DIFFICULT TRAVELING—HE LEAVES THE LAKE—
THE KASONSO FAMILY—A HOSPITABLE CHIEF—THE RIVER LOFU
—FAMINE—ILL—ARRIVES AT CHAMA'S TOWN—A DIFFICULTY—
AN IMMENSE SNAKE—ACCOUNT OF CASEMBE'S DEATH—CHUNGU
—REACHES THE RIVER LOPOPSI—MISLED AND BAFFLED—AR-
RIVES AT CHITUNKUE'S—TERRIBLE MARCHING—THE DOCTOR IS
BORNE THROUGH THE FLOODED COUNTRY..........................

CHAPTER XXXI.
COASTING ALONG LAKE BANGWEOLO.

GREAT PRIVATIONS—RETURNS TO CHITUNKUE'S—AGREEABLY SUR-
PRISED WITH THE CHIEF—DIFFICULT MARCH—FRESH ATTACK
OF ILLNESS—SENDS SCOUTS OUT TO FIND VILLAGES—AWAITS
NEWS FROM MATIPA—DISTRESSING PERPLEXITY—THE BOUGAS
OF BANGWEOLO—SUSI AND CHUMA SENT TO MATIPA—THE DON-
KEY SUFFERS—TRIES TO GO ON TO KABINGA'S—MAKES A DEM-
ONSTRATION—EXTRAORDINARY EXTENT OF FLOOD—REACHES
KABINGA'S—AN UPSET—CROSSES THE CHAMBEZE—THEY SEPA-
RATE INTO COMPANIES BY LAND AND WATER—DANGEROUS
STATE OF DR. LIVINGSTONE..

CHAPTER XXXII.
LAST ILLNESS AND DEATH OF DR. LIVINGSTONE.

DR. LIVINGSTONE RAPIDLY SINKING—LAST ENTRIES IN HIS DIARY
—GREAT AGONY—CARRIED ACROSS RIVERS AND THROUGH
FLOOD—KALUNGANJOVU'S KINDNESS—ARRIVES AT CHITAMBO'S,
IN GREAT PAIN—THE LAST NIGHT—LIVINGSTONE EXPIRES IN
THE ACT OF PRAYING—COUNCIL OF THE MEN—THE CHIEF
DISCOVERS THAT HIS GUEST IS DEAD—NOBLE CONDUCT OF CHI-
TAMBO—THE PREPARATION OF THE CORPSE—HONOR SHOWN TO
DR. LIVINGSTONE—INTERMENT OF THE HEART AT CHITAMBO'S
—AN INSCRIPTION AND MEMORIAL SIGN—POSTS LEFT TO DE-
NOTE THE SPOT ....

CONTENTS.

CHAPTER XXXIII.
THE BODY BROUGHT HOME.

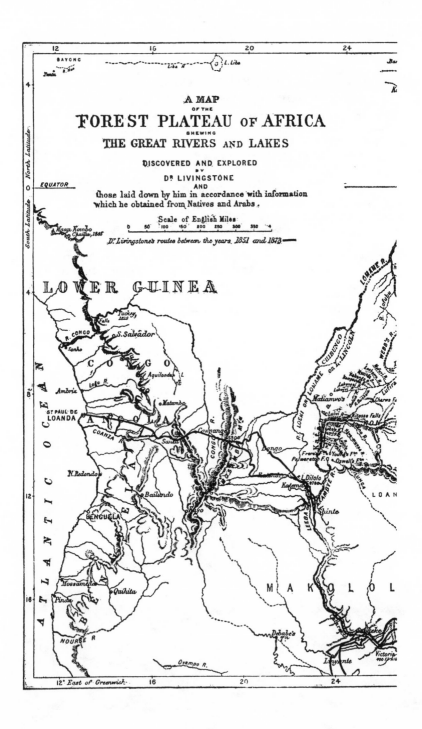

A MAP
OF THE
FOREST PLATEAU OF AFRICA
SHEWING
THE GREAT RIVERS AND LAKES

DISCOVERED AND EXPLORED
BY
DR LIVINGSTONE
AND
those laid down by him in accordance with information
which he obtained from Natives and Arabs.

Scale of English Miles

Dr Livingstone's routes between the years 1851 and 1873

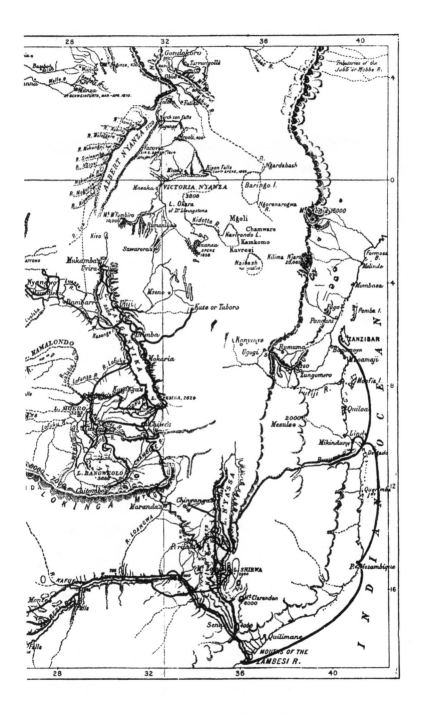

EXPLORATIONS IN AFRICA,

BY

LIVINGSTONE, STANLEY,

AND OTHERS.

————◆————

CHAPTER I.

INTRODUCTORY.

A Brief Account of Africa—Its Ancient Civilization—Little Information extant in Relation to Large Portions of the Continent—The Great field of Scientific Explorations and Missionary Labor—Account of a Number of Exploring Expeditions, Including those of Mungo Park, Denham and Clapperton, and others—Their Practical Results—Desire of Further Information Increased— Recent Explorations, Notably those of Dr. Livingstone and Mr. Stanley, Representing the New York "Herald" Newspaper.

A work of standard authority among scholars says that "Africa is the division of the world which is the most interesting, and about which we know the least." Its very name is a mystery; no one can more than approximately calculate its vast extent; even those who have studied the problem the most carefully widely disagree among themselves as to the number of its population, some placing it as low as 60,000,000, others, much in excess of 100,000,000 souls; its superficial configuration in many portions is only guessed at; the sources of its mightiest river are unknown. The heats, deserts, wild beasts, venomous reptiles and savage tribes of this great continent have raised the only barrier against the spirit of discovery and progress, elsewhere irrepressible, of the age, and no small proportion of Africa is to-day as much a *terra incognita* as when the father of history wrote. Many of its inhabitants are among the most barbarous and depraved of all the people of the world, but in ancient times some of its races were the leaders of all men in civilization and were unquestionably possessed of mechanical arts and processes which have long been lost in the lapse of ages. They had vast cities, great and elaborate works of art, and were the most successful of agriculturists. Noted for their skill in the management of the practical affairs of life, they also paid profound attention to the most abstruse questions of religion; and it was a people of Africa, the Egyptians, who first announced belief in the resurrection of the body and the immortality of the soul. Large numbers of mummies, still existing, ages older than the Christian era, attest the earnestness of the ancient faith in dogmas which form an essential part of the creed of nearly every Christian sect. The most magnificent of women in the arts of coquetry and voluptuous love belonged to this continent of which so much still sits in darkness. The art of war was here cultivated to the greatest perfection ; and it was before the army of an African general that the Roman legions went down at Cannæ, and by whom the Empire came near being completely ruined. Indeed,

It may with much show of argument be claimed that the continent over so much of which ignorance and superstition and beasts of prey now hold thorough sway, was originally the cradle of art, and civilization, and human progress.

But if the northern portion of the continent of Africa was in the remote past the abode of learning and of the useful arts, it is certain that during recent periods other portions of the continent, separated from this by a vast expanse of desert waste, have supplied the world with the most lamentable examples of human misery and the most hideous instances of crime. Nor did cupidity and rapacity confine themselves in the long years of African spoliation to ordinary robbers and buccaneers. Christian nations took part in the horrid work; and we have the authority of accredited history for the statement that Elizabeth of England was a smuggler and a slave-trader. Thus Africa presents the interesting anomaly of having been the home of ancient civilization, and the prey of the modern rapacity and plunder of all nations. It is natural, therefore, that in regard to the plundered portions of this devoted continent, the world at large should know but little. It is also natural that with the advancement of the cause of scientific knowledge, humanity, genuine Christianity, and the rage for discovery, this vast territory should receive the attention of good and studious men and moral nationalities. Accordingly we find that during a comparatively recent period Africa has become a great field of scientific explorations and missionary labor, as well as of colonization.

The first people to give special and continued attention to discoveries in Africa, were the Portuguese
During the fifteenth century, noted for the great advance made in geographical discoveries, the kingdom
of Portugal was, perhaps, the greatest maritime power
of christendom. Her sovereigns greatly encouraged
and many of their most illustrious subjects practically engaged in voyages of discovery. They were preëminently successful both in the eastern and western
hemisphere, and one of the results of their daring
enterprise is the remarkable fact that Portuguese colonies are much more powerful and wealthy to-day
than the parent kingdom.

" The Child is father of the Man."

The Portuguese sent many exploring expeditions
along the coast of Africa, and in the course of a century they had circumnavigated the continent and
planted colonies all along the shores of the Atlantic
and the Indian oceans. Bartholmew Dias having
discovered the Cape of Good Hope, the reigning
sovereign of Portugal determined to prosecute the
explorations still further, with the object of discovering a passage to India. This discovery was made by
the intrepid and illustrious mariner, Vasco de Gama,
November 20, 1497, a little more than five years after
the discovery of America. He pursued his voyage
along the eastern coast of Africa, discovering Natal,
Mozambique, a number of islands, and finding people
in a high stage of commercial advancement, with
well-built cities, ports, mosques for the worship of
Allah according to the Mohammedan faith, and carrying on a considerable trade with India and the Spice

Islands. Of this trade, Portugal long retained supremacy. Other European powers also meantime established colonies at different places on the African coast, so that in the sixteenth century a considerable portion of the outer shell, so to say, had been examined. The vast interior, however, long remained unexplored, and much of it remains an utterly unknown primeval wilderness to this day. The settlements and colonies of the Portuguese, French, Dutch, and English were for commercial purposes only, and added very little to the general stock of information.

It was not until a year after the adoption of the Constitution of the United States that any organized effort in behalf of discoveries in Africa was made. In the city of London a Society for the Exploration of Interior Africa was formed in 1788, but it was not until seven years afterwards, that the celebrated Mungo Park undertook his first expedition. Thus it was more than three hundred years from the discovery of the Cape of Good Hope before even a ray of light began to penetrate the darkness of benighted Africa. Meantime, great empires had been overthrown and others established in their place and beneficent governments founded on both continents of the western world.

The life and adventures of Mungo Park form a story of exceeding interest, between which and the life and adventures of Dr. Livingstone there are not a few points of remarkable coincidence. Park was a native of Scotland, and one of many children. He was educated also in the medical profession. Moreover, while he was making his first tour of discovery

in Africa, having long been absent from home, reports
of his death reached England and were universally
credited.   His arrival at Falmouth in December
1797, caused a most agreeable surprise throughout
the kingdom.   An account of his travels abounding
with thrilling incidents, including accounts of great
suffering from sickness and cruelty at the hands of
Mohammedan Africans on the Niger, was extensively circulated.   Many portions of this narrative were
in about all the American school books during the
first half of the nineteenth century, and the name of
Mungo Park became as familiar as household words in
the United States.   In 1805, Park undertook another
tour of discovery, which he prosecuted for some time
with indomitable courage and against difficulties before
which an ordinary mind would have succumbed.   He
navigated the Niger for a long distance, passing Jen-
nee, Timbuctoo, and Yaoori, but was soon after attacked in a narrow channel, and, undertaking to escape
by swimming, was drowned.   His few remaining white
companions perished with him.

The discoveries of this celebrated man were in that
part of Africa which lies between the equator and
the 20th degree of north latitude.   They added much
to the knowledge of that portion of the country, and
keenly whetted the desire of further information.
Several journeys and voyages up rivers followed, but
without notable result till the English expedition
under Denham and Clapperton in 1822.   This expedition started with a caravan of merchants from
Tripoli on the Mediterranean, and after traversing
the great desert, reached Lake Tsad in interior Africa.

Denham explored the lake and its shores, while Lieut. Clapperton pursued his journey westward as far as Sakatu, which is not greatly distant from the Niger. He retraced his steps, and having visited England, began a second African tour, starting from near Cape Coast Castle on the Gulf of Guinea. Traveling in a northeastern direction, he struck the Niger at Boussa, and going by way of Kano, a place of considerable commercial importance, again arrived at Sakatu, where he shortly afterwards died. He was the first man who had traversed Africa from the Mediterranean sea to the Gulf of Guinea. Richard Lander, a servant of Lieut. Clapperton, afterwards discovered the course of the Niger from Boussa to the gulf, finding it identical with the river Nun of the seacoast.

Other tours of discovery into Africa have been made to which it is not necessary here to refer. The practical result of all these expeditions, up to about the middle of the ninetenth century, was a rough outline of information in regard to the coast countries of Africa, the course of the Niger, the manners and customs of the tribes of Southern Africa, and a little more definite knowledge concerning Northern and Central Africa, embracing herein the great desert, Lake Tsad, the river Niger, and the people between the desert and the Gulf of Guinea. Perhaps the most comprehensive statement of the effect of this information upon Christian peoples was that it seemed to conclusively demonstrate an imperative demand for missionary labors. Even the Mohammedans of the Moorish Kingdom of Ludamar, set loose a wild boar upon Mungo Park. They were astonished that the wild beast assailed the Moslems instead of the Christian, and afterwards shut the two together in a hut, while King and council debated whether the white man should lose his right arm, his eyes, or his life. During the debate, the traveler escaped. If the Mohammedan Africans were found to be thus cruel, it may well be inferred that those of poorer faith were no less bloodthirsty. And thus, as one of the results of the expeditions to which we have referred, a renewed zeal in proselytism and discovery was developed.

Thus, the two most distinguished African travellers, and who have published the most varied, extensive, and valuable information in regard to that continent, performed the labors of their first expeditions cotemporaneously, the one starting from the north of Africa, the other from the south. I can but refer to the distinguished Dr. Heinreich Barth, and him who is largely the subject of this volume, Dr. David Livingstone. The expeditions were not connected the one with the other, but had this in common that both were begun under the auspices of the British government and people. A full narrative of Dr. Barth's travels and discoveries has been published, from which satisfactory information in regard to much of northern and central Africa may be obtained. The narrative is highly interesting and at once of great popular and scientific value. Hence the world has learned the geography of a wide expanse of country round about Lake Tsad in all directions; far toward Abyssinia northeasterly, as far west by north as Timbuctoo, several hundred miles southeasterly, and as

far toward the southwest, along the River Benue, as
the junction of the Faro. Dr. Barth remained in
Africa six years, much of the time without a single
white associate, his companions in the expedition
having all died. Dr. Overweg, who was the first
European to navigate Lake Tsad, died in September,
1852. Mr. Richardson, the official chief of the expedition, had died in March of the previous year.

But unquestionably the most popular of African
explorers is Dr. Livingstone, an account of whose
first expedition—1849–52—has been read by a great
majority of intelligent persons speaking the English
language. Large and numerous editions were speedily demanded, and Africa again became an almost
universal topic of discourse. Indeed, intelligence of
Dr. Livingstone's return after so many years of toil
and danger, was rapidly spread among the nations,
accompanied by brief reports of his explorations, and
these prepared the way for the reception of the
Doctor's great work by vast numbers of people.
Every one was ready and anxious to carry the war of
his reading into Africa. And afterwards, when Dr.
Livingstone returned to Africa, and having prosecuted
his explorations for a considerable period reports
came of his death at the hands of cruel and treacherous natives, interest in exact knowledge of his fate
became intense and appeared only to increase upon
the receipt of reports contradicting the first, and then
again of rumors which appeared to substantiate those
which had been first received. In consequence of the
conflicting statements which, on account of the universal interest in the subject, were published in the

public press throughout the world, the whole Christian church, men of letters and science became fairly agitated. The sensation was profound, and, based upon admiration of a man of piety, sublime courage, and the most touching self-denial in a great cause to which he had devoted all his bodily and intellectual powers, it was reasonable and philosophical.

It is not surprising, therefore, that the English government should have fitted out an expedition in search of Livingstone. Accordingly, the Livingstone Search Expedition, as it is called, was organized early in the winter of 1871–72, and under command of Lieut. Dawson, embarked on its destination, on the 9th of February of the last year. The expedition reached Zanzibar April 19, and the members were most kindly received by the Sultan, Sayid Bergash, and greatly assisted by his Grand Vizier, Sayid Suliman. A company of six Nasik youths, originally slaves in a part of Africa through which the Search Expedition would pass, were being drilled for the purpose, and were expected to be of great assistance.

But before intelligence of the Livingstone Search Expedition at Zanzibar awaiting favorable weather, had arrived, the world was startled by the news that a private expedition, provided solely by the New York "Herald" newspaper, and in charge of Mr. Henry M. Stanley, had succeeded, after surmounting incredible difficulties, in reaching Ujiji, where a meeting of the most remarkable nature took place between the great explorer and the representative of the enterprising journal of New York. Unique in its origin, most remarkable in the accomplishment of its beneficent purpose, this Herald-Livingstone expedition has received the considerate approval of mankind, and Mr. Stanley has become with justice regarded as a practical hero of a valuable kind. His accounts of his travel, his dispatches to the "Herald" from time to time, the more formal narratives furnished by him, compose a story of the deepest interest and, when properly considered, of the greatest value. It is to preserve this story in permanent form—and wherever possible in the language of Mr. Stanley himself —connecting with it such portions of Dr. Livingstone's life and explorations, such accounts of discoveries and affairs in Africa generally, and such mention of the newspaper enterprise itself as may serve to make a volume of interesting and useful information upon a subject of confessedly universal interest among Christian people, that this work has been undertaken.

CHAPTER II.

BIOGRAPHICAL SKETCH OF LIVINGSTONE.

His Birth and Parentage—Hard Work and Hard Study—The Factory Boy Becomes a Physician—The Opium War in China Causes Him to Sail for Africa.

David Livingstone, whose name has become so distinguished on account of discoveries in southern and central Africa, is a native of Scotland. In the introductory chapter to his interesting " Missionary Travels and Researches in South Africa," Dr. Livingstone makes passing mention of a few of his ancestors, showing that he came of good honest stock. " Our great-grandfather," he says, " fell at the battle of Culloden, fighting for the old line of kings; and our grandfather was a small farmer in Ulva, where my father was born. It is one of that cluster of the Hebrides thus alluded to by Walter Scott :

> ' And Ulva dark and Colonsay,
> And all the group of Islands gay
> That guard famed Staffa round !'

" Our grandfather was intimately acquainted with all the traditionary legends which that great writer has since made use of in the ' Tales of a Grandfather ' and other works. As a boy I remember listening to him with delight, for his memory was stored with a never-ending stock of stories, many of which were wonderfully like those I have since heard while sit-

ting by the African evening fires." Finding the resources of his farm unable to support a large family,
the grandfather transferred the scene of his story-tel-
ling and industry to Blantyre Works, a large cotton
manufactory on the Clyde not far from the City of
Glasgow. In these extensive works he and his sons
were honorably employed by the proprietors. It
would be difficult to speak of Dr. Livingstone's father
and mother and of his early life in more appropriate
words than he has himself used. He says :

" Our uncles all entered his majesty's service during the last French war, either as soldiers or sailors ;
but my father remained at home, and, though too
conscientious ever to become rich as a small tea-deal-
er, by his kindliness of manner and winning ways
he made the heart-strings of his children twine around
him as firmly as if he had possessed, and could have
bestowed upon them, every worldly advantage. He
reared his children in connection with the Kirk of
Scotland,—a religious establishment which has been
an incalculable blessing to that country ; but he afterward left it, and during the last twenty years of his
life held the office of deacon of an independent church
in Hamilton, and deserved my lasting gratitude and
homage for presenting me, from my infancy, with a
continuously consistent pious example, such as that
the ideal of which is so beautifully and truthfully
portrayed in Burns's ' Cotter's Saturday Night.' He
died in February, 1856, in peaceful hope of that
mercy which we all expect through the death of our
Lord and Saviour. I was at the time on my way
below the Zumbo, expecting no greater pleasure in

this country than sitting by our cottage-fire and telling him my travels. I revere his memory.

"The earliest recollection of my mother recalls a
picture so often seen among the Scottish poor—that
of the anxious housewife striving to make both ends
meet. At the age of ten I was put into the factory
as a 'piecer,' to aid by my earnings in lessening her
anxiety. With a part of my first week's wages I
purchased Ruddiman's 'Rudiments of Latin,' and
pursued the study of that language for many years
afterward, with unabated ardor, at an evening school,
which met between the hours of eight and ten. The
dictionary part of my labors was followed up till
twelve o'clock, or later, if my mother did not interfere by jumping up and snatching the books out of
my hands. I had to be back in the factory by six in
the morning, and continue my work, with intervals
for breakfast and dinner, till eight o'clock at night. I
read in this way many of the classical authors, and
knew Virgil and Horace better at sixteen than I do
now. Our schoolmaster—happily still alive—was
supported in part by the company ; he was attentive
and kind, and so moderate in his charges that all who
wished for education might have obtained it. Many
availed themselves of the privilege ; and some of my
schoolfellows now rank in position far above what
they appeared ever likely to come to when in the
village school. If such a system were established in
England, it would prove a never-ending blessing to
the poor."

In this happily-described scene of his boyhood,
David Livingstone had been born in 1815. He be-

gan this occupation of a " piecer " in the cotton works
at the age of ten years. It will be seen from the
foregoing quotations that, what with " piecing," reading, and studying, the ambitious lad did not leave
many hours to sleep. He says he read everything
that he could lay his hands on except novels, scientific
works and books of travels being, however, his special
delight. It appears that his father was of opinion
that works of science were inimical to religion, and
insisted upon David's reading those works which were
supposed to be the most conducive to his religious
education. Upon this point the son at length rose
in open rebellion, and tells us that the last application of the rod to him—from which we may infer
that the parental government did not always take the
form of moral suasion—was upon his refusal, point-
blank, to read Wilberforce's " Practical Christianity."
This dislike to what Dr. Livingstone calls " dry doc-
trinal reading " continued for several years, when he
discovered a number of religious works which were in
themselves interesting, and agreed with him in the idea
that religion and science were not hostile to each other.
Such being David Livingstone's course of intellectual culture during boyhood and youth, his manual labor continued for many years without cessation,
and it is believed, without complaint. It cannot be
doubted that as boy and youth, he was a good "hand"
in the factory. So we find him promoted from the
situation of a "piecer" to that of a "spinner," the
latter being a position at once less laborious, though
requiring more skill, and better paid. His moral education meantime proceeded apace. This it will be
best to relate in his own language :

"Great pains had been taken by my parents to instil the doctrines of Christianity into my mind, and I had no difficulty in understanding the theory of our free salvation by the atonement of our Saviour ; but it was only about this time that I really began to feel the necessity and value of a personal application of the provisions of that atonement to my own case. The change was like what may be supposed would take place were it possible to cure a case of color-blindness. The perfect freeness with which the pardon of all our guilt is offered in God's book drew forth feelings of affectionate love to Him who bought us with his blood, and a sense of deep obligation to Him for his mercy has influenced, in some small measure, my conduct ever since. But I shall not again refer to the inner spiritual life which I believe then began, nor do I intend to specify with any prominence the evangelistic labors to which the love of Christ has since impelled me. This book will speak, not so much of what has been done, as of what still remains to be performed before the gospel can be said to be preached to all nations. In the glow of love which Christianity inspires, I soon resolved to devote my life to the alleviation of human misery. Turning this idea over in my mind, I felt that to be a pioneer of Christianity in China might lead to the material benefit of some portions of that immense empire, and therefore set myself to obtain a medical education, in order to be qualified for that enterprise."

Young Livingstone pursued his medical education in a manner similar to that which had characterized

A Narrow Escape from a Lion

his studies theretofore. He continued to work hard as well as to study hard, and though of slender physical proportions, he certainly had a vigorous constitution, sustained by great force of will. He found time to make many excursions into the country round about his home, whereby his practical knowledge of botany and also of geology, to which he gave much attention, was greatly extended. It must be agreed that Livingstone's course of education, general and professional, was much out of the ordinary track. He appears to have been by nature broad-minded; catholic, or as it is often expressed, liberal in view. It was, perhaps, impossible for him to have become, at any rate in the age in which he was fortunately born, a sectarian in religion or a dogmatist in anything. He might, however, have become more inclined to sectarianism had his course of education been marked out by others instead of almost wholly by himself. His success in classical, general, and professional knowledge, is one of many illustrations of the gratifying truth that a boyhood and youth of hard manual labor may be so employed as to bring about the most admirable intellectual culture and men of prodigious influence in directing the progress of the world. It appears that Dr. Livingstone himself, after his name had become known throughout the world, was still firmly convinced that his early life of labor had been beneficial to him. In an interesting bit of autobiography he remarks:

" My reading while at work was carried on by placing the book on a portion of the spinning-jenny, so that I could catch sentence after sentence as I passed

3

at my work; I thus kept up a pretty constant study
undisturbed by the roar of the machinery. To this
part of my education I owe my present power of
completely abstracting the mind from surrounding
noises, so as to read and write with perfect comfort
amid the play of children or near the dancing and
songs of savages. The toil of cotton-spinning, to
which I was promoted in my nineteenth year, was
excessively severe on a slim, loose-jointed lad, but it
was well paid for; and it enabled me to support myself while attending medical and Greek classes in
Glasgow in winter, as also the divinity lectures of
Dr. Wardlaw by working with my hands in summer.
I never received a farthing of aid from any one, and
should have accomplished my project of going to
China as a medical missionary, in the course of time,
by my own efforts, had not some friends advised my
joining the London Missionary Society, on account
of its perfectly unsectarian character. It 'sends neither
Episcopacy, nor Presbyterianism, nor Independency,
but the gospel of Christ, to the heathen.' This exactly agreed with my ideas of what a missionary society ought to do; but it was not without a pang
that I offered myself, for it was not quite agreeable
to one accustomed to work his own way to become
in a measure dependent on others ; and I would not
have been much put about though my offer had been
rejected.

" Looking back now on that life of toil, I cannot
but feel thankful that it formed such a material part
of my early education; and, were it possible, I
should like to begin life over again in the same

lowly style, and to pass through the same hardy training."

Having finished his medical curriculum, Livingstone presented himself for examination, having prepared a thesis on a subject which required the use of the stethoscope (an instrument for the examination of the chest), on which account he had to go through a course of questions and experiments longer and more severe than usual. He passed the ordeal with entire success, however, and expresses great delight at becoming a member of a profession " which is preëminently devoted to practical benevolence, and which with unwearied energy pursues from age to age its endeavours to lessen human woe."

It had been Dr. Livingstone's purpose to go to China as a Missionary. He hoped to gain access to that empire whose vastness appears to have fascinated his imagination, by means of the healing art. England being engaged at this time, however, in the " opium war" with China, it was impracticable for him to make his way among the Celestials. Wherefore he remained in England and pursued certain theological studies, proficiency in which he thought would greatly aid him as a missionary. Meantime, he became deeply interested in Africa, through the labors of Dr. Moffat, who had long been a missionary at Kuruman, and who at this time was engaged in translating the Bible into the language of the Bechuanas. Accordingly, Dr. Livingstone, in 1840, sailed for that wonderful country which has become more and more interesting ever since.

CHAPTER III.

MISSIONARY LIFE IN SOUTHERN AFRICA.

Dr. Livingstone's Departure from Cape Town and Journey to the Missionary Station, Kuruman—Proceeds to Shokuane, the Chief Village of Sechele, Chief of the Bakwains—Sketch of the Chieftain's Life and Character—Missionary Life—Characteristics of the People—Graphic Sketch of a Combat with Lions—Many Facts about the "King of Beasts."

After a voyage of three months, Dr. Livingstone reached Cape Town, and soon afterwards proceeded to the interior, starting inland from Algoa Bay whence he had gone by a coastwise journey. At this time Kuruman, in the territory of the Bechuanas was a missionary station the farthest inland from Cape Town. This place is about seven hundred miles in a nearly northeastern direction, from Cape Town, and about five hundred, due north, from Algoa Bay. The route of travel from either place is, of course, farther. From Algoa Bay Dr. Livingstone took his departure in the aboriginal mode of travel, or, rather, the pioneer mode, namely, wagons drawn by oxen. The journey was tedious, but remaining at Kuruman only long enough to recruit his oxen, Dr. Livingstone pushed on northward, not halting for any length of time until he had reached Shokuane, where he met Sechele, a noted African chieftain, exercising great power among the people who inhabit what is called the Bakuena or Bakwain country. He was, indeed, sovereign of the tribe of Bakwains, and certainly one of the most interesting Africans of whom modern explorers give us any account.

Sechele was descended from what the Africans would call an illustrious ancestry. His great grandfather, Mochoasele, was a noted traveller and is said to have been the first to tell the Bakwains of the existence of white men. The father of Sechele was also named Mochoasele. One of his predominating characteristics was covetousnesss, and he appears especially to have coveted the wives of other chieftains. Because he had taken to himself many of the wives of his under chiefs they rebelled against him and put him to death. His children were spared and their adherents called in the aid of the powerful Sebituane, chief of the Makololo, far to the northward. Sebituane, with a large force surrounded the principal town of the Bakwains by night, and at the dawn of the following day, proclaimed that he had come to revenge the death of Mochoasele. The proclamation was accompanied by a tremendous beating of shields and African drums, whose rub-a-dub is rarely stilled in the southern and central protions of the continent, and the Bakwains fell into a panic. As they rushed from the town pell-mell, like the crowd from a burning theatre, many were taken and slain, the Makololo being the most expert of all Africans in throwing the javelin. The children of the murdered chief were ordered to be spared by Sebituane, and a Makololo meeting Sechele, took him in safe custody by giving him a blow over the head which rendered him insensible. The usurper being put to death, Sechele was

placed in power. He immediately began to augment
his influence and render his chieftainship secure by
marrying the daughters of his under-chiefs, of whom
he forthwith took three to wife. This is one of the
usual modes adopted in Africa for perpetuating the
allegiance of a tribe. The government is patriarchal, each man being, by virtue of paternity, chief of
his own children. They build their huts around his,
and the greater the number of his children the more
his importance increases. "Hence," says Dr. Livingstone, "children are esteemed one of the greatest
blessings, and are always treated kindly." In the
course of his narrative Dr. Livingstone relates a
number of incidents illustrating the universal affection of Africans for children.

The Chief Sechele had thus been placed at the
head of his tribe by the aid of Sebituane not long
before Dr. Livingstone reached the principal town
of the Bakwains. It was here that the great explorer held his first public religious exercises. Sechele
was present an attentive listener. But not disposed
to take things upon trust, he asked many questions,
and was particularly anxious to know why, if Dr.
Livingstone's forefathers had been told of a future
judgment his forefathers were left in ignorance and
to pass away into darkness, The chief was impressed, however, with the arguments in favor of
Christianity and at once went to work learning to
read. He learned the alphabet in a day, and very
soon began to read in the Bible. The prophet Isaiah
was his favorite. "He was a fine man, that Isaiah," Sechele used to say; "he knew how to speak."

Perceiving that Dr. Livingstone was anxious for the Africans to believe in Christianity, Sechele said to him one day, " Do you imagine these people will ever believe by your merely talking to them ? I can make them do nothing except by thrashing them and if you like I shall call our head men and with our litupa (whips of rhinoceros' hide) we will soon make them all believe together." Sechele, in fine, became a convert, always advocated Christianity, but was greatly troubled as to how to get rid of his su-perfluous wives. This was a real difficulty; because he could not put them aside without appearing to be ungrateful to their parents who had so materially aided him in his adversity. At length he did so, however, and with great natural politeness gave each one new toilets and other presents, including all his own goods which they had kept for him, and returned them to their parents with the message that he had no fault to find with them but wished to follow the will of God. He remained steadfast, and was ever a valuable friend and aid to Dr. Livingstone. When first known he was tall and slender, but active and strong. His studies and in-door life made him cor-pulent. About the time Dr. Livingstone was to be-gin his second journey into the interior, and while at the village of Kuruman awaiting repairs to his wagon, Sechele's town of Kolobeng was attacked by the Boers, and sacked. The discomfited chief sent the following account of the affair to the Rev. Mr. Mof-fat, at Kuruman, the bearer of the letter being Se-chele's wife Masebele :

" Friend of my heart's love, and of all the confi

dence of my heart, I am Sechele. I am undone by
the Boers, who attacked me, though I had no guilt
with them. They demanded that I should be in their
kingdom, and I refused. They demanded that I
should prevent the English and Griquas from passing (northward). I replied, 'These are my friends,
and I can prevent no one (of them).' They came on
Saturday, and I besought them not to fight on Sunday, and they assented. They began on Monday
morning at twilight, and fired with all their might,
and burned the town with fire, and scattered us.
They killed sixty of my people, and captured women
and children, and men. And the mother of Baleril-
ing (a former wife of Sechele) they also took prisoner. They took all the cattle and all the goods of the
Bakwains; and the house of Livingstone they plundered, taking away all his goods. The number of
wagons they had was eighty-five, and a cannon; and
after they had stolen my own wagon and that of Ma-
cabe, then the number of their wagons (counting the
cannon as one) was eighty-eight. All the goods of
the hunters (certain English gentlemen hunting and
exploring in the north) were burned in the town;
and of the Boers were killed twenty-eight. Yes, my
beloved friend, now my wife goes to see the children,
and Kobus Hae will convey her to you.

"I am SECHELE,
"The son of Mochoasele."

This disaster to Sechele caused a considerable delay in Dr. Livingstone's departure for the north upon
that remarkable expedition which has become so celebrated. At length, however, guides were procured,

and the journey was begun, November 20, 1852.
That which we further learn of the intelligent Sechele, whom misfortunes of the severest nature were
unable to dishearten, is thus related by Dr. Livingstone:

"When we reached Motito, forty miles off, we met
Sechele on his way, as he said, 'to the Queen of England. Two of his own children, and their mother, a
former wife, were among the captives seized by the
Boers; and, being strongly imbued with the then
very prevalent notion of England's justice and generosity, he thought that in consequence of the vio-
lated treaty he had a fair case to lay before her majesty. He employed all his eloquence and powers of
persuasion to induce me to accompany him, but I excused myself on the ground that my arrangements
were already made for exploring the north. On ex-
plaining the difficulties of the way, and endeavoring
to dissuade him from the attempt, on account of the
knowledge I possessed of the governor's policy, he
put the pointed question, 'Will the queen not listen
to me, supposing I should reach her?' I replied, 'I
believe she would listen, but the difficulty is to get
to her.' 'Well, I shall reach her,' expressed his final
determination. Others explained the difficulties more
fully, but nothing could shake his resolution. When
he reached Bloemfontein he found the English army
just returning from a battle with the Basutos, in
which both parties claimed the victory, and both
were glad that a second engagement was not tried.
Our officers invited Sechele to dine with them, heard
his story, and collected a handsome sum of money to

enable him to pursue his journey to England. The commander refrained from noticing him, as a single word in favor of the restoration of the children of Sechele would have been a virtual confession of the failure of his own policy at the very outset. Sechele proceeded as far as the Cape ; but, his resources being there expended, he was obliged to return to his own country, one thousand miles distant, without accomplishing the object of his journey.

" On his return he adopted a mode of punishment which he had seen in the colony, namely, making criminals work on the public roads. And he has since, I am informed, made himself the missionary to his own people. He is tall, rather corpulent, and has more of the negro feature than common, but has large eyes. He is very dark, and his people swear by ' Black Sechele.' He has great intelligence, reads well, and is a fluent speaker. Great numbers of the tribes formerly living under the Boers have taken refuge under his sway, and he is now greater in power than he was before the attack on Kolobeng."

And here we bid farewell to "the Black Sechele" trusting that his wise government, incipient statesmanship among the tribal Africans, may have full development worthy of its interesting and auspicious beginning.

The foregoing sketch of the life and character of this singular man has been given because believed to be interesting in itself and because one may hence get a glimpse at any rate of the people among whom Dr. Livingstone lived and labored for so many years. The calamity which befel Sechele did not occur, of

course, until after the traveler had been long in Africa.
Meantime, he had acquired the language of the Bakwains, had married a daughter of the missionary, Mr.
Moffat, and had become the father of several children. After several journeys in exploration of the
country, Dr. Livingstone finally determined to select "the beautiful valley of Mabotsa" as the site of a
missionary station, and thither he removed in 1843.
His purchase of land for the purposes he had in view
was the first instance of a sale, with regular transfer
of title, which had occurred in that country. The
price paid for a large lot was five pounds sterling, and
it was stipulated that a similar piece of land should
be allotted to any other missionary at any other place
to which the tribe might remove.

It were needless to enter into the details of Dr.
Livingstone's missionary life among the Bakwains.
His relations with the people, he tells us, were simply
relations between strangers. His influence depended
entirely upon persuasion. He disclaimed having
either authority or power, and it may be safely concluded, from the beneficent result in the case of
Sechele and the improved stage of civilization and
prosperity to which he brought his tribe, that his
course of kindness and affection was also the course
of wisdom Not only this, but the influence of the
missionaries was good in bringing new motives into
play among these ignorant people. There were no
less than five instances, during Dr. Livingstone's sojourn at Kolobeng, of the prevention of war through
influences which may be claimed as wholly Christian.
The people in general, he **says, were slow in coming**

to a decision on religious subjects; but in questions
affecting their worldly affairs they were keenly alive
to their own interests.   They might be called stupid
in matters which had not come within the sphere of
their own observation, but in other things, he proceeds to say, they showed more intelligence than is
to be met with in our own uneducated peasantry
They are remarkably accurate in their knowledge of
cattle, sheep, and goats, knowing exactly the kind of
pasturage suited to each; and they select with great
judgment the variety of soil best suited to different
kinds of grain.   They are also familiar with the habits of wild animals, and in general are well up in the
maxims which embody their ideas of political wisdom.   A little further on, Dr. Livingstone gives a
lively account of what may be called his private life:
"Our house at the river Kolobeng, which gave a
name to the settlement, was the third which I had
reared with my own hands.   A native smith taught
me to weld iron; and having improved from scraps
of information in that line from Mr. Moffat, and also
in carpentering and gardening, I was becoming handy
at almost any trade, besides doctoring and preaching;
and as my wife could make candles, soap, and clothes,
we came nearly up to what may be considered as indispensable in the accomplishments of a missionary
family in central Africa, namely, the husband to be a
jack-of-all-trades without doors and the wife a maid-
of-all-work within."

But it is not to be supposed that missionary life in
a country infested by large numbers of beasts of prey
would at all times pass smoothly on.   Indeed. it was

not long after Dr. Livingstone had taken up his abode at Kolobeng, that he took part in a lion hunt, in which he personally had an encounter with one of the beasts, the result of which was a wound which permanently disabled his left arm. His graphic account of this affair presents a vivid picture of one phase of African life, and relates besides certain habits and characteristics of the lion which will be found interesting to all students of natural history. Wherefore, the narative bearing upon the incident is given in full:

" Here an occurrence took place concerning which I have frequently been questioned in England, and which, but for the importunities of friends, I meant to have kept in store to tell my children when in my dotage. The Bakatla of the village Mabotsa were much troubled by lions, which leaped into the cattle-pens by night and destroyed their cows. They even attacked the herds in open day. This was so unusual an occurrence that the people believed that they were bewitched—'given,' as they said, 'into the power of the lions by a neighboring tribe.' They went once to attack the animals ; but, being rather a cowardly people compared to Bechuanas in general on such occasions, they returned without killing any.

" It is well known that if one of a troop of lions is killed, the others take the hint and leave that part of the country. So, the next time the herds were attacked, I went with the people, in order to encourage them to rid themselves of the annoyance by destroying one of the marauders. We found the lions on a small hill about a quarter of a mile in length and covered with trees. A circle of men was formed round it, and they gradually closed up, ascending pretty near to each other. Being down below on the plain with a native schoolmaster, named Mebalwe, a most excellent man, I saw one of the lions sitting on a piece of rock within the now closed circle of men. Mebalwe fired at him before I could, and the ball struck the rock on which the animal was sitting. He bit at the spot struck, as a dog does at a stick or stone thrown at him, then, leaping away, broke through the opening circle and escaped unhurt. The men were afraid to attack him, perhaps on account of their belief in witchcraft. When the circle was re-formed, we saw two other lions in it; but we were afraid to fire, lest we should strike the men, and they allowed the beasts to burst through also. If the Bakatla had acted according to the custom of the country, they would have speared the lions in their attempt to get out. Seeing we could not get them to kill one of the lions, we bent our footsteps toward the village: in going round the end of the hill, however, I saw one of the beasts sitting on a piece of rock as before, but this time he had a little bush in front. Being about thirty yards off, I took good aim at his body through the bush, and fired both barrels into it. The men then called out, ' He is shot! he is shot!' Others cried, 'He has been shot by an-other man too; let us go to him!' I did not see any one else shoot at him, but I saw the lion's tail erected in anger behind the bush, and, turning to the people, said, 'Stop a little, till I load again.' When in the act of ramming down the bullets, I heard a shout.

Starting, and looking half round, I saw the lion just in the act of springing upon me. I was upon a little height; he caught my shoulder as he sprang, and we both came to the ground below together. Growling horribly close to my ear, he shook me as a terrier dog does a rat. The shock produced a stupor similar to that which seems to be felt by a mouse after the first shake of the cat. It caused a sort of dreaminess, in which there was no sense of pain nor feeling of terror, though quite conscious of all that was happening. It was like what patients partially under the influence of chloroform describe, who see all the operation, but feel not the knife. This singular condition was not the result of any mental process. The shake annihilated fear, and allowed no sense of horror in looking round at the beast. This peculiar state is probably produced in all animals killed by the carnivora, and, if so, is a merciful provision by our benevolent Creator for lessening the pain of death. Turning round to relieve myself of the weight, as he had one paw on the back of my head, I saw his eyes directed to Mebalwe, who was trying to shoot him at a distance of ten or fifteen yards. His gun, a flint one, missed fire in both barrels ; the lion immediately left me, and, attacking Mebalwe, bit his thigh. Another man, whose life I had saved before, after he had been tossed by a buffalo, attempted to spear the lion while he was biting Mebalwe. He left Mebalwe and caught this man by the shoulder, but at that moment the bullets he had received took effect, and he fell down dead. The whole was the work of a few moments, and must have been his paroxysms of dying

rage. In order to take out the charm from him, the
Bakatla on the following day made a huge bonfire
over the carcass, which was declared to be that of the
largest lion they had ever seen. Besides crunching
the bone into splinters, he left eleven teeth-wounds
on the upper part of my arm.

"A wound from this animal's tooth resembles a
gun-shot wound; it is generally followed by a great
deal of sloughing and discharge, and pains are felt in
the part periodically ever afterward. I had on a tar-
tan jacket on the occasion, and I believe that it wiped
off all the virus from the teeth that pierced the flesh,
for my two companions in this affray have both suffered from the peculiar pains, while I have escaped
with only the inconvenience of a false joint in my
limb. The man whose shoulder was wounded showed
me his wound actually burst forth afresh on the same
month of the following year. This curious point
deserves the attention of inquirers."

It is very evident that Dr. Livingstone does not
hold the lion, famed as the king of beasts, in high
respect. He might almost appear to hold him in a
certain contempt, notwithstanding the fact that he will
carry to his grave the inconvenient evidence of the
maned brute's power. The traveler gives a full account
of these animals in the seventh chapter of his "Researches in South Africa." He says:

"When a lion becomes too old to catch game he
frequently takes to killing goats in the villages; a
woman or child happening to go out at night falls a
prey too; and as this is his only source of subsistence
now, he continues it. From this circumstance has

THREE LIONS ATTEMPTING TO DRAG DOWN A BUFFALO, AS SEEN BY THE EXPLORERS.

arisen the idea that the lion, when he has once tasted human flesh, loves it better than any other. A man-eater is invariably an old lion; and when he has overcome his fear of man so far as to come to villages for goats, the people remark, ' His teeth are worn, he will soon kill men.' They at once acknowledge the necessity of instant action, and turn out to kill him. When living far away from population, or when, as is the case in some parts, he entertains a wholesome dread of the Bushmen and Bakalahari, as soon as either disease or old age overtakes him he begins to catch mice and other small rodents, and even to eat grass; the natives, observing undigested vegetable matter in his droppings, follow up his trail in the certainty of finding him scarcely able to move under some tree, and dispatch him without difficulty The grass may have been eaten as medicine, as is observed in dogs.

"That the fear of man often remains excessively strong in the carnivora is proved from well-authenticated cases in which the lioness, in the vicinity of towns where the large game had been unexpectedly driven away by fire-arms, has been known to assuage the paroxysms of hunger by devouring her own young. It must be added that though the effluvium which is left by the footsteps of man is in general sufficient to induce lions to avoid a village, there are exceptions: so many came about our half-deserted houses at Chonuane while we were in the act of removing to Kolobeng, that the natives who remained with Mrs. Livingstone were terrified to stir out of doors in the evening.

4

"When a lion is met in the daytime, a circumstance by no means unfrequent to travelers in these parts, if preconceived notions do not lead them to expect something very 'noble' or 'majestic,' they will see merely an animal somewhat larger than the biggest dog they ever saw, and partaking very strongly of the canine features: the face is not much like the usual drawings of a lion, the nose being prolonged like a dog's; not exactly such as our painters make it,—though they might learn better at the Zoological Gardens,—their ideas of majesty being usually shown by making their lion's faces like old women in night-caps. When encountered in the daytime, the lion stands a second or two, gazing, then turns slowly round and walks as slowly away for a dozen paces, looking over his shoulder, then begins to trot, and when he thinks himself out of sight, bounds off like a greyhound. By day there is not, as a rule, the smallest danger of lions which are not molested attacking man, nor even on a clear moonlight night, except when they possess the breeding *storge* (natural affection:) this makes them brave almost any danger; and if a man happens to cross to the windward of them, both lion and lioness will rush at him, in the manner of a bitch with whelps. This does not often happen, as I only became aware of two or three instances of it. In one case a man, passing where the wind blew from him to the animals, was bitten before he could climb a tree; and occasionally a man on horseback has been caught by the leg under the same circumstances. So general, however, is the sense of security on moonlight nights, that we seldom tied up our oxen, but let them lie loose by the wagons; while on a dark, rainy-night, if a lion is in the neighborhood, he is almost sure to venture to kill an ox. His approach is always stealthy, except when wounded; and any appearance of a trap is enough to cause him to refrain from making the last spring. This seems characteristic of the feline species; when a goat is picketed in India for the purpose of enabling the huntsmen to shoot a tiger by night, if on a plain, he would whip off the animal so quickly by a stroke of the paw that no one could take aim; to obviate this, a small pit is dug, and the goat is picketed to a stake in the bottom; a small stone is tied in the ear of the goat, which makes him cry the whole night. When the tiger sees the appearance of a trap, he walks round and round the pit, and allows the hunter, who is lying in wait to have a fair shot.

" When a lion is very hungry, and lying in wait, the sight of an animal may make him commence stalking it. In one case a man, while steathily crawling toward a rhinoceros, happened to glance behind him, and found to his horror a lion *stalking him;* he only escaped by springing up a tree like a cat. At Lopepe a lioness sprang on the after-quarter of Mr. Oswell's horse, and when we came up to him we found the marks of the claws on the horse, and a scratch on Mr. O.'s hand. The horse, on feeling the lion on him sprang away, and the rider, caught by a wait-a-bit thorn, was brought to the ground and rendered insensible. His dogs saved him. Another English gentleman (Captain Codrington) was surprised in the same way, though not hunting the lion at the

time, but turning round he shot him dead in the neck.
By accident a horse belonging to Codrington ran away,
but was stopped by the bridle catching a stump ; there
he remained a prisoner two days, and when found
the whole space around was marked by the footprints
of lions. They had evidently been afraid to attack
the haltered horse, from fear that it was a trap. Two
lions came up by night to within three yards of oxen
tied to a wagon, and a sheep tied to a tree, and stood
roaring, but afraid to make a spring. On another
occasion, one of our party was lying sound asleep and
unconscious of danger between two natives behind a
bush at Mashue ; the fire was nearly out at their feet
in consequence of all being completely tired out by
the fatigues of the previous day: a lion came up to
within three yards of the fire, and there commenced
roaring instead of making a spring: the fact of their
riding-ox being tied to the bush was the only reason
the lion had for not following his instinct and making
a meal of flesh. He then stood on a knoll three
hundred yards distant, and roared all night, and continued his growling as the party moved off by daylight next morning.

"Nothing that I ever learned of the lion would
lead me to attribute to it either the ferocious or noble
character ascribed to it elsewhere. It possesses none
of the nobility of the Newfoundland or St. Bernard
dogs. With respect to its great strength there can
be no doubt. The immense masses of muscle around
its jaws, shoulders and forearms proclaim tremendous
force. They would seem, however, to be inferior in power to those of the Indian tiger Most of those feats of

strength that I have seen performed by lions, such as
the taking away of an ox, were not carrying, but
dragging or trailing the carcass along the ground:
they have sprung, on some occasions, on to the hind-
quarters of a horse, but no one has ever seen them
on the withers of a giraffe. They do not mount on
the hind-quarters of an eland even, but try to tear
him down with their claws. Messrs. Oswell and Vardon once saw three lions endeavoring to drag down
a buffalo, and they were unable to do so for a time,
though he was then mortally wounded by a two-ounce
ball.*

"In general, the lion seizes the animal he is attacking by the flank, near the hind-leg, or by the throat
below the jaw. It is questionable whether he ever
attempts to seize an animal by the withers. The
flank is the most common point of attack, and that
is the part he begins to feast on first. The natives
and lions are very similar in their tastes in the selection of titbits: an eland may be seen disemboweled

* This singular encounter, in the words of an eye-witness, happened as follows:—

" My South African Journal is now before me, and I have got hold of the account of the lion and buffalo affair ; here it is:—'15th September, 1846. Oswell
and I were riding, this afternoon, along the banks of the Limpopo, when a water-
buck started in front of us. I dismounted, and was following it through the jungle,
when three buffaloes got up, and after going a little distance, stood still, and the
nearest bull turned round and looked at me. A ball from the two-ouncer
crashed into his shoulder, and they all three made off. Oswell and I followed,
as soon as I had reloaded, and when we were in sight of the buffalo, and gaining on him at every stride, three lions leaped on the unfortunate brute ; he bellowed most lustily as he kept up a kind of running fight, but he was, of course,
soon overpowered and pulled down. We had a fine view of the struggle, and
saw the lions, on their hind-legs, tearing away with teeth and claws, in most
ferocious style. We crept up within thirty yards, and, kneeling down, blazed
away at the lions. My rifle was a single barrel, and I had no spare gun. One

by a lion so completely that he scarcely seems cut up at all. The bowels and fatty parts form a full meal for even the largest lion. The jackal comes sniffing about, and sometimes suffers for his temerity by a stroke from the lion's paw, laying him dead. When gorged, the lion falls fast asleep, and is then easily dispatched. Hunting a lion with dogs involves very little danger compared with hunting the Indian tiger, because the dogs bring him out of cover and make him stand at bay, giving the hunter plenty of time for a good deliberate shot.

"Where game is abundant, there you may expect lions in proportionately large numbers. They are never seen in herds, but six or eight, probably one family, occasionally hunt together. One is in much more danger of being run over when walking in the streets of London than he is of being devoured by lions in Africa, unless engaged in hunting the animal. Indeed, nothing that I have seen or heard about lions would constitute a barrier in the way of men of ordinary courage and enterprise.

lion fell dead almost *on* the buffalo; he had merely time to turn toward us, seize a bush with his teeth, and drop dead with the stick in his jaws. The second made off immediately ; and the third raised his head, coolly looked round for a moment, then went on tearing and biting at the carcass as hard as ever. We retired a short distance to load, then again advanced and fired. The lion made off, but a ball that he received *ought* to have stopped him, as it went clean through his shoulder-blade. He was followed up and killed, after having charged several times. Both lions were males. It is not often that one *bags* a brace of lions and a bull-buffalo in about ten minutes. It was an exciting adventure, and I shall never forget it.'

"Such, my dear Livingstone, is the plain, unvarnished account. The buffalo had, of course, gone close to where the lions were lying down for the day ; and they, seeing him lame and bleeding, thought the opportunity too good a one to be lost.   Ever yours,   FRANK VARDON."

"The same feeling which has induced the modern
painter to caricature the lion, has led the sentimen-
talist to consider the lion's roar the most terrific of
all earthly sounds. We hear of the 'majestic roar
of the king of beasts.' It is, indeed, well calculated
to inspire fear if you hear it in combination with the
tremendously loud thunder of that country, on a
night so pitchy dark that every flash of the intensely
vivid lightning leaves you with the impression of
stone-blindness, while the rain pours down so fast
that your fire goes out, leaving you without the protection of even a tree, or the chance of your gun
going off. But when you are in a comfortable house
or wagon, the case is very different, and you hear
the roar of the lion without any awe or alarm. The
silly ostrich makes a noise as loud ; yet he never was
feared by man. To talk of the majestic roar of the
lion is mere majestic twaddle. On my mentioning
this fact some years ago, the assertion was doubted,
so I have been careful ever since to inquire the opinions of Europeans, who have heard both, if they
could detect any difference between the roar of a
lion and that of an ostrich ; the invariable answer
was, that they could not, when the animal was at any
distance. The natives assert that they can detect
a variation between the commencement of the noise
of each. There is, it must be admitted, considerable
difference between the singing noise of a lion when
full, and his deep, gruff growl when hungry. In general, the lion's voice seems to come deeper from the
chest than that of the ostrich ; but to this day, I can
distinguish between them with certainty only by

knowing that the ostrich roars by day and the lion by night.

"The African lion is of a tawny color, like that of some mastiffs. The mane in the male is large, and gives the idea of great power. In some lions, the ends of the hair of the mane are black ; these go by the name of black-maned lions, though, as a whole, all look of the yellow tawny color. At the time of the discovery of the lake, Messrs. Oswell and Wilson shot two specimens of another variety. One was an old lion, whose teeth were mere stumps, and his claws worn quite blunt ; the other was full grown, in the prime of life, with white, perfect teeth : both were entirely destitute of mane. The lions in the country near the lake give tongue less than those farther south. We scarcely ever heard them roar at all.

"The lion has other checks on inordinate increase besides man. He seldom attacks full-grown animals ; but frequently, when a buffalo-calf is caught by him, the cow rushes to the rescue, and a toss from her often kills him. One we found was killed thus ; and on the Leeambye another, which died near Sesheke, had all the appearance of having received his death-blow from a buffalo. It is questionable if a single lion ever attacks a full-grown buffalo. The amount of roaring heard at night, on occasions when a buffalo is killed, seems to indicate there are always more than one lion engaged in the onslaught.

"On the plain, south of Sebituane's ford, a herd of buffaloes kept a number of lions from their young by the males turning their heads to the enemy. The young and the cows were in the rear. One toss from

a bull would kill the strongest lion that ever breathed.
I have been informed that in one part of India even
the tame buffaloes feel their superiority to some wild
animals, for they have been seen to chase a tiger up
the hills, bellowing as if they enjoyed the sport.
Lions never go near any elephants except the calves,
which, when young, are sometimes torn by them;
every living thing retires before the lordly elephant,
yet a full-grown one would be an easier prey than
the rhinoceros; the lion rushes off at the mere sight
of this latter beast."

Dr. Livingstone afterwards says, however, that he
saw lions above Libonta, which roared more and
louder than those of more Southern Africa; and he
makes special mention of seeing two which were as
large as donkeys.

CHAPTER IV.

Departure for the Central Portion of South Africa—Discovery of Lake Ngami
—Elephants—Journey to the Country of the Makololo—Their Sovereign,
Sebituane—A Remarkable Career—Discovery of the River Zambesi—The
Slave Trade—Return to Cape Town—The Tsetse Fly.

During all these years of missionary labor, first at Shokuane, and, upon the abandonment of that village, at Kolobeng, Dr. Livingstone had made explorations of the country round about, and had become familiar with the language, manners, and customs of those dark-colored people who were in most respects so different from those among whom he had been born, reared, and educated. It might appear that the traveler, like the poet, is born, not made by education. *Viator nascitur, non fit*, is as amply demonstrated by the examples of Columbus, Gama, Park, Marco Polo, Sir John Franklin, Dr. Livingstone, and very many others, as the original quotation is by Homer, or its author, or Shakespeare, or Milton or any of the rest of the grand old masters,

"—————————— the bards sublime,
Whose distant footsteps echo
Through the corridors of Time."

Dr. Livingstone's genius for exploration was again gratified on the 1st of June, 1849, when, in company with two noted travelers, Messrs. Oswell and Mur-

ray, who had joined him for the purpose, he set out
from Kolobeng in search of Lake Ngami. The existence of this lake, according to the reports of natives, had long been known, but its exact locality had
not been ascertained, nor had it ever been seen by
the eye of any white man. The fact of the existence
of the lake was not better known than that to approach it must be a task of great difficulty and a
thousand perils.

The difficulties and perils of the journey chiefly
lay in the nature of the country lying between the
explored portions of South Africa and the lake. To
the northward of the country of the Bechuanas is a
vast sterile, dry, and most uninviting territory, known
as the Kalahari Desert. It is not destitute of vegetation or inhabitants. Indeed, the quantity of grass
growing on these trackless plains is said to be astonishing even to those who are familiar with India, of
whom Mr. Oswell, accompanying Dr. Livingstone on
this journey, was one. There are also large patches
of bushes and even trees. Great herds of certain
kinds of antelopes, which require little or no water,
roam over the flat expanse. It is inhabited by Bushmen and Bakalahari, who subsist on game. The former are said to be the aborigines of the southern portion of the continent, the latter the remnants of the
first emigration of Bechuanas. Both possess an intense love of liberty, but in other respects are greatly
different the one tribe from the other. For whereas
the Bushmen are exceptions to Africans generally in
language, race, habits, and appearance, being the only
real nomads in the country, never cultivating the

soil, nor rearing any domestic animals save wretched dogs, and subsisting almost entirely upon game, the Bakalahari retain the Bechuana love for agriculture and domestic animals. They regularly hoe their gardens, which produce melons and pumpkins, and carefully rear small herds of goats, though Dr. Livingstone has seen them lift water for these animals out of little wells with a bit of ostrich egg-shell or by spoonfuls. They carry the skins of animals which they kill to the tribes on the border of the desert, and exchange them for their simple implements of agriculture, spears, knives, tobacco, and dogs. Some of these skins and furs are much valued.

The inhospitality of the Desert, its terror to travelers, is in the want of water. There are several beds of rivers in the vast plain, but they are perfectly dry, and it is sometimes three and even four days' journey between places where a supply of water for animals can be had. The inhabitants of the country are forced to use the greatest ingenuity and watchfulness that they may not succumb to thirst. At one time on his journey through the Desert Dr. Livingstone's cattle were three days without water. At length, upon reaching a pool, they dashed in until the the water was deep enough to be nearly level with their throats, where they stood drawing slowly in the long, refreshing mouthfuls, until their formerly collapsed sides distended as if they would burst. "So much do they imbibe," says the narrative, "that a sudden jerk, when they come out on the bank, makes some of the water run out again from their mouths." It will readily be supposed that a journey through this dry desert, with the sun broiling hot by day, was accompanied by much suffering on the part of the explorers, their servants, horses, and cattle.

On the 4th of July, the party reached the Zouga river at a point opposite a village inhabited by negroes who seemed to be closely allied to the Hottentots. Informed that the river came out of Lake Ngami, the travelers were greatly rejoiced, and proceeded on their journey near the river's bank with high courage and hearty enthusiasm. Having traveled thus nearly one hundred miles, all the oxen and wagons of the expedition, except Mr. Oswell's, were left at the village of Ngabisane, and the party pushed on for the lake. Twelve days afterwards they came to the north east end of Lake Ngami, and on August 1st the whole party "went down to the broad part, and for the first time, this fine-looking sheet of water was beheld by Europeans." The lake is thus described by Dr. Livingstone:

"The direction of the lake seemed to be N. N. E. and S. S. W. by compass. The southern portion is said to bend round to the west, and to receive the Teoughe from the north at its northwest extremity. We could detect no horizon where we stood looking S. S. W., nor could we form any idea of the extent of the lake, except from the reports of the inhabitants of the district; and as they professed to go round it in three days, allowing twenty-five miles a day would make it seventy-five, or less than seventy geographical miles in circumference. Other guesses have been made since as to its circumference, ranging between seventy and one hundred miles. It is shallow, for I subsequently saw a native punting his canoe over seven or eight miles of the northeast end; it can never, therefore, be of much value as a commercial highway. In fact, during the months preceding the annual supply of water from the north, the lake is so shallow that it is with difficulty cattle can approach the water through the boggy, reedy banks. These are low on all sides, but on the west there is a space devoid of trees, showing that the waters have retired thence at no very ancient date. This is another of the proofs of dessication met with so abundantly throughout the whole country. A number of dead trees lie on this space, some of them embedded in mud, right in the water. We were informed by the Bayeiye, who live on the lake, that when the annual inundation begins, not only trees of great size, but antelopes, as the springbuck and tsessebe (*Acronotus lunata*), are swept down by its rushing waters; the trees are gradually driven by the winds to the opposite side, and become embedded in the mud.

"The water of the lake is perfectly fresh when full, but brackish when low; and that coming down the Tamunak'le we found to be so clear, cold and soft, the higher we ascended, that the idea of melting snow was suggested to our minds. We found this reigon, with regard to that from which we had come, to be clearly a hollow, the lowest point being Lake Kumadau; the point of the ebullition of water, as shown by one of Newman's barometric thermometers, was only between $207\frac{1}{4}°$ and $206°$, giving an elevation of not much more than two thousand feet above the level of the sea. We had descended above two thousand feet in coming to it from Kolobeng. It is the southern and lowest part of the great river system beyond, in which large tracts of country are inundated annually by tropical rains."

The chief object of Dr. Livingstone in going to Lake Ngami was to visit Sebituane, the great chief of the Makololo, who was said to live some two hundred miles beyond. Nothwithstanding great exertions, however, and the most earnest appeals to Lechulatebe, the young chief of a half-tribe of the Bamangwato, called Batuana, who inhabit this part of Africa, he was unable to procure guides, and was reluctantly compelled to return to Kolobeng.

On their return, Livingstone and party passed down the Zouga river. He pronounces its banks very beautiful, closely resembling those of the Clyde above Glasgow. They are perpendicular on the side to which the water swings, and sloping and grassy on the other. The trees which adorn the banks are magnificent. There are two enormous baobabs, or mowanas, near the confluence of the lake and river, the larger of which measures 76 feet in girth. The palmyra also appears here and there. The mockuchong is quite plentiful. It bears an edible fruit of indifferent quality, but the tree itself is said to be very beautiful. It is so large that the trunk is often used for constructing canoes. The motsouri is a species of plum, and in its dark evergreen foliage resembles the orange-tree and the cypress in its form.

The sloping banks of the Zouga are selected by the natives for pit-falls designed to entrap wild animals as they come to drink. These pits are from seven to eight feet deep, three or four feet wide at the mouth, gradually decreasing until they are only about a foot wide at the bottom. The mouth is an oblong square, and the long diameter at the surface is about equal to the depth. The decreasing width in the earth is intended to make the animal wedge himself more firmly in by his weight and struggles. The pitfalls are usually in pairs, with a wall a foot thick between the two. Thus if the animal, feeling his four legs descending, should undertake to leap forward, he would only jump into the second pit with such force as to insure his capture. They are covered with the greatest care, and the earth removed so that no suspicion may be aroused in the instinct of the animals. They are, in fact, so skilfully made that several of the exploring party's men fell into them while actually in their search to prevent the cattle from falling in.

There are vast numbers of wild animals in this region. Among them was discovered a new species of antelope, called leche or lechwi. It is a beautiful water-antelope of a light brownish-yellow color, with horns rising from the head with a slight bend backward, then curving forward toward the points. It is never found a mile from water, and is unknown except in the central humid basin of Africa. Having a good deal of curiosity, it presents a noble appearance as it stands gazing, with head erect, at the approaching stranger. When beginning to escape, it lowers its head, lays its horns down to a level with its withers, and first starting on a waddling trot, soon begins to gallop and spring, leaping bushes like the pallahs. It invariably runs to the water and crosses

BUFFALO COW DEFENDING HER CALF.

it by a succession of bounds, each of which appears to be from the bottom. The party soon tired of its flesh. Countless numbers of other animals were seen, and the river was found to be well stocked with fish of different kinds, while alligators were plenty.

The number of elephants in this region was astonishing even to Dr. Livingstone, who had often before seen them in herds of incredible extent. They came from the southern side of the river to drink in prodigious numbers. They are smaller than the elephants farther south, being only eleven feet high, whereas at the Limpopo they are twelve feet in height. Still farther north Dr. Livingstone afterwards found them to be only nine feet high. The difference of three feet in height between animals of such immense size would probably give to the larger beast a quantity of flesh equal in weight to that of an ordinary yoke of oxen. The elephants are very sagacious as to the pit-falls of the country. Old elephants precede the troops, and whisk off the coverings with their trunks all the way to the river's edge. Instances have been known in which the old animals have actually lifted the young out of the trap. They come to drink by night, and after slaking their thirst—in doing which they throw large quantities of water over themselves, screaming all the time with delight—they evince their horror of pit-falls by setting off in a straight line to the desert, never diverging till they are eight or ten miles distant.

The journey from the Zouga to Kolobeng was performed without incident requiring particular mention.

5

In April 1850, Dr. Livingstone made a second attempt to visit Sebituane, chief of the Makololo. He was accompanied by Mrs. Livingstone, the three children, and Sechele, chief of the Bakwains. Taking a route somewhat farther eastward than the one pursued before, the party in due time though not without great difficulties in traveling along the northern bank of the Zouga, reached Lake Ngami. After a great deal of diplomacy with Lechulatebe, of which chief mention has already been made, Dr. Livingstone made arrangements for guides to show him the way, by journey on ox-back, to the country of Sebituane. Just as he was ready to depart, however, his wife and children all fell sick with the African fever, and he was compelled to remain. For their benefit he returned to the Desert, and actually again reached Kolobeng before the sick ones had become well enough to make the journey. During their convalescence at home, Dr. Livingstone made a trip to Kuruman and return. Upon the return, on that journey which was successful in bringing them to Sebituane's country, the whole family came near perishing of thirst. From the village of Nchokotsa on the Zouga, their present route was northward, so that Lake Ngami was left far westward. There are here many extensive "salt pans," one of which, called Ntwetwe, is fifteen miles broad and one hundred long. After passing this singular country, the route lay by the river Mahabe, the Sonta, and the Chobe. When Dr. Livingstone reached Sesheke, the capital town so to speak, at the time, of the Makololo, he and his companions had traversed deserts, forests, salt-pans, and swamps, through regions abounding in ferocious wild animals, venomous reptiles, and poisonous insects, and had traveled a distance of more than a thousand miles.

Sebituane, however, hearing of the white men's coming—an event which he had long desired and tried to bring about—magnanimously proceeded a long distance to welcome his visitors. There is scarcely a native chief of Africa, perhaps, who has had a more remarkable career than that of Sebituane. It will be most proper to give the account of his meeting with the first and only white persons he ever saw, and the graphic sketch of his life in the words of Dr. Livingstone:

"The Makololo whom we met on the Chobe were delighted to see us; and as their chief, Sebituane, was about twenty miles down the river, Mr. Oswell and I proceeded in canoes to his temporary residence. He had come from the Barotse town of Naliele down to Sesheke as soon as he heard of white men being in search of him, and now came one hundred miles more to bid us welcome into his country. He was upon an island with all his principal men around him, and engaged in singing when we arrived. It was more like church music than the sing-song e e e, æ æ æ of the Bechuans of the south, and they continued the tune for some time after we approached. We informed him of the difficulties we had encountered, and how glad we were that they were all at an end by at last reaching his presence. He signified his own joy, and added, 'Your cattle are all bitten by the tsetse, and will certainly die; but never mind, I have oxen, and will give you as many as you need.' We, in our ignorance, then thought that as so few tsetse had bitten them, no great mischief would follow. He then presented us with an ox and a jar of honey as food, and handed us over to the care of Mahale, who had headed the party to Kolobeng, and would now fain appropriate to himself the whole credit of our coming. Prepared skins of oxen, as soft as cloth, were given to cover us through the night; and as nothing could be returned to this chief, Mahale became the owner of them. Long before it was day Sebituane came, and, sitting down by the fire, which was lighted for our benefit behind the hedge where we lay, he narrated the difficulties he had himself experienced when a young man, in crossing that same desert which we had mastered long afterwards. As he has been most remarkable in his career and was unquestionably the greatest man in all that country, a short sketch of his life may prove interesting to the reader.

"Sebituane was about forty-five years of age; of a tall wiry form, an olive or coffee-and-milk color, and slightly bald; in manner cool and collected, and more frank in his answers than any chief I ever met. He was the greatest warrior ever heard of beyond the colony; for, unlike Mosilikatse, Dingaan, and others, he had led his men into battle himself. When he saw the enemy, he felt the edge of his battle-axe, and said 'Aha! it is sharp, and whoever turns his back on the enemy will feel its edge.' So fleet of foot was he, all his people knew there was no escape for the cowards, as any such would be cut down without mercy.

In some instances of skulking he allowed the individual to return home; then calling him, he would
say, 'Ah! you prefer dying at home to dying in the
field, do you? You shall have your desire?' This
was the signal for his immediate execution.

"He came from the country near the sources of
the Litwa and Namagari rivers, in the south, so we
met him eight hundred or nine hundred miles from
his birth-place. He was not the son of a chief, though
related closely to the reigning family of the Basutu;
and, when in an attack by Sikouyele, the tribe was
driven out of one part, Sebituane was one in that
immense horde of savages driven back by the Griquas
from Kuruman in 1824. He then fled northward
with an insignificant party of men and cattle. At
Melita the Bangwaketse collected the Bakwains,
Bakatla, and Bahurutse, to 'eat them up.' Placing
his men in front, and the women behind the cattle, he
routed the whole of his enemies at one blow. Having thus conquered Makabe, the chief of the Bangwaketse, he took immediate possession of his town
and all his goods.

"Sebituane subsequently settled at the place called
Litubaruba, where Sechele now dwells, and his people
suffered severely in one of those unrecorded attacks
by white men, in which murder is committed and
materials laid up in the conscience for a future judgment.

"A great variety of fortune followed him in the
northern part of the Bechuana country; twice he lost
all his cattle by the attacks of the Matabelle, but always kept his people together and retook more than

he lost. He then crossed the Desert by nearly the same path that we did. He had captured a guide, and, as it was necessary to travel by night in order to reach water, the guide took advantage of this and gave him the slip. After marching till morning, and going as they thought right, they found themselves on the trail of the day before. Many of his cattle burst away from him in the phrensy of thirst, and rushed back to Serotli, then a large piece of water, and to Mashue and Lopepe, the habitations of their original owners. He stocked himself again among the Batletli, on Lake Kamadau, whose herds were all of the long horned species of cattle. Conquering all around the lake, he heard of white men living at the west coast; and, haunted by what seems to have been the dream of his whole life, a desire to have intercourse with the white man, he passed away to the southwest into the parts opened up lately by Messrs. Galton and Anderson. There suffering intensely from thirst, he and his party came to a small well. He decided that the men, not the cattle, should drink it, the former being of most value, as they could fight for more should these be lost, In the morning they found the cattle had escaped to the Damaras.

"Returning to the north poorer than he started, he ascended the Teoughe to the hill Sorila, and crossed over a swampy country to the eastward. Pursuing his course onward to the low-lying basin of the Leeambye, he saw that it presented no attractions to a pastoral tribe like his, so he moved down that river among the Bashubia and Batoka, who were then living in all their glory. His narrative resem-

bles closely the 'Commentaries of Cæsar,' and the
history of the British in India. He was always forced
to attack the different tribes, and to this day his men
justify every step he took as perfectly just and right.
The Batoka lived on large islands in the Leeambye
or Zambesi, and, feeling perfectly secure in their fast-
ness, often allured fugitive or wandering tribes on to
uninhabited islets on pretense of ferrying them across
and then left them to perish for the sake of their
goods. Sekomi, the chief of the Bamangwatse, was,
when a child, in danger of meeting this fate; but a
man still living had compassion on him, and enabled
his mother to escape with him by night. The river
is so large that the sharpest eye cannot tell the difference between an island and a bend of the opposite
bank; but Sebituane, with his usual foresight, requested the island chief who ferried him across to
take his seat in the canoe with him, and detained
him by his side till all his people and cattle were
safely landed. The whole Batoka country was then
densely populated, and they had a curious taste for
ornamenting their villages with the skulls of strangers. When Sebituane appeared near the Great falls,
an immense army collected to make trophies of the
Makololo skulls; but instead of succeeding in this,
they gave him a good excuse for conquering them,
and capturing so many cattle that his people were
quite incapable of taking any note of the sheep and
goats. He overran all the high lands toward the
Kafue, and settled in what is called a pastoral country, of gentle undulating plains, covered with short

grass and but little forest. The Makololo have never lost their love for this fine, healthy region.

"But the Matebele, a Caffræ or Zulu tribe, under Mosilikatse, crossed the Zambesi, and, attacking Sebituane in this choice spot, captured his cattle and women. Rallying his men, he followed and recaptured the whole. A fresh attack was also repulsed, and Sebituane thought of going farther down the Zambesi, to the country of the white men. He had an idea, whence imbibed I never could learn, that if he had a cannon he might live in peace. He had led a life of war, yet no one apparently desired peace more than he did.

"Sebituane had now not only conquered all the black tribes over an immense tract of country but had made himself dreaded even by the terrible Mosilikatse. He never could trust this ferocious chief, however, and, as the Batoka on the islands had been guilty of ferrying his enemies across the Zambesi, he made a rapid descent upon them, and swept them all out of their island fastnesses. He thus unwittingly performed a good service to the country by completely breaking down the old system which prevented trade from penetrating into the great central valley. Of the chiefs who escaped, he said, ' They loved Mosilikatse, let them live with him ; the Zambesi is my line of defense ;' and men were placed all along it as sentinels. When he heard of our wish to visit him, he did all he could to assist our approach. Sechele, Sekomi, and Lechulatebe owed their lives to his clemency; and the latter might have paid dearly for his obstructiveness. Sebituane knew everything that had happened in the country, for he had the art of gaining the affections both of his own people and that of strangers. When a party of poor men came to his town to sell their hoes or skins, no matter how ungainly they might be, he soon knew them all. A company of these indigent strangers, sitting far apart from the Makololo gentlemen around the chief, would be surprised to see him come alone to them, and sitting down, inquire if they were hungry. He would order an attendant to bring meal, milk, and honey, and, mixing them in their sight, in order to remove any suspicion from their minds, make them feast perhaps for the first time in their lives, on a lordly dish. Delighted beyond measure with his affability and liberality, they felt their hearts warm toward him and gave him all the information in their power; and as he never allowed a party of strangers to go away without giving every one of them, servants and all, a present, his praises were sounded far and wide. 'He has a heart! he is wise!' were the usual expressions we heard before we saw him.

"He was much pleased with the proof of confidence we had shown in bringing our children, and promised to take us to see his country, so that we might choose a part in which to locate ourselves. Our plan was, that I should remain in the pursuit of my objects as a missionary, while Mr. Oswell explored the Zambesi to the east. Poor Sebituane, however, just after realizing what he had so long ardently desired, fell sick of inflammation of the lungs, which originated in and extended from an old wound got at Melita. I saw

his danger, but, being a stranger, I feared to treat him
medically, lest, in the event of his death, I should be
blamed by his people. I mentioned this to one of
his doctors, who said, 'Your fear is prudent and wise :
this people would blame you.' He had been cured
of this complaint, during the year before, by the Barotse making a large number of free incisions in the
chest. The Makololo doctors, on the other hand, now
scarcely cut the skin. On the Sunday afternoon in
which he died, when our usual religious service was
over, I visited him with my little boy Robert. 'Come
near,' said Sebituane, 'and see if I am any longer a
man. I am done.' He was thus sensible of the
dangerous nature of his disease; so I ventured to as-
sent, and added a single sentence regarding hope after death. 'Why do you speak of death?' said one
of a relay of fresh doctors; 'Sebituane will never die.'
If I had persisted, the impression would have been
produced that by speaking about it I wished him to
die. After sitting with him some time, and commending him to the mercy of God, I rose to depart, when
the dying chieftain, raising himself up a little from
his prone position, called a servant, and said, 'Take
Robert to Maunku, (one of his wives,) and tell her to
give him some milk.' These were the last words of
Sebituane.

"We were not informed of his death until the next
day. The burial of a Bechuana chief takes place in
his cattle-pen, and all the cattle are driven for an
hour or two around and over the grave, so that it may
be quite obliterated. We went and spoke to the
people, advising them to keep together and support

the heir. They took this kindly; and in turn told us not to be alarmed, for they would not think of ascribing the death of their chief to us; that Sebituane had just gone the way of his fathers; and, though the father had gone, he had left children, and they hoped that we would be as friendly to his children as we intended to have been to himself.

"He was decidedly the best specimen of a native chief I ever met. I never felt so much grieved by the loss of a black man before; and it was impossible not to follow him in thought into the world of which he had just heard before he was called away, and to realize somewhat of the feelings of those who pray for the dead. The deep, dark question of what is to become of such as he must, however, be left where we find it, believing that, assuredly, the 'Judge of all the earth will do right.'"

Upon the death of this remarkable man, the government of the Makololo devolved upon a daughter named Ma-mochisane. The explorers now had to look to her for permission to traverse the country as they desired. She gave them perfect liberty to visit any part of the country they chose. In the exercise thereof, Mr. Oswell and Dr. Livingstone proceeded one hundred and thirty miles to the northeast, to Sesheke, and toward the end of June discovered the Zambesi river in the centre of the continent, where it had not been previously known to exist at all. It is a magnificent stream, navigable from the bars inside the delta to Victoria Falls, discovered by Dr. Livingstone, a distance of 940 miles, and above them for nearly 400 miles more. Victoria Falls are about forty

miles from the mouth of the Chobe.   Here the river,
about half a mile wide, rushes over a precipice 100
feet in height, and suddenly turning almost at a right
angle, flows for some thirty miles between two walls
of rock not more than twenty yards apart.   Here the
river sometimes rises perpendicularly more than sixty
feet.   The entire length of the river is, perhaps, about
1,500 miles.

The discovery of the Zambesi in central South
Africa, and the acquaintance formed with Sebituane,
and the consequent good will of the powerful and
numerous Makololo were the great events of this
expedition, making it one of the most important
which had yet been made by African explorers.

As these were the first white men who had ever
penetrated this country they were visited by great
numbers of natives.   Among the visitors were several who were clothed in stuff which had come from
the Portuguese on the western coast.   Upon inquiry,
it was discovered that these goods had been purchased from a tribe called Mambari, far distant, in exchange for boys.   The tribe of Makololo had begun
the slave trade only in 1850, and then under the great
temptation of procuring muskets in exchange for
boys.   These were always captives, and Dr. Livingstone testifies that he never knew an instance in Africa where a parent had sold his own offspring.

Unable at this time to procure a healthy location
for the site of a missionary station in the Makololo
country, Dr. Livingstone determined to send his family to England, and himself to undertake a new expedition in this behalf.   He accordingly returned with

his family, reaching Cape Town in April, 1852, and for the first time in eleven years visiting the scenes of civilization. Having placed his family on board a homeward-bound ship, he at once began preparations for that journey across the continent in two directions, which has immortalized his name and added immensely to the world's stock of knowledge.

One of the greatest scourges to explorers in South Africa, often mentioned by Livingstone, makes an additional illustration of the contradictory character of that continent. Whilst it is summer pretty much everywhere else, inhabited by people who are civilized, it is winter there. The gradations of heat and cold appear to go the wrong way. One would naturally suppose that the immense troops of elephants might overrun the country. They are harmless. But a little insect, smaller than the honey bee, is so great an enemy to man that it must be utterly destroyed before the country can be cultivated by the agriculturist, or inhabited by people for whom the domestic animals are necessary. This is the Tsetse Fly, whose bite is certain death to horses, cattle, and other animals, though harmless to man and wild beasts. Dr. Livingstone thus describes this fearful pest :

"A few remarks on the Tsetse, or *Glossina morsitans*, may here be appropriate. It is not much larger than the common house-fly, and is nearly of the same brown color as the common honey-bee; the after-part of the body has three or four yellow bars across it; the wings project beyond this part considerably, and it is remarkably alert, avoiding most dexterously all

attempts to catch it with the hand at common temper-
atures; in the cool of the mornings and evenings it
is less agile. Its peculiar buzz when once heard can
never be forgotten by the traveler whose means of
locomotion are domestic animals; for it is well known
that the bite of this poisonous insect is certain death
to the ox, horse, and dog. In this journey, though
we were not aware of any great number having at
any time lighted on our cattle, we lost forty-three fine
oxen by its bite. We watched the animals carefully,
and believe that not a score of flies were ever upon
them.

"A most remarkable feature in the bite of the tsetse
is its perfect harmlessness in man and wild animals,
and even calves, so long as they continue to suck the
cow. We never experienced the slightest injury from
them ourselves, personally, although we lived two
months in their *habitat*, which was in this case as
sharply defined as in many others, for the south bank
of the Chobe was infested by them, and the northern
bank, where our cattle were placed, only fifty yards
distant, contained not a single specimen. This was
the more remarkable as we often saw natives carrying over raw meat to the opposite bank with many
tsetse settled upon it.

" The poison does not seem to be injected by a sting,
or by ova placed beneath the skin; for, when one is
allowed to feed freely on the hand, it is seen to insert the middle prong of three portions, into which
the proboscis divides, somewhat deeply into the true
skin; it then draws it out a little way, and it assumes
a crimson color as the mandibles come into brisk

operation. The previously-shrunken belly swells out, and, if left undisturbed, the fly quietly departs when it is full. A slight itching irritation follows, but not more than in the bite of a mosquito. In the ox this same bite produces no more immediate effects than in man. It does not startle him as the gad-fly does; but a few days afterward the following symptoms supervene: the eye and nose begin to run, the coat stares as if the animal were cold, a swelling appears under the jaw and sometimes at the navel; and, though the animal continues to graze, emaciation commences, accompanied with a peculiar flaccidity of the muscles, and this proceeds unchecked until, perhaps months afterward, purging comes on, and the animal, no longer able to graze, perishes in a state of extreme exhaustion. Those which are in good condition often perish soon after the bite is inflicted, with staggering and blindness, as if the brain were affected by it. Sudden changes of temperature produced by falls of rain seem to hasten the progress of the complaint; but, in general, the emaciation goes on uninterruptedly for months, and, do what we will, the poor animals perish miserably.

"When opened, the cellular tissue on the surface of the body beneath the skin is seen to be injected with air, as if a quantity of soap-bubbles were scattered over it, or a dishonest, awkward butcher had been trying to make it look fat. The fat is of a greenish-yellow color and of an oily consistence. All the muscles are flabby, and the head often so soft that the fingers may be made to meet through it. The lungs and liver partake of the disease. The stomach and bowels are pale and empty, and the gall-bladder is distended with bile.

"The mule, ass, and goat enjoy the same immunity from the tsetse as man and game. Many large tribes on the Zambesi can keep no domestic animals except the goat, in consequence of the scourge existing in their country. Our children were frequently bitten, yet suffered no harm; and we saw around us numbers of zebras, buffaloes, pigs, pallahs and other antelopes, feeding quietly in the very *habitat* of the tsetse, yet as undisturbed by its bite as oxen are when they first receive the fatal poison."

This insect has been classed by different naturalists as the same as the *zimb* of Bruce, and the *zebub* in Hebrew. The Marquis of Spineto identifies the zimb with the dog-fly of the Greeks, with the flies under different names of other countries, and with the *arob* of Scripture, the fly which caused the fourth of the plagues of Egypt. The Portuguese in Africa believe that the tsetse lives only in regions where there are elephants, and that upon the extermination of those animals the great scourge of the fly will cease.

SLAVERS REVENGING THEIR LOSSES.

CHAPTER V.

FROM CAPE TOWN TO LOANDA.

Dr. Livingstone Departs for the Country of Makololo—Life and Labors There —The Chief Sekeletu—Departs for the West Coast of Africa—Narrative of the Journey—Arrival Among the Portuguese Colonists—His Opinion of this Portion of Africa—Determines upon Another Great Expedition.

Dr. Livingstone had now been in Africa about twelve years. For eleven years he had been beyond the borders of civilization, so that when he appeared at Cape Town, taking his family thither for their departure to England, wearing a suit of the same fashion as that which he had worn away from London in 1840, he had to acknowledge that in this respect at any rate he had fallen behind the age, and was preposterously out of the mode. A far-away colony is not the best place in the world at which to procure intelligence of passing events. But with such means of intelligence as were at hand, Dr. Livingstone must have been astonished at the greatness and importance of events which had occurred while he had been preaching to the Bakwains, fighting lions, elephants, hyenas, rhinoceroses, hippopotami, exploring vast regions before unknown, by means of travel which had been in vogue since the time of Abraham, and amongst a people who had advanced but little if any from a barbarism hundreds of centuries old. During the brief period in which the great African explorer was conducting the expeditions of which an account has

been given in the   preceding pages, more important
events had occurred in the world than had occurred
in Africa during many ages.   And among these were
great inventions and progress in vastly developing
interprises with which his own name was destined to
be intimately associated.   While Dr. Livingstone had
been inwalled, as it were, within the deserts and
wilds of Africa, Europe had been convulsed by revolution and war.   If the cause of popular freedom had
not greatly gained, it had at least made way for liberty to gain victories in the future and this by many
deeds of soul-stirring heroism on the field and acts of
statesmanship during temporary control of governments by the people in revolution.   The republic of
the United States had waged a war with the republic of Mexico which terminated in success for the
stronger party, and the addition of a vast extent of
territory.   It was during this period that the great
empire of Brazil in South America became tranquil
and firmly established in independence of the Portuguese Cortes.   But far more important events than
these, and sure to confer lasting benefits upon man
kind, were taking place during the period of Dr. Livingstone's first series of explorations.   It was while
Livingstone was successful in the good old way of
discovery, in Africa, that Morse was successful, in a
new way, in America.   In 1844 the electric telegraph
became a practical success.   With the practical suc
cess of this momentous invention, the newspaper press
entered upon a career of enterprise and influence of
which those of former times had no conception.   And
it is a noteworthy fact that it was one of the great-

est of these newspaper establishments—the New York "Herald"—whose enterprise at length discovered the great discoverer after he had been given up as lost, and that full particulars of the interesting event, by means of this same magnetic telegraph, now connecting continents together in instantaneous intercourse, were at once flashed all over Christendom. But, without anticipating, the facts as they existed when Dr. Livingstone visited Cape Town were enough to arouse his highest ambition and his best endeavors. Perhaps through him the old and the new might clasp hands. Columbus, in the good old way of voyaging, had discovered a new world, now beneficently aiding mankind. Why might not he, exploring in the old manner—the only one possible—prepare the way whereby a continent for so many ages in the gloom of barbarism would let in the light and the glorious good of these great trophies of civilization? It will only add one to the many remarkable anomalies of Africa if there the sun should rise in the west after all.

Early in the month of June, 1852, Dr. Livingstone left Cape Town for the country of the Makololo, with the object of establishing a missionary station there. He traveled in the usual conveyance of the country, a heavy Cape Town wagon, drawn by five yoke of oxen. Of course the journey was slow; nor need it be said to those who have read the pages which have gone before, that it was often accompanied by dangers and difficulties not mastered except by those who have brave natures. In addition to the slow mode of travel, there were several causes of detention, and half the month of January, 1853, had passed before Dr. Livingstone left the scene of his long missionary labors among the Backwains, and again entered the Kalahari Desert. At this season of the year a hot wind frequently blows over the desert from north to south. It resembles in its effects the harmattan of North Africa, and when the missionaries first settled here, it came loaded with clouds of red-colored sand. This forms no part of the phenomenon of late years, but the wind blows hot as formerly, appearing to come from some vast oven in the north. It is so devoid of moisture, that everything made of wood, not manufactured in the country, greatly shrinks and warps. The atmosphere on such occasions is highly charged with electricity, so that even the movement of a native on his bed of skins will be accompanied by a luminous appearance and often by brilliant sparks. These winds do not appear to bear anything unhealthy on their heated wings. On the contrary, Dr. Livingstone expressly avows the opinion that the whole of the country adjacent to the Desert, and from Kuruman to the latitude of Lake Ngami, is extremely salubrious and especially healthy and restorative to those who are affected by pulmonary complaints.

The journey to the Makololo country did not pursue exactly the same route either to the region of Lake Ngami or farther on, as the explorations which have heretofore been described; but it did not differ from them so greatly as to require a detailed narration of its somewhat hum-drum incidents. On parts of the journey, the animals of the country were uncommonly tame. Giraffes and koodoos came close up to the wagon and the " camp" by night, and on one occasion, a large lion came within thirty yards of the resting-place for the night, and went all around it, but so shrewdly that Dr. Livingstone was unable to get a shot at him.

Early in May the party reached the reed-walled banks of the Chobe, and after some time he was able, with a single companion, to get a small boat into the stream. The banks of this river are so densely covered with grass and reeds that it is almost impossible to reach the water except at places made by the natives or those huge beasts, the rhinoceroses or hippopotami. Going down the stream with the current, the explorer soon discovered a village of the Makololo chief Moremi on the north bank. With the assistance of these friendly natives, the whole party was soon able to move on, and reached Linyanti, then the capital town of Sekeletu, chief of the Makololo.

The Makololo were surprised, but greatly gratified by the sudden appearance of the missionary among them. When here before, the wagon had been left behind. It was now an object of the greatest curiosity, and the whole town, numbering between six and seven thousand souls, turned out *en masse* to see the vehicle. Dr. Livingstone was received with all the ceremonies of Makololo etiquette by Sekeletu and his under chiefs. A great number of pots of boyaloa, the beer of the country, were brought forth by women, each of whom takes a stout draught as she sets down the pot to show that there is no poison.

The court herald, an aged man, who had occupied that office during Sebituane's time, with many bodily antics, roared out a welcome: " Don't I see the white man ?" " Don't I see the comrade of Sebituane?" And a great many other short sentences, the summary of whose meaning was that the white man, companion of the late chief, and good sound sleep were very welcome to the Makololo.

It will be recollected that Dr. Livingstone's journey to the Zambesi, or Leeambye, as it is here called, of which account is now being written, was with the object of establishing a missionary station. That at which he had so long labored at Kolobeng had been destroyed by the enemies of Sechele and his people the Bechuanas, and it was at the time of this journey, it will be remembered, when Sechele wrote his touching letter to Mr. Moffat, and shortly afterwards, when on his way to see the Queen of England, as he vainly hoped, met Livingstone in the Desert. Two considerations were regarded by the explorer-missionary as essential—healthfulness of locality, which should also not be liable to attack and destruction by enemies of the people where it should be determined to locate the station. In search of such place, Dr. Livingstone spent about six months at this time among the Makololo. During this time he explored a large extent of territory and also continued his missionary labors. He held public religious services in the kotla at Linyanti, that is, the place of public meetings and general amusements. He says that the Makololo women behaved with decorum, from the first, except at the conclusion of the prayer. When all knelt down, many of those who had children bent over them so that there was a simultaneous scream in all parts of the kotla, which turned into an universal laugh on the part of the women when " Amen " was said. This peccadillo was at length overcome, and the missionary had respectful if not believing audiences. He says that among the Bechuanas, there never was first-rate decorum. If a woman should happen to sit on the dress of another, the latter would make a vigorous nudge with her elbow and a request, " Take the nasty thing away, will you ? " Whereupon several women would go to scolding, and the men emphatically swear with the object of enforcing silence. There was a good deal of opposition to learning to read among the Makololo, chiefly arising, it would appear, from a feeling that knowledge would result in the abolition of polygamy, but it was at length overcome and some progress made, though not with Sekeletu, who was obdurate in this respect. He appears to have been uncommonly uxorious, even for an African chief. But before any considerable progress had been made in this regard, Dr. Livingstone departed for the west coast. He found much of the country very beautiful, and quite goes into heroics in his descriptions of the valley of the Leeambye inhabited by that branch of the Makololo known as the Barotse. It is nearly a hundred miles in length, and in some places twenty or thirty miles wide. It is covered with small villages which are built on artificial mounds so that during the period of inundation it has the appearance of a large lake dotted with islands, thus greatly resembling the valley of the Nile when the waters of that river overflow their banks. The current of the Leeambye in this region is very rapid. On returning from the upper Barotse country to Linyanti, Dr. Livingstone floated with the stream sixty miles a day, and saw any number of alligators, hippopotami, and other of the huge beasts and reptiles of the torrid zone.

Having returned from a considerable journey among the tribes on the Leeambye and its confluents, the missionary thus records his conclusions upon heathenism and the efforts of religious societies to eradicate it:

"I had been, during a nine weeks' tour, in closer contact with heathenism than I had ever been before; and though all, including the chief, were as kind and attentive to me as possible, and there was no want of food (oxen being slaughtered daily, sometimes ten at a time, more than sufficient for the wants of all), yet to endure the dancing, roaring, and singing, the jesting, anecdotes, grumbling, quarreling, and murdering of these children of nature, seemed more like a severe penance than any thing I had before met with in the course of my missionary duties. I took thence a more intense disgust at heathenism than I had before, and formed a greatly-elevated opinion of the latent effects of missions in the south, among tribes which are reported to have been as savage as the Makololo. The indirect benefits which, to a casual observer, lie beneath the surface, and are inappreciable, in reference to the probable wide diffusion of Christianity at some future time, are worth all the money and labor that have been expended to produce them."

Sekeletu, the chief of the Makololo, seems to have impressed Dr. Livingstone as a man of considerable natural ability, courage, and generosity. He desired especially to have his country opened to communication and commerce with white men, but exhibited little or no desire to adopt the Christian faith. It would appear also that Sekeletu's practical ideas had much weight with his distinguished visitor; for we find Dr. Livingstone asserting the belief that commerce must accompany Christianity before it can be greatly successful in its conflicts with heathenism and barbarism. Perhaps this opinion had something to do with hastening forward the explorer's next great journey—that to the west coast of Africa. It is true that other considerations helped to make up the decision. Linyanti is on the river Chobe, and in the midst of a marshy, swampy country. The most of the region round about is periodically inundated The African fever prevails; and here it was that Dr. Livingstone was first attacked by this dread disease. But against the attacks of the enemies of the Makololo, Linyanti offered the greatest advantages, and the people could not well be asked to risk great dangers of spoliation and sack, even for the rich valley of the Barotse. And hence, at length, the Makololo chief and Dr. Livingstone came heartily to agree upon the explorer undertaking a journey to St. Paul de Loanda, the capital of the Portuguese colony of Angola, in Lower Guinea.

On November 11, 1853, the explorer and party accompanied by Sekeletu and train and a considerable number of guides, embarked in their canoes on

the Chobe, and proceeded down that tortuous stream
to its juncture with the Leeambye. The route determined upon lay up this magnificent river to the
confines of the Makololo country and beyond. The
journey against the rapid current was as slow as the
late journey down stream had been agreeable, on account of speed. The country every day became more
beautiful, however, and many fruit and other trees
lent a charm to the scenery, which was not decreased
by the sight and voices of innumerable birds, many
of which were entirely new to the European. At
times the canoes had to be carried around rapids and
cataracts. The Falls of Gonye are near the southern
extremity of the Barotse Valley. These falls have
not been made by wearing back, like Niagara, but are
of a fissure form. For many miles below the river
is confined in a narrow space through which the water
boils and tumbles, making all navigation and even
swimming impracticable. There are numbers of
islands above the falls, covered with rich foliage, and
making a scene, as viewed from the rocks near the
cataract, of surpassing beauty.

Before Dr. Livingstone's departure from Linyanti,
Sekeletu had sent forward couriers, informing the various head-men and tribes of the explorer's intended
journey, and commanding that he be received with
all due state and hospitality. Accordingly all the
wants of the party were kindly provided for. They
had enough to eat and to spare, the use of the best
huts, plenty of skilled boatmen, and everything that
could be procured in the country for their accom-
modation. Indeed, the commands of Sekeletu were

sometimes so generously construed as to put Dr Livingstone to inconvenience by reason of excessive hospitality. Thus he was forced, as it were, to wait on one occasion till a certain great personage should pay him respect, and then go off on a journey to a considerable distance accompanied and guided by a vigorous Amazon, a chieftainess of the region and noted for great powers of tongue and pedestrianism. The Doctor had no little difficulty in keeping up with either, but cheerfully submitted to many good-natured inflictions because of the evident kindness and liberality of the people.

On December 17th, the party reached Libonta. This village, near the upper part of the now narrowed Barotse valley, is built upon a mound and belongs to two women who were wives to Sebituane. They liberally supplied the expedition with food. This is the last town of the Makololo. In front were a few hamlets and cattle stations and a vast expanse of border country. Ten days afterwards the party reached the confluence of the Leeambye and the Leeba, the former here flowing westward, the latter from the north. The journey was pursued up the Leeba. Near the confluence of these rivers, game was exceedingly abundant, but Dr. Livingstone's expectations in this regard were not sustained as he pursued his expedition. The region to the north of the Makololo country is called Londa, and its inhabitants Balonda. They worship idols, and are extremely superstitious. They are thus described:

" The Balonda are real negroes, having much more wool on their heads and bodies than any of the Bech-

uana or Caffre tribes, They are generally very
dark in color, but several are to be seen of a lighter
hue; many of the slaves who have been exported to
Brazil have gone from this region; but while they
have a general similarity to the typical negro, I never
could, from my own observation, think that our ideal
negro, as seen in tobacconists' shops, is the true type.
A large proportion of the Balonda, indeed, have heads
somewhat elongated backward and upward, thick lips,
flat noses, elongated *ossa calces*, &c. &c.; but there
are also many good- looking, well shaped heads and
persons among them."

Shinte, the chief of the Balonda, while exhibiting
much kindness to Dr. Livingstone, and receiving him
with great state, must have been much of a "night-
hawk." He sent for the missionary at most unsea-
sonable hours, till at length, on account of his fever,
he had to decline going. If the Makololo ate like
vultures, the Balonda slept on the wing. They are
great pedestrians, even the women walking long journeys through the dense forests of these regions, which
have scattered throughout numbers of the ugly idols
of the gross superstition of the people. The Balonda
are given to much speaking in their Kotla and are a
quite musical people, their instruments being drums
and the marimba, a rude species of piano. The dress
of the Balonda men consists of the softened skins of
small animals, as the jackal or wild cat, hung before
and behind from a girdle round the loins. The women
were dressed in nature's toilet; but were not im-
modest.

After leaving Shinte, the same flat, forest country

was met with, and any quantity of rain. The rivers and gullies were full and the plains drenched. In crossing the Lokalueje, which flows into the Leeba, the whole party got thoroughly wet through, but a few articles were kept dry by being held up by the guides and natives. On such occasions, Dr. Livingstone carried his watch in his arm-pit, where it was preserved from rains above and waters below. With this superabundance of water, game became scarce and the party often went hungry to bed. Here it was observed that all the streams of a vast extent of central South Africa have their origin in oozy bogs and not in fountains. Such is the case with the Chobe, the Loeti, Kaisi, and other rivers. About this time, the party heard of the death of Metiamvo, who had been a powerful chief, having life and death at his absolute control. He used to go about in person beheading his subjects as he would meet them, because, as he said, they were becoming too numerous. The farther north Dr. Livingstone proceeded the more savage and superstitious did the people become. But the people under the chief Katema are exceptionally amiable, and have a great love of singing birds, of which they have large numbers similar to our canaries. They are kept in cages.

On the 30th of March, 1854, after one of the most remarkable of journeys through savage lands, the party passed out of the confines of barbarism into a land inhabited by those who, if not civilized themselves, were the subjects of a civilized people. This was when the explorer entered the magnificent valley of the Quango, which forms the eastern limit of

Portuguese authority in this part of Africa. The
Basinje tribe is on the east bank of the Quango, and
they treated the expedition with more inhospitality
and threatened cruelty than it had received during
thousands of miles of travel. On the west bank,
and between the river and Lower Guinea proper, is
the territory of the Bangala, or Cassanges, subjects
of the Portuguese. The following from Livingstone's
description of this great valley will give the reader
a fine conception of a beautiful country within ten
degrees of the equator:

"On the 30th we came to a sudden descent from the
high land, indented by deep, narrow valleys, over
which we had lately been traveling. It is generally
so steep that it can only be descended at particular
points. Below us lay the valley of the Quango. If
you sit on the spot where Mary Queen of Scots
viewed the battle of Langside, and look down on the
vale of Clyde, you may see in miniature the glorious
sight which a much greater and richer valley presented to our view. It is about a hundred miles
broad, clothed with dark forest, except where the light
green grass covers meadow lands on the Quango,which
here and there glances out in the sun as it wends its
way to the north. The opposite side of this great
valley appears like a range of lofty mountains, and
the descent into it about a mile, which, measured perpendicularly, may be from a thousand to twelve hundred feet. Emerging from the gloomy forests of
Londa, this magnificent prospect made us all feel as
if a weight had been lifted off our eyelids. A cloud
was passing across the middle of the valley, from

which rolling thunder pealed, while above all was glorious sunlight; and when we went down to the part where we saw it passing we found that a very heavy thunder-shower had fallen under the path of the cloud, and the bottom of the valley, which from above seemed quite smooth, we discovered to be intersected by great numbers of deep-cut streams. Looking back from below, the descent appears as the edge of a table-land, with numerous indented dells and spurs jutting out all along, giving it a serrated appearance. Both the top and sides of the sierra are covered with trees; but large patches of the more perpendicular parts are bare, and exhibit the red soil which is general over the region we have now entered."

Detained some days on the Quango by rains and scientific observations, it was not until near the middle of April that Dr. Livingstone reached Cassange, the farthest inland town of the Portuguese, and about three hundred miles from the Atlantic coast at St. Paul de Loanda.

Thenceforward until his arrival at Loanda, Dr. Livingstone met with unbounded hospitality and the distinguished consideration due to his discoveries, his sufferings, and his labors in behalf of humanity and science. The commandants at the various Portuguese towns and trading-posts through which he and his unique Makololo companions passed, showed him every attention and honor, whereby, it is plain, he was most highly gratified. His opinion of the Portuguese colonists as high-toned gentlemen is evidently very exalted. Nor can he find words of too

high praise in which to speak of the entire freedom
of caste in social and business intercourse between
the Europeans and the Africans. He contrasts the
customs herein in Angola, with those of Cape Colony
and greatly to the disadvantage of the English. He
also has much to say in praise of the former labors of
Jesuit missionaries, whose good results are still plainly observable among the natives, but regrets that
they did not translate and leave the Bible for their
instruction and guidance. He laments the visible
want of internal improvements. There are no roads
in the country; merely paths from place to place,
with canoe ferries across the rivers and deep streams.
He also laments the fact that the Portuguese do not
bring wives to the colonies with them, and become
permanent citizens. It is true, they raise families by
native women, and treat their children with great
kindness, but the want of the family as an institution
founded in affection and sustained by law must, so
long as it exists, keep the colonists in the situation of
mere traders, and repress intellectual and moral development.

When Livingstone reached Loanda he was still
greatly suffering from the effects of the fever, by
which he had been several times attacked. There
was but a single Englishman in the town and the
missionary worried himself in his illness, wondering
whether this sojourner were possessed of good nature, "or was one of those crusty mortals one would
rather not meet at all." "This gentleman," the sick
traveler goes on to say, "Mr. Gabriel, our commis-
sioner for the suppression of the slave-trade, had

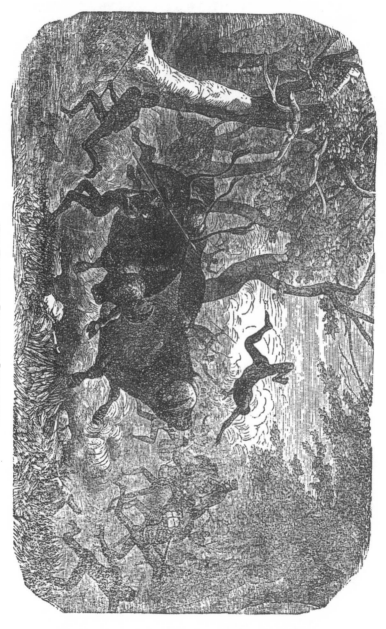

THE TRAVELING PROCESSION INTERRUPTED.

kindly forwarded an invitation to meet me on the
way from Cassange, but, unfortunately, it crossed me
on the road. When we entered his porch, I was delighted to see a number of flowers cultivated carefully, and inferred from this circumstance that he was,
what I soon discovered him to be, a real whole-hearted
Englishman. Seeing me ill, he benevolently offered
me his bed. Never shall I forget the luxurious pleasure I enjoyed in feeling myself again on a good English couch, after six months sleeping on the ground.
I was soon asleep ; and Mr. Gabriel coming in almost
immediately, rejoiced at the soundness of my repose."

Under the hospitable roof of Mr. Gabriel Dr.
Livingstone remained much longer than he had anticipated, for he continued for some time to grow more
and more reduced under the effects of the disease
from which he had long suffered. This was, doubtless,
owing to the fact that he was now " out of command,"
and the feeling of grave responsibility did not give
that strength and elasticity to the mind which have
so powerful an effect in counteracting bodily ailments. He was visited by a number of prominent
Portuguese gentlemen, and the acting governor of the
province sent his secretary to offer the services of
the government physician. Some British vessels also
came into port and offered to convey him to St.
Helena, or homeward, as he might choose. But there
were his Makololo friends, who had accompanied him
a vast distance, and would be unable, without his assistance, to pass through the country of the un-
friendly negroes near the borders of the Portuguese
colony. The explorer would not abandon his trusty

7

friends to such a fate. He therefore declined the
tempting offers of his naval friends, and came to the
determination to return to the Makololo chief, with
the object of proceeding from his country to the east
coast of Africa by way of the Leeambye or Zambesi
river, hoping thus to discover a route by which a
wagon road to central South Africa might be opened
up. This involved a journey across the continent,
through an unknown country, filled with wild animals,
hostile tribes, and noxious malaria. That Dr. Livingstone reached this determination while on a bed of
sickness, and importuned by kind friends to take his
ease for a season, is conclusive demonstration of his
sublime conscientiousness and his indomitable spirit.

CHAPTER VI.

ACROSS THE CONTINENT.

The Expedition Across the Continent from Loanda to Kilimane—Account of
the Journey—The Water-Shed of Central Africa—Lake Dilolo, and a River
Flowing in Two Directions—The Great Falls of Victoria on the Zambesi—
The Journey from Linyanti Eastward—The People of this Portion of Africa
—The Country—Animals and Vegetation—Arrival at Kilimane—Departure
for England—Resume of Events Connected with More Than 9,000 Miles of
Travel, and Many Discoveries.

Dr. Livingstone's journey through Angola on his
return to Linyanti was exceedingly slow. He was
detained at different times by different causes. Illness at times kept him laid up. Then again he would
depart from his direct route to the right or left, with
the object of examining the country. At other times
he was detained by the excessive hospitality of
Portuguese friends. His descriptions of the country
on his return are not so rose-colored as those accompanying his journey to the coast; and though he
loses none of his kind feelings for the colonists, he
is compelled to admit that they have not done so
much for the natives and the country as they ought
to have done, and that, under English control, the
country would have been far more prosperous and
wealthy. It is in speaking of some of the native
tribes who have here preserved their identity against
most untoward circumstances that he asseverates
that no African tribe has ever yet been destroyed.

He remained sometime at Cassange, and then proceeded for a very considerable distance by the same route upon which he had traveled on the previous journey. On account of the fever he made very slow progress. When he approached the vicinity of Lake Dilolo, he took a different course, with the object of more particular examinations into this portion of the country than he had before been able to make, the result being some remarkable and interesting discoveries in respect to the geography and geology of this portion of the globe.

In that extensive, undefined border country between the territory of the Makololo and that of the Balonda, there are vast level plains, which during the rainy season may be described, not inaccurately, as lakes of immense superficial area but of no great depth of water. In the midst of all is Lake Dilolo, from which flows the Lotembwa river, a small body of water which appears to form the water-shed of the African continent; certainly that vast portion known as South Africa. It seems to be established that this river on the one side of Lake Dilolo flows northward into the Kasai, a confluent of the Congo, emptying into the Atlantic ocean, and on the other side flows southward to the Leeambye which, under the name of Zambesi, discharges its waters into the Indian ocean. A statement so singular should be related in the words of the explorer himself. On June 8th, 1855, he forded the Lotembwa a short distance to the northwest of Lake Dilolo. He then goes on to say:

"The Lotembwa here is about a mile wide, about three feet deep, and full of the lotus, papyrus, arum,

mat-rushes, and other aquatic plants. I did not observe the course in which the water flowed while
crossing; but having noticed before that the Lotembwa on the other side of the Lake Dilolo flowed
in a southerly direction, I supposed that this was
simply a prolongation of the same river beyond Dilolo, and that it rose in this large marsh, which we
had not seen in our progress to the northwest. But
when we came to the Southern Lotembwa, we were
informed by Shakatwala that the river we had crossed
flowed in an opposite direction—not into Dilolo but
into the Kasai. This phenomenon of a river running in opposite directions struck even his mind as
strange; and, though I did not observe the current
simply from taking it for granted that it was toward
the lake, I have no doubt that his assertion corroborated as it was by others, is correct, and that the
Dilolo is actually the water-shed between the river
systems that flow to the east and west.

" I would have returned in order to examine more
carefully this most interesting point, but, having had
my lower extremities chilled in crossing the Northern Lotembwa, I was seized with vomiting of blood,
and, besides, saw no reason to doubt the native testimony. The distance between Dilolo and the valleys
leading to that of the Kasai is not more than fifteen
miles, and the plains between are perfectly level; and
had I returned, I should only have found that this
little Lake Dilolo, by giving a portion to the Kasai
and another to the Zambesi, distributes its waters to
the Atlantic and Indian oceans. I state the fact exactly as it opened to my own mind, for it was only

now that I apprehended the true form of the river
system and continent. I had seen the various rivers
of this country on the western side flowing from the
subtending ridges into the center, and had received
information from natives and Arabs that most of the
rivers on the eastern side of the same great region
took a somewhat similar course from an elevated
ridge there, and that all united in two main drains,
the one flowing to the north and the other to the
south, and that the northern drain found its way out
by the Congo to the west, and the southern by the
Zambesi to the east. I was thus on the water-shed,
or highest point of these two great systems, but still
not more than four thousand feet above the level of
the sea, and one thousand feet lower than the top of
the western ridge we had already crossed; yet instead of lofty snow-clad mountains appearing to ver-
ify the conjectures of the speculative, we had extensive
plains over which one may travel a month without
seeing anything higher than an ant-hill or a tree. I
was not then aware that any one else had discovered
the elevated trough-form of the centre of Africa."

Lake Dilolo is described as a fine sheet of water,
somewhat of a triangular shape, six or eight miles
long and from one to two broad. Moene Dilolo,
the " Lord of the Lake," was found to be a fat, jolly
fellow, who lamented the paradox that when there
were no strangers at the lake there was plenty of
beer, and when strangers were there the beverage
was always gone. He gave his guests plenty of
manioc meal, however, and a generous supply of
putrid buffalo-meat. Flesh is never too far gone for

these rather lazy natives whose chief food is the tasteless manioc. Here the idolater of central Africa and the epicure of fashionable civilization clasp hands over a common luxury; for tainted game and sauces in whose ingredients are the fluids of far-gone meats are greatly affected at our most stylish restaurants.

On his way from Lake Dilolo to the south, the explorer met again his old friends, Katema, Shinte, and Manenko. They treated him with cordial hospitality, and Manenko walked, if she did not talk, less than on the former visit. On July 27th, the expedition reached Libonta, and the traveler's Makololo companions—who had been constantly faithful and most valuable to their friend—were once more "home again." The party was welcomed, says Dr. Livingstone, "with demonstrations of joy such as I had never witnessed before. The women came forth to meet us, making their curious dancing gestures and loud lulliloos. Some carried a mat and stick, in imitation of a spear and shield. Others rushed forward and kissed the hands and cheeks of the different persons of their acquaintance among us, raising such a dust that it was quite a relief to get to the men assembled and sitting with proper African decorum in the kotla. We were looked upon as men risen from the dead, for the most skilful of their diviners had pronounced us to have perished long ago. After many expressions of joy at meeting, I arose, and, thanking them, explained the causes of our long delay, but left the report to be made by their own countrymen. Formerly I had been the chief speaker, now I would leave the task of speaking to them. Pit-

sane (a Makololo who had been with Livingstone)
then delivered a speech of upward of an hour in
length, giving a highly-flattering picture of the whole
journey, of the kindness of the white men in general,
and of Mr. Gabriel in particular. He concluded by
saying that I had done more for them than they expected ; that I had not only opened up a path for
them to the other white men, but conciliated all the
chiefs along the route. The oldest man present
rose and answered this speech, and, among other
things, alluded to the disgust I felt at the Makololo
for engaging in marauding-expeditions against Lechulatebe and Sebolamakwaia, of which we had heard
from the first persons we met, and which my companions most energetically denounced as 'mashue
hela,' entirely bad. He entreated me not to lose
heart, but to reprove Sekeletu as my child. Another
old man followed with the same entreaties. The following day we observed as our thanksgiving to God
for his goodness in bringing us all back in safety to
our friends. My men decked themselves out in their
best, and I found that, although their goods were
finished, they had managed to save suits of European
clothing, which, being white, with their red caps, gave
them rather a dashing appearance. They tried to
walk like the soldiers they had seen in Loanda, and
called themselves my 'braves' (batlabani). During
the service they all sat with their guns over their
shoulders, and excited the unbounded admiration of
the women and children. I addressed them all on
the goodness of God in preserving us from all the
dangers of strange tribes and disease. We had a

similar service in the afternoon. The men gave us
two fine oxen for slaughter, and the women supplied
us abundantly with milk, meal, and butter. It was all
quite gratuitous, and I felt ashamed that I could make
no return. My men explained the total expenditure
of our means, and the Libontese answered, grace-
fully, 'It does not matter: you have opened a path
for us, and we shall have sleep.' Strangers came
flocking from a distance, and seldom empty-handed.
Their presents I distributed among my men."

The progress down the Barotse valley was a constant ovation; a perpetual succession of barbecues,
and the number of oxen brought forth to the welcoming slaughter was great enough to make a respectable herd. But on reaching Naliele, a number
of Dr. Livingstone's Makololo fellow-travelers found
an unexpected source of sorrow in the fact that their
wives had taken to themselves other husbands. Most
of them having more wives than one they were not
altogether without consolation ; but it was plain that
they did not at all relish the fact that while they had
been toiling for two years others had eaten their
corn. The men who had married the only wives of
the traveling Makololo were compelled to restore
them. From which we may infer that ideas of the
marriage relation in central Africa, even at the best,
are still far from orthodox. On the canoe voyage
hence to Linyanti the craft, though moving near
shore was assailed by an immense hippopotamus,which
shoved against the boat, using its head for the purpose, with such strength that it was almost lifted out
of the water. Fortunately, no harm was done to life

or limb.   At Linyanti, where Dr. Livingstone arrived
early in September, he was received with great joy
by the chief Sekeletu and his people.

Having remained at the Makololo capital about
two months, Dr. Livingstone departed hence for the
east coast of Africa on the 3d of November. He
was accompanied by Sekeletu with about two hundred followers, and wherever they stopped in the
Makololo country, every arrangement for their hospitable entertainment was found to be provided for.
It was now, in his voyage down the Zambesi that Dr.
Livingstone visited the great falls of that river and
named them after the reigning sovereign of England,
Victoria.   These being among the most remarkable
of the many noteworthy scenes of Africa can only be
adequately described in the graphic words of the explorer, who here goes into more heroics, as it were,
than in almost any other portion of his great work :

" After twenty minutes' sail from Kalai we came
in sight for the first time, of the columns of vapor appropriately called 'smoke,' rising at a distance
of five or six miles, exactly as when large tracts of
grass are burned in Africa.   Five columns now arose,
and, bending in the direction of the wind, they seemed
placed against a low ridge covered with trees ; the
tops of the columns at this distance appeared to min-
gle with the clouds.   They were white below, and
higher up became dark, so as to simulate smoke very
closely.   The whole scene was extremely beautiful.
The banks and islands dotted over the river are
adorned with sylvan vegetation of great variety of
color and form.   At the period of our visit several

trees were spangled over with blossoms. Trees have
each their own physiognomy. There, towering over
all, stands the great burly baobab, each of whose
enormous arms would form the trunk of a large tree,
besides groups of graceful palms, which, with their
feathery-shaped leaves depicted on the sky, lend their
beauty to the scene. As a hieroglyphic they always
mean 'far from home,' for one can never get over
their foreign air in a picture or landscape. The sil-
very mohonono—which in the tropics is in form like
the cedar of Lebanon—stands in pleasing contrast
with the dark color of the motsouri, whose cypress
form is dotted over at present with its pleasant scar-
let fruit. Some trees resemble the great spreading
oak ; others assume the character of our own elms
and chestnuts ; but no one can imagine the beauty of
the view from anything witnessed in England. It
had never been seen before by European eyes ; but
scenes so lovely must have been gazed upon by angels
in their flight. The only want felt is that of mountains in the background. The falls are bounded on
three sides by ridges three hundred or four hundred
feet in height, which are covered with forest, with the
red soil appearing among the trees. When about
half a mile from the falls, I left the canoe by which
we had come down thus far, and embarked in a lighter
one, with men well acquainted with the rapids, who by
passing down the center of the stream in the eddies
and still places caused by many jutting rocks, brought
me to an island situated in the middle of the river
and on the edge of the lip over which the water rolls.
In coming hither there was danger of being swept

down by the streams which rushed along on each side
of the island; but the river was now low, and we
sailed where it is totally impossible to go when the
water is high.   But though we had reached the island,
and were within a few yards of the spot a view from
which would solve the whole problem, I believe that
no one could perceive where the vast body of water
went: it seemed to lose itself in the earth, the opposite lip of the fissure into which it disappeared being
only eighty feet distant.   At least I did not compre-
hend it until, creeping with awe to the verge, I peered
down into a large rent which had been made from
bank to bank of the broad Zambesi, and saw that a
stream of a thousand yards broad leaped down a
hundred feet and then became suddenly compressed
into a space of fifteen or twenty yards.   The entire
falls are simply a crack made in a hard basaltic rock
from the right to the left bank of the Zambesi, and
then prolonged from the left bank away through thirty
or forty miles of hills.   If one imagines the Thames
filled with low, tree-covered hills immediately beyond
the tunnel, extending as far as Gravesend, the bed of
black basaltic rock instead of London mud, and a
fissure made therein from one end of the tunnel to
the other down through the keystones of the arch,
and prolonged from the left end of the tunnel through
thirty miles of hills, the pathway being one hundred
feet down from the bed of the river instead of what it
is, with the lips of the fissure from eighty to one hundred feet apart, then fancy the Thames leaping boldly
into the gulf, and forced there to change its direction
and flow from the right to the left bank and then rush

boiling and roaring through the hills, he may have
some idea of what takes place at this, the most wonderful sight I had witnessed in Africa. In looking
down into the fissure on the right of the island, one
sees nothing but a dense white cloud, which, at the
time we visited the spot had two bright rainbows on
it. (The sun was on the meridian, and the declina-
tion about equal to the latitude of the place.) From
this cloud rushed up a great jet of vapor exactly like
steam, and it mounted two hundred or three hundred
feet high; there, condensing, it changed its hue to
that of dark smoke, and came back in a constant
shower, which soon wetted us to the skin. This
shower falls chiefly on the opposite side of the fissure
and a few yards back from the lip there stands a
straight hedge of evergreen trees, whose leaves are
always wet. From their roots a number of little rills
run back into the gulf; but, as they flow down the
steep wall there, the column of vapor, in its ascent,
licks them up clean off the rock, and away they mount
again. They are constantly running down, but never
reach the bottom.

"On the left of the island we see the water at the
bottom, a white rolling mass moving away to the prolongation of the fissure, which branches off near the
left bank of the river. A piece of the rock has fallen
off a spot on the left of the island, and juts out from
the water below, and from it I judged the distance
which the water falls to be about one hundred feet.
The walls of this gigantic crack are perpendicular,
and composed of one homogeneous mass of rock.
The edge of that side over which the water falls is

worn off two or three feet, and pieces have fallen
away, so as to give it somewhat of a serrated appearance. That over which the water does not fall is
quite straight, except at the left corner, where a rent
appears and a piece seems inclined to fall off. Upon
the whole, it is nearly in the state in which it was
left at the period of its formation. The rock is dark
brown in color, except about ten feet from the bottom, which is discolored by the annual rise of the
water to that or a greater height. On the left side
of the island we have a good view of the mass of
water which causes one of the columns of vapor to
ascend, as it leaps quite clear of the rock, and forms
a thick unbroken fleece all the way to the bottom.
Its whiteness gave the idea of snow, a sight I had
not seen for many a day. As it broke into (if I may
use the term) pieces of water all rushing on in the
same direction, each gave off several rays of foam,
exactly as bits of steel, when burned in oxygen gas,
give off rays of sparks. The snow-white sheet seemed
like myriads of small comets rushing on in one direction, each of which left behind its nucleus-rays of
foam. I never saw the appearance referred to noticed
elsewhere. It seemed to be the effect of the mass
of water leaping at once clear of the rock and but
slowly breaking up into spray.

"I have mentioned that we saw five columns of
vapor ascending from this strange abyss. They are
evidently formed by the compression suffered by the
force of the water's own fall into an unyielding wedge-
shaped space. Of the five columns, two on the right
and one on the left of the island were the largest,

and the streams which formed them seemed each to exceed in size the falls of the Clyde at Stonebyres when that river is in flood. This was the period of low-water in the Leeambye; but, as far as I could guess, there was a flow of five or six hundred yards of water, which, at the edge of the fall, seemed at least three feet deep."

From the falls, the explorer returned up the river to Kalai, where, on November 20th, he bade adieu to Sekeletu and the Makololo, and, with a company of 114 men furnished by the generous chief as escort and to carry tusks to the east coast, struck out on his long journey, first going northward, and for several hundred miles leaving the Zambesi far to his right. The journey for a long distance lay through the country of the Batoka. All the tribes of this people have the custom of knocking out their front upper teeth when the individuals arrive at the age of puberty. This is true of both males and females. The under teeth in consequence grow long and project outwards, giving the people a hideous appearance especially when they laugh. Sebituane with all his power was unable to eradicate this practice. The women are very scantily clothed, but the men go about *in puris naturalibus* and without the smallest sense of shame. Their mode of salutation is emphatic but singular. They throw themselves on their backs on the ground, and rolling from side to side slap the outside of their thighs as expressive of thankfulness and welcome, and uttering "kina bomba." The chief of the Batoka was Monze, who came one Sunday, wrapped in an extemporized shawl, and saluted the travelers, by rolling, clapping, and singing out " kina bomba" like all the rest of them. These people, though having many barbarous and repulsive customs, were friendly and in their savage way quite hospitable. While passing through the country of the Batoka the travelers were visited by a number of Bashukulompo, a tribe who live to the northward. They wear their hair in immense cones, most of which are constructed straight up from the head, but some obliquely. To keep these ornaments in order must require as much attention as a modern belle gives to head-dress, chignon, braid, waterfall, and all. But it may be claimed as a general truth, applying to all races of mankind, that much attention is given to the external portions of the head.

The country through which the expedition was now passing, was one of great beauty. The grass was green, trees were abundant, and instead of the vast plains of the Londa territory there were high ridges and hills, making the country such as is often called rolling. It was not long after leaving Kalai that the Lekene river was crossed, and soon afterwards the Unguesi. These both flow to the west, emptying into the Leeambye above the Falls of Victoria. In the vicinity of the Mozuma or River of Dila there were many ruins of large towns showing that the country had in former times been inhabited by large numbers of people. The depopulation had been caused by war, for the principal ruins were worn mill-stones and the round balls of quartz with which the grinding was effected. Had the people removed in peace, they would have taken these balls with

SLAVES ABANDONED.

them. Here Sebituane had formerly lived, and in
this beautiful pastoral region had formerly roamed
vast herds of cattle. The country was now well inhabited, for large numbers came daily to see the
white men, but they were not the same who had formerly lived here.

There was no diminution in the number of wild
animals. With the exception of ostriches, and giraffes,
"game" was even more abundant than Dr. Livingstone had ever found it in Africa. Elephants, buffaloes, zebras, and antelopes were thick as autumnal
leaves that strew the brooks in Vallambrosa. All
these beasts were exceedingly tame, and two or three
elephants were sometimes slain in a single day.
There were many birds of song, too, whose notes
were very pleasant, but appeared to the Scotchman
to have "a foreign accent." Their plumage, unlike
that of most of the birds of the tropics in the western hemisphere, is not brilliant. There are some
birds whose plumage is very gay and beautiful, and
specimens of these are found in museums; but as a
rule the feathers of the birds of central South Africa are as plain as those of the birds of England.
The animals generally are smaller than those of the
southern part of the continent, a singular fact, seeing
that they have more food and a greater variety.
Farther along this journey Dr. Livingstone found
that the people built their huts in gardens on stages,
as a protection against the spotted hyena, a cowardly
animal, but which will attack persons when asleep.
He has amazing powers of jaw, and will crunch the
bones of an ox into powder for his food.

The travelers did not want for food. Not only were the animals plenty, but many fruit trees grow in these parts, and Dr. Livingstone's companions and escort were constantly eating as they journeyed. The grass is shorter and richer than in most of the country which had heretofore been traversed and therefore better for the cattle. Flowers abounded also, so that on all accounts, the explorer-missionary appears to have been fully justified in claiming that years of experience in traveling had taught him how to make things comfortable. In addition, he was persuaded of the healthiness of the country, and observing many evidences of the existence of coal, confidence in the establishment of a missionary station in this region became strongly fixed in his mind. And the more he saw of the people and their many savage customs, the more was he convinced of the desirability of commerce and missionary work among them.

On January 14th, 1856, the explorers reached the confluence of the Loangwa and the Zambesi. Here are the ruins of Zumbo, once quite a missionary station of the Jesuits and a trading-post of the Portuguese. "I walked about some ruins I discovered," says Dr. Livingstone, " built of stone, and found the ruins of a church, and on one side lay a broken bell, with the letters I. H. S. and a cross, but no date. There were no inscriptions on stone, and the people could not tell what the Bazunga called their place." These ruins were in reality all that was left of Zumbo. There were ruins of eight or ten stone houses, which had evidently been surrounded by capacious grounds, a church, and, on the opposite side of the Zambesi, a

fort. The situation for a commercial site was excellent, and the locality itself beautiful, but it seems that
the slave trade had demoralized both Jesuits and
merchants, in consequence of which the place fell into
decay and the melancholy spectacle of ruin which it
now presents.

The Portuguese and the African tribes through
whose country Dr. Livingstone was now about to
pass, had recently been at war, and though peace had
been declared the effect of late hostilities appeared in
suspicion, the rigid enforcement of " game laws," and
a desire to compel strangers to pay toll or tribute.
Hence for a long distance the party traveled so as to
avoid the villages and to see as little of the people
as possible. In short, to avoid trouble, dispute, and,
perhaps, conflict, the travelers "took to the bush,"
first negotiating with persons familiar with the country to guide them out of sight of the towns, and
whither they desired to go. By thus avoiding the
Africans, the party met more animals. This resulted
in some singular incidents. One is thus related :
" The bush being very dense and high, we were going
along among the trees, when three buffaloes, which
we had unconsciously passed above the wind, thought
that they were surrounded by men, and dashed through
our line. My ox set off at a gallop, and when I could
manage to glance back I saw one of the men up in
the air about five feet above a buffalo which was
tearing along with a stream of blood running down
his flank, When I got back to the poor fellow, I
found that he had lighted on his face, and, though he
had been carried on the horns of the buffalo about

twenty yards before getting the final toss, the ski ,
was not pierced, nor was a bone broken. When the
beasts appeared, he had thrown down his load and
stabbed one in the side. It turned suddenly upon
him, and, before he could use a tree for defence, carried him off. We shampooed him well, and then went
on, and in about a week he was able to engage in the
hunt again."

Nevertheless, the great beauty of the country; the
richness and variety of the vegetation, from trees in
whose hollow trunks twenty men might easily have
reposed, to the most delicate flowers, some of which
came up in the morning, budded, bloomed, and passed
away before the day was done ; the frequent rains ;
the comparative coolness of the atmosphere; the
hills and the swiftly-flowing rivers rendering constant
change to the scenery,—all these things together, especially as contrasted with the long, fatiguing
wadings through the vast watery plains of Londa
and the dull, level views of Kolobeng, gave great
cheerfulness to the traveler, and it may well be
doubted whether he would at this time have regarded
his own tossing by a buffalo, provided no limbs had
been broken, as anything more than a good joke.
Moreover, though the party for a considerable period
avoided head-men and villages, as we have seen, its
treatment during the journey, upon the whole, was
excessively generous and kind. " In few other countries," remarks Dr. Livingstone, " would one hundred
and fourteen sturdy vagabonds be supported by the
generosity of the head-men and villagers, and whatever they gave be presented with politeness."

On February 1st of this year (1856) the party met a number of native traders, and as some of his escort were in the scant toilet of the Batoka, being that of the garden of Eden with the exception of the fig leaves, some American calico was bought for them. It was manufactured at " Lawrence Mills, Lowell," Massachusetts, and the price paid for the quantity here bought in " the kingdom of Chicova," as it has been called, though erroneously, was two small tusks of ivory. The explorer made careful examinations in the district of Chicova for evidences of silver mines reported to have been formerly worked there, but could learn nothing tending to persuade him that such had ever been the case. On the contrary, the people knew not the difference between tin and silver.

For a great distance now the expedition had been through the country of the Banyai. The Government of this people is peculiar, being a sort of feudal republicanism. The chief is elected, and they choose the son of a deceased chief's sister in preference to his own offspring. When dissatisfied with one candidate, they even go to a distant tribe for a successor, who is usually of the family of the late chief, a brother's or sister's son, but never his own son or daughter. The children of the chiefs have fewer privileges than the free men generally; but they can never be sold into slavery. The Banyai are a fine race. A great many of them are of a light coffee-and-milk color. As they draw out their hair into small cords a foot in length, and entwine the inner bark of a certain tree round each separate cord, and

dye this substance of a reddish color, they put the
explorer in mind of the ancient Egyptians. When
traveling, the Banyai draw this hair up into a bunch
and tie it on top of the head. They are very cleanly
in their habits.

On March 3d, the party reached Tete, a place on
the Zambesi, in possession of the Portuguese. The
commandant, Major Sicard, received Dr. Livingstone
with most generous welcome. He also presented his
men with abundance of provisions, and one of his
own houses in which to live, free from the bite of the
tampans, till they could construct their own huts.
The bite of this insect sometimes causes fatal fever.
" It may please our homœopathic friends," says Dr.
Livingstone, "to hear that in curing the bite of the
tampan, the natives administer one of the insects
bruised in the medicine employed."

Formerly a place of very considerable importance,
Tete had now become comparatively a ruin, with but
two or three thousand inhabitants and insignificant
trade. The cause of decadence of Portuguese power
here is very clearly stated by Dr. Livingstone. At
first, considerable quantities of wheat, millet, maize,
coffee, sugar, indigo, besides gold and ivory, were exported. The agricultural resources of the country
round about are very great. Gold dust was procured
at various washings north, south, and west of Tete.
The interior swarmed with elephants, and ivory could
be bought for a song. Slaves were used in agriculture, gold-washing, and elephant hunting. A market
for these was opened, and they were sold for trans-
portation. Thus the goose which laid the golden eggs

was slain. Tete declined, and is now of less importance than a great majority of the county towns of the
United States. There is a wall about the old town,
within which are a few European houses. Most of
the people (natives) live outside the walls and engage
in agricultural pursuits, At the time of Livingstone's
visit there were less than a score of Portuguese in
the place, with the exception of a few soldiers temporarily stationed there on account of sickness at a
post lower down the Zambesi. All the country round
about available for agricultural purposes, is under
cultivation. The value of goods now required for
the trade of Tete is only about $45,000 annually.
Plantations of coffee, formerly profitable, and export-
ing considerable quantities, are now entirely deserted,
and hardly a single tree can be found. The indigo
is found growing everywhere and large quantities of
the senna plant grow in and about Tete but neither
is collected. There are no less than three gold-wash-
ings near Tete, formerly quite productive, now but
little worked. Dr. Livingstone himself was the discoverer of coal deposits not far distant.

On the 22d of April, Dr. Livingstone left Tete,
and, a fine boat having been presented to him by
Major Sicard, the commandant, he proceeded by the
Zambesi to Senna, where he arrived on the 27th.
The voyage down the broad, deep, rapid river,
crowded with cultivated islands, and most of the way
bounded by shores of picturesque beauty, was like a
pleasure trip. The great traveler thought the state
of Tete quite lamentable, but found that of Senna
ten times worse. Every thing was in a state of stag-

nation and ruin. There was but a single exception,
and this not among the Portugese or half-castes.
Some Africans were building boats after the European model. They are very well made and sell at
prices ranging from $100 to $500.

On the 11th of May, the whole population of
Senna turned out to witness Dr. Livingstone's departure. His party was now small, a number having
been left at Tete and others here, hired to transport
government goods in canoes to the former place.
The commandant had liberally supplied provisions,
and the sail down the Zambesi to Mazaro, the begin-
ing of the great river's delta was very pleasant. At
Mazaro, the party took the way by the Kilimane
river, being that portion of the Zambesi known by
this name, and arrived at the town of Kilimane on
the 20th of May. This is a most disconsolate place,
in a marshy, unhealthful situation, several miles distant
from the ocean. Here the Missionary remained until July 12th, when, accompanied by his faithful Makololo companion, Sekwebu, he embarked on Her
Majesty's brig "Frolic" for Mauritius. The voyage
was made in precisely one month. Sekwebu was a
general favorite on shipboard, and rapidly picked up
a knowledge of English. At Mauritius a steamer
came out to tow the vessel into the harbor. Sekwebu, the strain on whose mind by new and constantly changing scenes had been severe, and had
given evidences of aberration, now became insane,
and on the following day cast himself into the sea,
and pulling himself down by the chain cable, was
drowned. Poor fellow! This was the last that was

ever seen of this fine Makololo gentleman. A long and careful search for his body was unsucessful.

—And here it will be proper to take a retrospective view of the missionary labors, explorations, scientific researches of Dr. Livingstone thus far made in the continent which had so long sat in darkness.

It will be recollected that he arrived at Cape Town, in the extreme southern portion of Africa in 1840. When, therefore, he sailed from Kilimane in July, 1856, he had been sixteen years engaged in laboring, in that part of the world about which the least had been known, for the advancement of the cause of Christian civilization and the progress of knowledge and science. If the preceding pages and extracts have not been prepared in vain, those who have read them have correctly concluded that Dr. Livingstone is no ordinary "missionary of the Gospel." It is much, very much, to be that. He is that, and more. We find in him, for instance, many of the elements of a successful statesman. If he cannot get all he thinks desirable, he will take all the good that he can accomplish, trusting to time, reflection, and God's good providence to bring about the remainder. This admirable characteristic was most happily illustrated, so far as individuals are concerned, in the notable case of Sechele, chief of the Bechuanas. Had it been undertaken to bring him into the church "with a rush," there might indeed have been a temporary success, but he probably would have gone out with a rush before long, and accomplished great and long-continued harm instead of good. Long established institutions—or habits and

customs, if you please, of tribes of men whose existence has continued for many centuries—are not to be
hastily overthrown, even though they may have been
established in error, or, if you please again, human
depravity. A child with a hammer in its hand, or a
lunatic, can undermine St. Peters and bring down the
majestic pile in ruins. Genius, patience, long years
of labor would be required even to rebuild it. The
faculty of tearing down is oftentimes admirable, but
when one can destroy evil by replacing it with good
he has the true inspiration of heaven and the magnificent genius of progress. If Dr. Livingstone did
not leave Kolobeng with so many professing believers in the religion which he espoused as might have
been encouraging to the sanguine, he at any rate
succeeded in eradicating some of the most lamentable notions of barbarism from the minds of the Bakwains, and implanting instead of them some of the
most beneficent teachings of the Christian system.
Thus were several wars prevented among the tribes
of South Africa by the power of the self-same truths
which have guided to illustrious triumphs of peace
the international polity of Mr. Gladstone and John
Bright, and this long before the Joint High Commission between Great Britain and the United States
had been dreamed of. If the Bakwains were not
taken at once from the gloom of barbarism and
placed on a plane of civilization, they were placed
fairly in the road leading thither, and year by year
they have been going on in the right direction.
They are no longer barbarians. A thousand degrading habits and customs and lamentable errors have

been abandoned. They are growing into civilized beings; and their civilization will be Christian.

A similar fact is true of Dr. Livingstone's influence among the Makololo. Sebituane, who established this singular people in permanent power and rude prosperity throughout a large proportion of central South Africa, though a man of war, possessed, indeed, by nature, with a military genius of most remarkable scope and versatility, was undoubtedly greatly the superior in moral attributes of his successor, Sekeletu, as he certainly was among the foremost of all modern Africans of whom we have any knowledge in practical statesmanship. He was in reality a much greater man than many a hero of classical story and song, and may with no little appropriateness be called the Robert Bruce of central Africa. Had Sebituane lived a few years longer, it cannot be doubted that, with Livingstone's practical assistance, the condition of the Makololo would have been vastly improved. But, though Sekeletu is much inferior in ability and ambition to Sechele, not to mention Sebituane, yet is he, through Livingstone's influence, a much wiser and abler ruler than, according to all probability, he could otherwise have been, and his people are more ambitious, more prosperous, more happy. They too are on the way to a better and higher stage of existence. Their huts are better than they were; they are improving their breeds of cattle; their system of agriculture has progressed; many savage punishments and customs have been abolished; their growth in moral and intellectual strength is evident. Sekeletu, though greatly inferior to Sebituane, rules over a superior people.

Now it is certain that in acquiring his prodigious influence over either the Bakwains or the Makololo, Dr. Livingstone preached and prayed on all proper occasions; and no one has a higher appreciation of the efficacy of preaching and praying. He did more. He taught the people how to build houses; how to mend wagons; how to do a thousand little things whereby they would be made more comfortable. Thus by degrees their minds were opened to receive the truth that the ways of civilization are good; and one by one old prejudices were eradicated, old errors were abandoned, and the power of truth and justice more and more acknowledged. It is probable that since the advent of Dr. Livingstone among them, the Bakwains and Makololo have progressed as much in government, trade, agriculture, as the Saxons of England did during several generations after the battle of Hastings. Had he devoted himself strictly to religious teaching, no such result could have taken place. The genius of common sense gave him a notable triumph; and let it never be forgotten that common sense ought ever to be regarded as one of the best of the Christian graces. To go without this to a heathen land is simply to cast pearls before swine.

Another fact that ought to be considered in any candid review of this explorer-missionary's labors in South Africa is his evident comprehension of the whole situation. He not only considered Africa from the Christian point of view—speaking here in somewhat of a technical sense—but he looked upon it as

a field also for humanitarian efforts; for scientific researches; for investigations of all kinds whereby the
sum of knowledge might be increased; for the spread
of commercial relations with other peoples; for advance in a knowledge of political economy. Hence
he had no qualms of conscience upon leaving his
Bakwain friends to look out for themselves for a season while he should undertake a journey to the interior. Thus he discovered Lake Ngami, whereby
his power as a missionary preacher was in no degree
increased, but his influence with the world of letters
and science was. So, too, his discovery of the Zambesi river in the central portion of South Africa
greatly aided in making his character respected by
many leading minds of the world, who by this means
were led, first, to have a respect for missionaries, and
then for the cause which missionaries represented.
Many a fine mind in christendom which had thought
of the Africans about as Cuvier might have thought
of a rhinoceros, Agassiz of a megatherium, or Colonel
Foster of a mound-builder, through these discoveries
was led to reflect at least upon the importance if not
the duty of preventing such vast masses of humanity
as lived round the lakes and along the magnificent
rivers of Africa from going to waste. Thus Christianity received a valuable reinforcement of allies if
not of devotees.

Patience, in great degree, is, perhaps, possessed only
by extraordinary minds. It enabled Dr. Livingstone,
having opened the way for civilization in Africa to
continue his explorations in other portions of the continent, with sublime confidence that the present and

the future would take all practicable advantages of
the past. It thus happened, as a consequence of his
comprehensive views and his sublime patience, not
only that men of letters and scientific savants everywhere became interested in Africa, in addition to the
various organized Christian societies for the spread
of the Gospel in heathen lands, but the spirit of commercial enterprise was aroused in that behalf. The
Christian church, the literati, including herein the
newspaper press, the devotees of science, have vast
influence in the world ; but when these are reinforced
by what we call the commercial world, they are sure
not only to carry the war for civilization, progress,
and profit, into Africa but through it, and bring to
development all the resources of the people and the
country. We know nothing that can stand against a
cause, sustained by the prayers of the Christian church
and supported by the power of the men on 'Change.

This three-fold character of Dr. Livingstone's labors and explorations in Africa is a demonstration
of his remarkable genius. Had he been only a missionary, his work might have demonstrated his personal piety and been long remembered by religious
societies. Had he been only a missionary and scientific explorer, he might have been long highly esteemed by both religious and learned bodies. Being
a missionary, a scientific explorer, and a man thoroughly acquainted with the necessities, the wants,
and the enterprising spirit of the commercial world,
he drew to the field of his labors the hearty
interest of those mighty powers which, when allied
together, never have known, and never will know,

such word as fail. America would perhaps be hardly better known than Africa to-day, had the conversion of the aborigines been the ONLY motive impelling to the exploration of the country. Now that the natural agricultural, manufacturing, and mineral resources of the country of the black man have become known, and the spirits of Christian propagandism, of intellectual progress, and of commercial enterprise have been aroused in behalf of that continent, there can be no reasonable doubt that its progress during the coming few years will be greater than that of the past hundreds of generations.

Such, it cannot be questioned, is but a fair outline of the general character of this great explorer-missionary's work in Africa and a justifiable prophecy of its probable results.

Those whose labors are purely intellectual—and these in all ages have been, upon the whole, the greatest benefactors of mankind—are apt to under-estimate the genius of those whom we generally call " men of action." Dr. Livingstone is a man of action not only but one whose whole life has been that of exceeding hard work. Bodily and intellectually he has ever been a working man. His labors in Africa, extending over a period of sixteen years, included moral instruction, medical attention, mechanical pursuits, scientific researches, astronomical observations, and a series of explorations in an unknown country and among savage, barbarous tribes, without a parallel, perhaps, all things considered, in all authentic history of personal adventure. When he went to South Africa, in 1840, the vast interior was wholly unknown. In the north-

ern part of South Africa on the west coast, there
were a number of Portuguese settlements. Along the
coast for several hundred miles and inland some two
or three hundred, the natives were semi-subject to
this foreign people. The trade of the country was
principally in slaves and ivory. Below this expanse,
known on the maps as Lower Guinea, the coast appeared to be a vast extent of bleak and barren desert. South of the Orange river and extending here
across the continent and on the east side still farther
north was a collection of English and Dutch Colonies, and provinces under somewhat civilized native
government, all being more or less under the influence of the British of Cape Colony, the largest of all.
Stretching northward along the east coast were Mozambique and Zanzibar under Portuguese and Mohammedan rule, but inhabited by tribes who were discon-
tented and warlike. These portions of the east
coast had long been in a state of decadence, a melancholy fact, which was in large measure owing, as
shown by Dr. Livingstone himself, when speaking of
the ruins of Zumbo, Tete, and Senna on the eastern
Zambesi, to the prevalence of the slave trade. As
to the vast interior of this continental rim all was
unknown or conjecture, except here and there a spot
where a missionary had established a station, and
whence had irradiated some rays of knowledge to the
outside world. Such was the situation of South
Africa when Dr. Livingstone, in the full vigor of
young manhood, appeared upon the scene, a recently-
graduated physician and an humble missionary. He
soon proceeded about a thousand miles into the in-

AN AFRICAN CHIEF RECEIVING DR. LIVINGSTONE.

terior, and, learning the language of a people who inhabit a wide expanse of country, established a missionary station. By a genuinely philosophical and liberal, comprehensive plan of education, he gradually brought this people to adopt many of the most beneficent rules and practices of civilization. Before he left Africa, it could not with truth be said that they were a barbarous people. Meantime, he had crossed the great desert of Kalahari and discovered Lake Ngami and the Zambesi river in the centre of South Africa. The contributions thus made to the geographical knowledge of the world have been universally and generously recognized, as have been also by the scientific his contributions in botany, geology, and natural history. This journey, by different routes, was made several times ; and it is not improbable that his suggestion of obtaining water—the only want of this " desert," wonderfully prolific in grasses and animals which require little water—by means of artesian wells may result in reclaiming a vast expanse to cultivation and wealth.

The journey from Cape Town to St. Paul de Loanda, particularly that portion of it between the region of Lake Ngami and the Portuguese colony must be regarded as a momentous undertaking, with results, at the the time and to come, of the greatest importance. By this journey, he traversed some thirty-one degrees of latitude and about fifteen de grees of longitude. The route, in general, was in the shape of the arc of an immense circle, and the journey could not have been much less than three thousand miles in length. Remaining a consider-

9

able period among the Makololo, a great people,
numbering many tribes inhabiting the central portion
of South Africa, from Lake Ngami on the south
nearly to the confluence of the Leeba, and the Leeambye on the north and a corresponding distance
east and west—a district about as large as France—
he became greatly influential among them, and was
the means of greatly benefiting their condition. It
was in the country of the Makololo that Dr. Livingstone discovered the Zambesi, with the great falls of
Gonye and the wonderful cataract of Victoria. Between here and the limits of the Portuguese power
he discovered vast plains for many weeks of the year
covered with water, and then with beautiful flowers
thick as grass. Here too he found a river part of
whose waters sought outlet in the Indian ocean, and
part in the Atlantic. He discovered that Lake Dilolo was the water-shed between the two oceans, and
yet that for vast distances on either side the general
elevation of the country, beyond the immense flat
plains in the midst of which is Dilolo, is thousands of
feet higher than that at the water-shed. Hence he
practically discovered that the general form of this
great portion of Africa was that of an immense basin,
with crevices here and there for the escape of the
water through the rims to the sea.* This practical
discovery was not made, however, until Dr. Living-

* When Dr. Livingstone arrived in England in 1856, he discovered that Sir
Roderick Murchison, the distinguished geologist, in his discourse before the
Royal Geographical Society in 1852, had enunciated, from Bain's geological
map of Cape Colony and a few other data, a hypothesis of the configuration of
the African continent, here entirely confirmed by Dr. Livingstone. The latter's
great work is dedicated to Sir Roderick, in fitting terms, with this fact happily
mentioned.

stone had, through incredible difficulties, reached the sea shore on the east coast, and was returning again on his journey "across the continent."

This journey, of which we have just given a rapid sketch traversed twenty-five degrees of longitude. It was in distance traveled about two thousand miles, and as the one from Linyanti, the capital of the Makololo, to Loanda, the capital of Portuguese Angola, demonstrated the practicability of a route to the ocean on the west, so did this in the opposite direction. When, therefore, Dr. Livingstone reached the delta of the Zambesi, he had shown by his own explorations that journeys could be made to central South Africa from the east, the west, and the south. He had become acquainted with large numbers of tribes, about all of whom were addicted to polygamy, some to repulsive customs and superstitions, idolatrous rites and degrading beliefs. He found many of these people who had large herds of cattle and who in a rude way gave considerable attention to agriculture. Many were little inclined either to superstition or true religion. Few had any notion of trade until he himself taught them by precept and example what it was. He had discovered several lakes and beautiful rivers, immense level plains of great fertility, many lovely valleys capable of producing heavy crops of grain. He had discovered several deposits of coal, and had visited gold washings which might again be made profitable. Portions of the country are without forest, others are covered with trees, some of which are the largest and most majestic in the world.

Thus in his travels of more than nine thousand miles, this great explorer had taught scholars how to make geographical and geological maps of a very large portion of the globe. He had interested in its people and in its growth and development the efforts of the Christian, the learned, and the commercial public. Those efforts, in the nature of things, will not cease until the continent shall everywhere become the abode of the friends of civilization and progress and the scene of many of their permanent and beneficent triumphs. Surely if man ever deserved rest from his labors, Dr. Livingstone now did.

CHAPTER VII.

DR. LIVINGSTONE IN ENGLAND.

His Reception by His Countrymen—The Preparation of His Work Entitled "Missionary Travels and Researches in South Africa"—Favorably Received by Christendom.

We left Dr. Livingstone on shipboard in the island of Mauritius, lamenting the untimely death of his long-time Makololo companion, Sekwebu. He remained here enjoying the good climate and English comfort, and getting well of an enlargement of the spleen—caused by some thirty different attacks of the African fever—for several months, and then departed for England. Taking the route by the Red Sea, and happily avoiding a threatened shipwreck, he reached home on the 12th of December as happy and grateful a man, no doubt, as there was in the three kingdoms.

One remarkable effect of Dr. Livingstone's long sojourn and travels among the tribes of Africa was that, so far as his native language was concerned, it almost untongued him. He had so long almost exclusively spoken in one or another foreign language or dialect, and for nearly five years had only met with an Englishmen now and then, that when he went aboard the "Frolic" off Kilimane, he found himself almost tongue-tied. "I seemed to know the language perfectly," says he, "but the words I wanted would not come at my call." By the time he reached England, however, this cause of embarrassment among Englishman had greatly diminished, and he could respond to the hearty receptions with which he was everywhere greeted in good vigorous Saxon. Soon there was no halt in his speech at all.

It is probably true that no returned missionary ever met with a more cordial reception by his countrymen than did Dr. Livingstone. He was welcomed by all classes of people, while religious bodies, missionary societies, and select circles of learned men hastened to express their appreciation of his great labors and discoveries. Medals, fellowships, and memberships of various associations for the cultivation and spread of knowledge and science were conferred upon him. Nor were these recognitions confined to associations in his own country, but came also from France, the United States, and other lands. During the period of his absence the public press of his native land and the United States had been so wonderfully enlarged in scope by the magnetic telegraph, and its influence had been so greatly increased in consequence thereof and of the enterprising spirit of certain journalists whose names have since become celebrated throughout the world, that it might well be said a new power had grown up in the state and society. Reports of meetings in honor of Dr. Livingstone were carried by ten thousand of the swiftest wings all over the kingdom, and very soon afterwards all over the United States. Thus, in all that vast portion of the world where the English is the language of the people, more was known in a few days of his explorations in Africa than would have been known to the learned few in many weeks or months had those explorations ended about the time at which they commenced.

It was impossible that the world should be satisfied with the mere outlines of a career which had been so adventurous and so useful as that of this great explorer in Africa. The more the press published in regard to it, the more the public perceived that a full account could not but contain a vast quantity of interesting and valuable reading matter. Accordingly, Dr. Livingstone was induced to prepare that volume—" Missionary Travels and Researches in South Africa "—upon which his literary fame with the world at large thus far rests, and which unfolded to the reading public a series of strange pictures upon which the public has ever since looked with deep and growing interest.

The preparation of this volume, which, it is believed, may with justice be pronounced a work which the world will not willingly let die, was, perhaps, the most difficult of all Dr. Livingstone's great undertakings. " The preparation of this narrative," he says in his preface, " has taken much longer time than, from my inexperience in authorship, I had anticipated." And he goes on to say that " those who have never carried a book through the press can form no idea of the amount of toil it involves. The process has increased my respect for authors and authoresses a thousand-fold." The work was really commenced upon the invitation of Sir Roderick Murchison, President of the Royal Geographical Society, which had given Dr. Livingstone a special meeting of welcome upon his return from Africa. The design came near being frustrated, however, by the explorer's inability to provide for his Makololo escort and companions, whom he had left at Tete, Senna, and Kilimane (often spelled Quilimane). This difficulty was overcome, however, by His Majesty Don Pedro V., of Portugal, who sent out orders for the support of these men until Dr. Livingstone should return. Thus freed from care on this account, he proceeded with his work of authorship, and gave to it, as must be evident to every one who has carefully examined it, the greatest study and pains. As a work of literary art, it is surely one of the most complete successes among books of the kind which have ever been published. Perhaps it may truthfully be called among books of its general kind the greatest success.

The work was completed and went to press in the year 1857, and at once met with the most generous reception by the reading public and the favorable judgment of critics. It was speedily republished in the United States, where very large editions were rapidly sold. No inexperienced author of a work of a serious nature ever found his way more rapidly to the general reading public than David Livingstone. His book was a faithful dauguerreotype of his labors in Africa, and these, as we have already seen, were of a three-fold nature; such, namely, as to be of special interest and value to all Christian denominations interested in the work of missionaries; to all men devoted to the acquisition and spread of scientific knowledge; and also to that large, influential, and practical class of men who conduct the trade and commerce of the world. For all these, he was inspired by his remarkable genius to construct a work which was at once instructive, interesting, and valuable. And hence the fact that his work was favorably received throughout Christendom was but natural, and one of the logical results of the liberal spirit with which he did everything that he was called upon to do.

And here, perhaps, it might be well enough to close the account of the literary labors and results connected with Dr. Livingstone's first sojourn in Africa. It may be well to remark, however, that even before the appearance of his great work, several attempts were made in England to impose upon the public, as his, spurious narratives of his travels. The journals of London, however, were quick to expose them, and the booksellers utterly refused to have anything to do with them, greatly to the credit and honor of the trade. Some two years after his work was published, a volume appeared in America, the title-page of which was almost identical with that of the original work, and upon which copyright was published as secured according to law. It is simply the work of Livingstone, greatly and most injuriously abridged, with an addendum giving an outline of a few discoveries in Africa, familiar to every school boy. So far as it goes, it is Livingstone, word for word, but very many pages to which he evidently gave the greatest study and in which he took the greatest pride, are entirely omitted. Thus, for example, the whole of his interesting account of the discovery of Lake Dilolo

as the water-shed of central South Africa, with that
singular river sending part of its waters to the Atlantic, part to the Indian Ocean, is expunged.   Other
equally interesting portions of the work are wanting.
And this book is duly " entered according to the act
of Congress."   It is like authorizing some one to take
out a copyright on the play of Hamlet, whose authorship in the business had consisted in removing Hamlet altogether from the drama.   Such murder of
genius in accordance with the forms of law is hardly
less than atrocious.   Perhaps that wretched travesty
of Mr. Dickens's most brilliant and powerful novel,
which travesty goes by the name of " Newman
Noggs" and is often represented on the American
stage, is copyrighted.   These things being so, do we
have any copyrights which white men, or any other
men, are bound to respect ?*

And here the great explorer might have rested
upon his laurels.   None of his cotemporaries had
done more, all things considered, for religion, science,
and mankind.   Had ambition only guided him he
would have been content; but genius and duty impelled him to again forsake those " English comforts,"

---

* There is a patent medicine originally compounded in the United States—
and it is understood to be good enough in its way—known as " Perry Davis's
Pain Killer."   Merit and reservoirs of printer's ink made it famous.   It was
proceeding in a perfect march of triumph against the combined pains—particularly those of the stomach—of America and Europe, when a noted manufacturer
of Mustang liniment got up a " pain killer" and labeled his vials with an exact
fac simile—Perry Davis's jolly head and all—of the other.   The fact becoming
known, he was compelled to peremptorily stop this spurious business.   It is
something that the great republic protects the regular workings of men's stom-
achs.   After a while it may give some proper protection to the labors of men's
brains.

which are, in fact, perhaps, the most comfortable in the world,* and proceed for the second time to that continent about which he had himself thrown a peculiar charm and interest which, it would appear, can only increase with time, and as modern enterprise and civilization extend their triumphs and their beneficent influences over the land on so large part of which he was long the solitary and intrepid ex plorer.

* I so conclude from a lecture which I happened once to hear in a Western town, entitled "English Hearts and Homes," by Mrs. Celia Logan—the most instructive and interesting essay I ever heard a lady read on the platform.

CHAPTER VIII.

Again Sails for Africa—Painful Reports of His Death—The Long Suspense in Regard Thereto—Conflicting Reports.

Among great men who have had much to do in directing the destinies of nations or any considerable number of mankind, there have been two kinds—one class, who supposed they controlled events and by imperial will and power mastered circumstances and the course of Providence; the other, composed of those who have modestly imagined they were but instruments in the hands of a Superior Power through whom some of his beneficent designs were to be accomplished. Among the former was Napoleon Bonaparte, who probably thought that in many particulars God was entitled to high respect, but that in the general conduct of military campaigns, He could not be compared with the French Emperor. It is historically true that the men of this class have generally inflicted great evils upon mankind. Of the other class of great men, David Livingstone is a conspicuous example; and the one thing of which he is the most unaffectedly ignorant is his own genius. "If the reader remembers," he modestly remarks near the close of his work, "the way in which I was led, while teaching the Bakwains, to commence exploration, he will, I think, recognize the hand of Providence." And he goes on to show how, previously to this, Se-

bituane had gone north and from a country larger
than France expelled hordes of bloody savages, and
occupied their country with a people speaking the
language of the Bakwains.   Then again he was singularly turned toward the west instead of the east
coast of Africa, it thus happening that when he returned upon his great expedition across the continent,
the country was at peace and his life saved.   Meantime, Sechele himself at Kolobeng had become a
missionary to his own people and they were becoming civilized.   " I think," he concludes, "that I see the
operation of the unseen hand in all this, and I hum-
bly hope that it will still guide me to do good in my
day and generation in Africa."

But this explorer was withal eminently practical.
He wanted British merchants as well as English missionaries to go to Africa, and thinking that philanthropy and profit were equally interested, he believed
that the explorations he had already made fully justified the opinion that still further discoveries might
completely demonstrate the fact that Africa was not
only a great missionary field but might become of
the greatest value in the commercial world through
the production especially of cotton and sugar.   "I
propose," he says, "to spend some more years of labor, and shall be thankful if I see the system fairly
begun in an open pathway which will eventually benefit both Africa and England."

From all which it is clear that the second expedition of Dr. Livingstone to Africa, and which has
not yet (in 1872) been concluded, was the result of
a deliberate opinion that, with the blessing of heaven,

he might be able to accomplish that which should result in great good to Africa and at the same time help to increase the trade and commerce of his own country. Impelled by such worthy and unselfish motives, he again left England in March, 1858, and sailed for Kilimane. He had resigned his position as missionary for the London Society, but the British government had appointed him consul at Kilimane, with the understanding that he was not on this account to give up his character of explorer. On the contrary, he was supplied with a small vessel, and accompanied by a number of scientific associates, made a number of exploring expeditions by which his ideas in respect to the production of cotton and sugar and the overthrow|of|the slave traffic were greatly encouraged, and the conclusion reached that it would not be long before the opening of commercial intercourse between European nations and the tribes of South Africa. It was afterwards discovered by Mr. Young, in charge of an English expedition of search, which proceeded far up the Zambesi river, that the memory of Dr. Livingstone was highly revered, and his influence manifested in the moral improvement of the people and the advancement of their material interests. Subsequently, Dr. Livingstone made an expedition in a large region of country drained by the river Rovuma, which, along the east coast of Africa is a sort of boundary between Mohammedan and Portuguese authority. For this expedition a steamer was provided, but it was found to be of too great draft of water to be of much service. Dr. Livingstone, therefore, with the object of accomplishing the great design of his second voyage to Africa, returned to England, having re-explored a large portion of country along the Zambesi and visited for the first time the tribes of a large extent of country several hundred miles north of the Zambesi in its eastward course. This return to England was, however, but a part of the expedition upon which he had started in 1858, or rather an episode in it, without which the original object—the discovery of the principal watershed of the African continent, including the sources of the Nile—would not have been accomplished. Whilst, therefore, Dr. Livingstone has made three voyages from England to Africa, it will be more convenient to group his series of explorations under the general heading of two great expeditions—the first, under the auspices of the London Missionary Society, the second under those of the Royal Geographical Society, with special assistance from the British government.

For the completion of the series of explorations of this expedition, upon which the explorer is, in 1872, still engaged, he left England, August 14th, 1865, accompanied by his daughter as far as Paris. Thence he proceeded to Bombay, and provided himself with *materiel* and men for the work before him. From Bombay he proceeded to Zanzibar, and on March 28th, 1866, left that island accompanied by two boys —Chanma and Wakotasie—a number of Sepoys, several men from Johanna Island, and some Suahili from a school at Bombay, and having reached the main land proceeded to the interior by the river Rovuma. As he proceeded he from time to time sent back accounts of his progress and the interesting incidents of his explorations. But late in this year the leader of the Johanna men arrived at Zanzibar with a story that Dr. Livingstone had been murdered on the shores of Lake Nyassa by a band of Mazitus. The tale had such an air of truth that no one doubted it. Moosa's story being fully credited, the world quite generally gave up Dr. Livingstone as lost. Dr. G. Edward Seward, resident agent of the English government at Zanzibar, condensed Moosa's information into a dispatch to Lord Stanley, Secretary of State for Foreign Affairs, of which the following is the principal portion:

"ZANZIBAR, Dec. 10, 1866.

"MY LORD—I send you the saddest news. Dr. Livingstone, in his despatch from Ngomano, informed your Lordship that he stood ' on the threshold of the unexplored.' Yet, as if that which should betide him had already thrown its shadow he added:—' It is but to say little of the future.'

"My Lord, if the report of some fugitives from his party be true, this brave and good man has 'crossed the threshold of the unexplored'—he has confronted the future and will never return. He was slain, so it is alleged, during a sudden and unprovoked encounter with those very Zulus of whom he says in his despatch, that they had laid waste the country round about him and had ' swept away the food from above and in the ground.' With an escort reduced to twenty by desertion, death and dismissals, he had traversed, as I believe, that *terra incognita* between the confluence of the Loende and Rovuma rivers, at Nyomano,

THE VILLAGE ON LAKE LIEMBA (TANGANYIKA).

and the eastern or northeastern littoral of Lake Nyassa ; had crossed the lake at some point as yet unascertained; had reached a station named Kompoonda or Mapoonda, on its western, probably its northwestern, shore, and was pushing west or northwest, into dangerous ground, when between Marenga and Mukliosowe a band of implacable savages stopped the way, a mixed horde of Zulus, or Mafilte and Nyassa folk. The Nyassa folk were armed with bow and arrow, the Zulus with the traditional shield, broad bladed spears, and axes. With Livingstone there were nine or ten muskets ; his Johanna men were resting with their loads far in the rear.

" The Mafilte instantly came on to fight; there was no parley, no avoidance of the combat ; they came on with a rush, with war cries and rattling on their shields their spears. As Livingstone and his party raised their pieces their onset was for a moment checked, but only for a moment. Livingstone fired and two Zulus were shot dead (his boys fired too but their fire was harmless); he was in the act of reloading when three Mafilte leaped upon him through the smoke. There was no resistance—there could be none—and one cruel axe cut from behind him put him out of life. He fell, and when he fell his terror stricken escort fled, hunted by the Mafilte. One at least of the fugitives escaped; and he, the eye-witness, it is who tells the tale—Ali Moosa, chief of his escort of porters.

" The party had left the western shores of Nyassa about five days. They had started from Kompoonda, on the lake's borders (they left the havildar of Sepoys

10

there dying of dysentery; Livingstone had dismissed
the other Sepoys of the Bombay Twenty-first at Mataka), and had rested at Marenga, where Livingstone
was cautioned not to advance. The next station was
Mahlivoora; they were traversing a flat country,
broken by small hills, and abundantly wooded.

"Indeed, the scene of the tragedy so soon to be
consumated would appear to have been an open forest glade. Livingstone, as usual, led the way, his
nine or ten unpractised musketeers at his heels. Ali
Moosa had nearly come up with them, having left
his own Johanna men resting with their loads far in
the rear. Suddenly he heard Livingstone warn the
boys that the Ma-zitus were coming. The boys in
turn beckoned Moosa to press forward. Moosa saw
the crowd here and there between the trees.

"He had just gained the party and sunk down behind a tree to deliver his own fire when his leader
fell. Moosa fled for his life along the path he had
come. Meeting his Johanna men, who threw down
their loads and in a body really passed Moosa, his escape and that of his party verges on the marvelous.
However, at sunset, they, in great fear, left their forest refuge, and got back to the place where they
hoped to find their baggage. It was gone, and then,
with increasing dread they crept to where the slain
traveler lay.

"Near him, in front, lay the grim Zulus who were
killed under his sure aim; here and there lay scattered some four dead fugitives of the expedition.
That one blow had killed him outright, he had no
other wound but this terrible gash; it must have

gone, from their description, through the neck and
spine up to the throat in front, and it had nearly de-
capitated him.   Death came mercifully in its instant
suddenness, for David Livingstone was ever ready.

" They found him stripped of his upper clothing,
the Ma-zitus had respected him when dead.   They
dug with some stakes a shallow grave and hid from
the starlight the stricken temple of a grand spirit—
the body of an apostle, whose martyrdom should
make sacred the shores of that sea which his labors
made known to us, and which now, baptized with his
life's blood, men should henceforth know as ' Lake
Livingstone.'"

Dr. Seward added the following postscript to his
despatch to the foreign office:

" The date of Dr. Livingstone's death is left as
much to conjecture as the place of his grave.   All
that we certainly know is that he was at Nyomano
on the 18th of May last; that he proceeded to Mataka, whence he sent a despatch to this Consulate.
From Mataka he is said to have made for and struck
Nyassa, which he crossed; but where, or where Mataka is, cannot be ascertained.   The runaway Reuben,
with the Sepoys, states that Livingstone left Mataka
a few days before they set out on their return journey to Zanzibar.   They were one month and twenty
days on the road to Keelwa, which they reached
during the latter days of September.   It may be inferred from this that Livingstone left Mataka about
the middle of last July.   The Johanna men named
six weeks as the probable time of their return journey from Mapoonda to Keelwa with the slave cara-

van. The fight with the Zulus took place sixteen days before they set out. They reached Keelwa in November, Zanzibar the 6th of December. Roughly then, we may conjecture the death of their leader to have happened during September. The statements of our informants as to time, distance, and direction are distressingly vague and untrustworthy."

The publication of this despatch at once created a profound sensation throughout the civilized world. There being no apparent reason to doubt the truthfulness of the story, it was quite universally accepted, and most men lamented the death of the great explorer with unfeigned sadness. The obituary notices which appeared in the public journals and proceedings of many learned bodies demonstrated the fame of Dr. Livingstone in a manner which will surely be exquisitely agreeable to him when he shall read the eulogiums, as, it is to be hoped, he may soon do. Dr. Kirk, of Zanzibar, who had, in former years, accompanied Dr. Livingstone in some of his explorations, gave the man Moosa a long and careful examination and cross-examination, and the longer he proceeded the more terrible the facts connected with Dr. Livingstone's death appeared. A letter from him, generally published and quoted by all journals, seemed to leave the painful reports fully and abundantly confirmed. The world's sorrow, therefore, expressed in every proper way, was, to all appearance, entirely reasonable.

Nevertheless, there were those who did not put their trust in Moosa's story. Among these was Sir Roderick Murchison, whose reputation for sagacity

In England was very high. So early as 1844, Sir Roderick had announced, from the examination of certain rocks brought to him for study, the existence of gold in Australia, and had vainly endeavored to enlist the aid of government in behalf of practically testing the question. We have seen that he correctly decyphered the general geological formation of central South Africa before the practical discovery of the fact by Livingstone. By these and other things of like nature, Sir Roderick had acquired the reputation of a prophet. He could give no special reason for his opinion, but he did not believe Moosa's story of Livingstone's death, and the fact of his want of faith in it made many suppose there might be ground for doubt after all. Sir Roderick was sustained in his doubts by Mr. E. D. Young, an African traveler of considerable experience who came forward and said that Ali Moosa belonged to a treacherous race. Suppose he had betrayed Dr. Livingstone, how else than by a cunningly-devised story of his death could he prevail upon the British consul to pay him. Here, at least, was a motive for the story, and it soon had many to believe in it. The consequence was a variety of conflicting reports and conflicting opinions, in the midst of which the Royal Geographical Society organized a search expedition and placed it under the charge of Mr. Young.

On the 8th of August, 1867, the little steel boat "Search," Mr. Young in command, was pointed up the Zambesi river, under the most explicit and comprehensive instructions from the Geographical Society. At Shupanga, the grave of Mrs. Livingstone

was visited, and such attention given it as was required.   On the 4th of September, Mr. Young heard
of a white man having been seen on Lake Pama-
lombi, which is far south of Lake Nyassa, the scene
of the reported death.   Young proceeded thither
and became convinced that the white man was Livingstone.   Continuing the search, he found that his
views were from day to day confirmed by the reports
of natives and articles which the explorer had left
with them subsequent to the time of his reported
murder.   The search was continued till toward the
close of the year, with the result that Dr. Livingstone
had certainly been seen at a long distance from the
Lake Nyassa, months after he had been reported
killed.   The expedition under Mr. Young did not
find Dr. Livingstone, but discovered enough to demonstrate that Ali Moosa's story was an ably and
cunningly devised romance.   Then the Geographical
Society received letters from Livingstone himself,
which proved that he was alive and well in February,
1867, some six months after Moosa's heroic but vain
defense near Lake Nyassa.   Authentic reports of his
presence on Lake Ujiji in October of the same year
were received.   But about this time Sir Roderick
Murchison published a letter in the London "Times"
newspaper, confidently predicting, on intelligence
which he supposed to be reliable, Dr. Livingstone's
return to England about the coming Christmas.   It
has since transpired that Sir Roderick was imposed
upon by a round-about story from Trincomalee in the
island of Ceylon, which had been based upon an entire misunderstanding of something that had been

said by Dr. Kirk, British Consul at Zanzibar, and the report of which was first transmitted from Trincomalee.

Dr. Livingstone did not appear in accordance with his friend's prediction, and the consequence was a new variety of reports of misfortune and death. Conjecture was free; nothing had been lately heard from him; the suspense of the public in regard to the fate of one in whom there was so deep and universal interest was absolutely painful. And it was at this time of intense public anxiety that an expedition was set on foot, the like of which had not previously been known and the complete success of which has bestowed upon its projector and commander imperishable renown.

CHAPTER IX.

THE HERALD EXPEDITION OF SEARCH.

The Great Development of Modern Journalism—The Telegraph—James Gordon Bennett, Horace Greeley, Henry J. Raymond—The Magnitude of American Journalistic Enterprise—The Herald Special Search Expedition for Dr. Livingstone—Stanley as a Correspondent—The Expedition on its Way Toward Livingstone.

It has already been remarked that among the many important events which had occurred in Christendom during Dr. Livingstone's first great series of explorations in Africa there were none of greater importance to mankind than the invention of the magnetic telegraph, and the prodigious development, consequent thereon—at least in great part—of the newspaper press. There is not so much difference in means of travel, between the great, lumbering wagon of Cape Colony, drawn by a number of oxen which get over a few miles in a whole day and the means of travel by the best of America's great railways, as there is between the means of current daily intelligence in 1872 and the means of that current daily intelligence as they existed when Dr. Livingstone first placed foot in Africa. If a daily journal of the manner and style of one of that time were to be now established, it would be looked upon like a curious relic of the past or an old almanac.

Nor is it strictly just to attribute the wonderful

development of public journalism since about the
year 1840 wholly to the success of Prof. Morse's
invention of the magnetic telegraph. His success
was largely due to the press, which at the time he
sought aid of Congress in behalf of his discovery had
already begun to be something more and something
better than the mere organ of power or of party. At
any rate it may with perfect safety be said that the
practical success of Prof. Morse's invention was considerably hastened by the influence of a public press
into which had recently been infused an independent
spirit and a consequent influence before unknown.
Up to about the time of which we speak the most
widely circulated journals of the United States had
been printed at the National Capital, a city which
had never been representative of the country's trade,
its literature, science, art, or labor. It was only the
seat of government, the centre of the political power
of a nation which claimed to lodge its political power
in the people. Here flourished a number of journalists of the old school, whose skill in political manipu-
lation, money making, and editorials without beginning and without end, can never be surpassed. There
is at this time more intelligence of the current events
of the day in the poorest daily journals of the "far
West" than there used to be in the "national organs"
of the respective political parties contending for the
control of our national polity. That neither one nor
the other could have justly claimed any great amount
of practical wisdom may be asserted with confidence
since the result of the rule of both—now one and
now the other—for a long period of years was a civil

war of long duration and exhaustive effects, growing out of a question which both the great parties of the times had "finally" settled by act of Congress and solemn resolution on more than one memorable occasion.

It was while this not very admirable fooling was about at its height, that certain knights of the quill, no less adventurous in their enterprises than Dr. Livingstone was in his explorations through the wilds of Africa, established themselves in the commercial metropolis of America, and soon became the head of a power in the land scarcely second to that of the government. If not a new estate in government, this power became a new estate in society. There sprang up an entirely new literature; a literature which, as regularly as the sun, appeared every morning, and soon came to be, to all well informed persons, about as necessary as the sun is to the physical world. There was no subject too abstruse, none too sacred, none too high, and few too low for the essays of the brilliant, daring, dashing minds which about this time threw themselves into the arena of journalism. Not a few who had been distinguished in the literature of former days became journalists, and the most celebrated of American novelists, the illustrious author of the "Leatherstocking Tales," finding himself too "slow" for the times, became incurably disgusted with men who cared little for venerable antiquity, and spoke of thrones and principalities, and powers, not to mention the writers of books, with all the sarcasm, wit, and irreverence of Junius and with infinitely more popular power. Here was,

as we have said, a new literature. What difference
was it that the individual essays were only for a day?
Every day there were essays equally good, and they
treated of political topics more fully and candidly
than political topics had ever been discussed before
by public journals, and they also treated of almost
everything else under the sun. Every advance in
science, every attempt at social or political reform,
every humanitarian endeavor, every attack upon
abuse and crime claimed to be hallowed by the lapse
of time, every current event of importance of every
kind, whether of fact or of idea, here in this wonderful kaleidescope could be seen, and then seen to give
way to new spectacles of equal interest. Here the
people were educated. There never has been discovered a means of education so powerful and so
universal. It is, doubtless, owing to the fact that so
many minds in America capable of creating a " permanent literature" devoted themselves to this potential means of influence, thereby losing their individu-
ality but for the time being augmenting their power,
that we have not yet produced an American Thack-
eray or even an American Dickens. In the formative
era of what may well be called journalism proper, a
very large proportion of existing genius has been
called into such active use, in America, that it has
not had leisure for books. And even in England,
many of the most distinguished thinkers have served
their regular terms as journalists.

Among the most celebrated of modern journalists
was James Gordon Bennett, the founder of the New
York " Herald" newspaper. A native of Scotland

and a Roman Catholic in religion, he was educated
for the priesthood, but whether, like John Randolph
of Roanoke, he perceived that he had "too much
spice of 'old Nick'" in his composition for the sacred
calling, or on other account, he did not take orders,
but emigrated to America instead.   After various
fortune—generally misfortune—embracing teaching,
translating, and associate-editorship, he embarked
upon the "Herald" enterprise in 1835.   It was not
until some years afterwards, however, that this journal acquired any considerable reputation outside the
city of New York, and inaugurated those news enterprises which made it so celebrated and a not un-
faithful chronicler of the passing events of the whole
world.   During the era of "special correspondence"
the "Herald" maintained an extensive corps of writers in Europe and other foreign countries, who ever
gave to the paper great interest and value.

Meantime, other young men, since distinguished,
had been educating themselves as journalists, and,
like Bennett, through various fortune.   Among them
was Horace Greeley, who established the first penny
daily paper ever published in the world, but its foundations soon gave way.   In 1841 the "Tribune" was
established, and Mr. Bennett discovered in the great
and varied abilities of Mr. Greeley and Henry J.
Raymond, assistant editor, rivals whom no assaults
could repress, and whose influence soon began to be
felt and acknowledged throughout the country.   The
warfare long waged between these journalistic giants
was always sharp, often fierce.   The intense rivalry
greatly augmented the enterprise of the printing

offices which at length became vast establishments, employing thousands of men, from the greatest intellects of the age to the ragged urchins on the street, and receiving and disbursing vast sums of money.

The invention of the telegraph added immensely to the scope and power of the daily press. Greatly increasing its expenditures, it also greatly augmented its circulation and profits. Its demand for brain-labor became perfectly prodigious, and it almost monopolized the genius of the land. In the city of New York there were established within a very few years after Morse's invention had begun regularly to click the news of the day no less than four morning journals of acknowledged reputation throughout the world, and which upon certain memorable occasions of current intelligence have contained in their combined columns nearly as great an amount of reading matter as the whole of Bancroft's history of the United States.* The average quantity of these journals' reading matter, of interest to the general public, is equivalent, every day, to from three to five volumes of Bancroft's distinguished work.

Other cities of the republic have been little if any behind the commercial and financial metropolis, excepting only the city of Washington whose most successful journalism of the old school has given way at last till quite recently to a series of wretched failures.

---

* As I write this, I take a copy of the Chicago "Tribune" of the day, and find, by actual calculation, that it contains reading matter, exclusive of advertisements, equivalent to more than 350 pages of Bancroft. Among this matter is a profoundly thoughtful speech by Horace Greeley, delivered hundreds of miles distant the night before. At this writing, he is a candidate for the chief office in the American republic.

Editorials of a journal published in the largest city of our Lake country, which was a straggling hamlet when Dr. Livingstone first went to Africa, have been known to make the proudest speculators of Wall street tremble, and powerful corporations to abandon long-conceived schemes of injustice. In an exhaustive article on the United States census of 1860, the New York "Tribune" said of the public press:

"The very great increase in the circulation of newspapers and periodicals during the last ten years is an evidence at once of a high degree of popular intelligence and of a high standard of journalistic ability. There is no doubt that this country has the best, and the best sustained public press in the world —the best, we mean, for the people and not merely the learned few. Newspapers penetrate to every part of the country, reach even the most obscure hamlet, and find their way to almost every household. Printing offices go with the vanguard of civilization toward the west, and in the 'new country' are about as numerous as the mills. The dailies of the great cities cannot be carried by the government mails; they have created, during the decade, an entirely new line of business, supporting thousands of families; on issues fairly joined they have defeated many of the most maturely considered measures of Congressional Committees."

Having given the statistics in regard to the number and circulation of the periodicals and papers of the country at the time under examination, the article goes on to say:

"The total number of daily papers thrown from the

press during the year is about half that of all the other papers and periodicals combined. Supposing each one to weigh an ounce, the weight of the whole number of daily papers printed in the United States during the year of the census was 28,644,678 pounds avoirdupois—enough to load 14,322 wagons with a ton each, or to make a train of them seventy miles in length. Were all the papers and periodicals printed in 1860 placed in such a train, it would reach from New York to Richmond. Should they be pasted into one vast sheet, they would make a covering for the continent, and leave a remnant large enough to shut out the sun from the British Islands.

"But, not to dwell upon the mere material aspect of the Public Press of America, it will suffice to say that if its records shall be preserved the historian of two thousand years hence who shall narrate the events which are now taking place, will find upon their dingy pages his best authorities and his most trustworthy sources of philosophical generalization. Not all that is left of Grecian literature, not all the grand works of the fine old Romans, give so correct a picture of the great peoples of antiquity as the daily papers of America are now taking of a people far greater than that whose phalanges swept down the barbarians from the Hellespont to the Indus, or than that 'the tramp of whose legions echoed round the world.'"

To such magnificent proportions and such stupendous influence had the American press grown during Livingstone's first sojourn in Africa. When he left England, its chief business was to chronicle small

beer. When he returned its power was more than
imperial, and all exercised through persuasion. As it
had grown in America, so it had been immensely developed in other lands, but in respect of the publication of current intelligence at the time of the happening of events, the American press is not approached by that of any other country. There is
more telegraphic news in almost any number of any
Chicago daily, for example, than the average quantity of such intelligence in the London "Times."

An additional impetus to the enterprise of journalism was given by the success of the Atlantic cable
during Dr. Livingstone's second great expedition to
Africa. It is difficult to believe these great facts
though they have occurred before our very eyes.
This wonderful achievement of science, aided by the
no less wonderful enterprise of the daily press of the
United States, made the inhabitants of Christendom
like next-door neighbors. A dispatch from Athens
in Greece, was once published by all the evening daily
journals of the United States at an earlier hour than
its date. The difference of time and the "girdle
round about the earth" put the inhabitants of the
Mississippi Valley, as they took their suppers, in a
situation in which they might have criticised an or-
ation by Demosthenes before he had gone to bed, had
Demosthenes belonged to this day and generation.

Thus had the press become the great means of the
dissemination of knowledge, and by reason of the
wonderful enterprise of its most distinguished representative men, far more potential in the affairs of the
world than any potentate or any government. It had

AN AFRICAN BRIDE BORNE TO HER HUSBAND.

come to be acknowledged as of the greatest consequence in the dissemination of science, in popular-
izing literature, in aiding moral, social, and political
reform. But the irrepressibility of its enterprising
spirit, its superiority even to the most powerful government in respect of obtaining intelligence remained
to be conclusively shown. And even this was done by
the expedition of Mr. Henry M. Stanley, in the employ of the New York "Herald," in search of Dr.
Livingstone, long lost from Christendom in the wilds
of central Africa.

So deep an interest did the government of Great
Britain take in discovering the truth of the reports
of the explorer's death, first given to the world
through the story of Ali Moosa, as condensed by Dr.
Seward, English Resident Agent at Zanzibar—the
substance of which appears in the preceeding chapter—that an expedition in that behalf was organized,
and after many hundred miles of journeyings by river
and land found unmistakable evidences that Moosa's
story was a cruel fabrication. So, too, when years
had elapsed without definite information from Dr.
Livingstone, and there arose a world of wild conjecture as to his fate, the British government again organized an expedition of search, which, as we have
seen, was at last accounts from it at Zanzibar, well
prepared for an expedition inland but waiting for a
proper season at which to begin the journey.

Meantime the great discoverer is discovered in the
heart of equatorial Africa by Mr. Henry M. Stanley,
in command of an expedition of search sent out under
the auspices of an American newspaper, the New

11

York "Herald." Thus did newspaper enterprise accomplish that in which the combined efforts of
wealthy religious societies, learned corporate bodies,
and one of the most powerful governments of earth
had failed. A brief account of this unique expedition
will be of interest :

During the civil war in the United States—1861–
65—among the many "war correspondents" of the
"Herald" was Mr. Stanley, just mentioned. He was
not so much distinguished as a writer as he was valuable to the journal on account of his fearless nature
and his restless activity. In imitation of Tennyson's
charge of the Light Brigade, he would pursue an
item if the search should carry him "into the jaws of
hell." Restrained by no danger, almost insensible to
fatigue, he could ride all day and write all night
almost, and keep up this hard work for an indefinite
period. After the war he went abroad and from various countries, generally out of the way of ordinary
lines of travel, corresponded with the "Herald."
When the proprietors of that journal—the elder Mr.
Bennett was then living—determined to organize a
"Herald Special Search Expedition," they naturally
selected Mr. Stanley as its commander. This was in
1868. Mr. Stanley at once accepted the charge, and,
after some hesitation as to whether he should proceed through Egypt up the Nile, or by way of Zanzibar and then westward overland, or by the line of the
river Rovuma, the route taken by Livingstone, he at
length resolved to go by way of Zanzibar. This is
an island, and town also of the same name, off the
coast of Zanguebar, and is toward the southern limit of

Mohammedan rule in Africa. Here Mr. Stanley arrived in due season, and hence wrote his first letter in this special service, under date of February 9, 1869 It chiefly had reference to Livingstone's previous explorations, the story of his death, and its refutation. But the report that he was only about a week's march inland from Zanzibar also received a quietus, and Mr. Stanley was well nigh persuaded to retrace his steps to Egypt and proceed by way of the Nile, in consequence of the following note from the United States Vice Consul:

"ISLAND OF ZANZIBAR, Dec. 26, 1868.

"DEAR SIR—I should be most happy to assist you in any way whatever; but, in reply to your note, I beg to assure you of my candid belief of his non-appearance. There is not the slightest probability of his ever coming again to this island. Dr. Kirk the British Vice Consul here, and who was with Dr. Livingstone for some years during his travels in Africa, thinks it more than probable that he will come out at the Nile, and has not the least expectation of having the pleasure of seeing him here. In September, 1868, Her Majesty's ship Octavia, Sir Leopold Heath, C. B., left here, and as I see by the Bombay papers, on her arrival at Trincomalee, which is in Ceylon, reported that when she left Zanzibar Dr. Livingstone was reported within a week's march of the coast. This, if you saw it, probably misled you also to believe he would come here, but it is hardly necessary to say that the statement was without the slightest foundation of truth, and was prob-

ably written from some entire misconception by the
writer of some conversation which took place between him and Dr. Kirk. Trusting, however, you
will succeed on the other side, I am, dear sir, very respectfully,

"FRANCIS R. WEBB,
"United States Vice Consul."

Nevertheless, Mr. Stanley determined to go on
and telegraphing to an acquaintance residing at
Khartoum, Upper Nubia, to send him word, if anything should be heard from Livingstone, went forward
with the preparations for his journey. He was doubtless cognizant of the fact also, that the "Herald" had
another Search expedition on foot to which the Khedive of Egypt was rendering generous encouragement and assistance. It may well be imagined that
the drafts upon the "Herald" at this time for necessary outlays in the purchase of horses, asses, and supplies and the employment of a sufficient escort—
mainly consisting of a number of Arabs—were not
light. The preparations, after months' delay, caused
by war in the interior, were at length made, and
the expedition left Zanzibar on the long-ago trail of
the great explorer.

And here it will be proper, while we are awaiting
intelligence of its difficulties and final great success,
to speak of the previous life of him who was to make
so many hearts glad by tidings of the safety of the
most distinguished explorer of our times.

CHAPTER X.

HENRY M. STANLEY.

Sketch of the Life of Mr. Stanley Before Beginning the Search for Livingstone —His Enthusiasm, Courage, and Endurance—Travels in Asia—Statement by the Hon. E. Joy Morris, Ex-United States Minister to Constantinople—Begins the Great Enterprise of His Life.

HENRY M. STANLEY, the leader of the "Herald" expedition of search, is a native of the State of Missouri where he spent his boyhood and youth. The system of popular education in Missouri was never successfully put in operation during the existence of slavery in that commonwealth. Like most of the boys of the State, Stanley grew up, having many more physical than intellectual exercises. He developed and strengthened sinew and muscle, however, and became accustomed to danger, and was therefore, all unconsciously to himself, being educated for the great work of his life. His parents died when he was about eighteen years of age, leaving him a small estate, but without a calling or profession by means of which to obtain a livelihood. This was during the late American civil war. Though the income from his patrimony would have gone a good way toward his support, he felt that it was his duty to earn his subsistence by his own exertions, herein manifesting a spirit of independence which is a quite general characteristic of Western people. He had already shown a literary

ambition, and some of his verses had appeared in
rural journals, and, though regretting the want of a
regular course of mental training, he resolved that he
would become a writer for the press. Looking about
for a field in which he might distinguish himself he
sought employment as a "war correspondent" of the
New York "Herald." "His chief recommendation
at this time," says a great journal, "was his energy
and industry and fearlessness in collecting facts, not
the style in which he told them; for although he had
previously shown some indications of literary ability,
his pen was as yet neither practiced nor fluent." His
energy, industry, and fearlessness were doubtless
better appreciated in the "Herald" office than by the
general public, but his reputation as a writer grew
with time, and he constantly performed his corres-
pondential duties to the satisfaction of his experienced employers.

Of an adventurous nature, he took a warm interest
in the attempt of the Cretans, in 1866, to throw off
the Turkish yoke and establish their independence.
With the object of joining the Cretan army he sailed
for Europe, first making arrangements for correspondence with the "Herald." He was not pleased
with the leaders of the revolution, and declined to
volunteer in the army of the famous little island.

It appears that he had a sort of roving commission from the "Herald," and now undertook a journey on foot with a few travelling companions of his
own country, by which it was contemplated to pass
through Asia Minor, the provinces of Russian Asia,
the Khanates, Bokhara, and Kiva, Eastern Turk-

estan, and so through China to the coast.   This project came, however, to a disastrous end.   The little
party had not penetrated more than about an hundred miles from Smyrna, when it was attacked by
Turkish brigands, completely plundered, and compelled, in consequence, to return.   Arriving at Constantinople in the most sorry plight, the members of
the party were kindly received by the Hon. E. Joy
Morris, then United States Minister to the Turkish
Sultan, and their wants supplied by a check upon the
generous Minister's private banker.   An account of
the affair, written by Mr. Stanley, had appeared in a
public journal of the country, so that Mr. Morris had
been apprised of the facts—afterwards fully substantiated in a court of justice—before the travellers
appeared, in shabby attire attesting a needy situation.

Inasmuch as one of Mr. Stanley's companions—
Noe by name—afterwards brought a charge of cruel
treatment against the "Herald" representative during this journey so disastrously terminated, it will
be well here to give a statement made by Mr. Morris.   It is all the more in place here, because it relates certain facts in Mr. Stanley's life, and deline-
ates certain prominent points of his character so
faithfully that it may be regarded as almost strictly
biographical.   After the appearance of Mr. Noe's
charge against Stanley, the "Herald" sent a reporter
to Atlantic City, New Jersey, where Mr. Morris was
temporarily residing, instructed to get such information from him as he might feel disposed to communicate.   An account of the interview was published

in the "Herald" of September 7th, 1872. The substantial portions follow:

"*Mr. Morris*—I first met Mr. Stanley, or at least
heard of him, in October, 1866. I was then at my
country residence in Bujukdere, on the Bosphorus,
and while there I received intelligence from Constantinople stating that three American travellers,
named Stanley, Noe, and Cook, had been barbar-
ously and cruelly treated and robbed of all their effects by a band of Turks in Asia Minor. In the advance of the arrival of the travellers at the Turkish
capital, Stanley sent an account of the occurrence to
the "Levant Herald," a paper published in English,
in which the particulars of the attack were all fully
narrated. I lost no time in taking the necessary
steps, when the tidings reached me, for the protection
and relief of my countrymen when they should arrive. Meantime the Turks, who were the perpetrators of the outrage, had been captured and conveyed, strongly guarded, to Broussa, a small town
near the Sea of Marmora.

"*Reporter*—Did you see the Americans on their
arrival?

"*Mr. Morris*—I did: the American Consul General and myself were both waiting to receive them
when they arrived, and of course they immediately
repaired to the Embassy when they got into the
city.

"*Reporter*—What appearance did they present?

"*Mr. Morris*—A most miserable appearance, sir.
If ever the condition of men presented the traces of
cruel treatment theirs did. Mr. Stanley's own plight

fully corroborated his story. He had been stripped of all his clothing, and though he had been enabled to procure some outside covering by the generosity of Mr. L. E. Pelesa, agent of the Ottoman Bank at Aflund-Karahissar, he had neither shirt nor stockings on when he came to me, and he showed other evidences of great suffering. I relieved his more pressing necessities and advanced him a loan of money to procure an outfit for himself and his companions. I considered it to be my duty to do this, both as American Minister and as an American who was bound by the tie of nationality to stand by my countrymen in distress. I gave Mr. Stanley a check on my banker and he drew the money—£150. The first thing he did was to repay the agent of the Ottoman Bank the amount advanced by him, and then he took his companions to a clothing bazaar, and both he and they procured the clothing of which they were so much in need.

"*Reporter*—What security had you for your loan?

"*Mr. Morris*—I had no security, nor did I ask any. The money was advanced without condition of any kind. I see it has been stated by Noe that the amount was given in consequence of a draft which Stanley offered, payable by a person in New York. This is false; no draft was given to me at that time, nor was any promise of a repayment made until subsequently. I advanced the money as a loan, asked for no security, nor was there any offered. Some time after Mr. Stanley inconsiderately did give me a draft, but I looked upon this as altogether superflous, and did not attach much value to the act, though it may have been well meant. The draft proved valueless, but it is unnecessary to enter into details of a transaction which has been long satisfactorily settled between Mr. Stanley and myself, and which does not, as I said before, concern any persons outside ourselves. I may state, however, that the action of Mr. Stanley was superfluous in another way, as Mr. Cook, Stanley's fellow traveller, came to me after the money had been sent and assumed all responsibility connected with the loan, stating that if the money was not recovered from the Turkish government he would personally indemnify me, giving me his American address.

"*Reporter*—What impression did you form about Mr. Stanley at the time?

"*Mr. Morris*—I regarded him as a young man of great courage and determination; his countenance showed this, it being stern, almost to severity but with nothing sinister about it.

"*Reporter*—Did Noe, at any time during the stay bring any charges of cruelty against Stanley?

"*Mr. Morris*—None that I recollect of, though he was at perfect liberty to do so. As stated before the Turkish outlaws were taken to Broussa, and after some time had elapsed they were placed upon trial. As there was no American Consul at the place, I obtained from Lord Lyons a promise that the British Consul, Mr. Sandison, should watch the trial and attend to the interests of my clients, Stanley, Cook, and Noe, who were all present as witnesses at Broussa. The Turks were placed upon trial and attempted to defend themselves, but the evidence against them was overpowering. Some of the effects of Stanley and his party were found upon their persons, including $300 which the party carried, and they were convicted and sentenced to various terms of imprisonment.

"*Reporter*—Did Noe swear to all the facts?

"*Mr. Morris*—*He did; and his sworn statement will, if I mistake not, be found in the archives of the State Department. I never was more astonished in my life than I was when I heard that he now states that everything he related at Broussa while under oath, was entirely false.*

"*Reporter*—What steps did you institute to obtain restitution from the Turkish government.

"*Mr. Morris*—I had Stanley and the others draw up an inventory of the effects which had been lost. and they attested to the losses upon oath as being in every instance correct. I then forwarded the claim to the Turkish Minister, including the money advanced by myself, which of course was included among the losses. The entire amount, as near as I can recollect, was about twelve hundred dollars, and the claim was prosecuted on our part with the greatest vigor and pertinacity.

"*Reporter*—Did Stanley and his friends remain in Constantinople after the trial?

"*Mr. Morris*—Not long. Stanley and Noe left for England, and Cook remained some time behind settling affairs. Before separating an agreement was entered into between them and me that if I recovered any money it was to be sent to Cook, as, I believe, it was he that bore the expenses of the journey to Smyrna. Soon after Cook left. I urged the claim

time after time upon the Turkish government, but
did not meet with much success, and at length I was
about to abandon the prosecution of the claim in despair, when the Turkish Minister of Foreign Affairs,
Saferet Pacha, called upon me at my residence and
offered to compromise the case by giving a smaller
amount. I had some conversation with the Grand
Vizier, Ali Pacha, about the same time and I accepted
the proposition in the amicable spirit in which it was
offered. The money was paid, and I first took out of
it the £150 which I had lent. The balance of the
money I sent to Cook.

"*Reporter*—Did any of the money go to Stanley?

"*Mr. Morris*—Not a cent. I received a letter from
Noe, in which he desired to have a part, but as I did
not wish to be dealing with too many parties I sent
the money as I said, to Cook; but Stanley did not
finger any of it, and if Noe was treated with any injustice Cook was the person he had got to look to,
not to Stanley or me. This closed the transaction
at the time, and I heard nothing more of the parties
for some years.

"*Reporter*—When did you see Mr. Stanley again?

"*Mr. Morris*—During the last year of my official
residence in Turkey. In that year a distinguished
American clergyman called upon me at the Embassy
and asked me did I remember anything about a person named Stanley. I answered in the affirmative,
and he then stated that Mr. Stanley had desired him
to call relative to a long-standing debt of £150, which
he believed was owing to me, which had never been
settled and which he was desirous to pay. I told the

clergyman that the matter had been long settled and
that I had been paid. The gentleman further stated
that Mr. Stanley desired to call upon me, and I replied that he was at perfect liberty to do so. The
same evening Mr. Stanley and the clergyman called
and by invitation remained to dinner. The two gentlemen had come on from Egypt together, and the
clergyman had an admiration which almost amounted
to veneration for the character of the 'Herald' correspondent.

"*Reporter*—Was Mr. Stanley much changed in his
appearance and manner?

"*Mr. Morris*—Wonderfully. The uncouth young
man whom I first knew had grown into a perfect
man of the world, possessing the appearance, the
manners and the attributes of a perfect gentleman.
The story of the adventures which he had gone
through and the dangers he had passed during his
absence were perfectly marvellous, and he became
the lion of our little circle. Scarcely a day passed
but he was a guest at my table, and no one was more
welcome, for I insensibly grew to have a strong admiration and felt an attachment for him myself. Instead of thinking he was a young man who had barely
seen twenty-six summers you would imagine that he
was thirty-five or forty years of age, so cultured and
learned was he in all the ways of life. He possessed
a thorough acquaintance with most of the eastern
countries, and, as I took an interest in all that related
to Oriental life, we had many a talk about what he
had seen and what I longed to see. He stated to
me that he had a sort of roving commission for the

Herald, but that he had exhausted all known countries and was at a loss to understand where he should go next. I said to him, 'Stanley, what do you think of trying Persia? That is an unexplored country, and would well repay a visit if you could get back with your life.' Stanley thought over the proposal, and rapidly came to the conclusion he would go. I busied myself in procuring him letters of introduction to the Russian authorities in the Caucasus, in Georgia and in other countries through which he would have to pass. He saw the Russian Ambassador at Constantinople in person, who was so well impressed with him that he made extra exertions to facilitate his progress to the mysterious home of the Grand Llama. I had some time previous to this had a Henry rifle sent me from a friend in New York, as a specimen of American art, and this I presented to Stanley, with my best wishes for the success of his undertaking. He started on the desperate enterprise some time after, and my table thereby lost one of its most entertaining guests. When I say desperate enterprise I mean it, for Persia is to a European a practically unexplored country; and, in consequence of its weak government and the marauders with which it abounds, a journey to Zanzibar or Unyanyembe would be a safe trip compared to it. How Mr. Stanley accomplished the task he undertook the columns of the Herald will tell. I received a letter from him, while on the way, narrating the hospitable manner in which he had been entertained by the Russian authorities, and the way in which he had astonished them by the performances of his Henry rifle. His journey through the Caucasus and Georgia was a sort of triumphal march, though he was looked upon as a lost man by all who knew anything of the East. The route he took was an entirely new one, as he went in a kind of zigzag way to Thibet, and he must have a charmed life to have come through so much peril in complete safety. After this affair I returned home, and I did not hear of Mr. Stanley again until I heard of him as the discoverer of Livingstone.

"*Reporter*—Were you astonished at hearing of the latter fact?

"*Mr. Morris*—Not in the slightest. I would be astonished at no feat in the line of travel that he would accomplish. He is a born traveller. He has all the qualities which the great explorers possessed— Mungo Park, Humboldt, and Livingstone himself— a hardy frame, unflinching courage, and inflexible perseverance. If such a thing were possible that I were forced to become a member of a band to undertake some forlorn hope, some desperate enterprise, I know of no one whom I would so readily select as the leader of such an undertaking as Henry Stanley. I receive his narrative of the discovery of Livingstone with implicit faith, and from my knowledge of him and his character I am lost in wonder that his story should be for an instant doubted. That he has found Livingstone is, in my opinion, as great a certainty as that you are now in Atlantic City. The perils of a journey into the interior of Africa would have no terrors for him."

A considerable portion of the year 1868 was spent

Mr Stanley in Abyssinia, where he accompanied the British expedition against King Theodore. He accompanied the English army as far as Magadla, and on several occasions was enabled to transmit accounts of the expedition, embracing most important news, to the "Herald" in advance of intelligence sent to the British government. The people of America were thus supplied with intelligence of this singular British foray in northeastern Africa before the people of England, and it may well be suspected that they know more of the Anglo-Abyssinian war to-day than the people of England generally know. Mr. Stanley's remarkable successes in Abyssinia were highly appreciated by the "Herald," and the quest for Dr. Livingstone being now fully determined upon, there was no hesitation in placing him in charge of the expedition.

Mr. Stanley is now about twenty-nine years of age. He is a thick-set, powerful man, though short of stature, being only about five feet seven inches in height. He is a sure shot, an expert swimmer, a fine horseman, a trained athlete. But few men living have had more experience in "roughing it." A better selection for the command of its singular undertaking the "Herald" could not possibly have made. And this the result, so astonishing to the world, proves.

And thus it was that the discoverer of the discover was prepared for his great work, which, as we saw at the close of the preceding chapter, he had entered upon, strongly feeling that while he should be in search of Livingstone from the east coast of

ATTACK ON A TRAVELER BY A NATIVE PARTY.

Africa, the explorer would be on his journey out of the country by way of the Nile. For he concludes his Zanzibar letter of February 9, 1869, to which we have referred, as follows:

"Now, the readers of this letter know really as much of the whereabouts of Dr. Livingstone as I do, but probably from conversations heard from different persons I have greater reasons for judging of the case, and I believe it will be a very long time yet before Dr. Livingstone arrives, and that his return will be by the River Nile."

With this opinion, but with a good stock of supplies for Livingstone's journey down the Nile, should he be found proceeding in that way, and with the best escort attainable, Stanley, in charge of the unique newspaper expedition, but not till after long delay, on account of wars, plunged into the wilderness, to be heard from no more until after many long months of suspense and conjecture.

CHAPTER XI.

MR. STANLEY IN AFRICA.

The Search for Dr. Livingstone Energetically Begun—Progress Delayed by
Wars—The Successful Journey from Unyanyembe to Ujiji in 1871—The
"Herald" Cable Telegram Announcing the Safety of Livingstone—The
Battles and Incidents of this Newspaper Campaign—Receipt of the Great
News—The Honor Bestowed on American Journalism.

Mr. Stanley found it much more difficult to get
into Africa than to that singular land. It was understood, according to the best intelligence to be had
that Dr. Livingstone would probably be found, if
found at all, not far from Ujiji. From Bagamoyo, on
the mainland of Africa, opposite the island of Zanzibar, there is a caravan route to Unyanyembe. The
journey generally takes some four months. At the
time Mr. Stanley undertook to proceed inland, he
found the country disturbed by wars, and though
starting now and again, he was delayed many weary
months on this account. "Forward and back" was
the necessary call of the situation. At length the
country became so far quiet between Bagamoyo and
Unyanyembe that the expedition, which terminated
in success, set forth very early in April, 1871, and,
after an unusually rapid journey, the caravan reached
Unyanyembe on the 23d of June. Hence letters
were dispatched home, but from this time for more
than a year, the world remained in ignorance of the
fate of the expedition.

AN AFRICAN CHIEF AND HIS STEED.

Upon the morning of the 2d of July, 1872, however, in the midst of the great Peace Jubilee at the city of Boston, appeared a cable telegram from Lon don to the New-York "Herald," announcing the discovery of Livingstone and the consequent complete success of the great American journal's enterprise. This telegram is worthy of preservation, though superseded by the fuller information in Mr. Stanley's letters, as an illustration of newspaper enterprise:

LONDON, July 1, 1872.

THE GLORIOUS NEWS.

It is with the deepest emotions of pride and pleasure that I announce the arrival this day of letters from Mr. Stanley, Chief of the HERALD Exploring Expedition to Central Africa. I have forwarded the letters by mail. Knowing, however, the importance of the subject and the impatience with which

RELIABLE NEWS

is awaited, I hasten to telegraph a summary of the HERALD explorer's letters, which are full of the most romantic interest, while affirming, emphatically,

THE SAFETY OF DR. LIVINGSTONE,

and confirming the meagre reports already sent on here by telegraph from Bombay and duly forwarded to the HERALD. To bring up the thread of

THE THRILLING NARRATIVE

where the last communication from him ended he proceeds with his account of the journey. It will be recalled that when last heard from he had arrived in the country of Unyanyembe, after a perilous march of eighty-two days from Bagamoyo, on the coast opposite the island of Zanzibar. The road up to this point had been in

THE REGULAR CARAVAN TRACK,

and the journey was performed in a much shorter
time than the same distance had been traversed by
previous explorers. The expedition

ARRIVED AT UNYANYEMBE

on the 23d of June, 1871, where he sent forward his
communication. The caravan had need of rest, and
it was necessary to refit while an opportunity was at
hand through the medium of the Arab caravans then
on their way to various points on the coast with ivory
and slaves. The expedition had suffered terribly,
but the heart of the HERALD explorer never gave
out.

THE TERRIBLE CLIMATE

of the countries through which it had passed told on
it even more than the difficulties of the tribes at war
among themselves and upon everything that came in
their way and which they were in sufficient force to
attack. The caravans met at the various halting
places threw every discouragement in the way, which
tended to destroy the *morale* of the expedition.

SEEDY BOMBAY,

however, the captain of the expedition, proved invaluable in controlling the disaffected, whether with
tact or a wholesome display of force when necessary.

THE INCESSANT RAINS,

alternated with a fierce African sun, made the atmosphere heavy, charged with moisture, and producing
a rank, rotten vegetation. In the mountainous regions which we traversed the climate was, of course,
much better, and the result was that the expedition

much improved in health.   The miasmatic vapors
and other hardships of the journey had played sad
havoc with its number and force.

THE TOTAL LOSS

up to this point by sickness had been one white man,
two of the armed escort, and eight of the pagazis
or native porters.   The two horses had also succumbed, and twenty-seven of the asses had either
fallen by the wayside and had to be abandoned or
else the rascally native donkey leaders had allowed
them to stray from the kraal at night.   As a consequence, a considerable quantity of the stores were
either lost or wasted, but the rolls of Merikani
(American   cloth) — for   shukkah   and   doti — the
beads and wire—had been as far as possible preserved, they being the only money in Central Africa.
In July

ALL WAS PREPARED TO MOVE

through Unyanyembe ; but before long it was found
that almost insuperable difficulties were interposed.
The country there is composed of thick jungle, with
large clearings for the cultivation of holcus.   The
utmost alarm and excitement were spread through the
native villages at

THE EXPECTATION OF A WAR.

The inhabitants were shy of intercourse, and it was
with great difficulty that supplies could be obtained.
A little further on the villages on either side of the
track were found to be filled with Arab

CARAVANS AFRAID TO ADVANCE.

and gathering together for security.   The cause of
all this alarm was soon discovered.   The ku . honga

or blackmail levied by the head men of the tribes as a sort of toll for passage through their territories, had been inordinately raised in the Ujowa country by

MIRAMBO,

King of the Wagowa. Obstinate fights had already occurred in which small bands of his soldiers had been beaten, several being killed. He had, therefore, declared to the traders that no caravan should pass to Ujiji except over his body. The Arabs hereupon held a council, and, finding themselves strong in fighting men,

DECLARED WAR ON MIRAMBO.

The HERALD commander took part in this. The Arabs appeared to anticipate a speedy victory, and preparations for a jungle fight were accordingly made. The ammunition was looked to, muskets inspected and matchlocks cleaned. The superior armament of the HERALD expedition made their assistance a matter of great importance to the Arabs.

THE HERALD GOES TO WAR.

An address was delivered to the members of the expedition through Selim, the interpreter, and the forces, with the American flag flying, were marshalled by Captain Seedy Bombay.

THE FIRST FIGHT.

At daybreak on the day following, according to previous arrangement, the armed men were divided into three parties. The vanguard for attack, the rear guard as immediate reserve, and the remainder, consisting of the less active, were stationed with the *impedimenta* and slaves in the kraals. The advance was ordered and responded to with alacrity, and the first village where the soldiers of Mirambo were lying was at once attacked and speedily captured. The inhabitants were

EITHER KILLED OR DRIVEN AWAY.

Another village followed the fate of the first, and both were left in ashes before nightfall. The troops were wearied with the hot day's work, but all were elate at their success thus far. The commander of the HERALD expedition, on his return to camp, passed a sleepless night, and morning found him

IN A HIGH FEVER.

He was therefore obliged to remain in camp, and his forces refused to fight except under his lead. This weakened the Arab force considerably, and, although the dreaded Mirambo and his followers, thirsting for vengeance, were known to be in the vicinity, the day was passed in fatal inactivity.

THE AMBUSH OF MIRAMBO.

The third day seemed as if about to pass like the preceding, the HERALD commander still suffering from the fever, when shots were heard in the direction of the Arab kraals, and it soon became evident that the wily Mirambo had ambushed the Arabs. This, in effect, was the case. A superior body of natives, armed with muskets, assegais (spears) and poisoned arrows, had suddenly burst upon the Arabs

A TERRIFIC SLAUGHTER ENSUED,

which ended in the rout with the Arabs, who took refuge in the jungle. The fourth day brought with it the fruit of the disaster. The Arabs could not be prevailed upon to renew the fight, and desertion and flight became the order of the day. Even the

MEN OF THE HERALD EXPEDITION DESERTED,

leaving but six with the commander. Mirambo now threatened the town of Unyanyembe. By stupendous exertion the commander collected one hundred and fifty of the fugitives; these being convinced by their numbers, when collected together, that resistance was still possible, resolved to obey the commander.

FORTIFYING FOR A SIEGE.

With five days provisions on hand the houses were loopholed and barricades erected, videttes stationed and the defenders told off as well as their numbers, armament and *morale* could be individually depended on.

THE AMERICAN FLAG WAS HOISTED

and the trembling inhabitants awaited the expected attack. This, however, was destined not to come off, for, to the general delight, a Wanyamwezi scout brought in the joyful intelligence that Mirambo, with all his forces, had retired, not caring to risk an engagement, except in the jungle. Mustering what force was possible, the intrepid HERALD commander then

STARTED FOR UJIJI,

on the Tanganyika Lake, or Sea of Ujiji. The Arabs endeavored in vain to dissuade him from this. Death, they said, was certain to the muzanyu (white man) and his followers. This frightened the already demoralized pagazis and caused a serious loss to the expedition in the person of Shaw, the English sailor. Undaunted by the forebodings of ill and the losses by desertion, the caravan once more was on the march and pushed forward.

BY ANOTHER ROAD,

to the one where Mirambo and his Africans were awaiting the first caravan. This road lay through an untrodden desert, and caused

A GREAT DETOUR

in order to come again upon the caravan road in the rear of the Wajowa. No great mishaps were met with, and when the villages and cultivated fields of sorghum, and holcus were reached everything progressed favorably.

AFTER A FOUR HUNDRED MILE JOURNEY

the outlying portions of the province of Ujiji were reached. Word had reached the expedition of the presence of Dr. Livingstone in the province within a recent period, and accordingly preparations were made for

A TRIUMPHIAL ENTRY INTO UJIJI.

The pagazis who chanced to be unladen proceeded, beating drums and blowing upon Kudu horns. The armed escort fired salutes every moment, keeping up a regular *feu de joie*, and the American flag floated proudly over all. In the distance lay the silver bosom of Tanganyika Lake, at the foot of the stately mountains in the background, and fringed with tall trees and lovely verdure. It was a wonderful relief to the pilgrims of progress. Before them lay the settlement or town of Ujiji, with its huts and houses looking dreamily like a land of rest.

THE ASTONISHED NATIVES

turned out at the unwonted display, and flocked in crowds to meet them with deafening shouts and beating of drums. Among the advancing throng was noticed a muscular group of turbaned Arabs. As they advanced still nearer

ONE OF THE GROUP

who walked in the centre was noticed to be different-ly attired from the others. The group halted, and the word was passed back that a muzangu was among them. Spurring forward the HERALD commander indeed saw that, strongly contrasting with the dusky, sunburnt Arab faces, was

A HALE-LOOKING, GRAY-BEARDED WHITE MAN,

wearing a navy cap, with a faded gold band and a red woolen jacket. It was a trying moment, wherein every emotion of hope and fear flashed through the brain. The fatigues faded in the intensity of the sit-uation. The questions, was this he who had so long been sought, or could it be a delusion of the mind, or was the white man some unknown waif of humanity? crowded the mind. bringing their changing feelings with them. A few feet in front of the group the HERALD commander halted, dismounted and ad-vanced on foot.

A HISTORIC MEETING.

Preserving a calmness of exterior before the Arabs which was hard to simulate as he reached the group, Mr. Stanley said :—

" Dr. Livingstone, I presume ?"

A smile lit up the features of the hale white man as he answered :

"YES, THAT IS MY NAME."

The meeting was most cordial, and the wearied caravan, joyous at the triumph of the expedition, were escorted by the multitude to the town. After a rest and a meal, in which milk, honey and fish from Tanganyika were new features,

LIVINGSTONE TOLD HIS STORY,

which is briefly as follows :—

In March, 1866, he informed the HERALD explorer that he started with twelve Sepoys, nine Johanna men and seven liberated slaves. He travelled

UP THE ROVUMA RIVER.

Before they had been gone very long the men became frightened at the nature of the journey, and the reports of hostile tribes up the country they were to pass through. At length they deserted him, and, as a cover to their cowardice in doing so, circulated

THE REPORT OF HIS DEATH.

Livingstone proceeded on his journey in spite of the isolation, and after some difficult marching reached the Chambezi River, which he crossed. He found that this was not the Portuguese Zambezi River, as had been conjectured, but, on the contrary, wholly separate. He traced its course, and found it called further on

THE LUALABA.

He continued his explorations along its banks for 700 miles, and has become convinced in consequence that the Chambezi is

DOUBTLESS THE SOURCE OF THE NILE,

and that this will make a total length for the mystic river of Africa of 2,600 miles. His explorations also establish that the Nile is not supplied by Lake Tanganyika. He reached within 180 miles of the source and explored the surrounding ground, when,

FINDING HIMSELF WITHOUT SUPPLIES,

he was obliged to return to Ujiji and was in a state of destitution there when met by the commander of the " Herald" expedition. On the 16th of October, 1871,

THE TWO EXPLORERS LEFT UJIJI

and arrived at Unyanyembe toward the end of November, where they passed twenty-eight days together exploring the district. They then returned and

SPENT CHRISTMAS TOGETHER

at Ujiji. The HERALD explorer arrived at the point of sending this important intelligence on the 14th o March, 1872, leaving Livingstone at Unyanyembe.

LIVINGSTONE'S FURTHER PLANS.

He will explore the north shore of Tanganyika Lake and the remaining 180 miles of the Lualaba River.

This herculean task he expects will occupy the next two years.

There have been but few "sensations" more profound than the sensation created by this despatch. As has been said, it threw the great Peace Jubilee into the shade. Sporting men who had just won on the race-horse "Longfellow" or lost on "Harry Bassett," paused for a while to think of the strange intelligence. The report of the trial of him who had been charged with the murder of the noted James Fisk, Jr. attracted but comparatively little attention. All through the section of the great city known as " Five Points" the news was discussed by the tatter-

demalions of the metropolis; all up and down Fifth
Avenue, thousands of the best representatives of
wealth and of culture canvassed the double-leaded telegram ; and Wall street gave it as much attention as
it gave to stocks and government securities. The
substance of the telegram was sent to the evening
papers all over the country and to Europe, and before sunset of July 2d a vast majority of intelligent
people of Christendom knew that Livingstone had
been found, and through the means of American private enterprise. It was a triumph in which the
" Herald" might have been excused, had it indulged
in no little self-glorification. Its article upon the
subject, however, was greatly national in spirit, and
awarded the credit of the success to American journalism, rather than claimed it for itself.*

*The leading article of the "Herald" upon this subject is worthy of quota-
tion here as a part of the journalistic history of this remarkable expedition :
The triumph of the HERALD exploring expedition to search in the heart of
Equatorial Africa for the long-lost Doctor David Livingstone is one which belongs to the entire press of America as well as to the journal whose fortune it
was to originate and carry it out. It marks the era in which the press, already
beyond the control of even the most exalted among men, who may hold states
and empires in their grasp, strikes out boldly into new fields and treads daringly
on *terra incognita*, whether of mind or matter. This is distinctively the work of
the American press, whose aspirations and ambitions have grown with the majesty of the land, and whose enterprise 'has been moulded on the national character. In even recent times the work of progress lay in government hands, or
else was wholly neglected. Sir John Franklin started out amid Polar snows to
work out the Northern passage only to leave his bones among the eternal ice
Hand or foot was not stirred to learn his fate until Lady Franklin, with woman's
devotion, fitted out the expeditions to search for him or his remains. When the
gentleman entrusted with the command of the HERALD expedition had arrived
at Unyanyembe, half way on his journey to Ujiji, he wrote:—"Until I hear
more of him, or see the long-absent old man face to face, I bid you farewell ; but
wherever he is, be sure I shall not give up the chase. If alive, you shall hear
what he has to say ; if dead, I will find and bring his bones to you." To those

who neither understood the man nor the *esprit de corps* which gives the representative of an American journal his stamp of vitality the words may have
sounded like bombast. For answer it is sufficient to point to the columns of the
HERALD of to-day. It may have seemed to those who reasoned from a foreign
standpoint that no man could so wrap himself up in his work as to give utter-
ance to such words with an earnestness of purpose, backed by a life at hazard
from day to day, They simply mistake the spirit of the American journal. If
it were in any other quarter of the globe, by land or sea, the same enthusiasm,
the same dash, enterprise and pluck would be exhibited, because of the race
which he runs for his journal against equally keen-witted rivals, and not alone
for the work itself. Enterprise, then, is the characteristic of the American
press. It is confined to no one paper, to no one locality. Whatever the HER-
ALD may have done in advancing the national reputation in this respect it is
proud to claim, as the victor in the Olympic games of old was proud of his laurel
crown above all gifts of gold or gems. But there is not a paper published between the Narrows and the Golden Gate which has not its own laurels in the
line of enterprise to glory in, and there is not one leaf of the wreath that has not
been snatched at and wrestled for by a hundred sinewy journalistic minds.
Thus no one journal on the Continent looks up to a permanent head of the profession. To-day one paper may be "ahead on the news ;" to-morrow another
will snatch the chaplet from its brows. The enterprise of a contemporary in the
late Franco-Prussian war was celebrated all over the land, as we have no doubt
the success of the HERALD will be when the HERALD's special columns are pe-
rused to-day.

In England the London *Times* is looked up to all over as a Triton among the
minnows. It is the great paper. The *Daily Telegraph* is the cheapest, spiciest
paper published there ; the *Standard* is a careful, able Tory organ ; the *Post* is a
quiet, aristocratic sheet, but the Thunderer overshadows them all. Instinct
with the democratic spirit of our institutions, the press of America looks up to
no lord among them. As each man born on the soil may be President of the
United States, so each paper—no matter what its origin or where its birthplace
—feels within itself the possibility of precedence in point of worth, brains and
news over all others. We, therefore, reassert that the triumph of the HERALD
Livingstone expedition is the triumph of American journalism in its broadest
sense.

To point this something more, we may say that an American war correspondent
has achieved what one of the most powerful governments in the world failed to
accomplish. How it was done is easily told. It is probable that an English
journal might have succeeded, if it had undertaken the task ; but, like Columbus
with the egg, the enterprise which knocked in the end of the oval difficulty and
made the expedition stand for itself is not a British article.

The story of the meeting of the greatest explorer of any time with the HERALD
correspondent, by the shores of Lake Tanganyika, with one thousand miles of
desert, jungle, jagged mountain path and sodden valley trail, peopled with
brutal, ignorant savages, behind him, is one which will long be remembered)

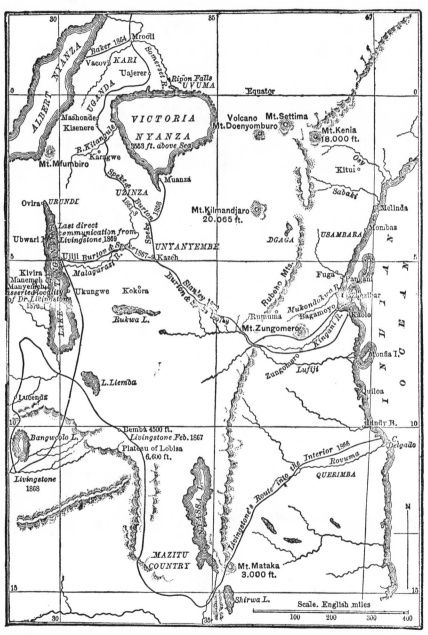

THE DISCOVERY OF DR. LIVINGSTONE.   MAP OF EQUATORIAL AFRICA, SHOWING THE
ROUTE EXPLORED.

The HERALD correspondent has kept his word. Happily for civilization there was no necessity to carry back to distant civilization the relics of her hero. He is alive and well and hopes to carry himself home when he has attained the object of his stay. In March, 1866, he started up the Rovuma, but was deserted, and the false Moosa spread the lying story of his death to cover his own poltroonery, as was hoped against hope when the baleful tidings first came to hand. The undaunted Livingstone then set forward and reached the Chambezi River, which he discovered has no connection with the Portuguese Zambesi River, which disembogues into the Mozambique Channel opposite Madagascar. But the gem of his discovery lies in the fact that the Chambezi is the true source of the Nile. He followed its course for seven hundred miles towards its source, but was obliged to turn back in want, with one hundred and eighty miles unexplored. The Chambezi towards its source is called the Lualaba, and is not supplied from Lake Tanganyika, and the latter lake has no effluence to the Nile. To solve the problem of the Lualaba and pass round the northern shore of Lake Tanganyika, Livingstone purposes spending two years more in Central Africa. Truly this is great news, and we congratulate the world that neither the life nor the toil of so great a man is lost to the world, as the fates seemed so grimly to threaten. The story of his solitary land-finding will now be read by joyful millions, who, if they cannot all appreciate fully his labors, will not grudge him the tribute of lasting admiration.

CHAPTER XII.

The "Land of the Moon"—Description of the Country and People—Horrid
Savage Rites—Journey from Unyanyembe to Ujiji—A Wonderful Country—
A Mighty River Spanned by a Bridge of Grass—Outwitting the Spoilers—
Stanley's Entry Into Ujiji and Meeting with Livingstone—The Great Triumph
of an American Newspaper.

With the object of presenting to the curious a *fac
simile* of the famous cable telegram announcing to
an anxious world the discovery of the great discoverer and of undertaking to preserve it in book
form, as vividly illustrative of the important part
borne by journalistic enterprise in opening up Africa
to progress and civilization, that despatch has been
literally copied in the preceding chapter. But the
full particulars of the journey of the "Herald" special
search expedition, after leaving the main caravan
track at Unyanyembe, are of thrilling interest. Instead of going directly from the last named place to
Ujiji, Mr. Stanley was compelled, by reason of hostile
tribes, to make an extensive detour to the southwest,
and then march up in a northwesterly direction, not
very far distant from the east shore of Lake Tanganyika. But first let us have quotations from the
letter written just before the fourth and finally successful journey written from Kwihara in the district
of Unyanyembe, on the 21st of September, 1871:

"In the storeroom where the cumbersome moneys

of the NEW YORK HERALD Expedition lie piled up
bale upon bale, sack after sack, coil after coil, and the
two boats, are this year's supplies sent by Dr. Kirk
to Dr. Livingstone—seventeen bales of cloth, twelve
boxes of wine, provisions, and little luxuries such as
tea and coffee. When I came up with my last caravan to Unyanyembe I found Livingstone's had arrived but four weeks before, or about May 23 last,
and had put itself under charge of a half-caste called
Thani Kati-Kati, or Thani 'in the middle,' or 'between.' Before he could get carriers he died of dys-
entry. He was succeeded in charge by a man from
Johanna, who, in something like a week, died of
smallpox; then Mirambo's war broke out, and here
we all are, September 21, both expeditions halted.
But not for long, let us hope, for the third time I will
make a start the day after to-morrow.

"Unyamwezi is a romantic name. It is 'Land of
the Moon' rendered into English—as romantic and
sweet in Kinyamwezi as any that Stamboul or Ispa-
han can boast is to a Turk or a Persian. The at-
traction, however, to a European lies only in the
name. There is nothing of the mystic, nothing of
the poetical, nothing of the romantic, in the country
of Unyamwezi. If I look abroad over the country I
see the most inane and the most prosaic country one
could ever imagine. It is the most unlikely country
to a European for settlement; it is so repulsive
owing to the notoriety it has gained for its fevers. A
white missionary would shrink back with horror at
the thought of settling in it. An agriculturist might
be tempted; but then there are so many better

countries where he could do so much better he would be a madman if he ignored those to settle in this. To know the general outline and physical features of Unyamwezi you must take a look around from one of the noble coigns of vantage offered by any of those hills of syenite, in the debatable ground of Mgunda Makali, in Uyanzi. From the summit of one of those natural fortresses, if you look west, you will see Unyamwezi recede into the far, blue, mysterious distance in a succession of blue waves of noble forest, rising and subsiding like the blue waters of an ocean. Such a view of Unyamwezi is inspiring; and, were it possible for you to wing yourself westward on to another vantage coign, again and again the land undulates after the same fashion, and still afar off is the same azure, mystic horizon. As you approach Unyanyembe the scene is slightly changed. Hills of syenite are seen dotting the vast prospect, like islands in a sea, presenting in their external appearance, to an imaginative eye, rude imitations of castellated fortresses and embattled towers. A nearer view of these hills discloses the denuded rock, disintegrated masses standing on end, boulder resting upon boulder, or an immense towering rock, tinted with the sombre color age paints in these lands. Around these rocky hills stretch the cultivated fields of the Wanyamwezi—fields of tall maize, of holcus sorghum, of millet, of vetches, &c.—among which you may discern the patches devoted to the cultivation of sweet potatoes and manioc, and pasture lands where browse the hump-shouldered cattle of Africa, flocks of goats and sheep. This is the scene which attracts

the eye, and is accepted as promising relief after the
wearisome marching through the thorny jungle plains
of Ugogo, the primeval forests of Uyanzi, the dim
plains of Tura and Rubuga, and when we have
emerged from the twilight shades of Kigwa. No
caravan or expedition views it unwelcomed by song
and tumultuous chorus, for rest is at hand. It is only
after a long halt that one begins to weary of Unyanyembe, the principal district of Unyamwezi. It is
only when one has been stricken down almost to the
grave by the fatal chilly winds which blow from the
heights of the mountains of Usagara, that one begins to criticize the beauty which at first captivated.
It is found, then, that though the land is fair to look
upon ; that though we rejoiced at the sight of its
grand plains, at its fertile and glowing fields, at sight
of the roving herds, which promised us abundance of
milk and cream—that it is one of the most deadly
countries in Africa; that its fevers, remittent and in-
termittent, are unequalled in their severity.

"Unyamwezi, or the Land of the Moon—from U
(country) nya (of the) mwezi (moon)—extends over
three degrees of latitude in length and about two
and a half degrees of longitude in breadth. Its
principal districts are Unyanyembe, Ugunda, Ugara,
Tura, Rubuga, Kigwa, Usagazi and Uyoweh. Each
district has its own chief prince, king, or *mtemt*, as
he is called in Kinyamwezi. Unyanyembe, however
is the principal district, and its king, Mkasiwa, is
generally considered to be the most important person in Unyamwezi. The other kings often go to war
against him, and Mkasiwa often gets the worst of it ;

as, for instance, in the present war between the King of Uyoweh (Mirambo) and Mkasiwa.

"All this vast country is drained by two rivers—the Northern and Southern Gombe, which empty into the Malagarazi River, and thence into Lake Tanganyika. On the east Unyamwezi is bounded by the wilderness of Mgunda Makali and Ukmibu, on the south by Urori and Ukonongo, on the west by Ukawendi and Uvniza, on the north by several small countries and the Ukereweh Lake. Were one to ascend by a balloon and scan the whole of Unyamwezi he would have a view of one great forest, broken here and there by the little clearings around the villages, especially in and around Unyanyembe."

On account of troubles in the country, the Search Expedition was detained some three months in Kwihara. Mr. Stanley lived in quite a large, strong house for that country, consisting of a main room and bathroom, built of mud about three feet thick. He thus describes "the daily round":

"In the early morning, generally about half-past five or six o'clock, I begin to stir the soldiers up sometimes with a long bamboo, for you know they are such hard sleepers they require a good deal of poking. Bombay has his orders given him, and Feragji, the cook, who, long ago warned by the noise I make when I rouse up, is told in unmistakable tones to bring 'chai' (tea), for I am like an old woman, I love tea very much, and can take a quart and a half without any inconvenience. Kalulu, a boy of seven all the way from Cazembe's country, is my waiter and chief butler. He understands my ways and mode of life exactly. Some weeks ago he ousted Selim from the post of chief butler by sheer diligence and smartness. Selim, the Arab boy, cannot wait at table. Kalulu—young antelope—is frisky. I have but to express a wish and it is gratified. He is a perfect Mercury, though a marvellously black one. Tea over, Kalulu clears the dishes and retires under the kitchen shed, where, if I have a curiosity to know what he is doing, he may be seen with his tongue in the tea cup licking up the sugar that was left in it and looking very much as if he would like to eat the cup for the sake of the divine element it has so often contained. If I have any calls to make this is generally the hour; if there are none to make I go on the piazza and subside quietly on my bearskin to dream, may be, of that far off land I call my own, or to gaze towards Tabora, the Kaze of Burton and Speke, though why they should have called it Kaze as yet I have not been able to find out; or to look towards lofty Zimbili and wonder why the Arabs, at such a crisis as the present, do not remove their goods and chattels to the summit of that natural fortress. But dreaming and wondering and thinking and marvelling are too hard for me; so I make some ethnological notes and polish up a little my geographical knowledge of Central Africa.

"I have to greet about four hundred and ninety-nine people of all sorts with the salutation 'Yambo,' This 'Yambo' is a great word. It may mean 'How do you do?' 'How are you?' 'Thy health?' The answer to it is 'Yambo!' or 'Yambo Sana!' (How are you; quite well?) The Kinyamwezi—the lan-

guage of the Wanyamwezi—of it is 'Moholo,' and the
answer is 'Moholo.' The Arabs, when they call, if
they do not give the Arabic 'Spal-kher,' give you the
greeting 'Yambo;' and I have to say 'Yambo.' And,
in order to show my gratitude to them, I emphasize
it with 'Yambo Sana! Sana! Sana?' (Are you
well? Quite well, quite, quite well?) And if they repeat the words I am more than doubly grateful, and
invite them to a seat on the bearskin. This bearskin
of mine is the evidence of my respectability, and if
we are short of common-place topics we invariably
refer to the bearskin, where there is room for much
discussion.

"Having disposed of my usual number of 'Yambos'
for the morning I begin to feel 'peckish,' as the sea
skipper says, and Feragji, the cook, and youthful
Kalulu, the chief butler, are again called and told to
bring 'chukula'—food. This is the breakfast put
down on the table at the hour of ten punctually every
morning:—Tea (ugali) a native porridge made out
of the flour of dourra, holcus sorghum, or matama, as
it is called here; a dish of rice and curry. Unyanyembe is famous for its rice, fried goat's meat, stewed
goat's meat, roast goat's meat, a dish of sweet potatoes, a few 'slapjacks' or specimens of the abortive
efforts of Feragji to make dampers or pancakes, to
be eaten with honey. But neither Feragji's culinary
skill nor Kalulu's readiness to wait on me can tempt
me to eat. I have long ago eschewed food, and only
drink tea, milk and yaourt—Turkish word for 'clab-
ber' or clotted milk.

"After breakfast the soldiers are called, and to-

gether we begin to pack the bales of cloth, string
beads and apportion the several loads which the escort must carry to Ujiji some way or another. Carriers come to test the weight of the loads and
to inquire about the inducements offered by the
'Muzungu.' The inducements are in the shape of so
many pieces of cloth, four yards long, and I offered
double what any Arab ever offered. Some are engaged at once, others say they will call again, but
they never do, and it is of no use to expect them
when there is war, for they are the cowardliest people under the sun.

"Since we are going to make forced marches I
must not overload my armed escort, or we shall be
in a pretty mess two or three days after we start;
so I am obliged to reduce all loads by twenty pounds,
to examine my kit and personal baggage carefully,
and put aside anything that is not actually and press-
ingly needed; all the amunition is to be left behind
except one hundred rounds to each man. No one
must fire a shot without permission, or waste his ammunition in any way, under penalty of a heavy fine
for every charge of powder wasted. These things
require time and thought, for the HERALD Expedition has a long and far journey to make. It intends
to take a new road—a road with which few Arabs
are acquainted—despite all that Skeikh, the son of
Nasib, can say against the project.

"It is now the dinner hour, seven P. M. Ferrajji
has spread himself out, as they say. He has all sorts
of little fixings ready, such as indigestible dampers,
the everlasting ngali, or porridge, the sweet potatoes,

chicken, and roast quarter of a goat; and lastly, a custard, or something just as good, made out of plantains. At eight P. M. the table is cleared, the candles are lit, pipes are brought out, and Shaw, my white man is invited to talk. But poor Shaw is sick and has not a grain or spirit of energy left in him. All I can do or say does not cheer him up in the least. He hangs down his head, and with many a sigh declares his inability to proceed with me to Ujiji."

On the 15th of July, war was declared between Mirambo and the Arabs. In this war, it will be recollected, Mr. Stanley with his men took part. The result was disaster, ensuing from Mirambo's stratagem, as so graphically related in the cable telegram. The continuation of this war is thus described:

" Mirambo, with one thousand guns, and one thousand five hundred Watuda's, his allies, invaded Unyanyembe, and pitched their camp insolently within view of the Arab capital of Tabora. Tabora is a large collection of Arab settlements, or tembes, as they are called here. Each Arab house is isolated by the fence which surrounds it. Not one is more than two hundred yards off from the other, and each has its own name, known, however, to but few outsiders. South by west from Tabora, at the distance of a mile and a half, and in view of Tarbora is Kwihara, where the HERALD expedition has its quarters. Kwihara is a Kinyamwezi word, meaning the middle of the cultivation. There is quite a large settlement of Arabs here—second only to Tabora. But it was Tabora aad not Kwihara that Mirambo, his forest thieves and the Watula came to attack. Khamis bin Abdallah, the bravest Trojan of them all—of all the Arabs—went out to meet Mirambo with eighty armed slaves and five Arabs, one of whom was his little son, Khamis. As Khamis bin Abdallah's party came in sight of Mirambo's people Khamis' slaves deserted him, and Mirambo then gave the order to surround the Arabs and press on them. This little group in this manner became the targets for about one thousand guns, and of course in a second or so were all dead—not, however, without having exhibited remarkable traits of character.

"They had barely died before the medicine men came up, and with their scalpels had skinned their faces and their abdominal portions, and had extracted what they call 'mafuta,' or fat, and their genital organs. With this matter which they had extracted from the dead bodies the native doctors or waganga made a powerful medicine, by boiling it in large earthen pots for many hours, with many incantations and shakings of the wonderful gourd that was only filled with pebbles. This medicine was drunk that evening with great ceremony, with dances, drum beating and general fervor of heart.

"Khamis bin Abdallah dead, Mirambo gave his orders to plunder, kill, burn, and destroy, and they went at it with a will. When I saw the fugitives from Tabora coming by the hundred to our quiet valley of Kwihara, I began to think the matter serious and began my operations for defence. First of all, however, a lofty bamboo pole was procured and planted on the roof of our fortlet, and the American flag was

run up, where it waved joyously and grandly, an omen
to all fugitives and their hunters.

"All night we stood guard; the suburbs of Tabora
were in flames; all the Wanyamwezi and Wanguana
houses were destroyed, and the fine house of Abid
bin Sulemian had been ransacked and then committed to the flames, and Mirambo boasted that 'to-morrow' Kwihara should share the fate of Tabora, and
there was a rumor that that night the Arabs were
going to start for the coast. But the morning came,
and Mirambo departed with the ivory and cattle he
had captured, and the people of Kwihara and Tabora breathed freer.

"And now I am going to say farewell to Unyanyembe for a while. I shall never help an Arab again.
He is no fighting man, or I should say, does not
know how to fight, but knows personally how to die.
They will not conquer Mirambo within a year, and I
cannot stop to see that play out. There is a good
old man waiting for me somewhere, and that impels
me on. There is a journal afar off which expects me
to do my duty, and I must do it. Goodby; I am off
the day after to-morrow for Ujiji; then, perhaps, the
Congo River."

After this followed a number of telegrams to the
"Herald" from the expedition, but their substance
has been given in what has preceded, to show the
general outline of explorations up to the time of the
meeting of Livingstone and Stanley at Ujiji. There
are, however, but few accounts of travel more interesting and valuable than the letter to the "Herald"
narrating the events of the journey from Unyan-

yembe to Ujiji, and the meeting with Livingstone.
The greater portion of this remarkable narrative is
appended:

"BUNDER, UJIJI, ON LAKE TANGANYIKA, }
"CENTRAL AFRICA, November 23, 1871. }

"Only two months gone, and what a change in my
feelings! But two months ago, what a peevish, fret-
ful soul was mine! What a hopeless prospect presented itself before your correspondent! Arabs
vowing that I would never behold the Tanganyika;
Sheikh, the son of Nasib, declaring me a madman to
his fellows because I would not heed his words.
My men deserting, my servants whining day by
day, and my white man endeavoring to impress me
with the belief that we were all doomed men! And
the only answer to it all is, Livingstone, the hero
traveller, is alongside of me, writing as hard as he
can to his friends in England, India, and America,
and I am quite safe and sound in health and limb.

"September 23 I left Unyanyembe, driving before
me fifty well-armed black men, loaded with the goods
of the expedition, and dragging after me one white
man. Once away from the hateful valley of Kwihara,
my enthusiasm for my work rose as newborn as when
I left the coast. But my enthusiasm was shortlived,
for before reaching camp I was almost delirious with
fever. When I had arrived, burning with fever, my
pulse bounding many degrees too fast and my temper
made more acrimonious by my sufferings, I found the
camp almost deserted. The men as soon as they had
arrived at Mkwenkwe, the village agreed upon, had
hurried back to Kwihara. Livingstone's letter-carrier

had not made his appearance—it was an abandoned
camp. I instantly dispatched six of the best of those
who had refused to return to ask Sheikh, the son of
Nasib, to lend or sell me the longest slave chain he
had, then to hunt up the runaways and bring them
back to camp bound, and promised them that for
every head captured they should have a bran new
cloth.

" Next morning fourteen out of twenty of those
who had deserted back to their wives and huts (as
is generally the custom) had reappeared, and, as the
fever had left me, I only lectured them, and they
gave me their promise not to desert me again under
any circumstances. Livingstone's messenger had
passed the night in bonds, because he had resolutely
refused to come. I unloosed him and gave him a
paternal lecture, painting in glowing colors the benefits he would receive if he came along quietly and
the horrible punishment of being chained up until I
reached Ujiji if he was still resolved not to come.
' Kaif Halleck' Arabic for ' How do you do ?' melted,
and readily gave me his promise to come and obey
me as he would his own master—Livingstone—until
we should see him, ' which Inshallah we shall ! Please
God, please God, we shall,' I replied, ' and you will
be no loser.' During the day my soldiers had captured the others, and as they all promised obedience
and fidelity in future, they escaped punishment.

" It is possible for any of your readers so disposed
to construct a map of the road on which the ' Herald' expedition was now journeying, if they draw a
line 150 miles long south by west from Unyanyembe,

then 150 miles west northwest, then ninety miles
north, half east, then seventy miles west by north,
and that will take them to Ujiji.

"We were about entering the immense forest that
separates Unyanyembe from the district of Ugunda.
In lengthy undulating waves the land stretches before us—the new land which no European knew, the
unknown, mystic land.   The view which the eyes
hurry to embrace as we ascend some ridge higher
than another is one of the most disheartening that
can be conceived.   Away, one beyond another, wave
the lengthy rectilinear ridges, clad in the same garb
of color.   Woods, woods, woods, forests, leafy
branches, green and sere, yellow and dark red and
purple, then an indefinable ocean, bluer than the blue-
est sky.   The horizon all around shows the same
scene—a sky dropping into the depths of the endless
forest, with but two or three tall giants of the forest
higher than their neighbors, which are conspicuous in
their outlines, to break the monotony of the scene.
On no one point do our eyes rest with pleasure; they
have viewed the same outlines, the same forest and
the same horizon day after day, week after week;
and again, like Noah's dove from wandering over a
world without a halting place, return wearied with the
search.

"It takes seven hours to traverse the forest between Kigandu and Ugunda, when we come to the
capital of the new district, wherein one may laugh at
Mirambo and his forest thieves.   At least the Sultan,
or Lord of Ugunda, feels in a laughing mood while
in his strong stockade, should one but hint to him

that Mirambo might come to settle up the long debt
that Chieftain owes him, for defeating him the last
time—a year ago—he attempted to storm his place.
And well may the Sultan laugh at him, and all others
which the hospitable Chief may permit to reside
within, for it is the strongest place—except Simba-
Moeni and Kwikuru, in Unyanyembe—I have as yet
seen in Africa. Having arrived safely at Ugunda we
may now proceed on our journey fearless of Mirambo,
though he has attacked places four days south of
this; but as he has already at a former time felt the
power of the Wanyamwezi of Ugunda, he will not
venture again in a hurry. On the sixth day of our
departure from Unyanyembe we continued our journey south. Three long marches, under a hot sun,
through jungly plains, heat-cracked expanses of
prairie land, through young forests, haunted by the
tsetse and sword flies, considered fatal to cattle,
brought us to the gates of a village called Manyara,
whose chief was determined not to let us in nor sell
us a grain of corn, because he had never seen a white
man before, and he must know all about this wonderful specimen of humanity before he would allow us
to pass through his country. Having arrived at the
khambi, or camp, I despatched Bombay with a pro-
pitiating gift of cloth to the Chief—a gift at once so
handsome and so munificent, consisting of no less
than two royal cloths and three common dotis, that
the Chief surrendered at once, declaring that the
white man was a superior being to any he had ever
seen. 'Surely,' said he, 'he must have a friend;
otherwise how came he to send me such fine cloths?

DR. LIVINGSTONE AND PARTY ARRIVE AT LAKE BANGWEOLO.

Tell the white man that I shall come and see him.'
Permission was at once given to his people to sell us
as much corn as we needed. We had barely finished
distributing five days' rations to each man when the
Chief was announced.

"Gunbearers, twenty in number, preceded him, and
thirty spearmen followed him, and behind these came
eight or ten men loaded with gifts of honey, native
beer, holcus sorghum, beans, and maize. I at once
advanced and invited the Chief to my tent, which had
undergone some alterations, that I might honor him
as much as lay in my power. Ma-manyara was a tall,
stalwart man, with a very pleasing face. He carried
in his hand a couple of spears, and, with the exception of a well-worn barsati around his loins, he was
naked. Three of his principal men and himself were
invited to seat themselves on my Persian carpet. The
revolvers and Winchester's repeating rifles were
things so wonderful that to attempt to give you any
idea of how awe-struck he and his men were would
task my powers. My medicine chest was opened
next, and I uncorked a small phial of medicinal brandy
and gave each a teaspoonful. Suffice it that I made
myself so popular with Ma-manyara and his people
that they will not forget me in a hurry.

"Leaving kind and hospitable Ma-manyara, after a
four hours' march we came to the banks of the
Gombe Nullah, not the one which Burton, Speke, and
Grant have described, for the Gombe which I mean
is about one hundred and twenty-five miles south of
the Northern Gombe. The glorious park land spreading out north and south of the Southern Gombe is a

14

hunter's paradise. It is full of game of all kinds—herds of buffalo, giraffe, zebra, pallah, water buck, springbok, gemsbok, blackbuck, and kudu,, besides several eland, warthog, or wild boar, and hundreds of the smaller antelope. We saw all these in one day, and at night heard the lions roar and the low of the hippopotamus. I halted here three days to shoot, and there is no occasion to boast of what I shot, considering the myriads of game I saw at every step I took. Not half the animals shot here by myself and men were made use of. Two buffaloes and one kudu were brought to camp the first day, besides a wild boar, which my mess finished up in one night. My boy gun-bearers sat up the whole night eating boar meat, and until I went to sleep I could hear the buffalo meat sizzing over the fires as the Islamized soldiers prepared it for the road.

"From Manyara to Marefu, in Ukonongo, are five days' marches. It is an uninhabited forest now, and is about eighty miles in length. Clumps of forest and dense islets of jungle dot plains which separate the forests proper. It is monotonous owing to the sameness of the scenes. And throughout this length of eighty miles there is nothing to catch a man's eye in search of the picturesque or novel save the Gombe's pools, with their amphibious inhabitants, and the variety of noble game which inhabit the forests and plain. A travelling band of Wakonongo, bound to Ukonongo from Manyara, prayed to have our escort, which was readily granted. They were famous foresters, who knew the various fruits fit to eat; who knew the cry of the honey-bird, and could follow it to the treasure of honey which it wished to show its human friends. It is a pretty bird, not much larger than a wren, and, 'tweet-tweet,' it immediately cries when it sees a human being. It becomes very busy all at once, hops and skips, and flies from branch to branch with marvellous celerity. The traveller lifts up his eyes, beholds the tiny little bird, hopping about, and hears its sweet call—'tweet-tweet-tweet.' If he is a Makonongo he follows it. Away flies the bird on to another tree, springs to another branch nearer to the lagging man as if to say, 'Shall I, must I come and fetch you?' but assured by his advance, away again to another tree, coquets about, and tweets his call rapidly; sometimes more earnest and loud, as if chiding him for being so slow; then off again, until at last the treasure is found and secured. And as he is a very busy little bird, while the man secures his treasure of honey, he plumes himself, ready for another flight and to discover another treasure. Every evening the Makonongo brought us stores of beautiful red and white honey, which is only to be secured in the dry season. Over pancakes and fritters the honey is very excellent; but it is apt to disturb the stomach. I seldom rejoiced in its sweetness without suffering some indisposition afterwards.

"Arriving at Marefu, we overtook an embassy from the Arabs at Unyanyembe to the Chief of the ferocious Watuta, who live a month's march southwest of this frontier village of Ukonongo. Old Hassan, the Mseguhha, was the person who held the honorable post of Chief of the embassy, who had volunteered to conduct the negotiations which were to se-

cure the Watuta's services against Mirambo, the
dreaded Chief of Uyoweh. Assured by the Arabs
that there was no danger, and having received the
sum of forty dollars for his services, he had gone on,
sanguine of success, and had arrived at Marefu, where
we overtook him.

"We left old Hassan the next day, for the prosecution of the work of the expedition, feeling much happier than we had felt for many a day. Desertions
had now ceased, and there remained in chains but
one incorrigible, whom I had apprehended twice after
twice deserting. Bombay and his sympathizers were
now beginning to perceive that after all there was
not much danger—at least not as much as the Arabs
desired us to believe—and he was heard expressing
his belief in his broken English that I would 'catch
the Tanganyika after all,' and the standing joke was
now that we could smell the fish of the Tanganyika
Lake, and that we could not be far from it. New
scenes also met the eye. Here and there were up-
heaved above the tree tops sugar-loaf hills, and,
darkly blue, west of us loomed up a noble ridge of
hills which formed the boundary between Kamirambo's territory and that of Utende. Elephant
tracks became numerous, and buffalo met the delighted eyes everywhere. Crossing the mountainous ridge
of Mwaru, with its lengthy slope slowly descending
westward, the vegetation became more varied and
the outlines of the land before us became more picturesque. We became sated with the varieties of
novel fruit which we saw hanging thickly on trees.
There was the mbembu, with the taste of an over

ripe peach; the tamarind pod and beans, with their grateful acidity, resembling somewhat the lemon in its flavor. The matonga, or *nux vomica*, was welcome, and the lucious singwe, the plum of Africa, was the most delicious of all. There were wild plums like our own, and grapes unpicked long past their season, and beyond eating. Guinea fowls, the moorhen, ptarmigans and ducks supplied our table; and often the lump of a buffalo or an extravagant piece of venison filled our camp kettles. My health was firmly established. The faster we prosecuted our journey the better I felt. I had long bidden adieu to the nauseous calomel and rhubarb compounds, and had become quite a stranger to quinine. There was only one drawback to it all, and that was the feeble health of the Arab boy Selim, who was suffering from an attack of acute dysentery, caused by inordinate drinking of the bad water of the pools at which we had camped between Manyara and Mrera. But judicious attendance and Dover's powders brought the boy round again.

" Mrera, in Ukonongo, nine days southwest of the Gombe Mellah, brought to our minds the jungle habitats of the Wawkwere on the coast, and an ominous sight to travellers were the bleached skulls of men which adorned the tops of tall poles before the gates of the village. The Sultan of Mrera and myself became fast friends after he had tasted of my liberality.

" After a halt of three days at this village, for the benefit of the Arab boy, we proceeded westerly, with the understanding that we should behold the waters of the Tanganyika within ten days. Traversing a dense forest of young trees, we came to a plain dotted with scores of ant hills. Their uniform height (about seven feet high above the plain) leads me to believe that they were constructed during an unusually wet season, and when the country was inundated for a long time in consequence. The surface of the plain also bore the appearance of being subject to such inundations. Beyond this plain about four miles we came to a running stream of purest water—a most welcome sight after so many months spent by brackish pools and nauseous swamps. Crossing the stream, which ran northwest, we immediately ascended a steep and lofty ridge, whence we obtained a view of grand and imposing mountains, of isolated hills, rising sheer to great heights from a plain stretching far into the heart of Ufipa, cut up by numerous streams flowing into the Rungwa River, which during the rainy season overflows this plain and forms the lagoon set down by Speke as the Rikwa. We continued still westward, crossing many a broad stretch of marsh and oozy bed of mellahs, whence rose the streams that formed the Rungwa some forty miles south.

"At a camping place beyond Mrera we heard enough from some natives who visited us to assure us that we were rushing to our destruction if we still kept westward. After receiving hints of how to evade the war-stricken country in our front, we took a road leading north-northwest. While continuing on this course we crossed streams running to the Rungwa south and others running directly north to the Malagarazi, from either side of a lengthy ridge

which served to separate the country of Unyamwezi
from Ukawendi. We were also attracted for the
first time by the lofty and tapering moule tree, used
on the Tanganyika Lake for the canoes of the natives, who dwell on its shores. The banks of the
numerous streams are lined with dense growths of
these shapely trees, as well as of sycamore, and gigantic tamarinds, which rivalled the largest sycamore
in their breadth of shade. The undergrowth of
bushes and tall grass, dense and impenetrable, likely
resorts of leopard and lion and wild boar were enough
to appal the stoutest heart. One of my donkeys
while being driven to water along a narrow path,
hedged by the awesome brake on either side, was attacked by a leopard, which fastened its fangs in the
poor animal's neck, and it would have made short
work of it had not its companions set up such a bray-
ing chorus as might well have terrified a score of
leopards. And that same night, while encamped
contiguous to that limpid stream of Mtambu, with
that lofty line of enormous trees rising dark and
awful above us, the lions issued from the brakes beneath and prowled about the well-set bush defence of
our camp, venting their fearful clamor without inter-
mission until morning.

"Our camps by these thick belts of timber, peopled as they were with wild beasts, my men never
fancied. But Southern Ukawendi, with its fair, lovely
valleys and pellucid streams nourishing vegetation to
extravagant growth, density and height, is infested
with troubles of this kind. And it is probable, from
the spread of this report among the natives, that this

is the cause of the scant population of one of the loveliest countries Africa can boast. The fairest of California scenery cannot excel, though it may equal, such scenes as Ukawendi can boast of, and yet a land as large as the State of New York is almost un-inhabited. Days and days one may travel through primeval forests, now ascending ridges overlooking broad, well watered valleys, with belts of valuable timber crowning the banks of the rivers, and behold exquisite bits of scenery—wild, fantastic, picturesque and pretty—all within the scope of vision whichever way one may turn. And to crown the glories of this lovely portion of earth, underneath the surface but a few feet is one mass of iron ore, extending across three degrees of longitude and nearly four of latitude, cropping out at intervals, so that the traveller cannot remain ignorant of the wealth lying beneath.

"What wild and ambitious projects fill a man's brain as he looks over the forgotten and unpeopled country, containing in its bosom such store of wealth, and with such an expanse of fertile soil, capable of sustaining millions! What a settlement one could have in this valley! See, it is broad enough to sup-port a large population! Fancy a church spire rising where that tamarind rears its dark crown of foliage, and think how well a score or so of pretty cottages would look instead of those thorn clumps and gum trees! Fancy this lovely valley teeming with herds of cattle and fields of corn, spreading to the right and left of this stream! How much better would such a state become this valley, rather than its pres-ent deserted and wild aspect! But be hopeful. The

day will come and a future year will see it, when happier lands have become crowded and nations have become so overgrown that they have no room to turn
about.   It only needs an Abraham or a Lot, an
Alaric or an Attila to lead their hosts to this land,
which, perhaps, has been wisely reserved for such a
time.

"After the warning so kindly given by the natives
soon after leaving Mrera, in Ukonongo, five days'
marches brought us to Mrera, in the district of Rusawa, in Ukawendi.   Arriving here, we questioned the
natives as to the best course to pursue—should we
make direct for the Tanganyika or go north to the
Malagarazi River?   They advised us to the latter
course, though no Arab had ever taken it.   Two days
through the forest, they said, would enable us to
reach the Malagarazi.   The guide, who had by this
forgotten our disagreement, endorsed this opinion, as
beyond the Malagarazi he was sufficiently qualified
to show the way.   We laid in a stock of four days'
provisions against contingencies, and bidding farewell
to the hospitable people of Rusawa, continued our
journey northward.

"The scenery was getting more sublime every day
as we advanced northward, even approaching the
terrible.   We seemed to have left the monotony of
a desert for the wild, picturesque scenery of Abyssinia and the terrible mountains of the Sierra Nevadas.   I named one tabular mountain, which recalled
memories of the Abyssinian campaign, Magdala, and
as I gave it a place on my chart it became of great
use to me, as it rose so prominently into view that I

was enabled to lay down our route pretty accurately
The four days' provisions we had taken with us were
soon consumed, and still we were far from the Malagarazi River. Though we eked out my own stores
with great care, as shipwrecked men at sea, these also
gave out on the sixth day, and still the Malagarazi
was not in sight. The country was getting more difficult for travel, owing to the numerous ascents and
descents we had to make in the course of a day's
march. Bleached and bare, it was cut up by a thousand deep ravines and intersected by a thousand dry
water courses whose beds were filled with immense
sandstone rocks and boulders washed away from the
great heights which rose above us on every side. We
were not protected now by the shades of the forest,
and the heat became excessive and water became
scarce. But we still held on our way, hoping that
each day's march would bring us in sight of the long-
looked-for and much-desired Malagarazi. Fortunately
we had filled our bags and baskets with the forest
peaches with which the forests of Rusawa had supplied us, and these sustained us in this extremity.

" Proceeding on our road on the eighth day every
thing we saw tended to confirm us in the belief that
food was at hand. After travelling two hours, still
descending rapidly towards a deep basin which we
saw, the foremost of the expedition halted, attracted
by the sight of a village situated on a table-topped
mountain on our right. The guide told us it must be
that of the son of Nzogera, of Uvinza. We followed a road leading to the foot of the mountain, and
camped on the edge of an extensive morass. Though

we fired guns to announce our arrival, it was unnecessary, for the people were already hurrying to our
camps to inquire about our intentions. The explanation was satisfactory, but they said that they had
taken us to be enemies, few friends having ever come
along our road. In a few minutes there was an
abundance of meat and grain in the camp, and the
men's jaws were busy in the process of mastication.

"During the whole of the afternoon we were engaged upon the terms Nzogera's son exacted for the
privilege of passing through his country. We found
him to be the first of a tribute-taking tribe which
subsequently made much havoc in the bales of the
expedition. Seven and a half doti of cloth were
what we were compelled to pay, whether we returned
or proceeded on our way. After a day's halt we proceeded under the guidance of two men granted to me
as qualified to show the way to the Malagarazi
River. We had to go east-northeast for a considerable time in order to avoid the morass that lay directly across the country that intervened between the
triangular mountain on whose top Nzogera's son
dwelt. This marsh drains three extensive ranges of
mountains which, starting from the westward, separated only by two deep chasms from each other, run
at wide angles—one southeast, one northeast, and
the other northwest. From a distance this marsh
looks fair enough; stately trees at intervals rise
seemingly from its bosom, and between them one
catches glimpses of a lovely champaign, bounded by
perpendicular mountains, in the far distance. After
a wide detour we struck straight for this marsh, which

presented to us another novelty in the watershed of the Tanganyika.

"Fancy a river broad as the Hudson at Albany, though not near so deep or swift, covered over by water plants and grasses, which had become so interwoven and netted together as to form a bridge covering its entire length and breadth, under which the river flowed calm and deep below. It was over this natural bridge we were expected to cross. Adding to the tremor which one naturally felt at having to cross this frail bridge was the tradition that only a few yards higher up an Arab and his donkey, thirty-five slaves and sixteen tusks of ivory had suddenly sunk forever out of sight. As one-half of our little column had already arrived at the centre, we on the shore could see the network of grass waving on either side, in one place like to the swell of a sea after a storm, and in another like a small lake violently ruffled by a squall. Hundreds of yards away from them it ruffled, and undulated one wave after another. As we all got on it we perceived it to sink about a foot, forcing the water on which it rested into the grassy channel formed by our footsteps. One of my donkeys broke through, and it required the united strength of ten men to extricate him. The aggregate weight of the donkey and men caused that portion of the bridge on which they stood to sink about two feet and a circular pool of water was formed, and I expected every minute to see them suddenly sink out of sight. Fortunately we managed to cross the treacherous bridge without accident.

"Arriving on the other side, we struck north, passing through a delightful country, in every way suitable for agricultural settlements or happy mission stations. The primitive rock began to show itself anew in eccentric clusters, as a flat-topped rock, on which the villages of the Wavinza were seen and where the natives prided themselves on their security and conducted themselves accordingly, ever insolent and forward. We were halted every two or three miles by the demand for tribute, which we did not, because we could not, pay.

" On the second day after leaving Nzogera's son we commenced a series of descents, the deep valleys on each side of us astonishing us by their profundity, and the dark gloom prevailing below, amid their wonderful dense forests of tall trees, and glimpses of plains beyond, invited sincere admiration. In about a couple of hours we discovered the river we were looking for below, at the distance of a mile, running like a silver vein through a broad valley. Halting at Kiala's, eldest son of Nzogera, the principal Sultan of Uvinza, we waited an hour to see on what terms he would ferry us over the Malagarazi. As we could not come to a definite conclusion respecting them we were obliged to camp in his village.

"Until three o'clock P. M. the following day continued the negotiations for ferrying us across the Malagarazi, consisting of arguments, threats, quarrels, loud shouting and stormy debate on both sides. Finally, six doti and ten fundo of sami-sami beads were agreed upon. After which we marched to the ferry, distant half a mile from the scene of so much contention. The river at this place was not more than

thirty yards broad, sluggish and deep; yet I would
prefer attempting to cross the Mississippi by swimming rather than the Malagarazi. Such another river
for the crocodiles, cruel as death, I cannot conceive.
Their long, tapering heads dotted the river everywhere, and though I amused myself, pelting them
with two-ounce balls, I made no effect on their numbers. Two canoes had discharged their live cargo on
the other side of the river when the story of Captain
Burton's passage across the Malagarazi higher up
was brought vividly to my mind by the extortions
which Mutware now commenced.

"Two marches from Malagarazi brought us to
Uhha. Kawanga was the first place in Uhha where
we halted. It is the village where resides the first
mutware, or chief, to whom caravans have to pay
tribute. To this man we paid twelve and a half doti,
upon the understanding that we would have to pay
no more between here and Ujiji. We left Kawanga
cheerfully enough. The country undulated gently
before us like the prairie of Nebraska, as devoid of
trees almost as our plains. The top of every wave
of land enabled us to see the scores of villages which
dotted its surface, though it required keen eyes to
detect at a distance the beehived and straw-thatched
huts from the bleached grass of the plain.

"Pursuing our way next day, after a few hours'
march, we came to Kahirigi, and quartered ourselves
in a large village, governed over by Mionvu's brother,
who had already been advised by Mionvu of the wind-
fall in store for him. This man, as soon as we had
set the tent, put in a claim for thirty doti, which I was

able to reduce, after much eloquence, lasting over five hours, to twenty-six doti. I saw my fine array of bales being reduced fast. Four more such demands as Mionvu's would leave me, in unclassic phrase, 'cleaned out.'

"After paying this last tribute, as it was night, I closed my tent, and, lighting my pipe, began to think seriously upon my position and how to reach Ujiji without paying more tribute. It was high time to resort either to a battle or to a strategy of some kind, possibly to striking into the jungle; but there was no jungle in Uhha, and a man might be seen miles off on its naked plains. At least this last was the plan most likely to succeed without endangering the prospects almost within reach of the expedition. Calling the guide, I questioned him as to its feasibility. He said there was a Mguana, a slave of Thani Bin Abdullah, in the Coma, with whom I might consult. Sending for him, he presently came, and I began to ask him for how much he would guide us out of Uhha without being compelled to pay any more Muhongo. He replied that it was a hard thing to do, unless I had complete control over my men and they could be got to do exactly as I told them. When satisfied on this point he entered into an agreement to show me a road—or rather to lead me to it—that might be clear of all habitations as far as Ujiji for twelve doti, paid beforehand. The cloth was paid to him at once.

"At half-past two A. M. the men were ready, and, stealing silently past the huts, the guide opened the gates, and we filed out one by one as quickly as possible. At dawn we crossed the swift Zunuzi, which

flowed southward into the Malagarazi, after which we
took a northwesterly direction through a thick jungle
of bamboo. There was no road, and behind us we
left but little trail on the hard, dry ground. At eight
A. M. we halted for breakfast, having marched nearly
six hours, within the jungle, which stretched for miles
around us.

"At ten A. M. we resumed our journey, and after
three hours camped at Lake Musuma, a body of water which during the rainy season has a length of
three miles and a breadth of two miles. It is one of
a group of lakes which fill deep hollows in the plain
of Uhha. They swarm with hippopotami, and their
shores are favorite resorts of large herds of buffalo
and game. The eland and buffalo especially are in
large numbers here, and the elephant and rhinoceros
are exceedingly numerous. We saw several of these,
but did not dare to fire. On the second morning after crossing the Sunuzi and Rugufu Rivers, we had
just started from our camp, and as there was no moonlight the head of the column came to a village, whose
inhabitants, as we heard a few voices, were about starting. We were all struck with consternation, but, con-
sulting with the guide, we despatched our goats and
chickens, and leaving them in the road, faced about,
retraced our steps, and after a quarter of an hour
struck up a ravine, and descending several precipitous
places, about half-past six o'clock found ourselves in
Ukaranga—safe and free from all tribute taking
Wahha.

"Exultant shouts were given—equivalent to the
Anglo-Saxon hurrah—upon our success. Addressing

GUHA HEAD-DRESSES.

the men, I asked them, 'Why should we halt when but a few hours from Ujiji? Let us march a few hours more and to-morrow we shall see the white man at Ujiji, and who knows but this may be the man we are seeking? Let us go on, and after to-morrow we shall have fish for dinner and many days' rest afterwards, every day eating the fish of the Tanganyika. Stop; I think I smell the Tanganyika fish even now.' This speech was hailed with what the newspapers call 'loud applause; great cheering,' and 'Ngema—very well, master;' 'Hyah Barak-Allah—Onward, and the blessing of God be on you.'

"We strode from the frontier at the rate of four miles an hour, and, after six hours' march, the tired caravan entered the woods which separate the residence of the Chief of Ukaranga from the villages on the Mkuti River. As we drew near the village we went slower, unfurled the American and Zanzibar flags, presenting quite an imposing array. When we came in sight of Nyamtaga, the name of the Sultan's residence, and our flags and numerous guns were seen, the Wakaranga and their Sultan deserted their village *en masse*, and rushed into the woods, believing that we were Mirambo's robbers, who, after destroying Unyanyembe, were come to destroy the Arabs and bunder of Ujiji; but he and his people were soon reassured, and came forward to welcome us with presents of goats and beer, all of which were very welcome after the exceedingly lengthy marches we had recently undertaken.

"Rising at early dawn our new clothes were brought forth again that we might present as decent an ap-

15

pearance as possible before the Arabs of Ujiji, and my helmet was well chalked and a new puggeree folded around it, my boots were well oiled and my white flannels put on, and altogether, without joking, I might have paraded the streets of Bombay without attracting any very great attention.

"A couple of hours brought us to the base of a hill, from the top of which the Kirangozi said we could obtain a view of the great Tanganyika Lake. Heedless of the rough path or of the toilsome steep, spurred onward by the cheery promise, the ascent was performed in a short time. On arriving at the top we beheld it at last from the spot whence, probably, Burton and Speke looked at it—'the one in a half paralyzed state, the other almost blind.' Indeed, I was pleased at the sight; and, as we descended, it opened more and more into view until it was revealed at last into a grand inland sea, bounded westward by an appalling and black-blue range of mountains, and stretching north and south without bounds, a gray expanse of water.

"From the western base of the hill was a three hours' march, though no march ever passed off so quickly. The hours seemed to have been quarters, we had seen so much that was novel and rare to us who had been travelling so long on the highlands The mountains bounding the lake on the eastward. receded and the lake advanced. We had crossed the Ruche, or Linche, and its thick belt of tall matete grass. We had plunged into a perfect forest of them, and had entered into the cultivated fields which supply the port of Ujiji with vegetables, etc., and we stood at last on the summit of the last hill of the myriads we had crossed, and the port of Ujiji, embowered in palms, with the tiny waves of the silver waters of the Tanganyika rolling at its feet was directly below us.

"We are now about descending—in a few minutes we shall have reached the spot where we imagine the object of our search—our fate will soon be decided. No one in that town knows we are coming; least of all do they know we are so close to them. If any of them ever heard of the white man at Unyanyembe they must believe we are there yet. We shall take them all by surprise, for no other but a white man would dare leave Unyanyembe for Ujiji with the country in such a distracted state—no other but a crazy white man whom Sheik, the son of Nasib is going to report to Syed or Burghash for not taking his advice.

"Well, we are but a mile from Ujiji now, and it is high time we should let them know a caravan is coming; so 'Commence firing' is the word passed along the length of the column, and gladly do they begin. They have loaded their muskets half full, and they roar like the broadside of a line-of-battle ship. Down go the ramrods, sending huge charges home to the breech, and volley after volley is fired. The flags are fluttered; the banner of America is in front waving joyfully; the guide is in the zenith of his glory. The former residents of Zanzita will know it directly, and will wonder—as well they may—as to what it means. Never were the Stars and Stripes so beautiful to my mind—the breeze of the Tanganyika has such an ef-

fect on them. The guide blows his horn, and the
shrill, wild clangor of it is far and near; and still the
cannon muskets tell the noisy seconds. By this time
the Arabs are fully alarmed; the natives of Ujiji,
Waguhha, Warundi, Wanguana, and I know not
whom, hurry up by the hundreds to ask what it all
means—this fusilading, shouting, and blowing of
horns and flag flying. There are Yambos shouted
out to me by the dozen, and delighted Arabs have
run up breathlessly to shake my hands and ask
anxiously where I came from. But I have no patience with them. The expedition goes far too slow. I
should like to settle the vexed question by one personal view. Where is he? Has he fled?

"Suddenly a man—a black man—at my elbow
shouts in English, ' How do you sir ?'

"Hello! who are you?' ' I am the servant of Dr.
Livingstone,' he says; but before I can ask any more
questions he is running like a madman toward the
town.

"We have at last entered the town. There are
hundreds of people around me—I might say thousands without exaggeration, it seems to me. It is a
grand triumphal procession. As we move they move.
All eyes are drawn towards us. The expedition at
last comes to a halt; the journey is ended for a time;
but I alone have a few more steps to make.

"There is a group of the most respectable Arabs,
and as I come nearer I see the white face of an old
man among them. He has a cap with a gold band
around it, his dress is a short jacket of red blanket

cloth and pants. I am shaking hands with him. We raise our hats, and I say:—

"Dr. Livingstone, I presume?

"And he says, 'Yes.'

"*Finis coronat opus.*"

And thus was the goal won after long and toilsome and dangerous journeyings, many hundred miles of them never before looked upon by the eye of white man. It was a triumph magnificently demonstrating the progress of humanity, science, and civilization; and it must be universally regarded as an achievement remarkably and most happily representative of the spirit of the age, since it was accomplished, not by the power and wealth of prince, or potentate, or government, but by the irrepressible enterprise of an AMERICAN NEWSPAPER.

CHAPTER XIII.

LIVINGSTONE AND STANLEY IN AFRICA.

The Great Explorer as a Companion—His Missionary Labors—The Story of His Latest Explorations—The Probable Sources of the Nile—Great Lakes and Rivers—The Country and People of Central Africa—A Race of African Amazons—Slave Trade—A Horrid Massacre—The Discoverer Plundered.

Mr. Stanley, rather contrary, it would seem, to his expectations, found Dr. Livingstone an exceedingly companionable and agreeable gentleman. He had been led to suppose that the explorer of Africa was haughty and reserved in manner. Instead, he found him hospitable, most generous, and as open and unaffected as a child. He deferred reading his own letters, brought by Mr. Stanley, until he had the general news of the world during the long period in which he had been "lost." Then, he read of home, and gave the commander of the "Herald" expedition an account of his explorations. The result of these interviews is contained in a letter dated at Bunder Ujiji on Lake Tanganyika, December 26, 1871, from which we largely extract as follows:

"The goal was won. *Finis coronat opus.* I might here stop very well—for Livingstone was found— only the 'Herald' I know will not be satisfied with one story, so I will sit down to another; a story so interesting, because he, the great traveller, the hero Livingstone, tells most of it himself.

"Together we turned our faces towards his tembe.
He pointed to the veranda of his house, which was
an unrailed platform, built of mud, covered by wide
overhanging eaves. He pointed to his own particular seat, on a carpet of goatskins spread over a thick
mat of palm leaf. I protested against taking his
seat, but he insisted, and I yielded. We were
seated, the Doctor and I, with our back to the wall,
the Arabs to our right and left and in front, the natives forming a dark perspective beyond. Then began conversation; I forget what about; possibly
about the road I took from Unyanyembe, but I am
not sure. I know the Doctor was talking, and I was
answering mechanically. I was conning the indomitable, energetic, patient and persevering traveller, at
whose side I now sat in Central Africa. Every hair
of his head and beard, every line and wrinkle of his
face, the wan face, the fatigued form, were all impart-
ing the intelligence to me which so many men so
much desired. It was deeply interesting intelligence
and unvarnished truths these mute but certain witnesses gave. They told me of the real nature of the
work in which he was engaged. Then his lips began
to give me the details—lips that cannot lie. I could
not repeat what he said. He had so much to say
that he began at the end, seemingly oblivious of the
fact that nearly six years had to be accounted for.
But the story came out bit by bit, unreservedly—as
unreservedly as if he was conversing with Sir R.
Murchison, his true friend and best on earth. The
man's heart was gushing out, not in hurried sentences,
in rapid utterances, in quick relation—but in still and

deep words. A happier companion, a truer friend
than the traveller, I could not wish for. He was always polite—with a politeness of the genuine kind—
and this politeness never forsook him for an instant,
even in the midst of the most rugged scenes and
greatest difficulties. Upon my first introduction to
him Livingstone was to me like a huge tome, with a
most unpretending binding. Within, the book might
contain much valuable lore and wisdom, but its exterior gave no promise of what was within. Thus
outside Livingstone gave no token—except of being
rudely dealt with by the wilderness—of what element
of power or talent lay within. He is a man of unpretending appearance enough, has quiet, composed
features, from which the freshness of youth has quite
departed, but which retains the mobility of prime
age just enough to show that there yet lives much
endurance and vigor within his frame. The eyes,
which are hazel, are remarkably bright, not dimmed
in the least, though the whiskers and mustache are
very gray. The hair, originally brown, is streaked
here and there with gray over the temples, otherwise
it might belong to a man of thirty. The teeth above
show indications of being worn out. The hard fare
of Londa and Manyema have made havoc in their
ranks. His form is stoutish, a little over the ordinary in height, with slightly bowed shoulders. When
walking he has the heavy step of an overworked and
fatigued man. On his head he wears the naval cap,
with a round vizor, with which he has been identified
throughout Africa. His dress shows that at times he
has had to resort to the needle to repair and replace

what travel has worn. Such is Livingstone externally.

"Of the inner man much more may be said than of
the outer. As he reveals himself, bit by bit, to the
stranger, a great many favorable points present themselves, any of which taken singly might well dispose
you toward him. I had brought him a packet of letters, and though I urged him again and again to defer conversation with me until he had read the news
from home and children, he said he would defer
reading until night; for the time he would enjoy being astonished by the European and any general
world news I could communicate. He had acquired
the art of being patient long ago, he said, and he had
waited so long for letters that he could well afford
to wait a few hours more. So we sat and talked on
that humble veranda of one of the poorest houses in
Ujiji. Talked quite oblivious of the large concourse
of Arabs, Wanguana, and Wajiji, who had crowded
around to see the new comer.

"The hours of that afternoon passed most pleasantly—few afternoons of my life more so. It seemed
to me as if I had met an old, old friend. There was
a friendly or good-natured *abandon* about Livingstone
which was not lost on me. As host, welcoming one
who spoke his language, he did his duties with a spirit
and style I have never seen elsewhere. He had not
much to offer, to be sure, but what he had was mine
and his. The wan features which I had thought
shocked me at first meeting, the heavy step which
told of age and hard travel, the gray beard and
stooping shoulders belied the man. Underneath

that aged and well spent exterior lay an endless fund
of high spirits, which now and then broke out in
peals of hearty laughter—the rugged frame enclosed a
very young and exuberant soul. The meal—I am not
sure but what we ate three meals that afternoon—
was seasoned with innumerable jokes and pleasant
anecdotes, interesting hunting stories, of which his
friends Webb, Oswell, Vardon, and Cumming (Gordon Cumming) were always the chief actors. ' You
have brought me new life,' he said several times, so
that I was not sure but that there was some little
hysteria in this joviality and abundant animal spirits,
but as I found it continued during several weeks I
am now disposed to think it natural.

"Another thing which specially attracted my attention was his wonderfully retentive memory. When
we remember the thirty years and more he has spent
in Africa, deprived of books, we may well think it an
uncommon memory that can recite whole poems of
Burns, Byron, Tennyson, and Longfellow. Even the
poets Whittier and Lowell were far better known to
him than me. He knew an endless number of facts
and names of persons connected with America much
better than I, though it was my peculiar province as
a journalist to have known them.

"Dr. Livingstone is a truly pious man—a man
deeply imbued with real religious instincts. The
study of the man would not be complete if we did
not take the religious side of his character into consideration. His religion, any more than his business,
is not of the theoretical kind—simply contenting itself with avowing its peculiar creed and ignoring all

other religions as wrong or weak. It is of the true,
practical kind, never losing a chance to manifest itself
in a quiet, practical way—never demonstrative or
loud. It is always at work, if not in deed, by shining
example. It is not aggressive, which sometimes is
troublesome and often impertinent. In him religion
exibits its loveliest features. It governs his conduct
towards his servants, towards the natives and towards
the bigoted Mussulmans—all who come in contact
with him. Without religion Livingstone, with his
ardent temperament, his enthusiastic nature, his high
spirit and courage, might have been an uncompanion-
able man and a hard master. Religion has tamed all
these characteristics; nay, if he was ever possessed
of them, they have been thoroughly eradicated.
Whatever was crude or wilful religion has refined,
and made him, to speak the earnest, sober truth, the
most agreeable of companions and indulgent of masters. Every Sunday morning he gathers his little
flock around him and has prayers read, in the tone
recommended by Archbishop Whately—viz, natural,
unaffected, and sincere. Following them he delivers
a short address in the Kisawahiti language about
what he has been reading from the Bible to them,
which is listened to with great attention.

"When I first met the Doctor I asked him if he did
not feel a desire to visit his country and take a little
rest. He had then been absent about six years, and
the answer he gave me freely shows what kind of man
he is. Said he :—

"' I would like very much to go home and see my
children once again, but I cannot bring my heart to

abandon the task I have undertaken when it is so
nearly completed. It only requires six or seven
months more to trace the true source that I have discovered with Petherick's branch of the White Nile, or
with the Albert Nyanza of Sir Samuel Baker. Why
should I go before my task is ended, to have to come
back again to do what I can very well do now?' 'And
why,' I asked, ' did you come so far back without fin-
ishing the short task which you say you have yet to
do?' 'Simply because I was forced; my men would
not budge a step forward. They mutinied and formed
a secret resolution that if I still insisted on going on
to raise a disturbance in the country, and after they
had effected it to abandon me, in which case I should
be killed. It was dangerous to go any farther. I had
explored six hundred miles of the watershed, had
traced all the principal streams which discharged
their waters into the central line of drainage, and
when about starting to explore the last one hundred
miles the hearts of my people failed, and they set
about frustrating me in every possible way. Now,
having returned seven hundred miles to get a new
supply of stores and another escort, I find myself destitute of even the means to live but for a few weeks,
and sick in mind and body.'

"Again, about a week after I had arrived in Ujiji, I
asked Livingstone if he had examined the northern
head of the Tanganyika. He answered immediately
he had not, and then asked if people expected he had.

" ' I did try before setting out for Manyema,' he said,
' to engage canoes and proceed northward, but I soon
saw that the people were all confederating to fleece

me as they had Burton, and had I gone under such
circumstances I should not have been able to proceed
to Manyema to explore the central line of drainage,
and of course the most important line—far more important than the line of the Tanganyika; for whatever connection there may be between the Tanganyika and the Albert the true sources of the Nile are
those emptying into the central line of drainage. In
my own mind I have not the least doubt that the Rusizi River flows from this lake into the Albert. For
three months steadily I observed a current setting
northward. I verified it by means of water plants.
When Speke gives the altitude of the Tanganyika at
only 1,880 feet above the sea I imagine he must have
fallen into the error by frequently writing the Anno
Domini, and thus made a slip of the pen; for the altitude is over two thousand eight hundred feet by
boiling point, though I make it a little over three
thousand feet by barometers. Thus you see that
there are no very great natural difficulties on the
score of altitude, and nothing to prevent the reasonable supposition that there may be a water connection by means of the Rusizi or some other river between the two lakes. Besides, the Arabs here are divided in their statements. Some swear that the river
goes out of the Tanganyika, others that it flows into
the Tanganyika.'

"Dr. Livingstone left the island of Zanzibar in
March, 1866. On the 7th of the following month he
departed from Mikindini Bay for the interior, with
an expedition consisting of twelve Sepoys from Bombay, nine men from Johanna, of the Comoro Isles

seven liberated slaves and two Zambesi men (taking
them as an experiment), six camels, three buffaloes,
two mules and three donkeys. He thus had thirty
men, twelve of whom—viz., the Sepoys—were to act
as guards for the expedition. They were mostly
armed with the Enfield rifles presented to the Doctor by the Bombay government. The baggage of
the expedition consisted of ten bales of cloth and
two bags of beads, which were to serve as currency
by which they would be enabled to purchase the nec-
essaries of life in the countries the Doctor intended
to visit. Besides the cumbrous moneys they carried
several boxes of instruments, such as chronometers,
air thermometers, sextant and artificial horizon, boxes containing clothes, medicines, and personal neces-
saries.

"The expedition travelled up the left bank of the
Rovuma River, a route as full of difficulties as any
that could be chosen. For miles Livingstone and
his party had to cut their way with their axes through
the dense and most impenetrable jungles which
lined the river's banks. The road was a mere foot-
path, leading in the almost erratic fashion, in and
through the dense vegetation, seeking the easiest
outlet from it without any regard to the course it
ran. The pagazis were able to proceed easily enough
but the camels on account of their enormous height,
could not advance a step without the axes of the
party first clearing the way. These tools of foresters were almost always required, but the advance
of the expedition was often retarded by the unwil-
lingness of the Sepoys and Johanna men to work.

Soon after the departure of the expedition from the
coast the murmurings and complaints of these men
began, and upon every occasion and at every opportunity they evinced a decided hostility to an advance.

"The Doctor and his little party arrived on the
18th day of July, 1866, at a village belonging to a
chief of the Mahiyaw, situated eight days' march south
of the Rovuma and overlooking the watershed of the
Lake Nyassa. The territory lying between the Rovuma river and this Mahiyaw chieftain was an uninhabited wilderness, during the transit of which Livingstone and the expedition suffered considerably
from hunger and desertion of men.

"Early in August, 1866, the Doctor came to
Mponda's country, a chief who dwelt near the Lake
Nyassa. On the road thither two of the liberated
slaves deserted him. Here, also, Wakotani (not
Wikotani) a *protege* of the Doctor, insisted upon his
discharge, alleging as an excuse, which the Doctor
subsequently found to be untrue, that he had found
his brother."

Hence the explorer proceeded to the heel of Lake
Nyassa where there is a village of a Babisa chief.
The chief was ill, and Doctor Livingstone remained
there for some time to give him medical aid. It was
here that he was deserted by his Johanna men, the
chief of whom, Ali Moosa (or Musa), pretended to
give credence to a mournful story of plunder per-
petrated upon a certain half-caste Arab who had been
along the western shore of the lake. Though the
explorer gave no faith to the Arab story, he determined not to go among the Ma-zitu, reported so

hostile, and proceeded in a southwestern course for a considerable distance. The correspondent's letter goes on to say:

"As soon as he turned his face westward Musa and the Johanna men ran away in a body. The Doctor says, in commenting upon Musa's conduct, that he felt strongly tempted to shoot Musa and another ringleader, but was nevertheless glad that he did not soil his hands with their vile blood. A day or two afterwards another of his men—Simon Price by name—came to the Doctor with the same tale about the Ma-Zitu, but, compelled by the scant number of his people to repress all such tendencies to desertion and faint-heartedness, the Doctor 'shut him up' at once and forbade him to utter the name of the Ma-Zitu any more. Had the natives not assisted him he must have despaired of ever being able to penetrate the wild and unexplored interior which he was now about to tread.

"'Fortunately,' as the Doctor says with unction, 'I was in a country now, after leaving the shores of the Nyassa, where the feet of the slave trader had not trodden. It was a new and virgin land, and of course, as I have always found it in such cases, the natives were really good and hospitable, and for very small portions of cloth my baggage was conveyed from village to village by them.' In many other ways the traveller in his extremity was kindly treated by the undefiled and unspoiled natives. On leaving this hospitable region in the early part of December, 1866, the Doctor entered a country where the Mazitu had excercised their customary spoliating propensities

Susi and Chuma.

The land was swept clean of all provisions and cattle, and the people had emigrated to other countries beyond the bounds of these ferocious plunderers. Again the expedition was besieged by famine, and was reduced to great extremity. To satisfy the pinching hunger it suffered it had recourse to the wild fruits which some parts of the country furnished. At intervals the condition of the hard-pressed band was made worse by the heartless desertion of some of its members, who more than once departed with the Doctor's personal kit—changes of clothes and linen, etc. With more or lesss misfortunes constantly dogging his footsteps, he traversed in safety the countries of the Babisa, Bobemba, Barungu, Baulungu, and Londa.

"In the country of Londa lives the famous Cazembe—made known to Europeans first by Dr. Lacerda, the Portuguese traveller. Cazembe is a most intelligent prince; is a tall, stalwart man, who wears a peculiar kind of dress, made of crimson print, in the form of a prodigious kilt. The mode of arranging it is most ludicrous. All the folds of this enormous kilt are massed in front, which causes him to look as if the peculiarities of the human body were reversed in his case. The abdominal parts are thus covered with a balloon-like expansion of cloth, while the lumbar region, which is by us jealously clothed, with him is only half draped bv a narrow curtain which by no means suffices to obscure its naturally fine proportions. In this state dress King Cazembe received Dr. Livingstone, surrounded by his chiefs and body guards. A chief, who had been deputed

16

by the King and elders to find out all about the
white man, then stood up before the assembly, and in
a loud voice gave the result of the inquiry he had in-
stituted. He had heard the white man had come to
look for waters, for rivers and seas. Though he did
not understand what the white man could want with
such things, he had no doubt that the object was
good. Then Cazembe asked what the Doctor proposed doing and where he thought of going. The
Doctor replied that he had thought of going south,
as he had heard of lakes and rivers being in that direction. Cazembe asked : ' What can you want to go
there for ? The water is close here. There is plenty
of large water in this neighborhood.' Before breaking up the assembly Cazembe gave orders to let the
white man go where he would through his country
undisturbed and unmolested. He was the first
Englishman he had seen, he said, and he liked him.

"Shortly after his introduction to the King the
Queen entered the large house surrounded by a body
guard of Amazons armed with spears. She was a
fine, tall, handsome young woman, and evidently
thought she was about to make a great impression
upon the rustic white man, for she had clothed herself after a most royal fashion, and was armed with a
ponderous spear. But her appearance, so different
from what the Doctor had imagined, caused him to
laugh, which entirely spoiled the effect intended, for
the laugh of the Doctor was so contagious that she
herself was the first who imitated, and the Amazons,
courtier-like, followed suit. Much disconcerted by
this, the Queen ran back, followed by her obedient

damsels—a retreat most undignified and unqueenlike
compared to her majestic advent into the Doctor's
presence.

" Soon after his arrival in the country of Londa, or
Lunda, and before he had entered the district of
Cazembe, he had crossed a river called the Chambezi, which was quite an important stream. The
similarity of the name with that large and noble
river south, which will be forever connected with his
name, misled Livingstone at that time, and he accordingly did not pay it the attention it deserved,
believing that the Chambezi was but the head-waters
of the Zambezi, and consequently had no bearing or
connection with the sources of the river of Egypt, of
which he was in search. His fault was in relying too
implicitly upon the correctness of Portuguese information. This error cost him many months of tedious labor and travel. But these travels and tedious
labors of his in Londa and the adjacent countries
have established beyond doubt first, that the Chambezi is a totally distinct river from the Zambezi of
the Portuguese, and secondly, that the Chambezi,
starting from about latitude eleven degrees south, is
none other than the most southerly feeder of the
great Nile, thus giving this famous river a length of
over two thousand six hundred miles of direct latitude, making it second to the Mississippi, the longest
river in the world. The real and true name of the
Zambezi is Dombazi. When Lacuda and his Portuguese successors came to Cazembe, crossed the
Chambezi and heard its name, they very naturally
set it down as 'our own Zambezi,' and without

further inquiry sketched it as running in that direction.

" During his researches in that region, so pregnant in discoveries, Livingstone came to a lake lying northeast of Cazembe, which the natives called Liemba, from the country of that name, which bordered it on the east and south. In tracing the lake north he found it to be none other than the Tanganyika, or the southeastern extremity of it, which looks on the Doctor's map very much like an outline of Italy. The latitude of the southern end of this great body of water is about nine degrees south, which gives it thus a length, from north to south, of 360 geographical miles.

" From the southern extremity of the Tanganyika he crossed Marungu and came in sight of Lake Moero. Tracing this lake, which is about sixty miles in length, to its southern head, he found a river called the Luapula entering it from that direction. Following the Luapula south he found it issue from the large lake of Bangweolo, which is as large in superficial area as the Tanganyika. In exploring for the waters which emptied into the lake he found by far the most important of these feeders was the Chambezi. So that he had thus traced the Chambezi from its source to Lake Bangweolo, and issue from its northern head under the name of Luapula, and found it enter Lake Moero. Again he returned to Cazembe, well satisfied that the river running north through three degrees of latitude could not be the river running south under the name of the Zambezi, though there might be a remarkable resemblance in their names.

" At Cazembe he found an old white-bearded half-caste named Mohammed ben Salih, who was kept as a kind of prisoner at large by the King because of certain suspicious circumstance attending his advent and stay in his country. Through Livingstone's influence Mohammed ben Salih obtained his release. On the road to Ujiji he had bitter cause to regret having exerted himself in the half-caste's behalf. He turned out to be a most ungrateful wretch, who poisoned the minds of the Doctor's few followers and ingratiated himself in their favor by selling the favors of his concubines to them, thus reducing them to a kind of bondage under him. From the day he had the vile old man in his company manifold and bitter misfortunes followed the Doctor up to his arrival in Ujiji, in March, 1869.

" From the date of his arrival until the end of June (1869) he remained in Ujiji, whence he dated those letters which, though the outside world still doubted his being alive, satisfied the minds of the Royal Geographical people and his intimate friends that he was alive, and Musa's tale an ingenious but false fabrication of a cowardly deserter. It was during this time that the thought occurred to him of sailing around the Lake Tanganyika, but the Arabs and natives were so bent upon fleecing him that, had he undertaken it the remainder of his goods would not have enabled him to explore the central line of drainage, the initial point of which he found far south of Cazembe, in about latitude 11 degrees, in

the river Chambezi. In the days when tired Captain
Burton was resting in Ujiji, after his march from the
coast near Zanzibar, the land to which Livingstone,
on his departure from Ujiji, bent his steps, was unknown to the Arabs save by vague report. Messrs.
Burton and Speke never heard of it, it seems.
Speke, who was the geographer of Burton's expedition, heard of a place called Uruwa, which he
placed on his map according to the general direction
indicated by the Arabs; but the most enterprising
of the Arabs, in their search after ivory, only touched
the frontiers of Rua, as the natives and Livingstone
call it; for Rua is an immense country, with a length
of six degrees of latitude and as yet an undefined
breadth from east to west.

"At the end of June, 1869, Livingstone took *dhow*
at Ujiji and crossed over to Uguhha, on the western
shore, for his last and greatest series of explorations,
the result of which was the discovery of a series of
lakes of great magnitude connected together by a
large river called by different names as it left one
lake to flow to another. From the port of Uguhha
he set off in company with a body of traders, in an
almost direct westerly course, through the lake country of Uguhha. Fifteen days march brought them
to Bambarre, the first important ivory depot in Manyema, or, as the natives pronounce it, Manuyema.
For nearly six months he was detained at Bambarre
from ulcers in the feet, with copious discharges of
bloody ichor oozing from the sores as soon as he set
his feet on the ground. When well, he set off in a
northerly direction, and, after several days, came to

a broad, lacustrine river, called the Lualaba, flowing northward and westward, and, in some places southward, in a most confusing way. The river was from one to three miles broad. By exceeding pertinacity he contrived to follow its erratic course until he saw the Lualaba enter the narrow but lengthy lake of Kamolondo, in about latitude 6 deg. 30 min. south. Retracing it south he came to the point where he had seen the Luapula enter Lake Moero.

"One feels quite enthusiastic when listening to Livingstone's description of the beauties of Moero scenery. Pent in on all sides by high mountainr clothed to their tips with the richest vegetation of the tropics, Moero discharges its superfluous waters through a deep rent in the bosom of the mountains. The impetuous and grand river roars through the chasm with the thunder of a cataract; but soon after leaving its confined and deep bed it expands into the calm and broad Lualaba—expanding over miles of ground, making great bends west and southwest, then, curving northward, enters Kamolondo. By the natives it is called the Lualaba, but the Doctor, in order to distinguish it from the other rivers of the same name, has given it the name of Webb's River, after Mr. Webb, the wealthy proprietor of Newstead Abbey, whom the Doctor distinguishes as one of his oldest and most consistent friends. Away to the southwest from Kamolondo is another large lake, which discharges its waters by the important river Locki, or Lomami, into the great Lualaba. To this lake, known as Chebungo by the natives, Dr. Livingstone has given the name of Lincoln, to be hereafter distinguished on maps and in books as Lake Lincoln, in memory of Abraham Lincoln, our murdered President. This was done from the vivid impression produced on his mind by hearing a portion of his inauguration speech read from an English pulpit, which related to the causes that induced him to issue his emancipation proclamation. To the memory of the man whose labors in behalf of the negro race deserved the commendation of all good men Livingstone has contributed a monument more durable than brass or stone.

"Entering Webb's River from the south-southwest, a little north of Kamolondo, is a large river called the Lufira, but the streams that discharge themselves from the watershed into the Lualaba are so numerous that the Doctor's map would not contain them, so he has left all out except the most important. Continuing his way north, tracing the Luabala through its manifold and crooked curves as far as latitude four degrees south, he came to another large lake called the Unknown Lake; but here you may come to a dead halt, and read it thus :—* * * * * Here was the furthermost point. From here he was compelled to return on the weary road to Ujiji, a distance of 600 miles.

"In this brief sketch of Doctor Livingstone's wonderful travels it is to be hoped that the most superficial reader, as well as the student of geography, comprehends this grand system of lakes connected together by Webb's river. To assist him, let him procure a map of Africa, embracing the latest discoveries. Two degrees south of the Tanganyika, and

two degrees west let him draw the outlines of a lake,
its greatest length from east to west, and let him call
it Bangweolo. One degree or thereabout to the
northwest let him sketch the outlines of another but
smaller lake and call it Moero; a degree again north
of Moero another lake of similar size, and call it
Kamolondo, and still a degree north of Kamolondo
another lake, large and as yet undefined limits, which,
in the absence of any specific term, we will call the
Nameless Lake. Then let him connect these several
lakes by a river called after different names. Thus,
the main feeder of Bangweolo, the Chambezi; the
river which issues out of Bangweolo and runs into
Moero, the Luapula; the river connecting Moero
with Kamolondo, Webb's river; that which runs
from Kamolondo into the Nameless Lake northward,
the Lualaba; and let him write in bold letters over
the rivers Chambezi, Luapula, Webb's River and the
Lualaba the 'Nile,' for these are all one and the same
river. Again, west of Moero Lake, about one degree
or thereabouts, another large lake may be placed on
his map, with a river running diagonally across to
meet the Lualaba north of Lake Kamolondo. This
new lake is Lake Lincoln, and the river is the Lomami River, the confluence of which with the Lualaba is between Kamolondo and the Nameless Lake.
Taken altogether, the reader may be said to have a
very fair idea of what Dr. Livingstone has been doing these long years, and what additions he has made
to the study of African geography. That this river,
distinguished under several titles, flowing from one
lake into another in a northerly direction, with all

its great crooked bends and sinuosities, is the Nile, the true Nile, the Doctor has not the least doubt. For a long time he did doubt, because of its deep bends and curves—west, and southwest even—but having traced it from its headwaters, the Chambezi, through seven degrees of latitude—that is, from latitude eleven degrees south to a little north of latitude four degrees south—he has been compelled to come to the conclusion that it can be no other river than the Nile. He had thought it was the Congo, but he has discovered the sources of the Congo to be the Kasai and the Quango, two rivers which rise on the western side of the Nile watershed in about the latitude of Bangweolo; and he was told of another river called the Lubilash, which rose from the north and ran west. But the Lualaba the Doctor thinks cannot be the Congo, from its great size and body and from its steady and continual flow northward through a broad and extensive valley, bounded by enormous mountains, westerly and easterly. The altitude of the most northerly point to which the Doctor traced the wonderful river was a little over two thousand feet, so that though Baker makes out his lake to be two thousand seven hundred feet above the sea, yet the Bahr Ghazal, through which Petherick's branch of the White Nile issues into the Nile, is only a little over two thousand feet, in which case there is a possibility that the Lualaba may be none other than Petherick's branch. It is well known that trading stations for ivory have been established for about five hundred miles up Petherick's branch. We must remember this fact when told that Gondokoro,

in latitude four degrees north, is two thousand feet
above the sea, and latitude four degrees south, where
the Doctor was halted, is only a little over two thousand feet above the sea. That two rivers, said to be
two thousand feet above the sea, separated from each
other by eight degrees of latitude, are the same
stream may, among some men, be regarded as a
startling statement. But we must restrain mere expressions of surprise and take into consideration that
this mighty and broad Lualaba is a lacustrine river
—broader than the Mississipi—and think of our own
rivers, which, though shallow, are exceedingly broad.
We must wait also until the altitude of the two rivers—the Lualaba, where the Doctor halted, and the
southern point on the Bahr Ghazal, where Petherick has been—are known with perfect accuracy.

"Webb's River, or the Lualaba, from Bangweolo is
a lacustrine river, expanding from one to three miles
in breadth. At intervals it forms extensive lakes,
then contracting into a broad river it again forms a
a lake, and so on to latitude four degrees north, and
beyond this point the Doctor heard of a large lake
again north. Now, for the sake of argument, suppose
we give this nameless lake a length of four degrees
latitude, as it may be the one discovered by Piaggia,
the Italian traveller, from which Petherick's branch
of the White Nile issues out through reeds, marshes
and the Bahr Ghazal into the White Nile south of
Gondokoro. By this method we can suppose the
rivers one—for the lakes extending over so many degrees of latitude would obviate the necessity of ex-
plaining the differences of latitude that must natu-

rally exist between the points of a river eight degrees
of latitude apart. Also, that Livingstone's instruments for observation and taking altitude may have
been in error, and this is very likely to have been the
case, subjected as they have been to rough handling
during nearly six years of travel.

"Despite the apparent difficulty about the altitude,
there is another strong reason for believing Webb's
River, or the Lualaba, to be the Nile. The water-
shed of this river, 600 miles of which Livingstone has
travelled, is drained by a valley which lies north and
south between the eastern and western ranges of the
watershed. This valley or line of drainage, while it
does not receive the Kasai and the Quango, receives
rivers flowing from a great distance west—for instance, the important tributaries Lufira and Lomami,
and large rivers from the east, such as the Lindi and
Luamo ; and while the most intelligent Portuguese
travellers and traders state that the Kasai, the Quango and Lubilash are the head waters of the Congo
river, no one as yet has started the supposition that
the grand river flowing north and known to the natives as the Lualaba, was the Congo. If this river
is not the Nile where, then, are the head waters of
the Nile ? The small river running out of the Victoria Nyanza and the river flowing out of the little
Lake Albert have not sufficient water to form the
great river of Egypt. As you glide down the Nile
and note the Asna, the Geraffe, the Sobat, the Blue
Nile and Atbara, and follow the river down to Egypt,
it cannot fail to impress you that it requires many
more streams, or one large river, larger than all yet

discovered, to influence its inundations and replace
the waste of its flow through a thousand miles of desert. Perhaps a more critical survey of the Bahr
Ghazal would prove that the Nile is influenced by
the waters that pour through 'the small piece of water resembling a duck pond buried in a sea of rushes,'
as Speke describes the Bahr Ghazal. Livinstone's
discovery answers the question and satisfies the intelligent hundreds, who, though Bruce and Speke and
Baker, each in his turn had declared he had found
the Nile, the only and true Nile sources, yet doubted
and hesitated to accept the enthusiastic assertions as
a final solution of the Nile problem. Even yet, according to Livingstone the Nile sources have not been
found; though he has traced the Lualaba through
seven degrees of latitude flowing north, and though
neither he nor I have a particle of doubt of its being
the Nile, not yet can the Nile question be said to be
ended for three reasons—

First—He has heard of the existence of four fountains, two of which give birth to a river flowing
north—Webb's River, or the Lualaba; two to a river
flowing south, which is the Zambezi. He has heard
of these fountains repeatedly from the natives.
Several times he has been within one hundred and
two hundred miles from them, but something always
interposed to prevent him going to see them. According to those who have seen them, they rise on
either side of a mound or hill which contains no
stones. Some have even called it an ant hill. One
of these fountains is said to be so large that a man
standing on one side cannot be seen from the other.

These fountains must be discovered, and their position taken. The Doctor does not suppose them to lie south of the feeders of Lake Bangweolo.

" *Second*—Webb's River must be traced to its connection with some portion of the old Nile.

" *Third*—The connection between the Tanganyika and the Albert Nyanza must be ascertained.

" When these three things have been accomplished, then, and not till then, can the mystery of the Nile be explained. The two countries through which this marvellous lacustrine river—the Lualaba—flows, with its manifold lakes and broad expanses of water, are Rua—the Uruwa of Speke—and Manyema. For the first time Europe is made aware that between the Tanganyika and the known sources of the Congo there exist teeming millions of the negro race who never saw or heard of the white peoples who make such noisy and busy stir outside of Africa. Upon the minds of those who had the good fortune to see the first specimen of these remarkable white races Livingstone seems to have made a favorable impression, though, through misunderstanding his object and coupling him with the Arabs who make horrible work there, his life has been sought after more than once.

" These two extensive countries, Rua and Manyema, are populated by true heathens—governed not as the sovereignties of Karagwah, Wumdi, and Uganda by despotic kings, but each village by its own sultan or lord. Thirty miles outside of their own immediate settlements the most intelligent of those small chiefs seem to know nothing. Thirty miles from the

Lualaba there were but few people who had ever
heard of the great river.   Such ignorance among the
natives of their own countries, of course, increased
the labors of Livingstone.   Compared with these all
tribes and nations in Africa with whom Livingstone
came in contact may be deemed civilized.   Yet in
the arts of home manufacture these wild people of
Manyema are far superior to any he had seen.   When
other tribes and nations contented themselves with
hides and skins of animals thrown negligently over
their shoulders the people of Manyema manufactured a cloth from fine grass which may favorably
compare with the finest grass cloth of India.   They
also know the art of dyeing in various colors—
black, yellow, and purple.   The Wanguana or freed
men of Zanzibar, struck with the beauty of this fine
grass frabric, eagerly exchange their cotton cloths
for fine grass cloth, and on almost every black man
returned from Manyema I have seen this native cloth
converted into elegantly made *damirs* (Arabic)—
short jackets.

"These countries are also very rich in ivory.   The
fever for going to Manyema to exchange their
tawdry beads for the precious tusks of Manyema is
of the same kind as that which impelled men to the
gulches and placers of California, Colorado, Mon-
tana, and Idaho; after nuggets to Australia, and
diamonds to Cape Colony.   Manyema is at present
the El Dorado of the Arabs and the Wamrima tribes.
It is only about four years since the first Arab returned from Manyema with such wealth of ivory and
reports about the fabulous quantities found there

that ever since the old beaten tracks of Karagwah,
Uganda, Ufipa, and Marungu have been comparatively deserted. The people of Manyema, ignorant
of the value of the precious article, reared their huts
upon ivory stanchions. Ivory pillars and doors were
common sights in Manyema, and hearing of these one
can no longer wonder at the ivory palace of Solo-
mon. For generations they had used ivory tusks as
doorposts and eave stanchions, until they had become perfectly rotten and worthless. But the advent
of the Arabs soon taught them the value of the
article. It has now risen considerably in price, though
yet fabulously cheap. At Zanzibar the value of ivory
per frarsilah of thirty-five pounds weight is from
fifty dollars to sixty dollars, according to its quality
In Unyanyembe it is about one dollar and ten cents
per pound; but in Manyema it may be purchased for
from half a cent to one and a quarter cent's worth of
copper per pound of ivory.

"The Arabs, however, have the knack of spoiling
markets by their rapacity and wanton cruelty. With
muskets a small party of Arabs are invincible against
such people as those of Manyema, who until lately
never heard the sound of a gun. The report of a
musket inspires mortal terror in them, and it is
almost impossible to induce them to face the muzzle
of a gun. They believe that the Arabs have stolen
the lightning, and that against such people the bow
and arrow can have but little effect. They are by
no means devoid of courage, and they have often
declared that were it not for the guns not one Arab
would leave the country alive, which tends to prove

The Effects of the Great Hurricane at Zanzibar.

that they would willingly engage in fight with the strangers, who have made themselves so detestable, were it not that the startling explosion of gunpowder inspires them with such terror.

"Into whichever country the Arabs enter they contrive to render their name and race abominated. But the mainspring of it all is not the Arab's nature, color, or name, but simply the slave trade. So long as the slave trade is permitted to be kept up at Zanzibar so long will these otherwise enterprising people, the Arabs, kindle against them throughout Africa the hatred of the natives. The accounts which the Doctor brings from that new region are most deplorable. He was an unwilling spectator of a horrible deed—a massacre committed on the inhabitants of a populous district—who had assembled in the market place, on the banks of the Lualaba, as they had been accustomed to for ages. It seems the Wa-Manyema are very fond of marketing, believing it to be the *summum bonum* of human enjoyment. They find unceasing pleasure in chaffering with might and main for the least mite of their currency—the last bead—and when they gain the point to which their peculiar talents are devoted they feel intensely happy. The women are excessively fond of their marketing, and as they are very beautiful, the market place must possess considerable attractions for the male sex. It was on such a day, with just such a scene, that Tagomoyo, a half-caste Arab, with his armed slave escort, commenced an indiscriminate massacre by firing volley after volley into the dense mass of human beings. It is supposed that there

17

were about two thousand present, and at the first
sound of the firing these poor people all made a rush
for their canoes. In the fearful hurry to avoid being
shot the canoes were paddled away by the first fortunate few who got possession of them. Those that
were not so fortunate sprang into the deep waters of
the Lualaba, and, though many of them became an
easy prey to the voracious crocodiles that swarmed
to the scene, the majority received their deaths from the
bullets of the merciless Tagomoyo and his villainous
band. The Doctor believes, as do the Arabs themselves,
that about four hundred people, mostly women and
children, lost their lives, while many more were made
slaves. This scene is only one of many such which
he has unwillingly witnessed, and he is utterly unable
to describe the loathing he feels for the inhuman
perpetrators.

"Slaves from Manyema command a higher price
than those of any other country, because of their fine
forms and general docility. The women, the Doctor
says repeatedly, are remarkably pretty creatures, and
have nothing except their hair in common with the
negroes of the West Coast. They are of very light
color, have fine noses, well-cut and not over full lips,
and a prognathous jaw is uncommon. These women
are eagerly sought after for wives by the half-castes
of the East Coast, and even the pure Amani Arabs
do not disdain connection with them. To the north
of Manyema Livingstone came to a light-complex-
ioned race of the color of Portuguese, or our own
Louisiana quadroons, who are very fine people, and
singularly remarkable for commercial 'cuteness' and

sagacity. The women are expert divers for oysters, which are found in great abundance in the Lualaba.

"Rua, at a place called Katanga, is rich in copper. The copper mines of this place have been worked for ages. In the bed of a stream gold has been found washed down in pencil-shaped lumps or particles as large as split peas. Two Arabs have gone thither to prospect for this metal, but as they are ignorant of the art of gulch mining it is scarcely possible that they will succeed.

"From these highly important and interesting discoveries Dr. Livingstone was turned back when almost on the threshold of success by the positive refusal of his men to accompany him further. They were afraid to go unless accompanied by a large force of men, and as these were not procurable in Manyema the Doctor reluctantly turned his face toward Ujiji.

"It was a long and weary road back. The journey had now no interest for him. He had travelled it before when going westward, full of high hopes and aspirations, impatient to reach the goal which promised him rest from his labors; now returning unsuccessful, baffled and thwarted when almost in sight of the end, and having to travel the same road back on foot, with disappointed expectations and defeated hopes preying on his mind, no wonder that the brave old spirit almost succumbed and the strong constitution almost wrecked. He arrived at Ujiji October 26, almost at death's door. On the way he had been trying to cheer himself up, since he had found it impossible to contend against the obstinacy of his men, with 'it won't take long, five or six months more; it matters not, since it can't be helped. I have got my goods in Ujiji and can hire other people and make a new start.' These are the words and hopes with which he tried to delude himself into the idea that all would be right yet; but imagine, if you can, the shock he must have suffered when he found that the man to whom was entrusted his goods for safe keeping had sold every bale for ivory.

" The evening of the day Livingstone had returned to Ujiji, Susi and Chuma, two of his most faithful men, were seen crying bitterly. The Doctor asked them what ailed them, and was then informed for the first time of the evil tidings that awaited him. Said they:—'All our things are sold, sir. Shereef has sold everything for ivory.' Later in the evening Shereef came to see him and shamelessly offered his hand, with a salutatory 'Yambo.' Livingstone refused his hand, saying he could not shake hands with a thief. As an excuse Shereef said he had divined on the Koran and that had told him the Hakim (Arabic for Doctor) was dead. Livingstone was now destitute. He had just enough to keep him and his men alive for about a month, after which he would be forced to beg from the Arabs. He had arrived in Ujiji October 26. The HERALD Expedition arrived November 10, from the coast—only sixteen days difference. Had I not been delayed at Unyanyembe by the war with Mirambo I should have gone on to Manyema, and very likely have been traveling by one road, while he would have been coming by another to Ujiji. Had I gone on two years ago, when I first received the instructions, I should have lost him without doubt. But I am detained by a series of circumstances, which chafed and fretted me considerably at that time, only to permit him to reach Ujiji sixteen days before I appeared. It was as if we were marching to meet together at an appointed rendezvous—the one from the west, the other from the east.

"The Doctor had heard of a white man being at Unyanyembe, who was said to have boats with him, and he had thought he was another traveller sent by the French government to replace Lieutenant Le Sainte, who died from a fever a few miles above Gondokoro. I had not written to him because I believed him to be dead, and of course my sudden entrance into Ujiji was as great a surprise to him as it was to the Arabs. But the sight of the American flag, which he saw waving in the van of the expedition, indicated that one was coming who could speak his own language, and you know already how the leader was received."

CHAPTER XIV.

LIVINGSTONE AND STANLEY IN AFRICA.

[CONTINUED.]

An Exploration of Tanganyika Lake—Result—Christmas at Ujiji—Livingstone Proceeds with Stanley to Unyanyembe—Account of the Journey—Alleged Neglect of Livingstone by the British Consulate at Zanzibar—Departure of the Explorer for the Interior, and of Mr. Stanley for Europe.

It had been supposed by Dr. Livingstone that the waters of Tanganyika Lake had outlet northward, and that they were, therefore, a part of the necessarily vast sources of the great river of the continent whose annual inundations are among the most wonderful illustrations in nature of the more than majestic power of Almighty God. His many discoveries of great lakes and rivers far to the westward of Tanganyika, their evident connection in a system, similar to that of the great lakes of North America at last forming the St. Lawrence river, flowing northward; the natural necessity there is for immense sources of supply to the Nile—these and other considerations left the explorer to imagine that Tanganyika formed a part of the same system with that lake which he named after an illustrious President of the United States. The commander of the "Herald" expedition, therefore, with a fine appreciation of the situation, offered his escort to Dr. Livingstone, with a proposal to accompany him to the head of the lake. The offer was accepted, and the explorer, as Mr. Stanley says, "like a hero, lost no time in starting."

The account of this journey, or voyage, rather, for the party travelled by boat, is given in a dispatch dated December 23, 1871, at Ujiji. It is as follows:

" On the 20th of November Dr. Livingstone and your correspondent, with twenty picked men of the HERALD Expedition Corps, started. Despite the assertion of Arabs that the Warundi were dangerous and would not let us pass, we hugged their coast closely, and when fatigued boldly encamped in their country. Once only were we obliged to fly—and this was at dead of night—from a large party which we knew to be surrounding us on the land side. We got to the boat safely, and we might have punished them severely had the Doctor been so disposed. Once also we were stoned, but we paid no heed to them and kept on our way along their coast until we arrived at Mokamba's, one of the chiefs of Usige. Mokamba was at war with a neighboring chief, who lived on the left bank of the Rusizi. That did not deter us, and we crossed the head of the Tanganyika to Mugihewah, governed by Ruhinga, brother of Mokamba.

"Mugihewah is a tract of country on the right bank of the Rusizi, extending to the lake. With Mokamba and Ruhinga we became most intimate · they proved to be sociable, good-natured chiefs, and gave most valuable information concerning the countries lying to the north of Usige ; and if their nformation is correct, Sir Samuel Baker will be obliged to curtail the ambitious dimensions of his lake by one degree, if not more. A Mgwana, living at Mokamba's, on the eastern shore of the lake, had informed us that the River Rusizi certainly flowed out of the lake, and after joining the Kitangule emptied into the Lake Nyanza (Victoria).

"When we entered Ruhinga's territory of Mugihe-wah, we found ourselves about 300 yards from the river about which a great deal has been said and written. At Unyanyembe I was told that the Rusizi was an affluent. At Ujiji all Arabs but one united in saying the same thing, and within ten miles of the Rusizi a freedman of Zanzibar swore it was an affluent.

"On the morning of the eleventh day of our departure from Ujiji, we were rowed towards the river. We came to a long, narrow bay, fringed on all sides with tall, dense reeds and swarming with crocodiles, and soon came to the mouth of the Rusizi. As soon as we had entered the river all doubt vanished before the strong, turbid flood against which we had to con-tend in the ascent. After about ten minutes we en-tered what seemed a lagoon, but which was the result of a late inundation. About an hour higher up the river began to be confined to its proper banks, and is about thirty yards broad, but very shallow.

"Two days higher up, Ruhinga told us, the Rusizi was joined by the Loanda, coming from the north-west. There could be no mistake then. Dr. Living-stone and myself had ascended it, had felt the force of the strong inflowing current—the Rusizi was an influent, as much so as the Malagarazi, the Linche,

and Rugufu, but with its banks full it can only be
considered as ranking third among the rivers flowing
into the Tanganyika. Though rapid it is extremely
shallow; it has three mouths, up which an ordinary
ship's boat loaded might in vain attempt to ascend.
Burton and Speke, though they ascended to within
six hours' journey by canoe from the Rusizi, were
compelled to turn back by the cowardice of the boatmen. Had they ascended to Meuta's capital, they
could easily have seen the head of the lake. Usige
is but a district of Wumdi, governed by several small
chiefs, who owe obedience to Mwezi, the great King
of Wumdi.

"We spent nine days at the head of the Tanganyika exploring the islands and many bays that indent
its shores.

"In returning to Ujiji we coasted along the west
side of the Tanganyika, as far as the country of the
Wasansi, whom we had to leave on no amicable terms,
owing to their hostility to Arabs, and arrived at
Ujiji on the 18th of December, having been absent
twenty-eight days.

"Though the Rusizi River can no longer be a subject of curiosity to geographers—and we are certain
that there is no connection between the Tanganyika
and Baker's Lake, or the Albert N'yanza—it is not
yet certain that there is no connection between the
Tanganyika and the Nile River. The western coast
has not all been explored; and there is reason to
suppose that a river runs out of the Tanganyika
through the deep caverns of Kabogo Mountain, far
under ground and out on the western side of Kabo-

go into the Lualaba, or the Nile. Livingstone has seen the river about forty miles or so west of Kabogo (about forty yards broad at that place), but he does not know that it runs out of the mountain.

"This is one of the many things which he has yet to examine."

It thus appearing that the Rusizi is an affluent, not an effluent, of Tanganyika Lake, the expedition failed to sustain the explorer's hypothesis, but added a useful item of geographical knowledge to the then existing stock. Nor does it follow that because the Rusizi flows into the Tanganyika, there is no river flowing out of it into that system of lakes which had before been discovered by the explorer, and of which the Chambesi—almost a system of rivers itself—is the largest affluent yet discovered. Should Dr. Livingstone's hypothesis of an effluent from the west shore of Tanganyika Lake not be sustained, and its waters found to procure outlet by Lake Nyassa and the Zambesi, his future discoveries will in all probability show a similar formation of the continent in east central Africa to that which he discovered to be the fact when he explored Lake Dilolo in the land of the Balonda.

The explorers remained in Ujiji until after "merry Christmas," both engaged much of the time in writing accounts of their explorations, which have appeared or will yet appear in this volume. Meanwhile, they had determined to make a journey together to Unyanyembe. This journey is described in telegraphic brevity:

KWIHARA, UNYANYEMBE, February 21, 1872.

After spending Christmas at Ujiji Dr. Livingstone, escorted by the NEW YORK HERALD Expedition, composed of forty Wanguana soldiers, well armed, left for Unyanyembe on the 26th of December, 1871.

In order to arrive safely, untroubled by wars and avaricious tribes, we sketched out a road to Unyanyembe, thus :—

Seven days by water south to Urimba.

Ten days across the uninhabited forests of Kawendi.

Twenty days through Unkonongo, direct east.

Twelve days north through Unkonongo

Thence five days into Unyanyembe, where we arrived without adventure of any kind, except killing zebras, buffaloes, and giraffes, after fifty-four days' travel.

The expedition suffered considerably from famine, and your correspondent from fever, but these are incidental to the march in this country.

The Doctor tramped it on foot like a man of iron. On arrival at Unyanyembe I found that the Englishman Shaw whom I had turned back as useless, had about a month after his return succumbed to the climate of the interior and had died, as well as two Wanguana of the expedition who had been left behind sick. Thus during less than twelve months William Lawrence Farquhar, of Leith, Scotland, and John William Shaw, of London, England, the two white men I had engaged to assist me, had died · also eight baggage carriers and eight soldiers of the expedition had died.

I was bold enough to advise the Doctor to permit the expedition to escort him to Unyanyembe, through the country it was made acquainted with while going to Ujiji, for the reason that were he to sit down at Ujiji until Mirambo was disposed of he might remain a year there, a prey to high expectations, ending always in bitter disappointment. I told him, as the Arabs of Unyanyembe were not equal to the task of conquering Mirambo, that it were better he should accompany the HERALD expedition to Unyanyembe, and there take possession of the last lot of goods brought to him by a caravan which left the seacoast simultaneously with our expedition.

The Doctor consented, and thus it was that he came so far back as Unyanyembe.

The " Herald" correspondent complains with much earnestness that Dr. Livingstone has been neglected by the British consulate at Zanzibar. Handsomely admitting the liberality of the British people and government, he has hearty denunciations for those in authority at Zanzibar. The contrast of their insufficiency with the enterprise of the " Herald" expedition is remarkable. Mr. Stanley says : " Within

the time that the British Consul's men took to convey Livingstone's goods and letters a distance of only
525 miles, the HERALD Expedition was formed, and
marched 2,059 English statute miles, and before the
fourteenth month of its departure from the seacoast
the HERALD Expedition will have arrived at the seacoast, be paid off and disbanded. In the matter of
supplies, then, being sent to Livingstone semi-an-
nually or annually there is no truth whatever. The
cause is extreme apathy at Zanzibar and the reckless
character of the men sent. Where English gentlemen are so liberal and money so plentiful it should be
otherwise."

Upon this very delicate subject the " Herald" itself
editorially remarks:

" On the question of Livingstone's having received
the supplies sent him by his friends in England these
letters will throw a startling light. The carelessness,
theft, and general mismanagement which overtook
the stores forwarded by the British Consulate at
Zanzibar, usually wasted and frittered these almost
entirely away before they had time to reach him. This
cannot be better stated than in the HERALD commander's words: ' Your correspondent begs to inform
his friends that the HERALD Expedition found him
turned back from his explorations when on the eve of
being terminated thoroughly by the very men sent to
him by the British Consulate; that the Expedition
found him sitting down at Ujiji utterly destitute,
robbed by the very men sent by the British Consulate at Zanzibar with his caravan; that the HERALD

Expedition escorted him to Unyanyembe only in
time to save his last stock of goods, for they were
rapidly being made away with by the very men entrusted by the British Consulate with the last lot of
goods; that it was only by an accident that your correspondent saw a packet of letters addressed to Livingstone, and so, forcibly, took one of Livingstone's
men to carry the letters to his employer.'"

The commander of the Search Expedition supplied
Dr. Livingstone with such supplies as he could command, in which were several bales of mixed cloths,
about one thousand pounds of assorted beads—all
this is African money—a large quantity of brass
wire, a portable boat, revolvers, carbines, and ammunition.

And thus Mr. Stanley was ready to depart for the
sea coast. Bidding the great explorer farewell, he
left Kwihara on March 14, 1872, bending his course
toward Zanzibar by the usual caravan track. At
Zanzibar he forwarded "men and means" to the explorer of whom he had learned to think so highly, by
the aid of which he has doubtless been able to make
his departure from Unyanyembe with confident anticipations of success. And so, we may be sure, the
iron man is wending his way on foot through the
wilds of Africa, inflexibly determined upon a complete solution of the great geographical problem of
the times.

Meanwhile, the chief of the successful search expedition discharged his men at Zanzibar, and by Bombay, thence to Aden in southwestern Arabia, the Red
Sea, and the Suez Canal, found his rapid way to the

abodes of those races of civilized men who had been astonished and gratified by the summary of the remarkable success of his enterprise which had preceded him.

CHAPTER XV.

DR. LIVINGSTONE STILL IN AFRICA.

The Great Explorer Still in Search of the Sources of the Nile—His Letters to the English Government on His Explorations—Correspondence with Lord Stanley, Lord Clarendon, Earl Granville, Dr. Kirk, and James Gordon Bennett, Jr.—His Own Descriptions of Central Africa and the Supposed Sources of the Nile—The Country and People—A Nation of Cannibals—Beautiful Women—Gorillas—The Explorer's Plans for the Future.

When Mr. Stanley bade good-bye to Dr. Livingstone in Unyanyembe, the explorer entrusted to the care of the corrrespondent despatches to the government, his journal, addressed to his daughter, and copies of letters of which former messengers had been robbed. The letters, old and new, to the representative of the British government at Zanzibar, Dr. Kirk, and to different members of the British cabinet, were allowed to be published. They give a full account of Dr. Livingstone's explorations among the supposed true sources of the Nile, and abundantly establish the complete success of the " Herald" search expedition. The letters to the British authorities thus sent to the press, August 1, 1872, through the courtesy of Earl Granville, were: 1. A letter from Dr. Livingstone to Lord Stanley, under date of November 15, 1870; 2. Two letters of November 1, 1871, to Lord Clarendon; 3. A letter of November 14, 1871, to Earl Granville; 4. Letter of October 30, 1871, to Dr. Kirk, British Consul at Zanzibar; 5. Letter of December 18, 1871 to Earl Granville; 6. Letter of February 20, 1872, to Earl Granville.

The first of these despatches to his government is from "Bambarre, Manyema country, say about one hundred and fifty miles west of Ujiji, Nov. 15, 1870," addressed to Lord Stanley, Secretary of State for Foreign Affairs. In this dispatch, much is contained which Dr. Livingstone orally related to Mr. Stanley, of the "Herald," and which has already appeared in this work. The country of the Manyema, reputed cannibals, is described generally thus:

"The country is extremely beautiful, but difficult to travel over. The mountains of light gray granite stand like islands in new red sandstone, and mountain and valley are all clad in a mantle of different shades of green. The vegetation is indescribably rank. Through the grass—if grass it can be called, which is over half an inch in diameter in the stalk and from ten to twelve feet high—nothing but elephants can walk. The leaves of this megatherium grass are armed with minute spikes, which, as we worm our way along elephant walks, rub disagreeably on the side of the face where the gun is held, and the hand is made sore by fending it off the other side for hours. The rains were fairly set in by November; and in the mornings, or after a shower, these leaves were loaded with a moisture which wet us to the bone. The valleys are deeply undulating, and in each innumerable dells have to be crossed. There may be only a thread of water at the bottom, but the mud, mire or (*scottice*) 'glaur' is grevious; thirty or forty yards of the path on each side of the stream are

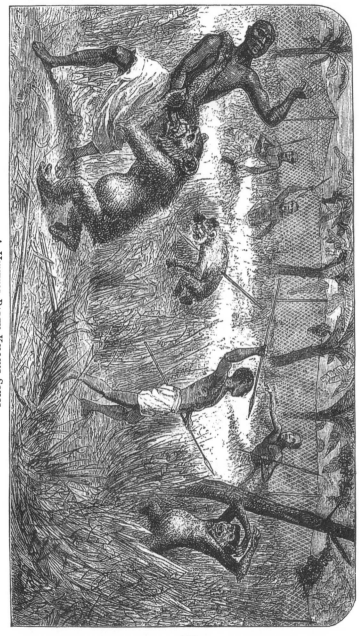

worked by the feet of passengers into an adhesive
compound. By placing a foot on each side of the
narrow way one may waddle a little distance along,
but the rank crop of grasses, gingers, and bushes cannot spare the few inches of soil required for the side
of the foot, and down he comes into the slough. The
path often runs along the bed of the rivulet for sixty
or more yards, as if he who first cut it out went that
distance seeking for a part of the forest less dense
for his axe. In other cases the muale palm, from
which here, as in Madagascar, grass cloth is woven
and called by the same name, 'lamba,' has taken possession of the valley. The leaf stalks, as thick as a
strong man's arm, fall off and block up all passage
save by a path made and mixed up by the feet of
elephants and buffaloes; the slough therein is groan-
compelling and deep.

" Some of the numerous rivers which in this region
flow into Lualaba are covered with living vegetable
bridges—a species of dark glossy-leaved grass, with
its roots and leaves, felts itself into a mat that covers
the whole stream. When stepped upon it yields
twelve or fifteen inches, and that amount of water
rises upon the leg. At every step the foot has to be
raised high enough to place it on the unbent mass in
front. This high stepping fatigues like walking on
deep snow. Here and there holes appear which we
could not sound with a stick six feet long; they gave
the impression that anywhere one might plump
through and finish the chapter. Where the water is
shallow the lotus, or sacred lily, sends its roots to the
bottom and spreads its broad leaves over the float-

18

ing bridge so as to make believe that the mat is its own, but the grass referred to is the real felting and supporting agent, for it often performs duty as bridge where no lilies grow. The bridge is called by Man-yema 'kintefwetefwe,' as if he who first coined it was gasping for breath after plunging over a mile of it.

"Between each district of Manyema large belts of the primeval forest still stand. Into these the sun, though vertical, cannot penetrate, except by sending down at midday thin pencils of rays into the gloom. The rain water stands for months in stagnant pools made by the feet of elephants; and the dead leaves decay on the damp soil, and make the water of the numerous rivulets of the color of strong tea. The climbing plants, from the size of whipcord to that of a man-of-war's hawser, are so numerous the ancient path is the only passage. When one of the giant trees falls across the road it forms a wall breast high to be climbed over, and the mass of tangled ropes brought down makes cutting a path round it a work of time which travellers never undertake."

At this time, Dr. Livingstone was not persuaded that the Manyema were men-eaters. Toward the conclusion of his letter to Lord Stanley, he thus de-cribes them:

"I lived in what may be called the Tipperary of Manyema, and they are certainly a bloody people among themselves. But they are very far from be-ing in appearance like the ugly negroes on the West Coast. Finely formed heads are common, and generally men and women are vastly superior to the slaves of Zanzibar and elsewhere. We must go deeper than phrenology to account for their low moral tone. If they are cannibals they are not ostentatiously so. The neighboring tribes all assert that they are men-eaters, and they themselves laughingly admit the charge. But they like to impose on the credulous, and they showed the skull of a recent victim to horrify one of my people. I found it to be the skull of a gorilla, or soko—the first I knew of its existence here—and this they do eat. If I had believed a tenth of what I heard from traders, I might never have entered the country. Their people told tales with shocking circumstantiality, as if of eye witnesses, that could not be committed to paper, or even spoken about beneath the breath. Indeed, one wishes them to vanish from memory. I have not yet been able to make up my mind whether the Manyema are cannibals or not. I have offered goods of sufficient value to tempt any of them to call me to see a cannibal feast in the dark forests where these orgies are said to be held, but hitherto in vain. All the real evidence yet obtained would elicit from a Scotch jury the verdict only of 'not proven.'"

The second despatch, a year later, is devoted to the expression of thanks to Lord Clarendon, on account of the expedition of search under Mr. Young, of which an account has already been given, to an explanation of Ali Moosa's story of the explorer's death, and an earnest request that the money expended on him and his fellow-imposters might be regained.

The third document of the series, being also a let-

ter to Lord Clarendon, presents an account of Dr.
Livingstone's explorations and views on the water-
shed of the Nile more *in extenso* than anywhere else
given. It is certainly one of the most interesting
and valuable contributions to modern science. The
readers of this volume cannot but feel that a large
share of this interesting document may appropriately
be quoted here.

" I have ascertained that the watershed of the Nile
is a broad upland between ten degrees and twelve degrees south latitude, and from 4,000 to 5,000 feet
above the level of the sea. Mountains stand on it at
various points, which, though not apparently very
high, are between 6,000 and 7,000 feet of actual altitude. The watershed is over 700 miles in length,
from west to east. The springs that rise on it are
almost innumerable—that is, it would take a large
part of a man's life to count them. A bird's-eye view
of some parts of the watershed would resemble the
frost vegetation on window panes. They all begin
in an ooze at the head of a slightly depressed valley.
A few hundred yards down the quantity of water from
oozing earthen sponge forms a brisk perennial burn
or brook a few feet broad, and deep enough to require a bridge. These are the ultimate or primary
sources of the great rivers that flow to the north in
the great Nile valley. The primaries unite and form
streams in general larger than the Isis at Oxford or
Avon at Hamilton, and may be called secondary
sources. They never dry, but unite again into four
large lines of drainage, the head waters or mains of
the river of Egypt. These four are each called by

the natives Lualaba, which, if not too pedantic, may
be spoken of as lacustrine rivers, extant specimens of
those which, in pre-historic times, abounded in Africa, and which in the south are still called by Bechuanas ' Melapo,' in the north, by Arabs, ' Wadys ;' both
words meaning the same thing—river bed in which
no water ever now flows. Two of the four great rivers mentioned fall into the central Lualaba, or
Webb's Lake River, and then we have but two main
lines of drainage as depicted nearly by Ptolemy.

" In passing over sixty miles of latitude I waded
thirty-two primary sources from calf to waist deep,
and requiring from twenty minutes to an hour and
a quarter to cross stream and sponge. This would
give about one source to every two miles. A Suaheli friend in passing along part of the Lake Bangweolo during six days counted twenty-two from thigh
to waist deep,   This lake is on the watershed, for the
village at which I observed on its northwest shore
was a few seconds into eleven degrees south. I tried
to cross it in order to measure the breadth accurately. The first stage to an inhabted island was
about twenty-four miles. From the highest point
here the tops of the trees, evidently lifted by the
mirage, could be seen on the second stage and the
third stage; the mainland was said to be as far as
this beyond it. But my canoe men had stolen the
canoe and got a hint that the real owners were in
pursuit, and got into a flurry to return home.

" The length of this lake is, at a very moderate estimate, 150 miles. It gives forth a large body of water in the Luapula ; yet lakes are in no sense sources,

for no large river begins in a lake; but this and otn-
ers serve an important purpose in the phenomena of
the Nile. It is one large lake, and, unlike the Okara,
which, according to Suaheli, who travelled long in our
company, is three or four lakes run into one huge
Victoria Nianza, gives out a large river which, on de-
parting out of Moero, is still larger. These men had
spent many years east of Okara, and could scarcely
be mistaken in saying that of the three or four lakes
there only one (the Okara) gives off its waters to the
north. The ' White Nile' of Speke, less by a full half
than the Shire out of Nyassa (for it is only eighty or
niety yards broad), can scarcely be named in comparison with the central or Webb's Lualaba, of from two
thousand to six thousand yards, in relation to the
phenomena of the Nile. The structure and economy
of the watershed answer very much the same end as
the great lacustrine rivers, but I cannot at present
copy a lost despatch which explained that. The
mountains on the watershed are probably what
Ptolemy, for reasons now unknown, called the Mountains of the Moon. From their bases I found that
the springs of the Nile do unquestionably arise.
This is just what Ptolemy put down, and is true geography. We must accept the fountains, and nobody
but Philistines will reject the mountains, though we
cannot conjecture the reason for the name.

" Before leaving the subject of the watershed, I
may add that I know about six hundred miles of it,
but am not yet satisfied, for unfortunately the seventh
hundred is the most interesting of the whole. I have
a very strong impression that in the last hundred

miles the fountains of the Nile, mentioned to Herodotus by the Secretary of Minerva in the city of Sais
do arise, not like all the rest, from   oozing earthen
sponges, but from an earthen mound, and half the
water flows northward to Egypt, the other half south
to Inner Ethiopia. These fountains, at no great distance off, become large rivers, though at the mound
they are not more than ten miles apart. That is, one
fountain rising on the northeast of the mound becomes Bartle Frere's Lualaba, and it flows into one
of the lakes proper, Kamolondo, of the central line of
drainage ; Webb's Lualaba, the second fountain rising
on the Northwest, becomes (Sir Paraffin) Young's
Lualaba, which passing through Lake Lincoln and
becoming Loeki or Lomame, and joining the central
line too, goes north to Egypt. The third fountain on
the southwest, Palmerston's, becomes the Liambia or
Upper Zambesi; while the fourth, Oswell's fountain,
becomes the Kafue and falls into Zambesi in Inner
Ethiopia.

" More time has been spent in the exploration than
I ever anticipated. Many a weary foot I trod ere I
got a clear idea of the drainage of the great Nile
valley. The most intelligent natives and traders
thought that all the rivers of the upper part of that
valley flowed into Tanganyika. But the barometers
told me that to do so the water must flow up hill.
The great rivers and the great lakes all make their
waters converge into the deep trough of the valley,
which is a full inch of the barometer lower than the
Upper Tanganyika.

" Let me explain, but in no boastful style, the mis-

takes of others who have bravely striven to solve
the ancient problem, and it will be seen that I have
cogent reasons for following the painful, plodding investigation to its conclusion.   Poor Speke's mistake was a foregone conclusion.   When he discovered the Victoria Nyansa he at once jumped to the
conclusion that therein lay the sources of the river
of Egypt, ' 20,000 square miles of water,' confused
by sheer immensity.   Ptolemy's small lake, ' Coloc,'
is a more correct representation of the actual size of
that one of three or four lakes which alone sends
its outflow to the north.   Its name is Okara.   Lake
Kavirondo is three days distant from it, but connected by a narrow arm.   Lake Naibash, or Neibash,
is four days from Kavirondo.   Baringo is ten days
distant, and discharges by a river, the Nagardabash,
to the northeast.

" These three or four lakes, which have been described by several intelligent Suaheli, who have lived
for many years on their shores, were run into one
huge Victoria Nyanza.   But no sooner did Speke
and Grant turn their faces to this lake, to prove that
it contained the Nile fountains, than they turned
their backs to the springs of the river of Egypt,
which are between four hundred and five hundred
miles south of the most southerly portion of the Victoria Lake.   Every step of their heroic and really
splendid achievement of following the river down
took them further and further from the sources they
sought.   But for the devotion to the foregone conclusion the sight of the little ' White Nile,' as unable to account for the great river, they must have

turned off to the west down into the deep trough
of the great valley, and there found lacustrine rivers
amply sufficient to account for the Nile and all its
phenomena.

" But all that can in modern times and in common
modesty be fairly claimed is the rediscovery of what
had sunk into oblivion, like the circumnavigation of
Africa by the Phœnician admirals of one of the
Pharaohs about B. C. 600. He was not believed
because he reported that in passing round Libya he
had the sun on his right hand. This, to us who have
gone round the Cape from east to west, stamps his
tale as genuine. The predecessors of Ptolemy
probably gained their information from men who
visited this very region, for in the second century of
our era he gave in substance what we now find to be
genuine geography.

" The geographical results of four arduous trips in
different directions in the Manyema country are
briefly as follows :—The great river, Webb's Lualaba,
in the center of the Nile valley, makes a great bend
to the west, soon after leaving Lake Moero, of at
least one hundred and eighty miles; then, turning to
the north for some distance, it makes another large
sweep west of about one hundred and twenty miles,
in the course of which about thirty miles of southing
are made; it then draws round to northeast, receives
the Lomani, or Loeki, a large river which flows
through Lake Lincoln. After the union a large lake
is formed, with many inhabited islands in it; but this
has still to be explored. It is the fourth large lake
in the central line of drainage, and cannot be Lake

Albert; for, assuming Speke's longitude of Ujiji to be pretty correct, and my reckoning not enormously wrong, the great central lacustrine river is about five degrees west of Upper and Lower Tanganyika.

"Beyond the fourth lake the water passes, it is said, into large reedy lakes, and is in all probability Petherick's branch—the main stream of the Nile—in distinction from the smaller eastern arm which Speke, Grant, and Baker took to be the river of Egypt. In my attempts to penetrate further and further I had but little hope of ultimate success, for the great amount of westing led to a continued effort to suspend the judgment, lest, after all, I might be exploring the Congo instead of the Nile, and it was only after the two great western drains fell into the central main, and left but the two great lacustrine rivers of Ptolemy, that I felt pretty sure of being on the right track.

"The great bends west probably form one side of the great rivers above that geographical loop, the other side being Upper Tanganyika and the Lake River Albert. A waterfall is reported to exist between Tanganyika and Albert Nyanza, but I could not go to it; nor have I seen the connecting link between the two—the upper side of the loop—though I believe it exists.

"The Manyema are certainly cannibals, but it was long ere I could get evidence more positive than would have led a Scotch jury to give a verdict of not proven.' They eat only enemies killed in war; they seem as if instigated by revenge in their man-eating orgies, and on these occasions they do not like a stranger to see them. I offered a large reward in vain to any one who would call me to witness a canibal feast. Some intelligent men have told me that the meat is not nice and made them dream of the dead. The women never partake, and I am glad of it, for many of them far down Lualaba are very pretty; they bathe three or four times a day and are expert divers for oysters.

" Markets are held at stated times and the women attend them in large numbers, dressed in their best. They are light colored, have straight noses, finely formed heads, small hands and feet and perfect forms; they are keen traders, and look on the market as a great institution; to haggle and joke and laugh and cheat seem the enjoyments of life. The population, especially west of the river, is prodigiously large.

" Near Lomani the Bakuss or Bakoons cultivate coffee, and drink it highly scented with vanilla. Food of all kinds is extremely abundant and cheap. The men smelt iron from the black oxide ore, and are very good smiths; they also smelt copper from the ore and make large ornaments very cheaply. They are generally fine, tall, strapping fellows, far superior to the Zanzibar slaves, and nothing of the West Coast negro, from whom our ideas of Africans are chiefly derived, appears among them; no prognathous jaws, barndoor mouth, nor lark heels are seen. Their defects arise from absolute ignorance of all the world.

" There is not a single great chief in all Manyema. No matter what name the different divisions of people bear—Manyema, Balegga, Babire, Bazire, Bokoos —there is no political cohesion; not one king or kingdom. Each head man is independent of every other. The people are industrious, and most of them cultivate the soil largely. We found them every where very honest. When detained at Bambarre we had to send our goats and fowls to the Manyema villages to prevent them being all stolen by the Zanzibar slaves.

"Manyema land is the only country in Central Africa I have seen where cotton is not cultivated, spun, and woven. The clothing is that known in Madagascar as 'lambas' or grass cloth, made from the leaves of the 'Muale' palm."

This despatch, it will be observed, is about a year later than the one to Lord Stanley, in which the statement occurs that the fact as to whether the Manyema were man-eaters was "not proven," though the explorer observed that they ate the gorilla, of which beast Dr. Livingstone evidently has a rather favorable opinion, as respects his disposition, and as surely holds his gross stupidity as clearly demonstrated. In the development of instinct, there appear to be several animals in Africa approaching nearer the capacity of reflection than the gorilla.

The next despatch is to Earl Granville, and is dated at Ujiji, November, 1871. It is almost wholly official, and relates in a clear and most forcible manner, the insurmountable difficulties by reason of which he had been forced to cease explorations at a time when a little longer work would most probably have been crowned with complete success. It is in this despatch that Dr. Livingstone relates the particulars of the horrid massacre at Nyanme, the fearful outlines of which have appeared in Mr. Stanley's letter, already quoted. On his return to Ujiji, Dr. Livingstone narrowly escaped death three times in a single day from the savages, who would not be persuaded that he did not belong to "the traders" guilty of the massacre.

The despatch to Dr. Kirk, Consul at Zanzibar, is of interest, as showing how the explorer had been annoyed, pained, and his plans frustrated by the inefficiency of those charged with sending him supplies from Zanzibar. In view of the dispute that has arisen upon this subject among certain representatives of public opinion in the United States and England, it may be well to show whether Dr. Livingstone himself thought he had been well or ill treated. In a postscript to this communicaiton, he says, with evident reluctance and evident feeling:

"P. S.—November 16, 1871.—I regret the necessity of bringing the foregoing very unpleasant subject before you, but I have just received letters and information which make the matter doubly serious. Mr. Churchill informed me by a letter of September 19, 1870, that Her Majesty's government had most kindly sent £1,000 for supplies, to be forwarded to me. Some difficulties had occurred to prevent £500 worth from starting, but in the beginning of November all were removed. But it appears that you had recourse to slaves again, and one of these slaves informs me that goods and slaves all remained at Bagamoio four months, or till near the end of February, 1871. No one looked near them during that time, but a rumor reached them that the Consul was

coming, and off they started, two days before your
arrival, not on their business, but on some private
trip of your own. These slaves came to Unyanyembe in May last, and there they lay till war broke
out and gave them, in July, a good excuse to lie there
still.

"A whole year has thus been spent in feasting
slaves on £500 sent by government to me. Like
the man who was tempted to despair when he
broke the photograph of his wife, I feel inclined to
relinquish hope of ever getting help from Zanzibar
to finish the little work I have still to do. I wanted
men, not slaves, and free men are abundant at Zanzibar; but if the matter is committed to Ludha instead of an energetic Arab, with some little superin-
tendence by your dragoman or others, I may wait
twenty years and your slaves feast and fail.

D. L.

"I will just add that the second batch of slaves
had, like the first, two freemen as the leaders, and
one died of smallpox. The freemen in the first party
of slaves were Shereef and Awathe. I enclose
also a shameless overcharge in Ludha's bill,
$364 06½.—D. L.

This should appear to be a complete justification
of Mr. Stanley's energetic animadversions upon the
general maladministration of affairs at Zanzibar by
the British Consulate there so far as they were related to Dr. Livingstone. It should be a source of
honest congratulation to every American that a
citizen of the United States, representing one of the
most widely circulated public journals of the nation,

energetically sent forward "men, not slaves," and furnished supplies by means of which, it may reasonably be expected, the explorer may proceed with his great work and accomplish the object so dear to his admirable ambition.

Dr. Livingstone's next dispatch is to Earl Granville, from Ujiji, December 18, 1871. It is almost wholly of an official nature, containing his theory, already herein set forth, of the watershed of the Nile, but contains a paragraph relating the arrival of the " Herald" expedition, which is well worthy of quotation :

"A vague rumor reached Ujiji in the beginning of last month that an Englishman had come to Unyanyembe with boats, horses, men, and goods in abundance. It was in vain to conjecture who this could be ; and my eager inquiries were met by answers so contradictory that I began to doubt if any stranger had come at all. But one day, I cannot say which, for I was three weeks too fast in my reckoning, my man Susi came dashing up in great excitement, and gasped out, 'An Englishman coming; see him!' and off he ran to meet him. The American flag at the head of the caravan told me the nationality of the stranger. It was Henry M. Stanley, the travelling correspondent of the NEW YORK 'Herald,' sent by the son of the editor, James Gordon Bennett, Jr., at an expense of £5,000, to obtain correct information about me if living, and if dead to bring home my bones. The kindness was extreme, and made my whole frame thrill with excitement and gratitude. I had been left nearly destitute by the moral idiot Shereef selling off my goods for slaves and ivory for himself. My condition was sufficiently forlorn, for I had but a few articles of barter left of what I had taken the precaution to leave here, in case of extreme need. The strange news Mr. Stanley had to tell to one for years out of communication with the world was quite reviving. Appetite returned, and in a week I began to feel strong. Having men and goods, and information that search for an outlet of the Tanganyika was desired by Sir Roderick Murchison, we went for a month's cruise down its northern end. This was a pleasure trip compared to the weary tramping of all the rest of my work; but an outflow we did not find."

The opening paragraph of the dispatch from which this is taken is so finely characteristic, that it should not be omitted. Dr. Livingstone began his letter to Lord Clarendon's successor in this beautifully courteous manner:

"MY LORD—The despatch of Lord Clarendon, dated 31st May, 1870, came to this place on the 13th ult., and its very kindly tone and sympathy afforded me a world of encouragement. Your lordship will excuse me in saying that with my gratitude there mingled sincere sorrow that the personal friend who signed it was no more."

The last of these despatches of the explorer was the longest, and, perhaps, the most worthy of his fame. Addressed to Earl Granville, it was a clear, full statement of the prevalence of the African slave trade and a terrible denunciaton of it, together with a proposition "which," he says, "I have very much at heart—the possibility of encouraging the native

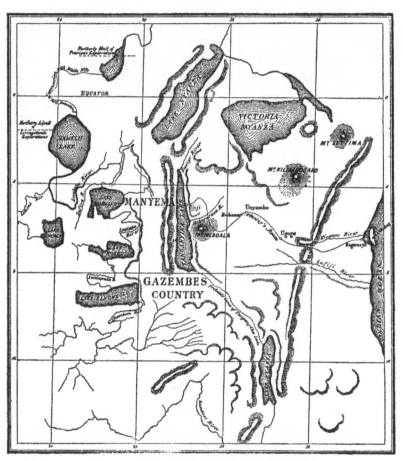

MAP OF THE WATERSHED OF AFRICA.

Christians of English settlements on the west coast
of Africa, to remove, by voluntary emigration, to a
healthy spot on this side the continent." There are
in Zanzibar a considerable number of British subjects
from India, called Banians. They are, like all British subjects, prohibited from engaging in the slave
trade, but shrewdly managing to throw the responsibility upon the Arabs, they are in fact responsible for
the slave trade of Zanzibar and all the horrible
" slaving" of East Africa. " The Manyema cannibals,"
says Dr. Livingstone, in this dispatch to Earl Granville, " among whom I spent nearly two years, are
innocents compared with our protected Banian fel-
low-subjects. By their Arab agents they compass
the destruction of more human lives in one year than
the Manyema do for their fleshpots in ten." " Slaves
are not bought," he says in another place, " in the
countries to which the Banian agents proceed. Indeed it is a mistake to call the system of Ujiji 'slave
trade' at all; the captives are not traded for, but
murdered for, and the gangs which are dragged coastwise are usually not slaves, but captive free people."
To eradicate this fearful wrong, the practical remedy
proposed by the explorer in his letter to Earl Granville is encouragement by the British government to
the voluntary emigration of native Christians from
the English settlements of the West Coast to the
East Coast. In reply to the argument of the un-
healthfulness of this portion of Africa he says that
the fevers are bad enough indeed, but that very much
more of the disease prevailing is due to intemperance
and gross licentiousness than fever. The whole dis-

19

patch is a demonstration of Dr. Livingstone's earnest piety, humanity, and practical sagacity. If there are some passages in it which show that his Highland blood is up, they may be attributed to a fiery hatred of injustice.

These quotations from Dr. Livingstone's letters of this important period of his life will be appropriately concluded with his letter of thanks to the editor of the "Herald":

"UJIJI, ON TANGANYIKA,
"EAST AFRICA, November, 1871.

"JAMES GORDON BENNETT, Esq., Jr.:—

"MY DEAR SIR—It is in general somewhat difficult to write to one we have never seen—it feels so much like addressing an abstract idea—but the presence of your representative, Mr. H. M. Stanley, in this distant region takes away the strangeness I should otherwise have felt, and in writing to thank you for the extreme kindness that prompted you to send him, I feel quite at home.

"If I explain the forlorn condition in which he found me you will easily perceive that I have good reason to use very strong expressions of gratitude. I came to Ujiji off a tramp of between four hundred and five hundred miles, beneath a blazing vertical sun, having been baffled, worried, defeated and forced to return, when almost in sight of the end of the geographical part of my mission, by a number of half-caste Moslem slaves sent to me from Zanzibar, instead of men. The sore heart made still sorer by the woful sights I had seen of man's inhumanity to man reached and told on the bodily frame and depressed it beyond measure. I thought that I was dying on my feet. It is not too much to say that almost every step of the weary sultry way was in pain, and I reached Ujiji a mere 'ruckle' of bones.

"There I found that some five hundred pounds sterling worth of goods which I had ordered from Zanzibar had unaccountably been entrusted to a drunken half-caste Moslem tailor, who, after squandering them for sixteen months on the way to Ujiji, finished up by selling off all that remained for slaves and ivory for himself. He had "divined" on the Koran and found that I was dead. He had also written to the Governor of Unyanyembe that he had sent slaves after me to Manyema, who returned and reported my decease, and begged permission to sell off the few goods that his drunken appetite had spared. He, however, knew perfectly well, from men who had seen me, that I was alive, and waiting for the goods and men; but as for morality, he is evidently an idiot, and there being no law here except that of the dagger or musket, I had to sit down in great weakness, destitute of everything save a few barter cloths and beads, which I had taken the precaution to leave here in case of extreme need. The near prospect of beggary among Ujijians made me miserable. I could not despair, because I laughed so much at a friend who, on reaching the mouth of the Zambezi, said that he was tempted to despair on breaking the photograph of his wife. We could have no success after that. Afterward the idea of despair had to me such a strong smack of the ludicrous that it was out of the question.

"Well, when I had got to about the lowest verge, vague rumors of an English visitor reached me. I thought of myself as the man who went down from Jerusalem to Jericho; but neither priest, Levite, nor Samaritan could possibly pass my way. Yet the good Samaritan was close at hand, and one of my people rushed up at the top of his speed, and, in great excitement, gasped out, 'An Englishman coming! I see him!' and off he darted to meet him. An American flag, the first ever seen in these parts, at the head of a caravan, told me the nationality of the stranger. I am as cold and non-demonstrative as we islanders are usually reputed to be; but your kindness made my frame thrill. It was, indeed, overwhelming, and I said in my soul, 'Let the richest blessings descend from the Highest on you and yours!'

The news Mr. Stanley had to tell was thrilling. The mighty political changes on the Continent; the success of the Atlantic cables; the election of General Grant, and many other topics rivited my attention for days together, and had an immediate and beneficial effect on my health. I had been without news from home for years save what I could glean from a few *Saturday Reviews* and *Punch* of 1868. The appetite revived, and in a week I began to feel strong again.

"Mr. Stanley brought a most kind and encouraging despatch from Lord Clarendon, whose loss I sincerely deplore, the first I have received from the Foreign Office since 1866, and information that the British government had kindly sent a thousand

pounds sterling to my aid. Up to his arrival I was
not aware of any pecuniary aid. I came unsalaried,
but this want is now happily repaired, and I am anxious
that you and all my friends should know that, though
uncheered by letter, I have stuck to the task which
my friend Sir Roderick Murchison set me with 'John
Bullish' tenacity, believing that all would come right
at last.

"The watershed of South Central Africa is over
seven hundred miles in length. The fountains thereon
are almost innumerable—that is, it would take a
man's lifetime to count them. From the watershed
they converge into four large rivers, and these again
into two mighty streams in the great Nile valley,
which begins in ten degrees to twelve degrees south
latitude. It was long ere light dawned on the ancient
problem and gave me a clear idea of the drainage. I
had to feel my way, and every step of the way, and
was, generally, groping in the dark, for who cared
where the waters ran? We drank our fill and let
the rest run by.

"The Portuguese who visited Cazemba asked for
slaves and ivory, and heard of nothing else. I asked
about the waters, questioned and cross-questioned,
until I was almost afraid of being set down as afflict-
ed with hydrocephalus.

"My last work, in which I have been greatly hindered
from want of suitable attendants, was following the
central line of drainage down through the country of
the cannibals, called Manyuema, or, shortly, Manyema.
This line of drainage has four large lakes in it. The
fourth I was near when obliged to turn. It is from

one to three miles broad, and never can be reached
at any point or at any time of the year. Two western drains, the Lupira, or Bartle Frere's River, flow
into it at Lake Kamolondo. Then the great River
Lomaine flows through Lake Lincoln into it, too,
and seems to form the western arm of the Nile, on
which Petherick traded.

"Now, I knew about six hundred miles of the
watershed, and unfortunately the seventh hundred
is the most interesting of the whole; for in it, if I am
not mistaken, four fountains arise from an earthen
mound, and the last of the four becomes, at no great
distance off, a large river. Two of these run north
to Egypt, Lupira and Louraine, and two run south
into inner Ethiopia, as the Liambai, or upper Zambezi, and the Kafneare, but these are but the sources
of the Nile mentioned by the Secretary of Minerva,
in the city of Sais to Herodotus. I have heard of
them so often, and at great distances off, that I cannot doubt their existence, and in spite of the sore
longing for home that seizes me every time I think
of my family I wish to finish up by their rediscovery.

"Five hundred pounds sterling worth of goods
have again unaccountably been entrusted to slaves,
and have been over a year on the way, instead of
four months. I must go where they lie at your expense, ere I can put the natural completion to my
work.

"And if my disclosures regarding the terrible
Ujijian slavery should lead to the suppression of the
east coast slave trade, I shall regard that as a greater
matter by far than the discovery of all the Nile sources

together. Now that you have done with domestic slavery forever, lend us your powerful aid toward this great object. This fine country is blighted, as with a curse from above, in order that the slavery privileges of the petty Sultan of Zanzibar may not be infringed, and the rights of the Crown of Portugal, which are mythical, should be kept in abeyance till some future time when Africa will become another India to Portuguese slave traders.

" I conclude by again thanking you most cordially for your great generosity, and am,

" Gratefully yours,
" DAVID LIVINGSTONE."

Dr Livingstone's plan of exploration for the future will lead him far southward of Ujiji. He will march southwestward from Unyanyembe and passing south of Tanganyika Lake traverse the country of Cazembe, and by a general circular course again reach the supposed sources of the Nile, and finish the work which was before so bravely begun and prosecuted, and so unfortunately brought to imperfect termination by reason of the neglect or incapacity of the representatives of the British government at Zanzibar.

CHAPTER XVI.

INTELLIGENCE OF THE SUCCESS OF THE HERALD ENTER-PRISE.

Mr. Stanley's Despacthes to the " Herald"—They Create a Profound Sensation·
The Question of the Authenticity of His Reports—Conclusive Proof Thereoi
—Testimony of the English Press, John Livingstone, Earl Granville, and the
Queen of England Herself.

Mr. Stanley's despatches to the "Herald," as we
have already seen, were sent through the London
bureau of that office. The noted telegram, printed
on the morning of July 2, 1872,—of which a copy has
been printed on preceding pages—created a profound
sensation. Followed by other cable telegrams giving
reports of the newspaper reporter's journey towards
Europe and his reception at Paris and elsewhere, the
intelligence was received with almost as much avidity
as the news which came from day to day of the late
Franco-German war, or that of the attempted revolution in Paris.

But to some, the reports of Mr. Stanley's great success were incredible. There were those who did not
believe he had seen Livingstone, and who did believe
that his story of the meeting—with, of course, all the
correspondence from Zanzibar, Unyanyembe, Ujiji,
and elsewhere—was but an adroitly-devised romance,
after the fashion of that of Ali Moosa, to cover up
inglorious failure. It is needless now to fully state

the arguments upon which this incredulity was based.
Perhaps newspaper jealousy had something to do
with it. Certainly it was a matter of deep chagrin to
many Englishmen that the British government, upon
whose soil the sun never sets, should have been totally
eclipsed by the enterprise of private citizens of a rival
nationality. Then there were certain little errors—
chiefly misprints and the excusable mistakes of telegraphing long despatches great distances—which were
claimed by the doubting as showing that the so-
called great Special Search Expedition of the " Herald" was but a magnificent hoax, after all. Moreover,
the universal interest manifested in the subject, gave
a splendid opportunity to adventurers, both male and
female, to ventilate themselves and become public
characters. Hence, those who had known Mr. Stanley as a native of Wales, and not of Missouri, or of
this, that, or the other country; who knew that he
had not been a correspondent as had been generally
stated ; and, in fine, who knew that many assertions
in regard to him were untrue—these adventurers became even more numerous than the celebrated cow
of the crumpled horn which originated the terrible
conflagration of Chicago, and then, with miraculous
self-multiplication, surpassed in number the cattle of
a thousand hills, and, mournfully ruminating over
her sad mishap in kicking over the kerosene lamp,
became the observed of all observers in all Christian
lands, and at the same instant of astronomical and
clock time.

It were needless to disguise the fact, however, that
the statements of those incredulous of the Search

Expedition's wonderful success, being for some time constantly iterated and reiterated through the press, had considerable effect upon the public mind, and actually left it for a period in a state of painful uncertainty in regard to the fate of the great explorer, the truth in regard to whom was earnestly desired by all intelligent persons throughout Christendom. Happily, the authenticity of Mr. Stanley's reports, and with it the recent safety of Dr. Livingstone have been placed beyond reasonable doubt by a mass of testimony against which no one can dispute who will not dispute against the sun.

Much of that testimony has already appeared in this volume, different portions in their appropriate places. These are:

1. The statement of the Hon. E. Joy Morris, Ex-Minister of the United States at Constantinople. He abundantly establishes the character of Mr. Stanley as that of a most energetic, fearless, and honest man. The first two qualities greatly enabled him to achieve success in the search expedition; the last is a sure guaranty that, had he not won success, he would not have claimed it. Mr. Morris's statement is also of value because utterly disproving and forever putting to rest a certain tissue of misrepresentations in regard to Mr. Stanley's history in Asia Minor.

2. The letters of Dr. Livingstone to Earl Granville, which were published by authority of the British government. In these letters, the African explorer not only gratefully alludes to Mr. Stanley but expressly says his despatches are entrusted to his care, because

of the great traveller's belief in Mr. Stanley's enterprise and capacity to accomplish whatever he might undertake. In one of these despatches, Dr. Livingstone also states that he had given to the custody of Mr. Stanley his journal of explorations, sealed, to be delivered to his daughter, when the commander of the Search Expedition of the "Herald" should arrive in England.

3. Upon Mr. Stanley's arrival in England, this journal was promptly forwarded to Miss Livingstone. Her acknowledgment was published in many English and American journals. It was as follows:

KELLY WEMYSS BAY, by GREENOCK,
August 6, 1872.

DEAR SIR—I write to say that I received last Saturday my father's letters and the diary which were entrusted to you by him.

I wish also to express to you my heartfelt gratitude for going in search of my father and aiding him so nobly and bringing the long-looked-for letters safely.

Believe me yours truly,   AGNES LIVINGSTONE.

HENRY M. STANLEY, Esq.

4. Dr. Livingstone's letter of thanks to James Gordon Bennett, Esq., Jr., the handwriting of which was published, in *fac simile*, in the "Herald," and fully substantiated by Mr. John Livingstone, of Canada, brother of the explorer, and more familiar with him and his handwriting than any man living.

5. The letter of John Livingstone to Mr. Blake, American Consul at Hamilton, Ontario, in Canada, which was accompanied by a letter from Dr. Livingstone, proving handwriting, and forwarded to the "Herald" through the Department of State at Washington. This letter follows:

LISTOWELL, August 24, 1872.

F. N. BLAKE, Esq., United States Consul, Hamilton, Ontario:

DEAR SIR—Would you kindly oblige me by conveying in your official capacity to Mr. Bennett, proprietor of the NEW YORK 'Herald,' and also to Mr. Stanley, the leader of the "Herald Livingstone Search Expedition," my warmest congratulations on the succeseful issue of that expedition.

Having noticed a number of articles in the public press reflecting doubts on the veracity of Mr. Stanley and the 'Herald,' I am glad to be able to say that I place the most implicit confidence in the statements of Mr. Stanley and the ' Herald.

I can also assure you that Dr. Livingstone holds the American government and people in the highest estimation, principally on account of the late abolition of slavery in the United States, and I trust that his persistent efforts to check the nefarious traffic in slaves in Africa will be crowned with success.

I am, yours respectfully,   JOHN LIVINGSTONE.

6. The Royal Geographical Society of London, fully persuaded of the authenticity of Mr. Stanley's reports, tendered him a formal reception at Brighton. The meeting occurred and caused a great deal of comment.

7. The Sovereign of England has herself on more than one occasion tendered special honors to Mr. Stanley on account of his success in finding Dr. Liv ingstone.

Evidence like this is not to be shaken by the asseverations of penny-a-liners. It must be regarded by the candid as absolutely conclusive. Such, it is believed, would be the result, had Mr. Stanley been a British subject instead of an American citizen. As the fact is, the case for the "Herald" Expedition is almost immeasurably stronger. It was a matter of profound chagrin to most of the English people that an American enterprise should be successful in the search for one of the most illustrious of Englishmen, whilst English expeditions should have failed. Under such circumstances, Mr. Stanley's proofs had to be absolutely unassailable and his credentials unanswerably satisfactory, or they would not have been received at all.   Both majesty and ministry would have given the commander of the American enterprise the coldest possible shoulder.   Instead, they crowned him with laurels.   The only conclusion with reasonable minds must be that the " Herald" expedition was a splendid success, and further doubt of it can only be a stupid and cruel skepticism.*

* It is not believed that anything further is needed to convince the public of what most of the intelligent public is already convinced ; but it may be well to place on record the statements of a number of prominent journals of the world, and reference to the action of certain learned societies.

On July 4th, 1872, the Lodon "Morning Post" said :

" Far surpassing everything of local import in interest just now is the information afforded by the New York 'Herald' to the London press of the discovery of Dr. Livingstone. Far surpassing everything which has been hitherto achieved by journalistic enterprise is the discovery of the great African explorer—concerning whose fate the peoples of every civilized State in the world have been anxious for many years—by the special correspondent of a daily newspaper commissioned to find him. We are accustomed to laugh on this side of the Atlantic at the rage which prevails for a knowledge of what are classed as 'big things' among our American kinsmen ; but it is not only with a feeling of satisfaction, but also of kindred pride, that we express our admiration of this wonderful undertaking, which was conceived and has been carried to such a successful issue by the proprietor of our New York contemporary."

The London "Telegraph" of the same date says :

" Yesterday we, in company with the whole people of Britain, listened to the narration of the outlines of a tale describing the accomplishment of a work as daring in its execution as that of Vasco de Gama, as solitary in its accompaniment as that of Robinson Crusoe, and quite as romantic in its progress as that of Marco Polo. The mind delights to realize, even in imagination, the moment when the gallant and indefatigable Stanley won his way in front of his little band of followers—making up in noise what it lacked in numbers—to the outskirts of Ujiji, and we must, all of us, envy the republic of the United States the fact that the American flag was carried proudly at the head of his force in happy agreement, and that under the banner of the Stars and Stripes he afforded succor to the lonely Briton."

And thus the London " Daily News :"

" The extraordinary narrative which has just been communicated to the world by the New York ' Herald' supplies one of the most exciting stories which civilization has had since the revelation of the startling truths of Bruce. Mr. Stanley gives to his collation a somewhat picturesque coloring, but the grand fact remains that he found Livingstone notwithstanding, and not, as Sir Henry Rawlinson conjectured lately, that Livingstone found Stanley. It is not easy to imagine an enterprise more full of toil and peril than this strange journey of the lonely American, attended, to be sure, by a small but reluctant escort, in the hitherto trackless wilds of Africa and among people of native tribes of unknown names. It is wholly impossible not to admire the daring and perseverance which the American discovery has crowned with triumph."

Said the Edinburgh (Scotland) "Courant:"

"It is long since the columns of a newspaper have contained so vividly romantic and so startlingly wonderful a story as that which has just been told to us of the fortunes that befell Mr. Stanley in his quest after Livingstone, and of the most strange circumstances under which the object of that quest was fulfilled The whole narrative reads, indeed, more like a forgotten episode from the travels of some Marco Polo or Vasco de Gama than, as it is, a truthful and unvarnished extract from the severe chronicle of nineteenth century fact."

This brief extract from the London "Globe" of July 9:

"The final discovery of Dr. Livingstone would seem to have been a bitter disappointment to a large class of his fellow countrymen. The doubt and mystery which hung around his fate promised to produce a perennial stream of quasi-scientific gossip, and to yield an endless crop of letters to the 'Times.' As it is, those 'interested' in the matter are reduced to patching the rags of the worn out controversy."

The London "Times" of July 15th contained a long letter from Mr. Charles Beke in which he fully answers a number of criticisms upon the Livingstone-Stanley despatches, the said criticisms having originated in British chagrin, not altogether inexcusable, at the fine success of the American enterprise. That great journal of July 27th editorially says: .

"To the enterprise of an American newspaper we are indebted for trustworthy information that Dr. Livingstone still lives and prosecutes his unexampled researches."

The London "Advertiser" of the date last mentioned also published a long leading article upon the subject, beginning:

"In another column we publish the first letter from Dr. Livingstone which has been received in England. By the energy of the proprietor of the New York 'Herald' the great English traveller has been found and succored at a moment when he seemed to be upon his 'last legs.' In his own words, when Stanley arrived at Ujiji 'he thought he was dying upon his feet.'"

The London "Standard" of July 26th remarked with emphasis:

"All doubts concerning the *bona fides* of Mr. Stanley's narratives of his adventures in Africa will now be laid at rest by the arrival of Dr. Livingstone's letters. We shall, apparently, have to wait a little for the publication of the geographical despatches, as the report of an intended meeting of the Geographical Society on Monday for the purpose of hearing them read is unfounded. But it is satisfactory to feel that even the very faint suspicions cast on the authenticity of Mr. Stanley's story are dissipated, and that we may absolutely rely upon the information which that gallant and triumphant traveller has brought home."

The Manchester (England) "Guardian" of July 29th, in an elaborate article in criticism of the English authorities because they had not organized a successful expedition, and had given the great explorer just cause for complaint, says the subject is one "which can be matter of no agreeable examination for any Englishman." And it concludes:

"Our magnificently equipped expedition did simply nothing; and it was reserved for Mr. Stanley, after his return to the coast, to organize a caravan with stores for Dr. Livingstone. 'Before we left Zanzibar,' says Mr. New, 'a caravan numbering fifty-seven men was packed, signed, sealed, addressed, and despatched, like so many packets of useful commodities, to the service and succor of Dr. Livingstone.' What says England to all this?"

The Leeds (England) "Mercury" of the date last mentioned remarks:

"The success of Mr. Stanley in his search for Dr. Livingstone is one of the most brilliant chapters in the history of newspaper enterprise. The expedition was an unprecedented one, and when it was first reported in this country there were few who did not laugh at it as a Yankee notion, conceived and started for the glorification of the New York 'Herald' and to gratify the vanity of Mr. James Gordon Bennett. The result has shown not only how little there was to laugh at, but how much there was to admire in such a project."

The journals of continental Europe were not less emphatic in awarding unmixed praise to the successful expedition of the American journal, and Geographical Societies, from Italy to Russia, awarded gold medals to Mr. Stanley in recognition of his services in behalf of geographical knowledge.

By this array of irresistible testimony—and even more will be forthcoming in natural order in the account of Mr. Stanley's reception in Europe—the most of American journals acknowledged the success of the expedition, and awarded unstinted praise to the "Herald." To clinch the conclusive testimony already adduced, however, and leave no possible room for doubt, it may be well to bring forth witnesses of the highest station, not even excepting the Queen of England herself.

Earl Granville, upon the receipt of Dr. Livingstone's despatches, forwarded from Paris by Mr. Stanley, directed an official acknowledgement, which was as follows:

"FOREIGN OFFICE, August 1, 1872.

"SIR—I am directed by Earl Granville to acknowledge the receipt of a package containing letters and despatches from Dr. Livingstone, which you were good enough to deliver to Her Majesty's Ambassador at Paris for transmission to this department, and I am to convey to you His Lordship's thanks for taking charge of these interesting documents.

"I am, your most obedient, humble servant,

"ENFIELD.

"HENRY M. STANLEY, Esq."

And on the next day Earl Granville himself wrote the following letter:

"AUGUST 2, 1872.

SIR—I was not aware until you mentioned it that there was any doubt as to the authenticity of Dr. Livingstone's despatches, which you delivered to Lord Lyons on the 31st of July; but, in consequence of what you have said, I have inquired into the matter, and I find that Mr. Hammmond, the Under Secretary of the Foreign Office, and Mr. Wyld, the head of the Consular and Slave Trade Department, have not the slightest doubt as to the genuineness of the papers which have been received from Lord Lyons, and which are being printed.

" I cannot omit this opportunity of expressing to you my admiration of the qualities which have enabled you to achieve the object of your mission, and to attain a result which has been hailed with so much enthusiasm both in the United States and in this country.

"I am, sir, your obedient,

"GRANVILLE.

" HENRY M. STANLEY, Esq."

As if all this were not enough we have the testimony of the Queen's speech, delivered for Queen Victoria by commission, on the occasion of the prorogation of Parliament, on Saturday, August 10, 1872. The Queen said: " My government has taken steps intended to prepare the way for dealing more effectually with the slave trade on the East Coast of Africa." The London "Times" of the following Monday, in commenting on this portion of Her Majesty's speech, said:

" This paragraph is the most significant part of the throne speech, and we suppose it is not an error to connect the announcement which has just been made by Her Majesty with the recent discovery of Dr. Livingstone and the despatches to the Foreign Office brought by Mr. Stanley, of the New York 'Herald,' from the great traveller."

It would be impossible, it is believed, to more completely demonstrate the hearty acknowledgement of the British government of the success of the American enterprise; an acknowledgment which no earthly power but that of unanswerable truth could have compelled that government to make.

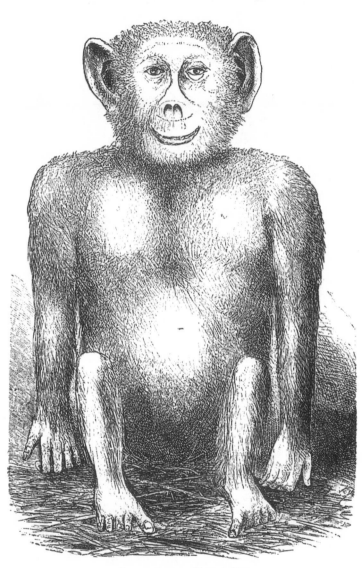

PORTRAIT OF A YOUNG SOKO.

CHAPTER XVII.

MR. STANLEY'S RECEPTION IN EUROPE.

Mr. Stanley is Everywhere Received with Marked Attention—Reception at Paris—In London—The Brighton Banquet—Honors from the Queen of England.

It is now time again to take up the further adventures of Mr. Stanley, and follow him upon his long journey back to the abode of civilization. From Zanzibar he sailed across the Indian Ocean to Bombay, whence he transmitted despatches announcing the success which had crowned his long labors and journeyings. It was this intelligence, transmitted so fully through the London office of the New York "Herald," which so gratifyingly startled the world about the time of the anniversary of American independence in 1872. From Bombay, Mr. Stanley proceeded to Europe by way of the Suez canal, reaching Aden, southwestern Arabia, July 11; Port Said, the head of the Suez canal on the 18th; and arrived at Marseilles in France on the 24th. Here he was received with kindest welcome, and to some extent besieged by gentlemen of his own profession, who transmitted to their journals accounts of his doings. At Paris a few days afterwards he was received with exhilerating hospitality by the American residents of the city, and was greatly lionized generally. Breakfasting with Hon. Elihu B. Washburne, American Minister, he there met among other distinguished

guests, General William T. Sherman, the commanding officer of the army of the United States, about
completing a tour of Europe and the Levant. The
General occupied much of the time in examining Mr.
Stanley's maps, and discharging some of his fund of
caustic humour on the prevalence of the East African
slave trade. On July 30th, Minister Washburne and
many other Americans in Paris extended a formal invitation to Mr. Stanley to meet them at a banquet
where they might in a body testify their " high appreciation of the indomitable courage, energy, and per-
severence which crowned with such brilliant success
your efforts to find Dr. Livingstone, as well as to express their sense of the enterprise and liberality of
the New York ' Herald' in sending you forth on such
an extraordinary mission."

Mr. Stanley's reply to this cordial invitation was so
modest, so happily expressed, that it is worthy of a
place here :

HOTEL DU HELDER, PARIS, July 30, 1872.

GENTLEMEN—I have received your letter of this date, asking me to accept the
compliment of a dinner from my compatriots and friends now resident in Paris,
to be given in acknowledgment of the "enterprise and liberality of the New
York Herald" in sending out an expedition in search of Dr. Livingstone, as
well as of the extraordinary good fortune and perfect success which, under
Providence, attended the footsteps of the expedition I had the honor to command. Gentlemen, believe me, I am deeply conscious of the great honor you
would do me, and through me not only to the journal I have the pleasure of
serving, but to the patient, resolute, brave and Christian gentleman whom I left
in Central Africa. I therefore gladly accept your invitation, and shall be pleased
to meet you July 31 at any house or place that may be deemed most convenient.
I have the honor to be, gentlemen, your obedient and humble servant,

HENRY M. STANLEY..

To His Excellency E. B. WASHBURNE, Minister Plenipotentiary of the United
States of America, and many others.

The meeting was one of great enjoyment. The

American Minister, after a happy speech, richly flavored with American allusions, proposed the guest of the evening—" Henry M. Stanley, the discoverer of the discoverer: we honor him for his courage, energy, and fidelity. We rejoice in the triumphant success of his mission, which has gained him imperishable renown and conferred additional credit on the American name." To this the traveller responded felicitously, and was specially eloquent when speaking of the great explorer of Africa. A number of distinguished gentlemen—artists, journalists, public men—addressed the meeting. The assemblage adjourned at a late hour, Mr. Stanley strongly impressed with the difference between a Parisian banquet and an African supper of manioc and hippopotamus. Other like honors flew upon him, thick and fast. From scientific and literary bodies and from distinguished persons he received invitations to accept which would have occupied him a year. These things do not go to the author of a hoax, however magnificent.

The traveller-correspondent could not long remain at the fashionable metropolis, and at once departed for England. His reception in England was most cordial on the part of most intelligent persons, but there was a feeling of national chagrin, if one may so speak, on account of the discovery of Dr. Livingstone having been brought about through American enterprise, which vented itself in no little carping criticism and the discharge of British atrabilariousness. Hence at once originated that skepticism in regard to the discovery of the great explorer which continued to becloud some minds and journals for a number of weeks. But the publication of Dr. Livingstone's several official despatches—already largely quoted from in this work—and the prompt production of other evidence, heretofore mentioned, brought the English people quite generally to an acknowledgment of the truth. At the annual meeting of the British Association for the Advancement of Science, which convened at Brighton, August 14th, W. B. Carpenter, LL.D., in the chair, Mr. Stanley's successful mission was handsomely mentioned. He was twice compelled to rise, in acknowledgment of calls and cheers. Ex-Emperor Napoleon III. of France, was present and joined in the applause. Here at another meeting, Mr. Stanley read a paper on Tanganyika Lake, which was greatly praised. About this time there are meetings of many scientific associations at Brighton, to all of which Mr. Stanley was invited. On the occasion of what has been called "the Brighton Banquet," it being a dinner given to the British Association by the Brighton and Sussex Medical Society, Mr. Stanley appeared late in the evening, and, being soon called out, responded to some remarks of a previous speaker in such way as to create some feeling. Good nature at last prevailed, and harmony was restored among the English savants.

But his honors in England did not stop below the recognition of his fine success by royalty itself. Early in September he was invited to an interview with Queen Victoria, and afterwards dined with her and the members of the royal family present at Balmoral. Upon this occasion the Queen is reported to have expressed to him in the most warm and friendly terms her congratulations on the successful result of the American enterprise in furnishing intelligence of the English traveller in Africa, his condition of health, his discoveries, and his hopes for the future previous to his return to Great Britain.

Mr. Stanley could hardly be left in a happier situation than partaking of a right royal dinner with Her Majesty of England.

CHAPTER XVIII.

THE SLAVE TRADE OF EAST AFRICA.

Dr. Livingstone's Letter upon the Subject to Mr. Bennett—Compares the Slave Trade with Piracy on the High Seas—Natives of Interior Africa Average Specimens of Humanity—Slave Trade Cruelties—Deaths from Broken Hearts —The Need of Christian Civilization—British Culpability.

While waiting for supplies in Unyanyembe, Dr. Livingstone wrote a second letter to Mr. James Gordon Bennett, which was principally devoted to the slave trade of East Africa, to greatly aid in the abolition of which would be more gratifying to the explorer's ambition than to discover all the sources of the Nile. This might well be supposed from what has already been quoted from Dr. Livingstone's despatches to his government; but inasmuch as he here directly appeals to the American people, this volume would be incomplete without the remarkable and most thrillingly interesting statements of the letter in question. They were sent by cable telegram from London and appeared in the "Herald" newspaper of July 27, 1872:

"At present let me give a glimpse of the slave trade, to which the search and discovery of most of the Nile fountains have brought me face to face. The whole traffic, whether by land or ocean, is a gross outrage on the common law of mankind. It is carried on from age to age, and, in addition to the evils it inflicts, presents almost insurmountable obstacles to intercourse between different portions of the human family. This open sore in the world is partly owing to human cupidity, partly to the ignorance of the more civilized of mankind of the blight which lights chiefly on more degraded piracy on the high seas. (*sic.*) It was once as common as slave trading is now, but as it became thoroughly known the whole civilized world rose against it.

"In now trying to make Eastern African slave trade better known to Americans, I indulge the hope I am aiding on, though in a small degree, the good time coming yet when slavery as well as piracy will be chased from the world. Many have but a faint idea of the evils that trading in slaves inflicts on the victims and authors of its atrocities. Most people imagine that negroes, after being brutalized by a long course of servitude, with but few of the ameliorating influences that elevate the more favored races, are fair average specimens of the African man. Our ideas are derived from slaves of the west coast, who have for ages been subject to domestic bondage and all the depressing agencies of a most unhealthy climate. These have told most injuriously on their physical frames, while fraud and the rum trade have ruined their moral natures so as not to discriminate the difference of the monstrous injustice.

"The main body of the population is living free in the interior, under their own chiefs and laws, cultivating their own farms, catching fish in their own rivers, or fighting bravely with the grand old denizens of the forest, which, in more recent continents, can only be reached in rocky strata or under peren-

nial ice. Winwood Reade hit the truth when he said
the ancient Egyptian, with his large, round, black
eyes, full, luscious lips, and somewhat depressed nose,
is far nearer the typical negro than the west coast
African, who has been debased by the unhealthy land
he lives in. The slaves generally, and especially
those on the west coast, at Zanzibar and elsewhere,
are extremely ugly. I have no prejudice against their
color; indeed, any one who lives long among them
forgets they are black and feels they are just fellow-
men; but the low, retreating forehead, prognathous
jaws, lark-heels and other physical peculiarities common among slaves and West African negroes, always
awaken some feelings of aversion akin to those with
which we view specimens of the Bill Sykes and
'Bruiser' class in England. I would not utter a syl-
lable calculated to press down either class more
deeply in the mire in which it is already sunk, but I
wish to point out that these are not typical Africans
any more than typical Englishmen, and that the natives on nearly all the high lands of the interior
Continent are, as a rule, fair average specimens of
humanity.

" I happened to be present when all the head men
of the great Chief Msama—who lives west of the
south end of Tanganyika—had come together to
make peace with certain Arabs who had burned their
chief town, and I am certain one could not see more
finely formed, intellectual heads in any assembly in
London or Paris, and the faces and forms corresponded finely with the well-shaped heads. Msama himself
had been a sort of Napoleon for fighting and con-

quering in his younger days. He was exactly like the Ancient Assyrians sculptured on the Nineveh marbles, as Nimrod and others, and he showed himself to be one of ourselves by habitually indulging in copious potations of beer, called pombe, and had become what Nathaniel Hawthorne called 'bulbous below the ribs.' I do not know where the phrase 'bloated aristocracy' arose. It must be American, for I have had glimpses of a good many English noblemen, and Msama was the only specimen of a 'bloated aristocrat' on whom I ever set eyes.

"Many of the women are very pretty, and, like all ladies, would have been much prettier if they had only let themselves alone. Fortunately the dears could not change charming black eyes, beautiful foreheads, nicely rounded limbs, well shaped forms and small hands and feet, but must adorn themselves, and this they do by filing splendid teeth to points like cats' teeth. It was distressing, for it made their smile like that of crocodile ornaments, scarce. They are not black, but of light, warm brown color, and so very sisterish, if I may use the word, it feels an injury done one's self to see a bit of grass stuck through the cartilage of the nose so as to bulge out the *alæ nasi*, or wing of the nose of the anatomists.

"Cazembe's Queen, Moaria Nyombe by name, would be esteemed a real beauty either in London Paris, or New York, and yet she had a small hole through the cartilage, near the tip of her fine, slightly aquiline nose. But she had only filed one side of two of the front of her superb snow-white teeth, and then, what a laugh she had! Let those who wish to

know go see her. She was carried to her farm in a
pony phæton, which is a sort of throne, fastened on
two very long poles and carried by twelve stalwart
citizens. If they take the Punch motto of Cazembe
—'Niggers don't require to be shot here'—as their
own, they may show themselves to be men; but
whether they do or not Cazembe will show himself a
man of sterling good sense.

"Now, these people, so like ourselves externally,
have brave, genuine human souls. Rua, large sections of country northwest of Cazembe, but still in
same inland region, is peopled with men very like
those of Wsama and Cazembe. An Arab, Syed Ben
Habib, was sent to trade in Rua two years ago, and,
as Arabs usually do where natives have no guns, Syed
Ben Habib's elder brother carried matters with a high
hand. The Rua men observed the elder brother
slept in a white tent, and, pitching spears into it by
night, killed him. As Moslems never forgive blood,
the younger brother forthwith 'ran a muck' on all in-
discriminately in a large district.

"Let it not be supposed any of these people are,
like American Indians, insatiable, blood-thirsty savages, who will not be reclaimed or entertain terms of
lasting friendship with fair-dealing strangers. Had
the actual murderers been demanded, and a little time
granted, I feel morally certain, from many other instances among tribes who, like the Ba Rua, have not
been spoiled by Arab traders, they would all have
been given up.

"The chiefs of the country would, first of all, have
specified the crime of which the elder brother was

guilty, and who had been led to avenge it. It is very likely they would have stipulated no other should be punished but the actual perpetrator, the domestic slave acting under his orders being considered free of blame.

"I know nothing that distinguishes the uncontaminated African from other degraded peoples more than their entire reasonableness and good sense. It is different after they have had wives, children, and relatives kidnapped, but that is more than human nature, civilized or savage, can bear. In the chase in question indiscriminate slaughter, capture, and plunder took place. A very large number of very fine young men were captured and secured in chains and wooden yokes.

"I came near the party of Syed Ben Habib, close to a point where a huge rent in the Mountain of Rua allows the escape of the great river Lualaba out of Lake Moora, and here I had for the first time an opportunity of observing the difference between slaves and freemen made captive. When fairly across the Lualaba, Syed Ben Habib thought his captives safe, and got rid of the trouble of attending to and watching the chained gangs by taking off both chains and yokes. All declared joy and a perfect willingness to follow Syed to the end of the world or elsewhere, but next morning twenty-two made clear of two mountains.

"Many more, seeing the broad Lualaba roll between them and the homes of their infancy, lost all heart, and in three days eight of them died. They had no complaint but pain in the heart, and they

pointed out its seat correctly; though many believe
the heart situated underneath the top of the sternum,
or breast bone. This to me was the most startling
death I ever saw. They evidently die of broken-
heartedness, and the Arabs wondered, seeing they
had plenty to eat.

" I saw others perish, particularly a very fine boy
ten or twelve years of age. When asked where he
felt ill, he put his hand correctly and exactly over the
heart. He was kindly carried, and, as he breathed
out his soul, was laid gently on the side of the path
The captors are not unusually cruel. They were cal-
lous. Slaving hardened their hearts.

" When Syed, an old friend of mine, crossed Lualaba, he heard I was in the village, where a company
of slave traders were furiously assaulted for three
days by justly incensed Bobemba. I would not fight
nor allow my people to fire if I saw them, because
Bobemba had been especially kind to me. Syed sent
a party of his own people to invite me to leave the
village and come to him. He showed himself the
opposite of hard-hearted ; but slavery hardens within,
petrifies the feelings, is bad for the victims and ill for
the victimizers. Once, it is said, a party of twelve,
who had been slaves in their own country—Cunda or
Conda, of which Cazemba is chief or general—were
loaded with large, heavy yokes, which were forked
trees, about three inches in diameter and seven or
eight feet long, the neck inserted in the fork and an
iron bar driven across one end of the fork to the
other and riveted to the other end, tied at night to
the tree or ceiling of the hut, and the neck being fi/m

in the fork and the slave held off from unloosing it, was excessively troublesome to the wearer, and, when marching, two yokes were tied together by tree ends and loads put on the slaves' heads beside.

"A woman, having an additional yoke and load, and a child on her back, said to me on passing, ' They are killing me. If they would take off the yoke I could manage the load and child; but I shall die with three loads.' The one who spoke this did die; poor little girl! Her child perished of starvation.

" I interceded some, but when unyoked off they bounded into the long grass, and I was greatly blamed for not caring in presence of the owners of the property.

"After the day's march under a broiling, vertical sun, with yokes and heavy loads, the strongest were exhausted. The party of twelve, above mentioned, were sitting down singing and laughing. ' Hallo,' said I, ' these fellows take to it kindly. This must be the class for whom philosophers say slavery is the natural state;' and I went and asked the cause of their mirth.

" I had asked aid of their owner as to the meaning of the word ' Rukha,' which usually means fly or leap. They were using it to express the idea of haunting, as a ghost, inflicting disease or death, and the song was: ' Yes, we going away to Manga, abroad, or white man's land, with yoke on our necks; but we shall have no yokes in death, and shall return and haunt and kill you.' Chorus then struck in, which was the name of the man who had sold each of them, and then followed the general laugh, in which at first I saw no bitterness. Tarembee, an old man, at least one hundred and four years, being one of the sellers, in accordance with African belief, they had no doubt of being soon able, by ghost power, to kill even him.

" The refrain was as if:—'Oh! oh! oh! bird of freedom, you sold me.' 'Oh! oh! oh! I shall haunt you! Oh! oh! oh!' Laughter told not of mirth, but of tears, such as were oppressed, and they had no comforter. He that is higher than the highest regardeth."

" If I am permitted," says Dr. Livingstone in concluding the subject of the slave trade, " in any way to promote its suppression, I shall not grudge the toil and time I have spent. It would be better to lessen this great human woe than to discover the sources of the Nile."

The moral degradation of these people is only to be reached and cured, in the deliberate judgment of the explorer-missionary, through the means of Christian civilization. " The religion of Christ," he says with emphasis, " is unquestionably the best for man. I refer to it not as the Protestant, the Catholic, the Greek, or any other, but to the comprehensive faith which has spread more widely over the world than most people imagine, and whose votaries, of whatever name, are better than any outside the pale." The great end of placing the numerous tribes of East and Central Africa under the pure and elevating morality of the Christian religion cannot be successful until the suppression of the inhuman slave trade, which has its headquarters at Zanzibar, shall have been accomplished. It would be unjust to forget that Great Britain has done much, very much, for the suppression of this terrible traffic in other portions of the globe. It would be unjust to charge the government of Great Britain with intentional criminality in this case. But it stands proved, by the failure of English expeditions to find Dr. Livingstone, and by his own positive, earnest testimony, now that an American expedition has succeeded in discovering him, that it is the subjects of the British monarchy who are responsible for the existence of the slave trade of Zanzibar and all the nameless horrors of the interior resulting therefrom. The moral culpability, by reason of neglect—not to put the case too strongly—of the British government is therefore made manifest; and of this great national turpitude that government must stand convicted before the bar of Christendom.

CHAPTER XIX.

THE ANIMAL KINGDOM OF AFRICA,

Some Account of the Beasts, Birds, Reptiles, and Insects of Africa—Livingstone's Opinion of the Lion—Elephants, Hippopotami, Rhinoceroses, etc.—Wild Animals Subject to Disease—Remarkable Hunting Explorations—Cumming Slays more than One Hundred Elephants—Du Chaillu and the Gorilla—Thrilling Incidents—Vast Plains Covered with Game—Forests Filled with Birds—Immense Serpents—The Python of South Africa—Ants and other Insects.

No portion of the globe is so productive of wild animals as Africa. There animal life is more extensive, if we may so say, and more varied than anywhere else. The domestic animals of that continent are not to such extent different from those of other parts of the world as to merit special mention, with the exception of the camel, without whose aid a large portion of the country would be not only uninhabitable but untraversable. The invaluable services which this patient but obstinate beast of burden renders to the inhabitants of Northern Africa are known to all men. In northern Africa and in the central portions, horses are numerous and many of them of excellent breeds. Here and in many parts of South Africa, there are many cattle, used as beasts of burden and for beef. Some of them are noted for the prodigious size of their horns. Sheep abound in some portions of the continent, but in South Africa the flocks are composed almost entirely of goats, which

A Dangerous Prize.

subsist better on the dry herbs of the dessert, yield more milk, and are considered more palatable food. But in respect to wild beasts—all kinds of "game" as the sportsman would say—Africa, as has been said by Mr. John Bonner, "may be called the region of animal life, since there are more than twice the number of species in it than in the other quarters of the globe." Here are found, in immense numbers, all those kinds of animals which fill the strong cages of the menageries of Europe and America, of parks, and zoological gardens, and many more besides. Here are the most abject and degraded specimens of mankind and the most sagacious and lordly wild animals. Here are the most beautiful and gentle of birds and the most venomous and terrible serpents and reptiles. Here are small insects whose attacks are fatal to many useful animals, and others—the devouring locusts—which in a single day devastate vast sections of country.

The lion, so long regarded as the king of beasts, is found in most parts of interior Africa. We have already seen that Dr. Livingstone's opinion of this beast is not very exalted. It is certainly inferior to the African leopard both in beauty and courage. In strength and prowess this latter animal is not inferior to the Asiatic tiger. The hippopotamus, supposed to be the Behemoth of Job, is found in nearly all the rivers of Central and South Africa and the Nile. His body is often as large as that of a full-grown elephant. A noted African hunter killed one with a single ball, which was six feet broad across the belly. The skin of an adult hippopotamus, accord-

21

ing to Du Chaillu, who shot several and stuffed one, is from one and a-half to two inches thick, and extremely solid and tough—quite bullet-proof, in fact, except in a few thinner spots, as behind the ear and near the eyes. It is devoid of hair with the exception of a few short bristly hairs in the tail, and a few scattered tufts near the muzzle. The color of the skin is a clayey yellow, assuming a roseate hue under the belly. After death, the animal becomes a dull brownish color. It is successfully hunted by the natives of east equatorial Africa, who approach within a few feet of it, fire their "slugs" at his eye and then run for dear life ; for if the animal be not killed the hunter surely will be. Cumming, the most successful of African Nimrods, once slew some ten hippopotami in the course of a couple of days, and secured the carcasses of most of them, dragging them with oxen to which were attached strong cables fastened to the beasts. The bagging of several tons of edible game—the meat of the beast is described by some as like beef, by others as like pork—in a day or two could not be accomplished elsewhere than in Africa.

Most of the perennial rivers and even small streams of a few feet depth abound in crocodiles. Those of South Africa, whose nature and habits are described by Dr. Livingstone and Cumming, are a different species from the crocodile of the Nile, one of the sacred animals of the Egyptians. They are as great in size, however, and, perhaps, greater in voracity. Their great numbers, particularly in the waters of equatorial Africa, are astonishing. The natives hunt them, going in canoes and using a sort of harpoon with which the stout armour, elsewhere impenetrable, of the animal is pierced behind the legs. The natives are fond of the flesh. Though a full grown crocodile will weigh as much as an ox, there is not much flesh that is edible. Cumming shot one more than twenty feet in length in a stream not more than twelve feet wide. " On our return to Damagondai's town," says Du Chaillu, "as we were paddling along, I perceived in the distance ahead a beautiful deer, looking meditatively into the waters of the lagoon, of which from time to time it took a drink. I stood up to get a shot, and we approached with the utmost silence. But just as I raised my gun to fire, a crocodile leaped out of the water, and, like a flash, dove back again with the struggling animal in his powerful jaws. So quickly did the beast take his prey that though I fired at him I was too late. I would not have believed that this huge and unwieldy animal could move with such velocity; but the natives told me that the deer often falls prey to the crocodile. Sometimes he even catches the leopard, but then there is a harder battle than the poor little deer could make."

The rhinoceros, formerly found on the slopes of Table Mountain, has now been driven far into the interior of South Africa, but here these huge animals, second only to the elephant and hippopotamus in bulk, are found along all the streams and in the neighborhood of fountains and pools of water. Dr. A. Smith in his " Zoology of South Africa" makes three species of rhinoceros. The great hunter, Cumming, describes what he considers as four different

kinds. * Dr. Livingstone, however, asserts that there
are but two species—the white and the black—insisting that all the species made by naturalists beyond

* He says : Of the rhinoceros there are four varieties in South Africa distinguished by the Bechuanas by the names of the borèlé, or black rhinoceros, the
keitloa, or two-horned black rhinoceros, the muchocho, or common white rhinoceros, and the kobaoba, or long-horned white rhinoceros. Both varieties of ·
the black rhinoceros are extremely fierce and dangerous, and rush headlong and
unprovoked at any object which attracts their attention. They never attain
much fat, and their flesh is tough, and not much esteemed by the Bechuanas.
Their food consists almost entirely of the thorny branches of the wait-a-bit
thorns. Their horns are much shorter than those of the other varieties, seldom
exceeding eighteen inches in length. They are finely polished with constant
rubbing against the trees. The skull is remarkably formed, its most striking
feature being the tremendous thick ossification in which it ends above the nostrils. It is on this mass that the horn is supported. The horns are not con
nected with the skull, being attached merely by the skin, and they may thus be
separated from the head by means of a sharp knife. They are hard and per
fectly solid throughout, and are a fine material for various articles, such as drinking cups, mallets for rifles, handles for turner's tools, etc., etc. The horn is
capable of a very high polish. The eyes of the rhinoceros are small and spark-
ling, and do not readily observe the hunter, provided he keeps to leeward of
them. The skin is extremely thick, and only to be penetrated by bullets hardened with solder. During the day the rhinoceros will be found lying asleep or
standing indolently in some retired part of the forest, or under the base of the
mountains, sheltered from the power of the sun by some friendly grove of um-
brella-topped mimosas. In the evening they commence their nightly ramble,
and wander over a great extent of country. They usually visit the fountains
between the hours of nine and twelve o'clock at night, and it is on these occasions that they may be most successfully hunted, and with the least danger. The
black rhinoceros is subject to paroxysms of unprovoked fury, often plowing up
the ground for several yards with its horns, and assaulting large bushes in the
most violent manner. On these bushes they work for hours with their horns, at
the same time snorting and blowing loudly, nor do they leave them in general
until they have broken them into pieces. The rhinoceros is supposed by many,
and by myself among the rest, to be the animal alluded to by Job, chap. xxxix.,
verses 10 and 11, where it is written, "Canst thou bind the unicorn with his
band in the furrow? or will he harrow the valleys after thee? Wilt thou trust
him because his strength is great? or wilt thou leave thy labor to him?" evidently alluding to an animal possessed of great strength and of untamable disposition, for both of which the rhinoceros is remarkable. All the four varieties
delight to roll and wallow in mud, with which their rugged hides are gener
erally incrusted.—*Adventures in South Africa*, 1. pp. 215-16.

these two are based on mere differences in size, age, and direction of horns, all which vary much in each variety. The rhinoceros has a "guardian spirit" in the rhinoceros-bird, his constant companion and devoted friend. * Those of the black species are very wary, fierce, and difficult to take. Their flesh is tough also, whilst that of the white rhinoceros is fat, tender, and, to the South African tribes, delicious. He is of a comparatively gentle spirit also, and more easily found and dispatched.

But the most interesting of the wild animals of Africa is the elephant, which, as is well known, is in several respects different from the elephant of Asia. His ears are larger, and the formation of his tough,

---

* These singular birds are thus described by Cumming :—These rhinoceros-birds are constant attendants upon the hippopotamus and the four varieties of rhinoceros, their object being to feed upon the ticks and other parasitic insects that swarm upon these animals. They are of a grayish color and are nearly as large as a common thrush ; their voice is very similar to that of the mistletoe thrush. Many a time have these ever-watchful birds disappointed me in my stalk, and tempted me to invoke an anathema upon their devoted heads. They are the best friends the rhinoceros has, and rarely fail to awaken him even in his soundest nap. "Chukuroo" perfectly understands their warning, and, springing to his feet, he generally first looks about him in every direction, after which he invariably makes off. I have often hunted a rhinoceros on horseback, which led me a chase of many miles, and required a number of shots before he fell, during which chase several of these birds remained by the rhinoceros to the last. They reminded me of mariners on the deck of some bark sailing on the ocean, for they perched along his back and sides ; and as each of my bullets told on the shoulder of the rhinoceros, they ascended about six feet into the air uttering their harsh cry of alarm, and then resumed their position. It sometimes happened tnat the lower branches of trees, under which the rhinoceros passed, swept them from their living deck, but they always recovered their former station ; they also adhere to the rhinoceros during the night. I have often shot these animals at midnight when drinking at the fountains, and the birds, imagining they were asleep, remained with them till morning, and on my approaching, before taking flight. they exerted themselves to their utmost to awaken Chukuroo from his deep sleep.—*Ibid.*, 292-3.

elastic feet is very different. His tusks also are larger and he reaches a greater size than the Asiatic elephant. He has been found in nearly all parts of interior Africa which have been explored, and to this day may be seen from vessels sailing along the West Coast near the equator, as he comes down to the sea to bathe his ponderous body. These animals are found in troops, varying in number from a few to several hundred. At times different troops have been seen together, whose heavy tread, in escaping, would make the earth tremble. They are exceedingly delicate as to their food, of which, however, they require immense quantities. Docile by nature, they are wonderfully fearful of man, whom, with a favorable wind, they can scent at a great distance; but in defence of their young or when attacked they fight with the greatest courage and effect. The elephant is unquestionably recognized by all animals of the forest as their undoubted master. They often retain life long after being mortally wounded, and when about to die, the agony of the dissolution of such an immense physical system forces tears from their eyes, but they expire without convulsions and in heroic silence. It might almost appear that their predominating feeling is that of sorrow that the vast forests through which they have roamed for years—perhaps a century—shall know them no more. It is difficult to believe one can kill these sublime animals, for gain alone, unless he be, at bottom, a genuine scoundrel.

It is doubtless different, however, when the gratification of the sporting propensity is the impelling motive. It was this which carried the Scottish hunter, Roualeyn Gordon Cumming, into the interior of South Africa, only about two years after the arrival there of Dr. Livingstone, and where he remained, hunting elephants, lions, rhinoceroses, hippopotami camelopards, and other great game, for the period of nearly five years. Mr. Cumming's "Adventures in South Africa" were published, if my memory does not err, in the year 1850. They were speedily republished in America, and were at first received with no little incredulity, as, by the way, most accounts of adventures in Africa, from Mungo Park to Stanley, have been. Adventures there appear to be naturally incredible to the rest of the world. It is as it is with respect to the rebuilding of Chicago; no one believes it all until he sees it all, and after that he can believe that almost anything is within the power of man's spirit of enterprise once fully aroused.* The

---

*We cannot all go to Africa, but the testimony of Dr. Livingstone, who received visits from this hunter every year during the five years of his warfare with wild animals, will be regarded as conclusive upon the general truthfulness of Mr. Cumming's reports. Dr. Livingstone says :

As the guides of Mr. Cumming were furnished through my influence, and usually got some strict charges as to their behavior before parting, looking upon me in the light of a father, they always came to give me an account of their service, and told most of those hunting-adventures which have since been given to the world, before we had the pleasure of hearing our friend relate them himself by our own fireside. I had thus a tolerably good opportunity of testing their accuracy, and I have no hesitation in saying that, for those who love that sort of thing, Mr. Cumming's book conveys a truthful idea of South African hunting. Some things in it require explanation, but the numbers of animals said to have been met with and killed are by no means improbable, considering the amount of large game then in the country. Two other gentlemen hunting in the same region destroyed in one season no fewer than seventy-eight rhinoceroses alone. Sportsmen, however, would not now find an equal number ; for, as guns are introduced among the tribes, all these fine animals melt away

incredulity in regard to Mr. Cumming's wonderful
success in securing great game in Africa has long
since passed away, and his narrative is now regarded
as altogether trustworthy. He remained in Africa,
hunting, the greater part of five years. During this
time he slew more than one hundred elephants, besides those, mortally wounded, which escaped. He
was equally successful with the camelopard, rhinoceros, hippopotamus, lion, buffalo, eland, and the
great variety of antelope which live in South Africa
in countless numbers. One of his first adventures
with large animals was with a troop of camelopards.
It is thus graphically described:

"We halted beside a glorious fountain, the name of
which was Massouey, but I at once christened it 'the
Elephant's own Fountain.' This was a very remarkable spot on the southern border of endless elephant
forests, at which I had at length arrived. The fountain was deep and strong, situated in a hollow at the
eastern extremity of an extensive vley, and its margin was surrounded by a level stratum of solid old
red sandstone. Here and there lay a thick layer of
soil upon the rock, and this was packed flat with the
fresh spoor of elephants. Around the water's edge
the very rock was worn down by the gigantic feet
which for ages had trodden there. We drew up the
wagons on a hillock on the eastern side of the water.
I had just cooked my breakfast, and commenced to

like snow in spring. In the more remote districts, where fire-arms have not yet
been introduced, with the single exception of the rhinoceros the game is to be
found in numbers much greater than Mr. Cumming ever saw.—*Researches in
South Africa*, 169-70.

feed, when I heard my men exclaim, 'Almagtig keek de ghroote clomp cameel;' and raising my eyes from my sassayby stew, I beheld a truly beautiful and very unusual scene. From the margin of the fountain there extended an open level vley, without a tree or bush, that stretched away about a mile to the northward, where it was bounded by extensive groves of wide-spreading mimosas. Up the middle of this vley stalked a troop of ten colossal giraffes, flanked by two large herds of blue wildebeests and zebras, with an advanced guard of pallahs. They were all coming to the fountain to drink, and would be within rifle-shot of the wagons before I could finish my breakfast. I, however, continued to swallow my food with the utmost expedition, having directed my men to catch and saddle 'Colesberg.' In a few minutes the giraffes were slowly advancing within two hundred yards, stretching their graceful necks, and gazing in wonder at the unwonted wagons. Grasping my rifle, I now mounted 'Colesberg,' and rode slowly toward them. They continued gazing at the wagons until I was within one hundred yards of them, when, whisking their long tails over their rumps, they made off at an easy canter. As I pressed upon them they increased their pace; but 'Colesberg' had much the speed of them, and before we had proceeded half a mile I was riding by the shoulder of a dark-chestnut old bull, whose head towered high above the rest. Letting fly at the gallop, I wounded him behind the shoulder; soon after which I broke him from the herd, and presently going ahead of him, he came to a stand. I then gave him a second bullet, somewhere near the first. These two shots had taken effect, and he was now in my power, but I would not lay him low so far from camp; so, having waited until he had regained his breath, I drove him half way back toward the wagons. Here he became obstreperous; so loading one barrel, and pointing my rifle toward the clouds, I shot him in the throat, when, rearing high, he fell backward and expired. This was a magnificent specimen of the giraffe, measuring upward of eighteen feet in height. I stood for nearly half an hour engrossed in the contemplation of his extreme beauty and gigantic proportions; and, if there had been no elephants, I could have exclaimed, like Duke Alexander of Gordon when he killed the famous old stag with seventeen tine, 'Now I can die happy.' But I longed for an encounter with the noble elephants, and I thought little more of the giraffe than if I had killed a gemsbok or an eland."

And in another place he describes his second success with the camelopard :

"We now bent our steps homeward. We had not ridden many miles when we observed a herd of fifteen camelopards browsing quietly in an open glade of the forest. After a very severe chase, in the course of which they stretched out into a magnificent widely extended front, keeping their line with a regularity worthy of a troop of dragoons, I succeeded in separating a fine bull, upward of eighteen feet in height, from the rest of the herd, and brought him to the ground within a short distance of the camp. The Bechuanas expressed themselves delighted at my success. They kindled a fire and slept beside the carcass, which they very soon reduced to bil-tongue and marrow-bones."

Mr. Cumming's first successful encounter with elephants was one of the most exciting of all. It is thus related :

" Having followed the spoor for a short distance, old Mutchuisho became extremely excited, and told me that we were close to the elephants. Two or three men quickly ascended the tallest trees that stood near us, but they could not see the elephants. Mutchuisho then extended men to the right and left, while we continued on the spoor.

" In a few minutes one of those who had gone off to our left came running breathless to say that he had seen the mighty game. I halted for a minute, and instructed Issac, who carried the big Dutch rifle, to act independently of me, while Kleinboy was to assist me in the chase. I bared my arms to the shoulder, and, having imbibed a draught of aqua pura from the calabash of one of the spoorers, I grasped my trusty two-grooved rifle, and told my guide to go ahead. We proceeded silently as might be for a few hundred yards, following the guide, when he suddenly pointed, exclaiming, ' Klow !' and before us stood a herd of mighty bull elephants, packed together beneath a shady grove about a hundred and fifty yards in advance. I rode slowly toward them, and, as soon as they observed me, they made a loud rumbling noise, and, tossing their trunks, wheeled right about and made off in one direction, crashing through the forest and leaving a cloud of dust behind them I

was accompanied by a detachment of my dogs, who
assisted me in the pursuit.

"The distance I had come, and the difficulties I
had undergone to behold these elephants, rose fresh
before me. I determined that on this occasion at
least I would do my duty, and, dashing my spurs into
Sunday's' ribs, I was very soon much too close in
their rear for safety. The elephants now made an
inclination to my left, whereby I obtained a good
view of the ivory. The herd consisted of six bulls;
four of them were full-grown, first-rate elephants; the
other two were fine fellows, but had not yet arrived
at perfect stature. Of the four old fellows, two had
much finer tusks than the rest, and for a few seconds
I was undecided which of these two I would follow;
when, suddenly, the one which I fancied had the
stoutest tusks broke from his comrades, and I at once
felt convinced that he was the patriarch of the herd,
and followed him accordingly. Cantering alongside,
I was about to fire, when he instantly turned, and,
uttering a trumpet so strong and shrill that the earth
seemed to vibrate beneath my feet, he charged furiously after me for several hundred yards in a direct
line, not altering his course in the slightest degree for
the trees of the forest, which he snapped and over-
threw like reeds in his headlong career.

"When he pulled up in his charge, I likewise halted;
and as he slowly turned to retreat, I let fly at his
shoulder, 'Sunday' capering and prancing, and giving
me much trouble. On receiving the ball the elephant
shrugged his shoulder, and made off at a free majestic walk. This shot brought several of the dogs to

my assistance which had been following the other elephants, and on their coming up and barking another
headlong charge was the result, accompanied by the
never-failing trumpet as before. In his charge he
passed close to me, when I saluted him with a second
bullet in the shoulder, of which he did not take the
slightest notice. I now determined not to fire again
until I could make a steady shot; but, although the
elephant turned repeatedly, 'Sunday' invariably disappointed me, capering so that it was impossible to
fire. At length, exasperated, I became reckless of
the danger, and, springing from the saddle, approached the elephant under cover of a tree, and gave
him a bullet in the side of the head, when, trumpeting
so shrilly that the forest trembled, he charged among
the dogs, from whom he seemed to fancy that the
blow had come; after which he took up a position in
a grove of thorns, with his head toward me. I walked
up very near, and, as he was in the act of charging
(being in those days under wrong impressions as to
the impracticability of bringing down an elephant
with a shot in the forehead), stood coolly in his path
until he was within fifteen paces of me, and let drive
at the hollow of his forehead, in the vain expectation
that by so doing I should end his career. The shot
only served to increase his fury—an effect which, I
had remarked, shots in the head invariably produced;
and, continuing his charge with incredible quickness
and impetuosity, he all but terminated my elephant-
hunting forever. A large party of the Bechuanas
who had come up yelled out simultaneously, imagining I was killed, for the elephant was at one moment

almost on the top of me; I, however, escaped by my activity, and by dodging round the bushy trees.

"The elephant held on through the forest at a sweeping pace; but he was hardly out of sight when I was loaded and in the saddle, and soon once more alongside. He kept crashing along at a steady pace, with blood streaming from his wounds. It was long before I again fired, for I was afraid to dismount, and 'Sunday' was extremely troublesome. At length I fired sharp right and left from the saddle: he got both balls behind the shoulder, and made a long charge after me, rumbling and trumpeting as before. The whole body of the Bamangwato men had now come up, and were following a short distance behind me. Among these was Mollyeon, who volunteered to help; and being a very swift and active fellow, he rendered me important service by holding my fidgety horse's head while I fired and loaded. I then fired six broadsides from the saddle, the elephant charging almost every time, and pursuing us back to the main body in our rear, who fled in all directions as he approached.

"The sun had now sunk behind the tops of the trees; it would very soon be dark, and the elephant did not seem much distressed, notwithstanding all he had received. I recollected that my time was short, and therefore at once resolved to fire no more from the saddle, but to go close up to him and fire on foot. Riding up to him, I dismounted and, approaching very near, I gave it him right and left in the side of the head, upon which he made a long and determined charge after me; but I was now very reckless of his charges, for I saw that he could not overtake me, and in a twinkling I was loaded, and, again approaching, fired sharp right and left behind his shoulder. Again he charged with a terrific trumpet, which sent 'Sunday' flying through the forest. This was his last charge. The wounds which he had received began to tell on his constitution, and he now stood at bay beside a thorny tree, with the dogs barking around him. These, refreshed by the evening breeze, and perceiving that it was nearly over with the elephant, had once more come to my assistance. Having loaded, I drew near and fired right and left at his forehead. On receiving these shots, instead of charging, he tossed his trunk up and down, and by various sounds and motions, most gratifying to the hungry natives, evinced that his demise was near Again I loaded and fired my last shot behind his shoulder: on receiving it, he turned round the bushy tree beside which he stood, and I ran round to give the other barrel, but the mighty old monarch of the forest needed no more; before I could clear the bushy tree he fell heavily on his side, and his spirit had fled."

Such is a specimen of the "sport" which the wilds of Africa offer to the ambitious hunter. That it is in some respects rather serious sport may be imagined from the description as well as from Mr. Cumming's statement of his losses during his four expeditions into the interior. These were forty-five horses and seventy head of cattle, the value being at least $3,000. "I also," he says, "lost about seventy of my dogs," which would convey the idea of a considerable kennel, the dogs all told. But he usually had only about thirty at a time. Many were killed by lions, while elephants made way with a still larger number.

The expeditions of Mr. Du Chaillu, an American naturalist, in Equatorial Africa, were more valuable to the cause of science than those of Mr. Cumming in South Africa, and scarcely less interesting as the explorations of a hunter. Like Cumming, he was a highly successful hunter, and he was also much more —a student of natural history imbued with a love of science and having a genius for it. As Mr. Cumming's starting point was the extreme of South Africa, under English domination, Mr. Du Chaillu had his headquarters beneath the equator on the west coast, and under the immediate eyesight, so to speak, of the American Presbyterian Mission for the Gaboon country. Mr. Du Chaillu afterwards established his home in the Camma country, and building himself a little village of huts near the junction of the N'poulounay and Fernand Vas rivers, and not far from the coast, named it "Washington." From the Gaboon and then from this African "city of Washington," this celebrated traveller made several explorations of the interior, much of the time among idolatrous and cannibal tribes. Enduring many hardships, overcoming many almost insurmountable difficulties, he not only gave to the world an extremely interesting account of hunting expeditions, but a description of the singular people and wonderful country he was the first white man to visit which forms a valued acquisition to the stock of geographical and scientific knowledge.*

Whilst he was very successful in procuring specimens of most of the animals and birds in equatorial Africa to a distance of several hundred miles from the coast, he devoted special attention to hunting the ape, and was more successful in killing the species commonly known as the gorrilla than any one else of Christendom has ever been. The greater difficulty of hunting the animal considered, he was as successful with the gorrilla as Mr. Cumming had been with the elephant.

The *troglodytes gorilla*, or great chimpanzee of the equatorial region of West Africa has long been the most dreaded, perhaps, of all the wild beasts of that continent. And it is probably true that in unmixed ferocity when assailed he does not have his equal. The nature of this fierce animal—much like man in some particulars of physical formation, totally dissimilar in all other respects—may be learned from an instance or two of Mr. Du Chaillu's hunting him. The account of his killing his "first gorilla" is as follows :

" We started early and pushed for the most dense and impenetrable part of the forest (this was in the country of the Fan negroes, cannibals, a little more than one degree north of the equator and something less than two hundred miles east of the mouth of the Gaboon river), in hopes to find the very home of the

---

* It need not be stated to students of matters pertaining to Africa, that this gentleman's " Explorations and Adventures in Equatorial Africa" (published by the Harpers in 1868) is one of our most interesting books of travel.

22

beast I so much wished to shoot. Hour after hour
we travelled, and yet no signs of gorilla. Only the
everlasting little chattering monkeys—and not many
of these—and occasional birds. In fact, the forests of
this part of Africa are not so full of life as in some
other parts to the south.

"Suddenly Miengai uttered a little *cluck* with his
tongue, which is the native's way of showing that
something is stirring, and that a sharp look-out is necessary. And presently I noticed, ahead of us seemingly, a noise as of some one breaking down branches
or twigs of trees. This was the gorilla, I knew at
once, by the eager and satisfied looks of the men.
They looked once more carefully at their guns, to
see if by any chance the powder had fallen out of
the pans; I also examined mine, to make sure that
all were right; and then we marched on cautiously.
The singular noise of the breaking of tree-branches
continued. We walked with the greatest care, making no noise at all. The countenances of the men
showed that they thought themselves engaged in a
very serious undertaking; but we pushed on, until
finally we thought we saw through the thick woods
the moving of the branches and small trees which the
great beast was tearing down, probably to get from
them the berries and fruits he lives on.

"Suddenly, as we were yet creeping along, in a silence which made a heavy breath seem loud and distinct, the woods were at once filled with the tremendous barking roar of the gorilla. Then the under-
brush swayed rapidly just ahead, and presently before
us stood an immense male gorilla. He had gone

through the jungle on his all-fours; but when he saw our party he erected himself and looked us boldly in the face. He stood about a dozen yards from us, and was a sight I think never to forget. Nearly six feet high (he proved two inches shorter), with immense body, huge chest, and great muscular arms, with fiercely-glaring large deep gray eyes, and a hellish expression of face, which seemed to me like some nightmare vision : thus stood before us this king of the African forests.

" He was not afraid of us. He stood there, and beat his breast with his huge fists till it resounded like an immense bass-drum, which is their mode of offering defiance ; meantime giving vent to roar after roar.

" The roar of the gorilla is the most singular and awful noise heard in these African woods. It begins with a sharp *bark*, like an angry dog, then glides into a deep bass *roll*, which literally and closely resembles the roll of distant thunder along the sky, for which I have sometimes been tempted to take it where I did not see the animal. So deep is it that it seems to proceed less from the mouth and throat than from the deep chest and vast paunch.

" His eyes began to flash fiercer fire as we stood motionless on the defensive, and the crest of short hair which stands on his forehead began to twitch rapidly up and down, while his powerful fangs were shown as he again sent forth a thunderous roar. And now truly he reminded me of nothing but some hellish dream creature—a being of that hideous order, half man half beast, which we find pictured by old artists in some representations of the infernal regions. He advanced a few steps—then stopped to utter that hideous roar again—advanced again, and finally stopped when at a distance of about six yards from us. And here, as he began another of his roars and beating his breast in rage, we fired, and killed him.

" With a groan which had something terribly human in it, and yet was full of brutishness, it fell forward on its face. The body shook convulsively for a few minutes, the limbs moved about in a struggling way, and then all was quiet—death had done its work, and I had leisure to examine the huge body. It proved to be five feet eight inches high, and the muscular development of the arms and breast showed what immense strength it had possessed.

" My men, though rejoicing at our luck, immediately began to quarrel about the apportionment of the meat—for they really eat this creature. I saw that we should come to blows presently if I did not interfere, and therefore said I should give each man his share, which satisfied all. As we were too tired to return to our camp of last night, we determined to camp here on the spot, and accordingly soon had some shelters erected and dinner going on. Luckily, one of the fellows shot a deer just as we began to camp, and on its meat I feasted while my men ate gorilla."

Another hunt resulted fatally to one of the natives. It is thus related:

" The next day we went on a gorilla-hunt. All the olako was busy on the evening of my arrival with preparations; and as meat was scarce, everybody had joyful anticipations of hunger satisfied and plenty in the camp. Little did we guess what frightful death was to befall one of our number before the next sunset.

"I gave powder to the whole party. Six were to go off in one direction for bush-deer, and whatever luck might send them, and six others, of whom I was one, were to hunt for gorilla. We set off toward a dark valley, where Gambo, Igoumba's son, said we should find our prey. The gorilla chooses the darkest, gloomiest forests for its home, and is found on the edges of the clearings only when in search of plantains, or sugar-cane, or pine-apple. Often they choose for their peculiar haunt a piece of wood so dark that even at midday one can scarce see ten yards. This makes it the more necessary to wait till the monstrous beast approaches near before shooting, in order that the first shot may be fatal. It does not often let the hunter reload.

"Our little party separated, as is the custom, to stalk the wood in various directions. Gambo and I kept together. One brave fellow went off alone in a direction where he thought he could find a gorilla. The other three took another course. We had been about an hour separated when Gambo and I heard a gun fired but little way from us, and presently another. We were already on our way to the spot where we hoped to see a gorilla slain, when the forest began to resound with the most terrific roars. Gambo seized my arms in great agitation, and we hurried on, both filled with a dreadful and sickening fear. We had

not gone far when our worst fears were realized.
The poor brave fellow who had gone off alone was
lying on the ground in a pool of his own blood, and
I thought at first quite dead.   His bowels were pro-
truding through the lacerated abdomen.   Beside him
lay his gun.   The stock was broken, and the barrel
was bent and flattened.   It bore plainly the marks of
the gorilla's teeth.

" We picked him up, and I dressed his wounds as
well as I could with rags torn from my clothes.
When I had given him a little brandy to drink he
came to himself, and was able, but with great difficulty, to speak.   He said that he had met the gorilla suddenly and face to face, and that it had not attempted to escape.   It was, he said, a huge male, and
seemed very savage.   It was in a very gloomy part
of the wood, and the darkness, I suppose, made him
miss.   He said he took good aim, and fired when the
beast was only about eight yards off.   The ball
merely wounded it in the side.   It at once began
beating its breasts, and with the greatest rage advanced upon him.

" To run away was impossible.   He would have
been caught in the jungle before he had gone a dozen
steps.   He stood his ground, and as quickly as he
could reloaded his gun.   Just as he raised it to fire
the gorilla dashed it out of his hands, the gun going
off in the fall, and then in an instant, and with a terrible roar, the animal gave him a tremendous blow with
its immense paw, frightfully lacerating the abdomen,
and with this single blow laying bare part of the intestines.   As he sank, bleeding, to the ground, the

monster seized the gun, and the poor hunter thought he would have his brains dashed out with it. But the gorilla seemed to have looked upon this also as an enemy, and in his rage flattened the barrel between his strong jaws.

"When we came upon the ground the gorilla was gone. This is their mode when attacked—to strike one or two blows, and then leave the victims of their rage on the ground and go off into the woods."

During his explorations in equatorial Africa, Du Chaillu discovered two new species of ape—*Troglodytes calvus* and *T. Koola-Kamba*—and also a number of other mamalians, birds, serpents, and reptiles, before unknown to naturalists.

Contrary to a somewhat prevalent belief, many diseases prevail among wild animals. "The free life of nature" is subject to woes, and needs the physician's aid, after all. "I have seen," says Dr. Livingstone, "the gnu, kama or hartebeest, the tressebe, kukama, and the giraffe, so mangy as to be uneatable even by the natives. Great numbers also of zebras are found dead with masses of foam at the nostrils, exactly as occurs in the common 'horse-sickness.' I once found a buffalo blind from ophthalmia standing by the fountain Otse. The rhinoceros has often worms on the conjunction of his eyes. All the wild animals are subject to intestinal worms besides. The zebra, giraffe, eland, and kukuma have been seen mere skeletons from decay of their teeth as well as from disease. The carnivera, too, become diseased and mangy; lions become lean and perish miserably by reason of the decay of the teeth." Cumming also speaks of seeing extensive plains thickly covered with the bones of wild animals which had died of disease.

As a rule, however, the animals are healthy. Their variety and vast numbers are beyond calculation. In a single day, Cumming saw the fresh spoor of about twenty varieties of "large game" and most of the animals themselves. These included elephant, black and white rhinoceros, hippopotamus, camelopard, buffalo, blue wildebeest, zebra, water-buck, sassayby, koodoo, pallah, springbok, serolomootlooque, wild boar, duiker, steinbok, lion, leopard. This is the *habitat* also of keilton, eland, oryx, roan antelope, sable antelope, hartebeest, klipspringer, grys steinbuck, and reitbuck. A little farther on he thus speaks of the game he saw while taking breakfast:

"We resumed our march at daybreak on the 28th, and held on through boundless open plains. As we advanced, game became more and more abundant. In about two hours we reached a fine fountain, beside which was a small cover of trees and bushes, which afforded an abundant supply of fire-wood. Here we outspanned for breakfast: it was a fine cool morning, with a pleasant breeze. The country was thickly covered with immense herds of game, consisting of zebra, wildebeest, blesbok, and springbok. There could not have been less than five or six thousand head of game in sight of me as I sat at breakfast. Presently the whole of this game began to take alarm. Herd joined herd, and took away up the wind; and in a few minutes other vast herds came pouring on up the wind, covering the whole breadth of the plain with a living mass of noble game."

And again:

"When the sun rose next morning I took coffee, and then rode west with two after-riders, in the hope of getting some blesbok shooting. I found the boundless undulating plains thickly covered with game, thousands upon thousands checkering the landscape far as the eye could strain in every direction. The blesboks, which I was most desirous to obtain, were extremely wary, and kept pouring on, on up the wind in long continued streams of thousands, so swift and shy that it was impossible to get within six hundred yards of them, or even by any stratagem to waylay them, so boundless was the ground, and so cunningly did they avoid crossing our track."

It might thus appear that if there is a sportsman's paradise anywhere it is Africa.

Perhaps it would not be too much to say that about all the birds known to ornithology, and many yet unknown in the books upon that science are to be found in Africa. The ostrich, the largest of birds, is found only in Africa. It sometimes attains the height of eight feet. It is swift of foot, its cry is much like the roar of the lion, and its appearance at a distance is very stately; but it is extremely stupid. Its feathers have long been highly valued in commerce. Another most remarkable bird, peculiar to Africa, is the secretary. This is a bird of prey, feeding solely on serpents, which it pursues on foot and destroys in great numbers. It has been described as "an eagle, mounted on the long, naked legs of a crane." Waterfowl of all kinds abound, and there are wild geese which have brilliant and variegated plumage. The most of the forests of South Africa are alive with countless numbers of an almost end-less variety of birds, but in the equatorial regions they are much less numerous, though there are many of those varieties which are characterized by bright, gorgeous plumage.

"Snake stories" are proverbially tinged with the colors of the imagination; but the serpents and rep-tiles of Africa are no jesting topic to the inhabitants. Many of the serpents are particularly venomous. Dr. Livingstone states that the picakholu is so copi-ously supplied with poison, that "when a number of dogs attack it, the first bitten dies almost instantane-ously, the second in about five minutes, the third in an hour or so, while the fourth may live several hours." The puff adder and several vipers are very dangerous. There is one which "utters a cry by night exactly like the bleating of a kid. It is supposed by the natives to lure travellers to itself by this bleating." Several varieties, when alarmed, emit a peculiar odor, by which their presence is made known. The deadly cobra exists in several colors or varieties. There are various species of tree-climbing serpents, which ap-pear to have the power of fascination. This belief of Dr. Livingstone in the fascinating power of some ser-pents is also entertained by Mr. Du Chaillu, and avowed as correct by the eminent naturalist, Dr. Andrew Smith in his "Reptilia." The eminent hunter of the gorilla says the presence of serpents in Africa is a "great blessing to the country. They destroy great numbers of rats and mice, and other of the smaller quadrupeds which injure the native provisions; and it is but just to say they are peacefully inclined, and never attack man unless trodden on. They are glad enough to get out of the way; and the most feared snake I saw in Africa (the Echidna nasicornis) was one which is very slow in its movements, from which cause it happens that it oftener bites people than others, being unable to get out of the way quickly. Though serpents abound in all parts of the country, I have travelled a month at a time without seeing one." The natives, though bare legged, are rarely bitten. There are several species of boa, which attain great size and weight. The variety known as the natal rock python, which is often seen in interior south Africa, though entirely without venom, like other boas, is very destructive of birds and animals. " They are perfectly harmless," says Dr. Livingstone, " and live on small animals, chiefly the rodentia; occasionally the steinbuck and pallah fall victims, and are sucked into its comparatively small mouth in boa-constrictor fashion. The flesh is much relished by Bakalahari and Bushmen. They carry away each his portion, like logs of wood, over their shoulders." Cumming killed one of these boas measuring fourteen feet in length. They have been known to measure nearly thirty feet in length, and to capture and swallow half-grown cattle. The Caffre of South Africa is very skilful in slaying the python with his spear. He is thus often pinned to the earth by a single throw and dispatched at leisure; then cut up into snake-logs and carried off for food.

Among the innumerable insects of Africa—-the fa-

tal tsetse fly and the devastating locust have already
been mentioned—the most interesting, perhaps, is the
ant. It exists in great variety and prodigious numbers. There are countless ant-hills in different parts
of Africa, which are larger than a majority of the individual homes of the natives of the southern and
central portions of the continent. Human works, to
be of the same relative size as these homes of insects
would tower five or six times above the pyramids of
Egypt, and would require a base correspondingly
large. Among themselves in Africa some of the species are warriors and cannibals; they fight their enemies and eat the vanquished. Other species are exceedingly destructive of the timbers of houses, eating
out the insides and leaving useless shells. Others
consume vast quantities of decaying animal matter,
and still others the decaying vegetation, including
great trees, of the tropics. Many are exceedingly
fierce in nature. Among these is the bashikouay ant
of equatorial Africa. It is, perhaps, relatively the
most voracious of all living things, and the most destructive. Unlike other large-sized ants it does not
build houses, but excavates holes in the earth for
place of retreat during storms. Its nature and babits
are fully described by Du Chaillu:

"This ant is very abundant in the whole region I
have travelled over in Africa. It is the dread of all
living animals from the leopard to the smallest insect. It is their habit to march through the forests
in a long regular line—a line about two inches broad
and often several miles in length. All along this line
are larger ants, who act as officers, stand outside the

ranks, and keep this singular army in order. If they come to a place where there are no trees to shelter them from the sun, whose heat they can not bear, they immediately build underground tunnels, through which the whole army passes in columns to the forest beyond. These tunnels are four or five feet underground, and are used only in the heat of the day or during a storm.

"When they get hungry the long file spreads itself through the forest in a front line, and attacks and devours all it comes to with a fury which is quite irresistible. The elephant and gorilla fly before this attack. The black men run for their lives. Every animal that lives in their line of march is chased. They seem to understand and act upon the tactics of Napoleon, and concentrate, with great speed, their heaviest forces upon the point of attack. In an incredibly short space of time the mouse, or dog, or leopard, or deer is overwhelmed, killed, eaten, and the bare skeleton only remains.

"They seem to travel night and day. Many a time have I been awakened out of a sleep, and obliged to rush from the hut and into the water to save my life, and after all suffered intolerable agony from the bites of the advance-guard, who had got into my clothes. When they enter a house they clear it of all living things. Roaches are devoured in an instant. Rats and mice spring round the room in vain. An overwhelming force of ants kills a strong rat in less than a minute, in spite of the most frantic struggles, and in less than another minute its bones are stripped. Every living thing in the house is devoured. They will not touch vegetable matter. Thus they are in reality very useful (as well as dangerous) to the negroes, who have their huts cleaned of all the abounding vermin, such as immense roaches and centipedes at least several times a year.

"When on their march the insect world flies before them, and I have often had the approach of a bashikouay army heralded to me by this means. Wherever they go they make a clean sweep, even ascending to the tops of the highest trees in pursuit of their prey. Their manner of attack is an impetuous *leap.* Instantly the strong pincers are fastened, and they only let go when the piece gives away. At such times this little animal seems animated by a kind of fury which causes it to disregard entirely its own safety, and to seek only the conquest of its prey. The bite is very painful.

"The negroes relate that criminals were in former times exposed in the path of the bashikouay ants, as the most cruel manner of putting to death.

"Two very remarkable practices of theirs remain to be related. When, on their line of march, they must cross a stream, they throw themselves across and form a tunnel—a living tunnel—connecting two trees or high bushes on opposite sides of the little stream. This is done with great speed, and is effected by a great number of ants, each of which clings with its fore claws to its next neighbor's body or hind claws. Thus they form a high, safe tubular bridge, *through* which the whole vast regiment marches in regular order. If disturbed, or if the arch is broken by the violence

of some animal, they instantly attack the offender
with the greatest animosity.

" The bashikouay have the sense of smell finely developed, as indeed have all the ants I know of, and
they are guided very much by it. They are larger
than any ant we have in America, being at least half
an inch long, and are armed with very powerful fore
legs and sharp jaws, with which they bite. They are
red or dark-brown in color. Their numbers are so
great that one does not like to enter into calculations; but I have seen one continual line passing at
good speed a particular place for *twelve hours*. The
reader may imagine for himself how many millions
on millions there may have been contained here."

And yet the ants of Africa are the chief agents
employed in forming a fertile soil. " But for their
labors," remarks Dr. Livingstone, " the tropical forests, bad as they now are with fallen trees, would be
a thousand times worse. They would be impassible
on account of the heaps of dead vegetation lying on
the surface, and emitting worse effluvia than the comparatively small unburied collections do now. When
one looks at the wonderful adaptations throughout
creation, and the varied operations carried on with
such wisdom and skill, the idea of second causes looks
clumsy. We are viewing the direct handiwork of
Him who is the one and only Power in the universe;
wonderful in counsel; in whom we all live, and move
and have our being."

There are vast numbers of annoying insects in all
portions of the continent, which in this respect, perhaps, is neither better nor worse than other parts of

the world, where little annoyances make up the great
sum of human misery.   It is only one of many proofs
that Africa is the region of contrasts, that the greatest animals flee from a little insect, the life of scores
of whom might be stamped out by a single footstep,
yet the aggregate labors of which preserve the continent from desolation and decay.

CHAPTER XX.

AFRICAN TREES AND VEGETATION.

Brief Notice of the Vegetable Kingdom of Africa—Immense Deserts and Prodigious, Tower-like Trees—Grasses Higher than a Man on Horseback—The
Cotton Plant—General Remarks.

There are so many anomalies in this continent of
contrasts that it seems quite of course to observe that
nowhere else can be found such vast extent of sandy,
barren wastes, and such immense expanse of forest
whose trees, and vines, and jungle fairly shut out the
rays of the sun, and leave the earth in eternal shade
and gloom. Much the larger share of North Africa
is embraced within the limits of the great Desert of
Sahara, which, though in some respects not correctly
represented to the reading public, not only covers a
vast expanse on this continent, but extends its bleak
and dreary nature far eastward of Africa, not ending
until after it has passed through Arabia, Persia, central Asia, and penetrated the confines of the Chinese
Empire. So in South Africa we have the Kalahari
Desert, often mentioned in this work, which, though
singularly covered with herbage and abounding in
wild beasts, is much of the time almost entirely untraversable by man on account of the want of water
It is coursed by the beds of many rivers which, ages
ago, were doubtless perennial streams of flowing

water, now as dry and uninviting as the sands of Sahara.

There are also extensive treeless plains—in America called prairies—whose soil is rich, supporting great quantities of luxuriant grasses and an infinite variety of shrubs and flowers. Over these, as we have seen, roam countless numbers of wild animals. Over a large portion of the watershed of South Africa, are immense "flats," covered with water during the long season of rains, but in the dry season presenting to the eyes a boundless expanse of infinitely variegated flowers.

Bounding these deserts, treeless plains, and flats, are forests of almost inconceivable extent, covered with thick jungle and the greatest variety of trees.

The magnificent trees which Dr. Livingstone found along the banks of the Zouga river, have already been spoken of.* The baobab is equal in size to the famous great trees of California, the immense hollow trunk of one of which has been exhibited as a curiosity in most portions of the United States. In some parts of the Bechuana country the remains of ancient forests of wild olives and of the camel-thorn are still to be met with. "It is probable," says Dr. Livingstone, "that this (the camel-thorn—*Acacia giraffe*) is the tree of which the Ark of the Covenant and the Tabernacle were constructed, as it is reported to be found where the Israelites were at the time these were made. It is an imperishable wood, while that usually pointed out as the 'shittim' soon decays, and

* See page 67, *ante.*

wants beauty." The baobab, already mentioned, has a vitality almost imperishable. "No external injury," says Livingstone, "not even a fire, can destroy this tree from without; nor can any injury be done from within, as it is quite common to find it hollow; and I have seen one in which twenty or thirty men could lie down and sleep as in a hut. Nor does cutting down exterminate it, for I saw instances in Angola in which it continued to grow in length after it was lying on the ground." In fact the baobab, or mowana as it is often called, has the qualities of both exogenous and endogenous trees, and is rather a gigantic bulb than either. It is often seen with its branches extending down to the ground and taking root, after the manner of the banyan. The wood of this giant of the forest is so spongy and soft that an axe can be struck in so far with a good blow that there is great difficulty in pulling it out again.

The mopane tree (*bauhinia*) is remarkable for the little shade it affords, and its astonishing capacity for being struck by lightning. The natives say "lightning hates it." The wood is hard, of a light red color, and called iron-wood by the Portuguese. On the other hand, there is a fine tree, called the morala, which has never been known to be struck by lightning. Branches of it may be seen on the huts of the natives and the houses of the Portuguese of East Africa, as a protection against lightning.* A tree which the natives

---

* Cumming thus describes the baobab, or mowana, under the name of *nwana*. It is about this latitude that the traveller will first meet with the gigantic and castle-like nwana, which is decidedly the most striking and wonderful tree among the thousands which adorn the South African forests. It is chiefly re-

call the indoonoo exists in some portions of equatorial Africa, which is taller and more graceful than the

markable on account of its extraordinary size, actually resembling a castle or
tower more than a forest tree. Throughout the country of Bamangwato the
average circumference of these trees is from thirty to forty feet; but on subsequently extending my researches in a northeasterly direction, throughout the
more fertile forests which clothe the boundless tracts through which the fair
Limpopo winds, I daily met with specimens of this extraordinary tree averag-
ing from sixty to a hundred feet in circumference, and maintaining this thick
ness to a height from twenty to thirty feet, when they diverge into numerous
goodly branches, whose general character is abrupt and horizontal, and which seem
to terminate with a peculiar suddenness. The wood of this tree is soft and utterly
unserviceable ; the shape of the leaf is similar to that of the sycamore tree, but
its texture partakes more of the fig leaf; its fruit is a nut, which in size and
shape resembles the egg of the swan. A remarkable fact, in connection with
these trees, is the manner in which they are disposed throughout the forest.
They are found standing singly, or in rows, invariably at considerable distances
from one another, as if planted by the hand of man ; and from their wondrous
size and unusual height (for they always tower high above their surrounding
compeers), they convey the idea of being strangers or interlopers on the ground
they occupy.

And toward the close of his work he says: The shoulders and upper ridges
of the mountains throughout all that country are profusely adorned with the
graceful sandal-wood tree, famed on account of the delicious perfume of its
timber. The leaf of this tree emits at every season of the year a powerful and
fragrant perfume, which is increased by bruising the leaves in the hand. Its
leaf is small, of a light silvery-gray color, which is strongly contrasted by the
dark and dense ever-green foliage of the moopooroo tree, which also adorns the
upper ridges of the mountain ranges. This beautiful tree is interesting, as producing the most delicious and serviceable fruit that I have met with throughout
those distant parts, the poorer natives subsisting upon it for several months,
during which it continues in season. The moopooroo is of the size and shape
of a very large olive. It is at first green, but, gradually ripening, like the Indian mango, it becomes beautifully striped with yellow, and when perfectly ripe
its color is the deepest orange. The fruit is sweet and mealy, similar to the
date, and contains a small brown seed. It covers the branches, and when ripe
the golden fruit beautifully contrasts with the dark green leaves of the tree
which bears it. Besides the moopooroo, a great variety of fruits are met with
throughout these mountains and forests, all of which are known to, and gathered by, the natives. I must, however, forego a description of them, as it would
swell these pages to undue bounds. Throughout the densely-wooded dells
and hollows of the mountains the rosewood tree occurs, of considerable size
and in great abundance.

baobab, but not of such immense trunk. It is from eight to twelve feet in diameter near the base. The ebony-tree is found on high lands. It is met with all along the ridges and hills of equatorial Africa. It is described as one of the finest and most graceful trees of the African forest. Its leaves are long, sharp-pointed, dark green, and hang in clusters, producing a grateful shade. Its bark is smooth and of a dark green color. The trunk rises straight and often to the height of sixty feet without a branch; then large heavy branches are sent out. Some of these valuable trees have a diameter of five feet at the base. They are all hollow, when mature, even the branches. Next the bark is a white sap-wood which is not valuable. This in an average tree is three or four inches thick, and next to this lies the ebony of commerce. The ebony-tree is found intermixed with others in the forest, but generally in groups of three or four together, and none others within a little distance. In the same regions of equatorial Africa grows the *liamba* plant, whose leaves are used for smoking by the natives, very much as the tobacco leaf is used in some countries. Under its influence, the natives frequently become permanently insane. Here also the India-rubber vine grows in great luxuriance. Immense quantities of land round about Lake Anengue especially, are literally covered with this valuable vine.

The cotton-plant is indigenous in most portions of central and south Africa, but the natives have as yet paid little attention to its cultivation. The cannibal tribes of central Africa make mats and many of their garments of a "grass-cloth," which has been described by Dr. Livingstone and Mr. Stanley in letters heretofore quoted. The thread used in this material is obtained from a species of palm, a great number of the many different varieties of which abound in Africa. As for grasses, the great explorer of whom this volume principally treats often speaks of riding through immense extents of it, taller than a man on horseback. The vast quantities of grass and the great number of palms in Africa suggest the belief that the manufacture of "grass-paper" may some day become an important element in African commerce. The date-tree and many other fruit-bearers are plentiful.

If Christian civilization held her benign sway over all portions of Africa, much of the great forest area would be cultivated, and the fertile prairies would yield many of the fruits and grains by which the world is supplied with food. The natural agricultural advantages of the continent are undoubtedly very great. It is well known that the valley of the Nile was for ages the granary of the world. Much of it is no less fertile now than when its products fed mankind. The whole of central Africa, from the confines of the Desert of Sahara to beyond the sources of the Nile, the Zambesi, and the Congo, is mostly suitable to agriculture. A vast region of this country, south of the great desert, and nearly across the continent, was formerly the abode of large numbers of people, the remains of whose cities and towns attest their civilization and successful agriculture. Here was the battle-ground in Africa between Mohammedanism and paganism; and it is not improbable that the hosts of the Prophet were stayed in their victorious career and driven back upon regions previously overrun by the fierce cannibal tribes of equatorial Africa, who, from the time of Herodotus, have afforded some of the best specimens of physical man. Still farther south, natural agricultural advantages are notably good, except in the Desert of Kalahari — redeemable by means of Artesian wells—and the climate is extremely salubrious and healthy.

CHAPTER XXI.

THE DESERT OF SAHARA.

General Description of the Great Desert of North Africa—Its Different Divisions, Inhabitants, and Productions—Cities Buried Under the Sands—The Storms of Wind—Influence of the Desert upon the Climate and Civilization of Europe.

An opinion quite extensively prevails that the Desert of Sahara is a vast treeless plain; a level expanse of hot and dreary sand, with nothing to disturb the awful monotony but an occasional caravan winding its weary way through the pathless waste, or the dreadful simoon driving the sands from their accustomed place and hurling them wildly whithersoever it will. Such, indeed, would be no very inaccurate description of many portions, some of them considerable in extent, of this immense waste, but if such were taken as a picture of the whole it would convey a false impression.

Perhaps the first idea which occupies one's mind in thinking of Sahara is in regard to its prodigious extent. Its western boundary is the Atlantic ocean whose waves wash these arid sands from Cape Nuun, at the southern extremity of Morocco, to the mouth of the river Senegal, a distance of more than a thousand miles. Thence it extends eastward about three thousand miles to the valley of the Nile. It is estimated that within the limits thus generally described there is an area of nearly 2,000,000 square miles, being about ten times as great as the area of France, and more than twenty times greater than that of England, Scotland, Wales, and Ireland combined. It is to be furthermore considered that Sahara, vast as it is, embraces less than half of the desert system, if we may so speak, of which it forms the western portion, for, as is elsewhere remarked, it pushes itself, after interruption by the Nile, the rocky regions of Nubia and Abyssinia, and the Red sea, through Arabia, and thousands of miles eastward to far within the boundaries of the Celestial empire. The area of the whole is prohably about 7,000,000 square miles or something more than that of Europe and the United States. But Sahara itself in North Africa has three times the extent of the Mediterranean sea. So vast an expanse, with so much of it uninhabitable and unproductive, traversable only by those "ships of the desert," the patient camels, must impress the mind with gloomy reflections, to be replaced by brighter ones only upon considering further that in the wonderful workings of Nature hence have been borne and are constantly being borne upon the wings of the viewless winds the greatest blessings to the best portions of mankind.

The western portion of Sahara, which is called Sahel, is far more desolate than the eastern portion. In the latter part there are many oases, which are inhabitable and productive. Thus we have not far from the valley of the Nile, the oases of Darfoor, El Wah, Great Oasis, Takel, and some others, of which the first named is the greatest and the farthest south. Northward is the oasis of Siwah, or Jupiter Am-

mon, Aujilah, farther west, and the great oasis of Fezzan, with the important city of Murzuk.   The oasis
of A-ir or Asben, is in the south-central part of the
desert.   Between this and the Atlantic ocean on the
west and Morocco and Algeria on the north, the expanse is as desolate a region, perhaps, as there is any
where on the globe.   For a considerable distance from
the ocean, the scene is a bleak plain of sand, except
in the portion near Senegambia, where many acacias
are found—the trees which furnish the gum-arabic of
commerce.   This coast region has a considerable elevation, however, and the shore consists of sandstone,
generally about one hundred feet high.   Whilst there
are many low plains covered with drifting sands, their
desolation only increased in places by wide-spread
coatings of salt and vast fields of naked rock upon
which one might journey for days together without
seeing a grain of sand or a sign of vegetation or animal life, yet may Sahara be generally described as a
region of elevated plateaus which frequently rise into
mountains of 3,000 to 5,000 feet elevation, separated
from each other by valleys and immense tracts of
sand.   Traversing the Desert from Tripoli one
reaches the summit of the Gharian plateau at an
elevation of 2,000 feet whence it gradually slopes
away to 500 feet and in some places even below the
level of the sea.   Farther on is a long range of table
land called the Hamadah, stretching east and west
with an elevation of almost fifteen hundred feet.
Toward the west Hamadah becomes mountainous and
toward the east it breaks into a vast scene of huge
cliffs called El-Harouj.   Toward the Mediterranean

on the whole plateau of Hamadah and that of Murzuk, are dry channels, called wadys, and small deserts. The route then ascends several hundred feet and passing over a sandy region, with some expanses of bare granite, with an elevation above the sea of from 1,000 to 2,200 feet, continues to the mountainous region between Ghat and Asben, where there is a wady at an elevation of 2,956 feet amid mountain peaks not less than 4,000 feet high. Still further south the average elevation is believed by Barth to be about 1,900 feet. Vogel discovered similar features in the eastern portions of the Desert, and concluded that Sahara is a vast plateau formation of the general height of from 1,200 to 1,500 feet. Natives reported to him that there were high mountains in the southern part of the Desert, and two ranges, the Borghoo and the Madschunga, were specially spoken of as so elevated that the inhabitants dress in furs. Further west, the explorer Barth found the Tuariks clad in woollens and some in furs. The greatest expanse of sand and salt is between Asben and Timbuctoo and thence on west to the ocean. Hence caravans from Morocco to Timbuctoo have met with more difficulties and endured more sufferings than those which traverse the Desert from Tripoli, Barca, or Cairo.

In many portions of this western waste of Sahara have been found marine shells of recent species, showing that at no very remote geological period these now arid plains formed the bed of the ocean Not only so, but most astonishing changes have here occurred within what is commonly called the historic period. Careful investigations have discovered that

unknown cities are buried beneath the drifting sands
of western Sahara, and where in former ages were
fertile territories there is now only bleak and barren
waste. It is interesting to speculate upon the question, Who were the people thus engulfed by the
sands of Sahara ? The substantial nature of their
buildings, in so far as they have been disentombed,
would appear to make it certain that they far surpassed
in art and civilization any of the tribes which now live
near the scenes of the invisible ruins. There are but
two peoples, of whom we have historic knowledge,
inhabitants of Africa, who might have óccupied these
buried cities and cultivated the fruitful territories of
" the olden time long ago." These are the Egyptians
and the Carthagenians. The ruins can hardly be those
of the Egyptians, for they were essentially a stationary people. For ages they remained where they emigrated, or where they established themselves after
their first migration. If the era of Carthage were
early enough to account for these sand-submerged
cities it might not be unreasonable to claim that they
may have belonged to the race of which Hannibal
was one of the greatest minds. And the remarkable
fact that though Carthage was unquestionably one of
the most powerful nations of antiquity, nothing remains, by her own authority, of her history, may be
regarded as one of those mysterious coincidences of
engulfment, considered in connexion with the burial
of the entombed cities of Sahara, for which we cannot account and which yet have a powerful effect not
only upon the imagination but the reason. Carthage
left nothing of her literature, her arts, her language.

With the exception of a few coins there are no monuments remaining even of a commerce whose sails whitened every known sea. And yet this nation of which absolutely nothing remains, was able, on the very day when the Greeks defeated Xerxes, at Salamis (480 B. C.) to bring into action 300,000 men in Sicily. It is doubtful whether England could transport so large an army across the British Channel today. Though in after times, when Carthage maintained her wars with Rome, her armies were not so large, yet the country must have been both extensive and populous which could at once transport an army of a hundred thousand men across the Mediterranean. No less, with large numbers of horses, was the force with which Hannibal embarked on his last great campaign, and with whichhe succeeded, after various fortunes, in thundering at the very gates of Rome. Regions of fertility and dense population round about Carthage must, it would seem but natural, have been greater in those times than now. Perhaps valuable evidences of the literature, arts, and institutions of this extinguished nationality may some day be revealed under the sands of the Great Desert.

The western portion of the Desert is inhabited by Moors and Arabs, who live in tents and move about frequently from place to place. The Moors are a branch of those who dwell in Morocco. In color they are nearly black, with straight hair, slight physical frames, and slender legs. They are all able to read the Koran. Numerous tribes of the Tuariks inhabit the central portions of the desert. With the finest of physical natures they are a robber race, brave

cruel, and revengeful, but with a certain hospitality
which is the redeeming trait in the general unworthi-
ness of their character. The Tibboos occupy the
eastern and least desolate portion of the desert. They
much resemble the negroes in feature, and are an
agricultural and pastoral people, living in fixed abodes.
Not a few of the Tibboos are pagans, the other inhabitants of the Desert being all Mohammedans.

Throughout this vast expanse, there are, except on
the oases, but few productions of value to man. Iron
is found in considerable quantities east of Fezzan.
Salt is abundant all along the southern portion of the
desert west of Asben. Here and there are accacias,
here and there groves of the date-palm.

One of the greatest terrors of the Desert is the
wind which sometimes blows with great force and
velocity, lifting up vast quantities of sand and hurling
them madly through the air. The simoon which occurs in India and Arabia, and which would appear to
be a narrow wave of intensely hot, sulphurous air,
does not, perhaps, afflict any portion of Sahara. But
when the ordinary winds of the Desert grow into a
gale or a whirlwind, their effects are oftentimes fatal
and terrible in the extreme. Frequently a thick cloud
of sand may be seen rapidly borne by the wind at a
distance of about twenty feet from the ground. Such
sand-clouds often extend over vast expanses. If then a
whirlwind comes on, the effects are often no less than
awful. By such fearful storms whole caravans, consisting of thousands of camels and men have been
suddenly buried alive.

Perhaps the most interesting fact connected with

the Desert of Sahara is the effect it produces, if we may believe the testimony of men of science who have investigated the subject, upon the climate of Europe. It has been stated that what is now the Desert of Sahara was occupied by the ocean at a comparatively recent geological period. Some of the facts which have brought scientists to this conclusion will be set forth when we come to speak of the geology of Africa. Here taking the conclusion for granted, it may be interesting to speculate how far this great change of the earth's surface has affected the climate farther north. If the Desert of Sahara were ocean, the "Fohn," instead of being a burning, dry wind, which strikes the snow off the Alps both by melting and by evaporation, would be a moist, damp wind, When it reached the crests of those mountains it would produce dense clouds and thick fogs which would prevent the rays of the sun from warming the earth or melting the glaciers. In a word, the Desert of Sahara, so generally regarded as the most desolate portion of the earth, appears to be the furnace by which much of Europe has been warmed out of a state of frigid discomfort into a temperate and genial climate. For geology clearly teaches us that while what we now call Sahara was covered with water, the great glaciers were advanced far beyond their present limits, giving the region to a hyperborean climate and a hyperborean fauna. The reindeer and the musk-ox roamed south to the shores of the Mediterranean when man first made his appearance in Europe. Animals which we now find only in Greenland, and the coldest habitable countries lived where frosts now

rarely come, in those remote times when the Desert
of Sahara was ocean.

Not many years ago, Napoleon III., then Emper-
or of the French, with the object, it is believed, of
moderating the heated terms in the French colony
of Algeria, bordering on the northern boundary of
Sahara, directed a considerable corps of engineers to
examine into the practicability of transferring Sahara
back again to ocean. The idea was doubtless suggested to the astute mind of the Emperor by the fact
that Sahara had become dry land more recently than
any other portion of the globe, and it was well known
that there were many large expanses within its borders lower than the level of the sea. They reported
that a great portion of the Desert could be without
impracticable expense turned again into sea, but expressed the opinion that the meteorological effects
would be disastrous to the climate and eventually to
the civilization of Europe. And this opinion is, most
probably, entirely correct.

It is, then, however remarkable it may appear, the
fact that the continent of Europe owes all of its progress in civilization, the arts, and sciences, beyond
that made by such men as live where the reindeer
and musk-ox have their *habitat*, to bleak and dreary
Sahara. But for Sahara, the inhabitants of Europe
might now be little better than the Esquimaux, bur-
rowing in the ground under ice huts, living on blub-
ber, and dying on seal skins. Or if this be accounted
an extravagant illustration, it can hardly be doubted
that much of the continent whence has orginated in
the historic ages the noblest civilization and the most

beneficent institutions would not have been in the zone in which about all the great and good triumphs of the human intellect have been achieved from the beginning. Even the immortal literature and art of Greece and Rome were under obligations of gratitude to the Desert of Sahara, and they are the acknowledged parents of the best literature and art of modern Europe.

It is impossible to reflect upon this remarkable influence of the Desert of Sahara—in itself producing nothing, by its vast extent and singular formation the means of incalculable blessings to Europe and hence to all mankind—without being most profoundly impressed with the truth that in the disposition of affairs by Him who created all things there is no waste; nothing which may not be turned into good ; no curse which may not be turned into a blessing.

CHAPTER XXII.

GEOLOGY OF AFRICA—ANTIQUITY OF MAN.

The General Geological Formation of the Continent—The Want of Comprehensive Investigation—Singular Facts as to the Desert of Sahara—The Question of the Antiquity of Man—Is Africa the Birth-place of the Human Race? Opinions of Scientists Tending to Answer in the Affirmative—Darwinism.

It is to be greatly regretted that no comprehensive geological sur' eys of Africa have ever been made; because there are certain questions, eventually to be settled by geology, whose determination, it appears to be agreed, will be finally resolved by investigations in this continent. In a volume of this nature, designed for the general reader, those facts and reasonings only need be referred to which may be supposed to have the most interest. Reference has already been made to Sir Roderick Murchison's exposition of the trough-shaped form of South Africa in his discourse before the Royal Geographical Society in 1852 —an exposition which was so remarkably substantiated by Dr. Livingstone in his journey across the continent from Loanda to Kilimane. Though in its geographical configuration Africa is not greatly unlike South America, in its geological structure it much more resembles the northern continent of the western hemisphere. The Appalachian range of mountains extending through nearly the whole of the eastern portion of North America, parallel with the coast, and the Rocky Mountains and Sierra Nevadas in the west, bear a notable resemblance to those ranges of mountains in Africa, which, rising first in the northern portions of Senegambia, pursue a south-easterly, then a southerly course to near the southern limit of the continent, when they sharply bend toward the northeast, and with many lofty peaks, some of which reach the region of eternal snow, pass through Mozambique, Zanguebar, and end not until after they have passed through Abyssinia and Nubia, and penetrated the limits of Egypt. In Tripoli, Tunis, Algeria, and Morocco, is the Atlas range, between which and the beginning of the other the distance is hardly so great as that between the southern limits of the Appalachian range and the mountains of Mexico. The course of each of the great rivers of these continents is also across the degrees of latitude instead of generally parallel with the equator, as is the case with the great river of South America. There is a similarity also between North America and Africa in an extensive system of inland lakes of fresh water and vast extent.

The geological structure of the mountains of Africa, especially of South Africa, appears to be quite uniform. They have a neucleus of granite which often appears at the surface and forms the predominating rock, but in the greater proportion of the mountains, perhaps, the granite is overlain by vast masses of sandstone, easily distinguished by the numerous pebbles of quartz which are embedded in it. The summit, when composed of granite, is usually round and smooth, but when composed of the quartzose sandstone is often perfectly flat. Of this Table Mount, in South Africa, is a notable illustration. The thickness of this stratum of sandstone is sometimes not less than 2,000 feet. Such is the case in the Karoo mountains of Cape Colony. When thus appearing, it may be seen forming steep, mural faces, resembling masonry, or exhibiting a series of salient angles and indentations as sharp, regular, and well-defined as if they had been chiselled. With the granite are often associated primitive schists, the decomposition of which seems to have furnished the chief ingredients of the thin, barren clay which forms the characteristic covering of so much of the South African mountains. In some places, more recent formations appear, and limestone is seen piercing the surface. The geological constitution of the Atlas Mountains, in northwestern Africa, presents old limestone alternating with a schist, often passing to a well-characterized micaceous schist, or gneiss, the stratification of which is exceedingly irregular. Volcanic rocks have here been found in small quantities. There are veins of copper, iron, and lead.

In Egypt we find the alluvial soil a scarcely less interesting object of study than the rocks upon which it rests. These are limestone, sandstone, and granite, the latter of which, in Upper Egypt, often rises 1,000 feet above the level of the Nile. Not many years ago were discovered about 100 miles east of the Nile, and in 28 deg. 4 min. of north latitude the splendid ruins of the ancient Alabastropolis, which once derived wealth from its quarries of alabaster. Farther south are the ancient quarries of jasper, porphyry, and verd antique. The emerald mines of Zebarah lay near the Red Sea

The Atlas range in Algeria is better known than elsewhere. It is as described above, but at Calle, there are distinct traces of ancient volcanoes. Iron, copper, gypsum, and lead are found in considerable quantities. Cinnabar is found in small quantities. Salt and thermal springs abound in many parts of Algeria, amethysts in Morocco, slates in Senegambia, and iron in Liberia, Guinea, the Desert of Sahara and many other parts of Africa.

Gold, gold-dust, and iron are among the best known of the mineral riches of Africa, and are the most generally diffused throughout the continent. In the country of Bambouk, in Senegambia, most of the gold which finds its way to the west coast is found. Here the mines are open to all, and are worked by natives who live in villages. The richest gold mine of Bambouk, and the richest, it is believed, yet discovered in Africa, is that of Natakoo—an isolated hill, some 300 feet high and 3,000 feet in circumference, the soil of which contains gold in the shape of lumps, grains, and spangles, every cubic foot being loaded, it is said, with the precious metal. The auriferous earth is first met with about four feet from the surface, becoming more abundant with increase of depth. In searching for gold the natives have perforated the hill in all directions with pits some six feet in diameter and forty or fifty feet deep. At a depth of twenty feet from the surface lumps of pure gold of from two to ten grains weight are found. There are other mines in this portion of Africa, gold having been found distributed over a surface of 1,200 square miles. The precious metal is not only found

in hills, the most of which are composed of soft argil
laceous earth, but in the beds of rivers and smaller
streams, so that the lines of Bishop Heber's well-
known missionary hymn are truthful as well as
poetical: —

> "Where Afric's sunny fountains,
> Roll down their golden sands."

The gold mines of Semayla, which are some forty
or fifty miles northward of those of Natakoo, though
nearly as rich as the latter, are in hills of rock and
sandstone, which substances are pounded in mortars
that the gold may be extracted. Barth judged that
gold would be found in the Benue river, the principal
eastern tributary of the Niger. Gold, silver, iron
lead, and sulphur have been found in large quantities,
and were long profitably mined in the mountainous
districts of Angola. In Upper Guinea gold and iron
are deposited in granitic or schistose rocks. The interior contains vast quantities of iron which might be
easily mined, but the natives are not sufficiently enterprising to accomplish much in this respect. Gold
is also obtained in the beds of some of the rivers of
Guinea. In Mozambique, on the east coast, the
Portuguese have for a great length of time had a
considerable commerce in gold obtained from mines
near the Zambezi, in the region near the western
limit of that province. It has already been stated
that here Dr. Livingstone discovered deposits of
coal. Along the Orange and Vaal rivers, in extreme
South Africa, have recently been discovered diamond
fields which some noted scientists believe will yet
prove to be among the richest in the world.

Perhaps the portions of Africa which are the most interesting on account of geological investigations which have been made, are the valley of the Nile in Egypt, and the Desert of Sahara. It is well known that the river Nile annually overflows its banks in Egypt, and the inundation remaining a considerable period, a thin layer of soil is each year added to that which existed there before. This Nile mud, as it is called by geologists, has been the subject of considerable scientific examination for many years. In his work upon the " Geological Evidences of the Antiquity of Man," Sir Charles Lyell gives a full account of certain systematic borings in the Nile mud which were made between the years 1851 and 1854, under the superintendency of Mr. Leonard Horner, but who employed to practically conduct the examinations an intelligent, enterprising, and faithful Armenian officer of engineers, Hekekyan Bey, who had for many years pursued scientific studies in England, was in every way qualified for the task, and, unlike Europeans, was able to endure the climate during the hot months, when the waters of the Nile flow within their banks. Sir Charles Lyell states that the results of chief importance arising out of this inquiry were obtained from two sets of shafts and borings—sunk at intervals in lines crossing the great valley from east to west. One of these consisted of fifty-one pits and artesian perforations, made where the valley is sixteen miles wide between the Arabian and the Libyan deserts, in the latitude of Heliopolis, about eight miles above ‚the apex of the delta. The other line of pits and borings, twenty-seven in number, was in the parallel of Memphis where the valley is five miles wide. Besides Hekekyan Bey, several engineers and some sixty workmen, inured to the climate, were employed for several years, during the dry season, in the furtherance of these interesting investigations.

It was found that in all the works the sediment passed through was similar in composition to the ordinary Nile mud of the present day, except near the margin of the valley, where thin layers of quartzose sand, such as is sometimes blown from the adjacent desert by violent winds, were observed to alternate with the loam. A remarkable absence of lamination and stratification, the geologist goes on to say, was observed almost universally in the sediment brought up from all points except where the sandy layers above alluded to occurred, the mud closely agreeing in character with the ancient loam of the Rhine. Mr. Horner attributes this want of all indication of successive deposition to the extreme thinness of the film of matter which is thrown down annually on the great alluvial plain during the season of inundation. The tenuity of this layer must indeed be extreme, if the French engineers are tolerably correct in their estimate of the amount of sediment formed in a century, which they suppose not to exceed on the average five inches. It is stated, in other words, that the increase is not more than the twentieth part of an inch each year, or one foot in the period of 240 years. All the remains of organic bodies found during these investigations under Hekekyan Bey belonged to living species. Bones of

the ox, hog, dog, dromedary, and ass were not uncommon, but no vestiges of extinct mammalia were
found, and no marine shells were anywhere detected.
These excavations were on a large scale, in some instances for the first sixteen or twenty-four feet. In
these pits, jars, vases, and a small human figure in
burnt clay, a copper knife, and other entire articles
were dug up; but when water soaking through from
the Nile was reached, the boring instrument used
was too small to allow of more than fragments of
works of art being brought up. Pieces of burnt brick
and pottery were constantly being extracted, and
from all depths, even where they sank sixty feet below the surface toward the central parts of the valley. In none of these cases did they get to the bottom of the alluvial soil. If it be assumed that the
sediment of the valley has increased at the rate of
six inches a century, bricks at the depth of sixty feet
have been buried 12,000 years. If the increase has
been five inches a century, they have lain there during a period of 14,400 years. Lyell states further on
that M. Rosiere, in the great French work on Egypt,
has estimated the rate of deposit of sediment in the
delta at two inches and three lines in a century. A
fragment of red brick has been excavated a short
distance from the apex of the delta at a depth of
seventy-two feet. At a rate of deposit of two and a-
half inches a century, a work of art seventy-two feet
deep must have been buried more than 30,000 years
ago. Lyell frankly states, however, that if the boring was made where an arm of the river had been
silted up at a time when the apex of the delta was

somewhat further south, or more distant from the
sea than now, the brick in question might be comparatively very modern. It is agreed by the best
geologists that the age of the Nile mud cannot be
accurately, but only approximately calculated by the
data thus far furnished. The amount of matter
thrown down by the waters in different parts of the
plain varies so much that to strike an average with
any approach to accuracy must be most difficult.
The nearest approach, perhaps, as has been observed
by Baldwin, to obtaining an accurate chronometric
scale for ascertaining the age of the deposits of the
Nile at a given point, was made near Memphis, at the
statue of King Rameses. It is known that this
statue was erected about the year 1260 B. C.   In
1854 it had stood there 3,114 years. During that time
the alluvium had collected to the depth of nine feet
and four inches above its base, which was at the rate
of about three and a half inches in each century.
Mr. Horner found the alluvium, below the base of
the statue, to be thirty feet deep, and pottery was
found within four inches of the bottom of the alluvium. If the rate of accumulation previous to the
building of the statue had been the same as subsequently, the formation of the alluvium began, at that
point, about 11,660 years before the Christian era,
and men lived there some 12,360 years ago, cultivating the then thin soil of the valley. But it would
appear to be certain that the average deposit is so
slight annually that many centuries more than those
formerly quite universally received as the age of the
world for the stage of mankind's achievements must

have passed since the work of man's hands have been buried under these vast deposits of alluvium. Thus, geology insists, is the fact of man's existence, long before the historic era, conclusively established.

The Desert of Sahara presents some interesting facts of the same nature. It has already been stated that this part of Africa was ocean within a compara-tively recent geological period. Tristram and several French officers of scientific attainments, who have made geological examinations of large portions of the desert have shown that the northern margin is lined with ancient sea-beaches and lines of terraces—the "rock-bound coasts" of the old ocean. Numerous salt-lakes exist in the desert which are tenanted by the common cockle. A species of *Haligenes* which inhabits the Gulf of Guinea is found in a salt lake in latitude 30 deg. north and longitude 7 deg. east, sep-arated, therefore, from its present marine habitat by the whole extent of the great desert, and the vast ex-panse of Soudan and Guinea. Geologists hence con-clude that the existing fauna, including man, occupied Africa long before the Sahara became dry land. Ref-erence has been made in the preceding chapter to the supposed remarkably beneficent effect this great ex-panse of desert, heated sands, and hot air, has upon the climate, and consequently upon the civilization of Europe.

It is probable that from the fact that Sahara was about the last extensive portion of earth to be aban-doned by the ocean, that the general opinion became prevalent that the continent of Africa was, geologi-cally, the most recent of the grand divisions of the

earth. Though supposed to be the oldest in civiliza
tion, it has been supposed to be the youngest in geological constitution. I am informed by scientific men
that on account of recent investigations and reasonings, the opinion has for some time been gaining
ground that Africa is likely to be shown to be the
oldest part of the globe in both respects, and to have
been the original birthplace of the race of man.

The negroid race, comprehending the Negroes, Hottentots, and Algutos, are, it is claimed by many scientists, the most ancient of all the types of mankind,
and since their appearance on earth vast geographical changes have taken place. Continents have become ocean and sea has become land. "The negroes,"
says Lubbock, "are essentially a non-navigating race;
they build no ships, and even the canoes of the Fee-
jeeans are evidently copied from those of the Poly-
nesians. Now what is the geographical distribution
of the race? They occupy all Africa south of Sahara, which neither they nor the rest of the true African fauna have ever crossed. And though they do not
occur in Arabia, Persia, Hindoostan, Siam, or China,
we find them in Madagascar, and in the Andaman
Islands; not in Java, Sumatra, or Borneo, but in the
Malay Peninsula, in the Phillippine Islands, New
Guinea, the New Hebrides, New Caledonia, the Fee-
jee Islands, and in Tasmania. This remarkable distribution is perhaps most easily explicable on the hypothesis that since the negroid race came into existence there must have been an immense tract of land
or a chain of islands stretching from the eastern coast
of Africa right across the Indian ocean; and secondly

that the sea then occupied the area of the present
great desert. In whatever manner, however, these
facts are to be explained, they certainly indicate that
the race is one of very great antiquity." " It is manifest," says Baldwin in his Pre-Historic Nations, "that
Africa at a remote period was the theatre of great
movements and mixtures of peoples and races, and
that its interior countries had then a closer connection with the great civilizations of the world than at
any time during the period called historical." It is
the opinion of this writer that the Cushite race—the
Ethiopians of Scripture—appeared first in the work
of civilization, and that in remote antiquity that people exerted a mighty and wide-spread influence in
human affairs, whose traces are still visible from farther India to Norway. Nor is he by any means
alone in the opinion that the Carthagenians, ages ago,
sent their ships across the Atlantic to the American
continent. The Cushites, or original Ethiopians originated in Arabia, but their descendents are still found
in northern Africa from Egypt to Morocco. Of this
race are the Tuariks, the robbers of the Great Desert,
to this day among the most magnificent specimens
of physcal man to be found anywhere on the globe.

The final solution of these problems of the geological status of Africa, and the great antiquity of man
can but be of the greatest interest to all thoughtful
persons. Unquestionably their solution will be greatly hastened, should Dr. Livingstone succeed in the
great enterprise upon which he is now engaged, and
soon make known to the world the true sources of the
Nile. His success therein would stimulate endeavor,

study, exploration, and, it is to be hoped, comprehensive and systematic surveys of a continent the evidences of whose civilization in remote ages lie buried
among the debris of countless centuries.

We know, from the imperfect investigations which
have already been made, that cities have been engulfed in the sands of Sahara. We know that vast
changes have taken place in the physical structure of
the continent of Africa and of the world since the
negro race first appeared. It is not improbable, therefore, that where for so many ages beasts of prey and
savage tribes have occupied a land oppressed with
heat and burdened with many ills, there may yet be
found evidences of former civilization and power in
greatest possible contrast to present barbarism and
national weakness. And who shall say that when the
face of the continent was changed, whether by a great
convulsion or by a gradual process, some of the people
did not migrate northward, cross the Mediterranean
and populate the continent which has since become the
abode of the highest civilization and the greatest intellectual culture? Who shall say that these races of
remote antiquity were not possessed of culture and
arts and literature placing them very high in the scale
of civilization? Within the historic period those nations have passed away which were the acknowledged
parents of modern culture and art. The power and
versatility of the human mind, reason, eloquence, and
poetry, were most sublimely illustrated by the Greeks,
whose works still remain to benefit and instruct mankind. Yet the freedom and power of this wonderful
people have for more than twenty centuries been an-

nihilated. The people, in the eloquent diction of Macaulay, have degenerated into timid slaves ; the language into a barbarous jargon; and the beautiful temples of Athens " have been given up to the successive depredations of Romans, Turks, and Scotchmen." The vast empire of Rome has passed entirely away within a few centuries. She had herself annihilated Carthage leaving nothing, as we have seen, of the arts, literature, or institutions of a people whose ships had sailed on every wave from the Hellespont to the Baltic, and, not improbably, from the Mediterranean to the delta of the Mississippi. Other great nations are also known to have passed away or been destroyed, the nature of their civilization and institutions being left to conjecture based upon a few monuments or a few literary remains preserved by foreign writers. It being once established that man existed ages before what is commonly called the beginning of the historic period it would be simply logical, considering many national destructions which have occurred during the historic period, to conclude by analogy that races of remote antiquity flourished and passed away leaving no sign, which has been yet discovered, of their power and civilization. It is evident the historian Macaulay thinks it not improbable such may be the fate of England, and he expressly states in a well-known passage that the time may come when only a single naked fisherman may be seen in the river of the ten thousand masts. It is difficult, if not impossible, for mankind entirely to overcome the tendency to decay.

We shall presently see that Africa is a field upon

which must soon be decided a great issue of politico-social importance ; an issue which involves the abolition of polygamy, domestic slavery, and the suppression of the foreign slave trade. From what has gone before in this volume, it will have been seen that here, too, are likely to be most conclusively demonstrated the vast age of the world, the great antiquity of man, and the nature of his origin. In comparison of the settlement of this issue and the solution of these problems of science, even the discovery of the true sources of the Nile may be regarded as unimportant, except for the reason that Dr. Livingstone's great achievement will arouse other men of science to similar sacrifices, labors, and fortitude. Thus Africa is found to present another remarkable contrast for our contemplation ; for while civilization is there at a lower ebb than in any other grand division of the globe, the highest intellectual efforts of the most astute thinkers of the times are turning their best efforts thitherward, in the confident hope of greatly enlarging the sphere of human knowledge, and of extending the triumphs of science and civilization.

There are many, it is true, who imagine that the scientific inquiries which are being made in regard to the great age of the world, the races which existed long anterior to the historic period, and the origin of the human species are founded in a spirit of skepticism and hostility to Christian civilization, or, rather, to Christianity as a religion. Doubtless there are many scientists who put no faith in Holy Writ, as much of it has been commonly understood. Others, and those among the most distinguished of men, are no less devout believers in Christianity than they are firm believers in the great age of the world and antiquity of man. The devotees of Christianity have in not a few instances mistaken an ally for an enemy This was notably the fact, in an example which is here most appropriate, in the case of the modern origin of the science of astronomy. The Christian church, as then existing, pronounced as religious heresy the plain truth that the world moves, and that the sun neither rises nor sets, but is stationary—the sublime centre of a universe of planets and stars, and, perhaps, inhabited worlds, whose movements must be controlled, as the vast system must have been originated, by One of infinite wisdom and power and goodness. In due course of time it was discovered that astronomy did not militate against Christianity, and the church not only ceased putting astronomers in prison, but learned that the acceptance of all truth, come from whatever source it may, is a Christian duty. And many of the most distinguished astronomers have been no less earnest exemplars of the Christian system of religion than any monk who ever wore the pavements of a monastery and left the world no wiser or better than he found it.

As it was with astronomy, so it has been even of late years with the science of geology. The era of imprisonment for heresy had indeed passed by when men began to construct a comprehensive science on the study of rocks ; but as their revelations became more extensive and more wonderful, it again appeared to many that here had arisen a formidable foe of Christianity, and the new science was assailed accordingly. It has not turned out that these disputants were as wise as they were zealous and as they were undoubtedly sincere. Though the sun never rises and never sets, we should be stupid indeed were we always, when speaking of his appearance on our horizon, or his disappearance therefrom, to state the fact in words of scientific accuracy. The world has never yet been slow enough justly to permit such waste of time and words. Not only the almanac-makers, but the most celebrated astronomers persist in saying that the sun rises and the sun sets. And, properly understood, it is perfectly true though scientifically false. To all appearance and for all practical purposes to the inhabitants of earth the sun does rise and set, and when one so says, whether inspired or uninspired, one simply conveys the idea that he intends to convey, and this is the province of language. As astronomy appeared to be utterly opposed by certain expressions in Scripture, but was found not to be, upon more liberal construction of the language, as well as more philosophical, so geology appeared to be, in its apparent demonstration of the vast age of the world, and, later, of the great antiquity of man, hostile to the received canons of the church, and especially subversive of the Mosaic account of creation and the generally received system of chronology. The conflicts thus arising have dissipated many erroneous theological constructions and dogmas, but they have in no manner affected the foundations of Christianity. There are many eminent geologists who are earnest Christians, and though Dr. Livingstone himself has done geology

Incalculable service he has done Christianity incalculably more. It may well be doubted whether any single theologian of the age has conferred more valuable service upon Christianity than Hugh Miller, the great geologist of Scotland, whose scientific works are, perhaps, the most fascinating of any in the English language.

There can be, then, no well-grounded fear of science overturning Christianity. It is more likely thereby to be in the end not only more thoroughly and correctly understood, but more firmly established and more generally adopted. Even the inquiry which is now receiving so much attention from men of thought—that into the origin of man—need not be deemed as fraught with any real danger to the system which has given the world its present civilization. Were it possible to establish Mr. Darwin's theory of evolution—and that it is more than a theory cannot be claimed for it by its most devoted advocate—and establish man's origin in the ape, still would the act of his creation into man from ape be an act of infinite power and goodness. For the infinite power and goodness of the act consist in the creation, by some means, of a being of intellectual and moral attributes. The act of divine power is in breathing into the nostrils the breath of life, and causing the being to become a living soul. Even Mr. Darwin will not dispute that the ape was in the long ages evolved from dust, nor that, so far as science has shown or probably ever can show, there is no being in the universe with capacity to evolve thought except only God, as shown in His manifold works, and man.

Whatever may be the result, therefore, of the interesting inquiries in commerce, religion, geography, geology, ethnology which now are being more and more directed toward Africa with each passing year, we may quite safely conclude, judging from the results of the past, that Christianity will come forth out of the conflicts that may arise, whether they be scientific or of other nature, with renewed beauty and power; with more liberal and enlightened views, doubtless, upon some questions which have been erroneously considered, but with greater influence on this account, and with brighter prospects of more speedily than might have been but for these conflicts extending the rule of her pure and beneficent morality among all the nations and tribes of men.

CHAPTER XXIII.

THE RESULTS OF THE EXPLORATIONS IN AFRICA.

The Result in Behalf of Science, Religion, and Humanity of the Explorations and Missionary Labors of Dr. Livingstone and Others in Africa—Review of Recent Discoveries in Respect to the People and the Physical Nature of the African Continent—The Diamond Fields of South Africa—Bird's-Eye View of that Division of the World—Its Capabilities and Its Wants— Christianity and Modern Journalism Dissipating Old Barbarisms, and Leading the Way to Triumphs of Civilization.

It would be difficult to estimate the result present and sure to come, in behalf of science, religion, and humanity, of the explorations and missionary labors of Dr. Livingstone and others in Africa during a period which embraces but little more than a quarter of a century. The manner in which Livingstone conducted his missionary labors has already been pointed out, but more with reference to their connection with peoples outside of Africa: with men of letters, of science, and of trade in the civilized world: than with reference to the natives themselves. Nevertheless, it is a fact that the Christian religion has nowhere in Africa been anything like so generally adopted, practiced, and honored by the natives as in the country of the Bakwains. And it was among the Bakwains that Dr. Livingstone performed his principal missionary work. Among that people only did he establish a permanent missionary station. There he had his home in Africa; there his children were

427

born. Unquestionably the labors of the Rev. Dr. Moffat, Dr. Livingstone's father-in-law, were of the highest importance in some respects. The scene of his studies was at Kuruman, several hundred miles to the southward of Kolobeng where Livingstone was stationed. He translated the Scriptures into the Bechuana language, travelled and preached over a wide domain in South Africa, and accomplished vast good. But it was Livingstone who infused into the spirit of Christian propagandism practical wisdom and the argument of present as well as future good. He is the Franklin of missionaries, having wonderful power in showing pagans that, even so far as their temporal affairs and material prosperity are concerned, the religion of Him of Nazareth is the best policy. Much has been accomplished at the "Gaboon Mission" as it has been called, on the east coast, but it may be said that the principal good is in the mitigation of the woes of the slave trade, which here, with the aid of nations which keep cruisers off the coast, has received, perhaps, a mortal wound. Nevertheless, the tribes of this coast are exceedingly depraved, drunken, and ignorant. They are universally idolatrous and given to disgusting superstitions and habits. Scarcely more than a hundred miles in the interior are tribes of cannibals, which are doubtless succeeded by others practicing the horrid orgies of man-eating across the continent to Tanganyika Lake. But with the great decrease in the slave trade has sprung up among all these people a wish to engage in legitimate commerce. With half the ideas of Christain civilization which have been instilled into the Bakwains of South Africa, these unhappy people would soon find ways and means to conduct a large trade in ebony, India-rubber, ivory, and other products of their country so much prized by commerce. Those who live on the coast have become somewhat skilful and daring in navigation, their little vessels, made of great trees hollowed out and pointed, making considerable coastwise voyages. Upon the arrival of a vessel on the coast, great numbers of these canoes, filled with natives, are constantly moving about from ship to shore, too often carrying off the miserable beings from the baracoons. This terrible traffic completely done with, they must perforce seek other means of trade; and these their country happily affords in great abundance.

The Makololo of central South Africa, so often mentioned in this volume, were greatly improved by the restless genius of the warrior-statesman Sebituane, whose remarkable career has been delineated in these pages. These people, possessing a country of great beauty and fertility along the valley of one of the most magnificent rivers of the world; possessing also vast herds of cattle and many villages and towns; and endued by nature with tractable dispositions and ambitious spirit, continue greatly to profit by the teachings and example of Dr. Livingstone. Related to the Bakwains and with them speaking the Bechuana language, Christian ideas are rapidly gaining adherents, so that it is but reasonable to expect that ere long, that vast extent of country from Cape Colony to Londa, between the eastern and western coast "shells" of South Africa will have come under the be-

nignant and progressive influences of Christian civilization.

The value of the results of Dr. Livingstone's explorations to science can hardly be overestimated. Geography, geology, botany, natural history, ornithology, have all recived new facts of value by his labors,
while the latest intelligence from him clearly points
to his speedy success, should his life be spared, in the
solution of that problem in geography which for
many years has elicited the studies of the learned
and the adventures of the adventurous.

But Dr. Livingstone has not been alone in giving
the world intelligence of the long unknown continent.
In the interest of commerce, England sent an expedition to central Africa in 1850 under Captain Richardson, with whom were associated Dr. Overweg and
the celebrated Dr. Barth, upon the latter of whom the
work of the mission devolved on account of the death
of both of his colleagues. The result was published
in a most elaborate work of which mention has been
made in the early pages of this volume. Dr. Barth traversed the African Sahara from north to south and
again from south to north, near the middle, passing
through Murzuk, the capital of Fezzan, Ghat, Tintel-
lust, the capital of Asben, Agades, and Katsena,
whence on the journey out Dr. Barth proceeded to
Kano, Messrs. Richardson and Overweg going to
Lake Tsad. Dr. Barth remained in Africa about five
years, exploring the country from east of Lake Tsad
to Timbuctoo. All this vast country is inhabited by
a remarkable people, or a variety of remarkable peoples, who are good horsemen, sustaining large armies,

chiefly of cavalry, adroit robbers, cruel, vindictive, having the worst form of domestic slavery, but who number many millions of souls; cultivate vast tracts of land, raising corn, rice, millet, tobacco, cotton, and other products; have many extensive towns and walled cities; carry on great operations in manufactures, trade, and mining; and are almost constantly at war: for the different states are independent of each other, each empire governed by its own sheik, the lesser sovereignties by sultans. The common religion of the people is that of Mahomet, but there are remnants of pagan tribes, some of which are even yet independent, and wage deadly war with their cruel oppressors. The country is well watered, and may be generally described as a vast plain, diversified only at wide distances by insulated mountains of no great height. In this expanse, the general name of which is Soudan, or Soodan (Berr es-Soodan, "Land of the Blacks"), the most celebrated city, perhaps, is Timbuctoo, which, from remote antiquity, has been the meeting-place of many caravans and converging lines of traffic. Sokato, or Sukatu, was formerly a city of 50,000 inhabitants, but has of late years decreased in importance. It is noted for its excellent manufactures of leather and iron, and its general markets, which always bring together great numbers of people and a wonderful variety of articles for sale. Kano, the capital of the province of Houssa, has a population of forty thousand souls. The city is surrounded by a wall of clay, thirty feet high, and more than fifteen miles in extent. Much of the enclosed space is occupied by gardens and cultivated fields. The cotton cloth woven and dyed at Kano is the chief article of commerce. The fine cotton fabrics of the Timbuctoo market are really manufactured at Kano. Dyed sheep-skins, sandals, ivory, the kola nut are largely exported. Kuka, the capital of Bornu, is near Lake Tsad, but is a small city of inconsiderable importance. Yola, the capital of Adamwa, is larger than Kuka. It was in this province that Dr. Barth discovered the Benue river, a navigable stream and the principal afflu- ent from the east of the Niger. There are many cities in this portion of Africa of far more importance than the capitals of Bornu and Adamwa. Polygamy is universally practiced, and there are probably more slaves than freemen throughout all the vast expanse between the equator and the Desert of Sahara, and Senegambia and Abyssinia.

In 1856, Captain Burton, whose " Pilgrimage to El Medinah and Mecca" (which he made in the disguise of a dervish) had just made a sensation in the read- ing world, explored, with the lamented Speke, a con- siderable portion of East Africa. The explorations of Grant and Speke in this portion of the continent were also of the greatest value. Thus was a knowl- edge of the expanse lying between Lake Nyassa, Tanganyika Lake, Victoria Nyanza and the Indian ocean made known to the world. The explorations of Sir Samuel Baker and others in search of the sources of the Nile are familiar to the intelligent public. At this moment there are at least two expe- ditions engaged in attempting to solve this interest- ing geographical problem, one, under the patronage of the Prince of Wales, the other under that of the

Khedive of Egypt. With this latter is a representative of the same American journal whose Search Expedition under Mr. Stanley discovered the great discoverer on the shores of Tanganyika. The most interesting and valuable series of explorations from the west coast of Africa which have been made of late years were those by Paul B. Du Chaillu, an American traveller and student whose work has been freely quoted from in this volume. His explorations embraced some three degrees of latitude and six of longitude near the equator. He penetrated far into the country of the gorilla and the cannibal, and his researches in respect of the people, animals, vegetation, and birds of this part of the continent are confessedly of great value to science.

Thus, if we consider the known portions of Africa at the time Dr. Livingstone began his first expedition of discovery, and compare them with the known portions of Africa at the time of the finding of Livingstone by the " Herald" expedition, we shall see that nearly all South Africa and much of East Africa has been explored by Livingstone himself; that Baker, Burton, Speke, Grant have added much to our knowledge of the supposed regions of the upper Nile and the "lake country" of East Africa; that Richardson and Barth have informed us of the true nature of the Desert of Sahara, the latter adding a vast fund of information in respect to north-central Africa; that Du Chaillu's explorations and direct information almost impinge upon the vast area, both upon the east and the south, explored by Dr. Livingstone. The unexplored regions of Africa, therefore, are now small in comparison of the regions explored and in regard to which trustworthy information has been gathered. Whereas, when Dr. Livingstone went to Africa, only the outer portions of the continent had been examined, the regions now unknown are a wide belt eastward of Lake Tsad; a considerable expanse south of Abyssinia; portions of the Desert of Sahara, and of Kalahari; and that expanse in equatorial Africa between the recent explorations of Livingstone among the supposed sources of the Nile and the eastern limit of Du Chaillu's journeys. It is true that these still unexplored regions embrace the most interesting portion of the continent and extend over an area several times larger than that of France, but in comparison of the portions of this great division of the earth which have now come under the view and the study of civilized man, they are but like a little cloud in a clear sky.

Within the long explored regions of South Africa a most important discovery in respect to commerce has recently been made. Reference can be had, of course, only to the discovery of the diamond fields of the Orange and Vaal rivers, some seven or eight hundred miles, by a traversable route, northeastward of Cape Town, but considerably nearer either Port Elizabeth in Cape Colony, or Port Natal on the east coast. Some twenty years ago, England abandoned the tract of country now known as the Orange River Free State, and it was occupied by emigrant Boers, some of whom also proceeded still farther north and established the Trans-Vaal Republic—a region over which Great Britain never had dominion. The Boers are generally supposed to be descendants of the Dutch colonists, but by some they are believed to be de scended of certain warlike North Germans, whom the Dutch employed to guard their distant settlements, giving them lavish grants of lands in return for their services. This latter opinion would seem to be substantiated by the fierce and warlike nature of the present race of Boers. The diamond fields commence near the junction of the Orange and Vaal rivers, and extend indefinitely up both those streams. The diamond region is described as "a desert country of bare rock and sand, far from the upland pastoral districts" where the Boers successfully conduct agricultural pursuits. The fields are reached by a journey of some eight hundred miles from Cape Town. The distance from Port Elizabeth is about five hundred miles; that from Port Natal about four hundred and fifty. By the Port Elizabeth route, the traveller passes over the Zumberg mountains, and over the Drakensberg range, should he start from Port Natal. By either route, the scenery is described as magnificent and calculated to put the traveller at once in love with the country. But the region between Port Natal and the diamond fields is more wild and desolate than that on either of the other routes, and great suffering is often experienced by the way.

The first South African diamond is said to have been found in March, 1867. The fortunate person was a Dutch farmer named Schalk Van Niekerk, who was struck with the appearance of a stone with which some children were playing. It turned out to be a genuine diamond, and was purchased by Sir Philip

Wodehouse, then governor of the Colony, for $2,500. In a short time the governor purchased several other fine and valuable stones. In May, 1869, the magnificent diamond "Star of South Africa" was discovered by a man named Swatbooy, near Sandfontein, on the Orange river. This was a diamond of eighty-three and a-half carats and was purchased for $56,500. Being cut, it produced a fine gem of forty-six and a-half carats, valued at $100,000. The finder of this diamond sold it for 500 head of sheep, 10 head of cattle, and a horse. In a single year since their discovery these fields have yielded more than five stones above forty carats. Professor Tennant thinks we shall have diamonds from South Africa exceeding the famous Koh-i-noor in size and equaling it in beauty when cut and polished. The Sultan of Matan, of the island of Borneo, has a diamond of the first water, weighing 367 carats, and worth at least $3,500,000. The Orloff diamond, belonging to the Czar of Russia, weighs 195 carats, but is worth only about $500,000 on account of being a little off color. It is not too credulous to believe that the diamond fields of South Africa may produce stones equal to these, and which will throw the fabulous "Moonstone," about which Wilkie Collins has written one of his most fascinating stories, completely in the shade.

These diamond fields have already been visited by great numbers of explorers, many of whom have been exceedingly lucky, while others had better remained at home. Astonishingly few scenes of lawlessness and violence have been witnessed, a fact which is owing to the peaceful nature of the Africans who do the most of the digging. The result of the discovery of this extraordinary diamond region was greatly to lower the price of rough diamonds for a season. It is not believed that the price will be permanently affected. Only about one tenth of the African diamonds are of the first water. The ordinary trade in diamonds had been about $800,000 a month—$400,000 from the mines of South America and India, and $400,000 from private parties. The increase from the South African fields has not yet been $100,000 a month, or anything like it on the average. The introduction of machinery and of capital to direct and control the workings, will doubtless add largely to the yield of these precious stones. Rubies are also found here in large numbers, but they are generally small. The probability of the discovery of gold also is very great.

Reflecting upon all these recent explorations and discoveries in Africa, how different would be a bird's eye view of that continent now from what it was when Dr. Livingstone first went ashore at Cape Town! The extreme southern portion of the continent is under the dominion of Great Britain. On the east and northeast are Natal and the Boer republics of Orange River and Trans-Vaal. Here, of course, we find a people not unlike the peasantry of Europe, with towns and cities and farms and manufactures and commerce. The political institutions are liberal, and popular education supported by the state, is becoming general. The original inhabitants of this region were the Hottentots, a race bearing more resemblance to the Mongols than to the negroes having broad foreheads, high cheek bones, oblique eyes, thin beards, and a yellow complexion. They are of a docile disposition, and quick intellectual perception. They were possessed of vast herds of cattle and large flocks of sheep, but were enslaved by the Dutch. Emancipated in 1833 by England, they are still found all over this region—still enslaved by the Boers in their so-called republics—and in small bodies here and there to a great distance in the interior. The Caffres, who inhabit the eastern portion of South Africa north of the British possessions, and form a large proportion of the population of the northern part of Cape Colony, are described by Livingstone as "tall, muscular, and well made; they are shrewd, energetic, and brave; altogether they merit the character given them by military authorities of being magnificent savages! Their splendid physical development and form of skull show that, but for the black skin and woolly hair, they would take rank among the foremost Europeans." Near the east coast of Africa the Caffres are brown or copper-colored. Their government is patriarchal, a petty chief presiding over each kraal or village, who is tributary to a higher chief, and these higher chiefs owe allegiance to the great chief, with whom they form the National Council. They live by hunting and raising cattle. Their women attend to the agriculture. They have no notion of a Supreme Being, but are exceedingly superstitious in respect to witches, spirits, and the shades of their ancestors. The missionary labors of more than forty years have made no

EXPLORATIONS IN AFRICA.

perceptible impression upon this stalwart race except
those who live under the British Colonial government, and these have only been partially won over
to civilization. Caffre women are described as superior in beauty to the other native races of South
Africa. Then, and farther to the left, still looking
northward, we have the Bushmen, who are described
by Livingstone as true nomads. Then we come
to the Griquas, an independent people north of the
Orange river. By Griquas is meant any mixed race
sprung from natives and Europeans. These are
of Dutch extraction through association with Hotten-
tot and Bushwomen. Many of these have adopted
Christianity. The human inhabitants of the Kalahari Desert are Bushmen and Bakalahari, the former
supposed to be the aborigines of Southern Africa,
the latter the remnants of the first emigration of
Bakwains. Both of these singular people are possessed of an intense love of liberty, but the Bushmen
live almost exclusively on wild animals, while the
Bakalahari have an irrepressible love of flocks of domestic animals. They procure a precarious existence
over the dry expanse of Kalahari. East of the Desert are the Bakwains, among whom Moffat and Livingstone labored. These, numbering many different
tribes, inhabit a large portion of Southern Africa,
and by their migrations under Sebituane, have for
a number of years also held a vast territory on the
Chobe and Zambesi rivers, north of Lake Ngami.
Many of the Southern tribes have embraced Christianity and all are noted for intelligence and the desire of progress. Between the Southern Bechuanas

and their relatives the Makololo are the Bamangwato
and the Bayeiye, the latter "the Quakers of Africa,"
who do not believe in fighting. The former are sufficiently savage and indolent. They live round
about Lake Ngami. To the westward of Kalahari
and as far northward as the country under Portuguese dominion we observe a region possessing
many fertile tracts. A wide expanse is called Nam-
aqua Land, and is sparsely inhabited by Hottentots among whom live a few Dutch. Northward of
these are the Damaras, whose domains extend far
into the interior, but of whom little is known. Far
up the east coast extends the country of Mozambique,
long known to geography. Near the middle of this
country the waters of the Zambesi empty into the
Indian ocean. Far up this stream we find many
tribes of ignorant men, all polygamous, but none, until we reach the watershed of central South Africa,
devoted to disgusting fetiches. There, where the
country is for a vast distance an immense flat, with a
river, part of whose sluggish waters seek outlet in the
Atlantic and part in the Indian ocean, we see negroes
of the most savage nature and the most degrading
superstitions. And as we cast our vision westward
toward the Portuguese colony of Angola, we find them
becoming more and more degraded, through the immense territory of the Balonda, until we reach the
magnificent valley of the Quango, and begin to perceive the beneficent effects of civilization, even though
its representatives have not been of the best. We
shall look in vain over the whole expanse of Lower
Guinea for notable prospects cheering to the cause of

man's advancement. Then extending our vision northward and eastward over what may for convenience sake be called the equatorial region of Africa, we shall observe great lakes and rivers on the east, the lakes scarcely less great in surface extent than those of interior North America, while at the west we perceive extensive rivers, and immense forests. Here the nobler wild animals do not live, but repulsive apes and cannibals possess the gloomy shade of the vast wilderness. Near the eastern portion of this expanse the great explorer of Africa is at this time engaged in traversing that now most interesting portion of the globe whence spring the sources of the Nile. Still farther north, and extending nearly across the continent, we see an immense territory crowded with a commercial, trading people, whose cities have been noted for ages through the reports of caravans which have brought their goods and gold across the great desert to the Mediterranean sea. On the right of the desert we find Abyssinia, Nubia, and Egypt. The desert itself is seen to have many oases, stately mountains, and in places a growth of singular trees. Its caravans are sometimes submerged by the terrible simoon; but the robbers of the desert are more cruel and destructive than the winds and sands. On the north of Sahara we see the countries bordering on the Mediterranean, where in ancient times the great rival of Rome exercised supreme authority, which was doubtless wrested from Carthage in a calamity to mankind. To the westward of this famous seat of ancient empire, the French now have a numerous and prosperous colony. Still farther westward and look-

ing out upon the pillars of Hercules, live the remnants of that singular people who once possessed a
large part of Spain, and whose melancholy fate has
been rendered wonderfully interesting to the intelligent of all lands by the great and tender genius of
our American Irving. The descendants of the old
possessors of Granada, the builders of the Alhambra,
may now be found in northwestern Africa, and penetrating deeply into the regions of the Desert, with
little to suggest the ancient taste, and culture, and
warlike prowess. With the exception of Liberia, and
the English, Portuguese, Dutch, and French colonies,
and of late some of the Backwains who have become
Christianized, the people of whom we are taking this
rapid view are devoted to polygamy. As it exists
throughout nearly the whole of the vast continent it
is both a social and a political institution. Of all
these people, perhaps those only who are actually
progressive are the Bakwains, under Sechele, the Makololo, under Sekeletu, successor to the greatest of
South African chieftains, Sebituane, some of the colonists of extreme South Africa, and a province or two
of central West Africa.

Confining our view now to the physical aspect of
Africa, we perceive that the four great rivers are the
Nile, the Zambesi, the Quango, or Congo, and the
Niger. The Orange river of the south is of less magnitude, as is the Senegal of the west. Of these, the
Nile is the greatest and most interesting, the most
interesting river, perhaps, of the world. The Niger
drains much of western and central Africa, and with
its affluents forms a system of drainage for an in

mexse empire. The Quango is the principal river of central South Africa, but between it and the Niger are the Gaboon and the Fernand Vas with their many affluents. The Zambesi is seen to drain a region many times larger than Great Britain. The Orange with its affluents is at least equal to the Ohio in the United States. All these rivers, with the exception of the Nile, force their way through mountains which reach in almost unbroken range around the continent from Abyssinia southwestward to Cape Colony, then northwestward to Senegambia, whence they shoot off in broken fragments over the Desert of Sahara.

The northern half of Africa is chiefly Mohammedan, the southern half chiefly pagan. In the north we have sheikhs, khedives, sultans, harems, intrigues, treachery, vindictivenes, and tortures. In the south we have man-eating, superstitions, fetiches, degradation, but, unquestionably as I think, very much less of man's inhumanity to man. North and south, except where the English have control, domestic slavery exists in its most cruel forms, but nowhere in the world has it ever existed, perhaps, in such monstrous shape of iniquity as in central Africa under the rule of Islamism. Dr. Barth accompanied the sheikh of Bornoo on a predatory (slave-catching) expedition into the Musgu country on one occasion. He thus relates the principal business of a single day:

"The village we had just reached was named Kakala, and is one of the most considerable places in the Musgu country. A large number of slaves had been caught this day, and in the course of the evening, after some skirmishing, in which three Bornoo horsemen were killed, a great many more were brought in; altogether they were said to have taken one thousand, and there were certainly not less than five hundred. To our utmost horror, not less than one hundred and seventy full-grown men were mercilessly slaughtered in cold blood, the greater part of them being allowed to bleed to death, a leg having been severed from the body."

The number of "slaves" (that is, free persons captured) on this expedition was about 4,000, of whom nearly 1,000, being full-grown men, were disposed of in the horrible manner above described.

—Those who have read the preceding pages can hardly help arriving at the conclusion that the capabilities and the wants of Africa are very great. Leaving out those portions of the continent which were known when Dr. Livingstone first reached South Africa, we find that there have since been discovered lakes, rivers, mountains, regions abounding in precious stones and metals, vast fertile plains, forests rich in valuable trees and vines, animals producing rare articles of commerce, peoples rude indeed and degraded, but neither cruel by nature, vindictive, nor revengeful. Many of them are magnificent specimens of mankind, so far as physical nature is concerned, while a great majority of them are far above that which is too generally considered the typical African. They are by no means wanting in intellectual powers; and their almost universal love of children must be regarded as a most admirable and redeeming trait. Even the cannibals of the equatorial regions are unq uestionably less cruel and infinitely less treacherous than the Mohammedans of north Central Africa, while the numerous tribes of Bakwains and Makololo are for the most part by nature gentlemen; brave, magnanimous, and reasonable. The Bakalahari are a pastoral people; and those who are fond of both children and flocks cannot be irreclaimably depraved. Over a large part of South Africa, idolatry is unknown; and skepticism is a much less powerful antagonist of Christian civilization than fetiches.

These people have many navigable rivers, vast extents of arable lands, large numbers of domestic animals, and some of them are wonderfully skilful in the manufacture of certain fabrics and tools. Perhaps it is hardly too much to say that the Fans (cannibals) of equatorial Africa are the best blacksmiths in the world.

There can be little doubt that many of these people would have adopted Christian civilization before this time but for polygamy. As has been said a moment ago this is both a social and political institution. The more wives a chief has the more fathers-in-law, the more friends, and consequently the more influence. We have seen how this long kept the chief Sechele from espousing Christianity. It appeared to his generous nature like a cruelty to return his supernumerary "wives." It is difficult to see how any general progress can be made toward the adoption of Christian civilization by these people until this institution shall have been destroyed.

The abolition of domestic slavery is one of the greatest wants of the continent. In no part of pagan

Africa is this inhuman system upheld by such barbarous practices as in many large portions under the
sway of Islamism. In pagan Africa the captives of
war are made slaves, but the adult males are not
mangled and slain. Throughout a great extent of
Mohammedan Africa the system of slavery is upheld
by nameless atrocities in gratification of the terrible
cruelty and scarcely less terrible lust of the most
cruel and lustful people. The legend of Legree in
Mrs. Stowe's celebrated novel of "Uncle Tom's Cab-
in" is a pleasant fable in comparison of many acts
pertaining to African domestic slavery of which
truthful accounts might be given. It might appear
that time is necessary to prepare a people so cruel
for the reception of Christian civilization. The Boers
of South Africa are exceedingly hard task-masters
with their slaves, compelling them to do a great deal
of hard labor and drudgery, but they have not been
charged with blood-thirstiness.

This wide-spread system of domestic slavery is, of
course, an important ally of the foreign slave trade
but the slave trade is in some respects a wrong and
unutterable woe of itself. There is a certain introna-
tional slave trade, if we may so speak, in Africa,
carried on between tribes which are independent of
each other. The importance of a chief is often estimated by the number of his slaves and wives. Now
that the recent explorations of white men have made
intercourse between tribes of more frequent occurrence than formerly, a rude diplomacy has sprung
up, which is chiefly exercised in matters pertaining
to slaves and the purchase of wives. A chief

strengthens himself at home by marrying as many of the daughters of his "head men" as he can, and among other tribes by the same course among them. A large number of slaves adds to the consideration in which he is held at home and abroad. Thus polygamy, domestic slavery, and the foreign slave trade are the great obstacles which stand in the way of civilizing the continent of the black man. And of these the greatest obstacle is the foreign slave trade. This, not only because of its own cruelty, fearful wrongfulness, and hideous practices, but because it gives the black man a fairly unanswerable practical argument against civilization. Dr. Livingstone expressly tells us, in letters which we have quoted, that the practices of the slave-traders are more horrible and cruel than even those of the man-eating Manyema. Is it to be expected that the natives of Africa will adopt a system which, so far as they see, is more cruel than the most horrible customs of their most degraded tribes? Those Africans only who have to any considerable extent adopted Christain civilization live at the greatest distance from the scenes of the foreign slave trade.

The first great want of Africa, therefore, is the suppression of the slave trade. This has been to great extent accomplished on the West Coast. It has not been accomplished on the East Coast because of the neglect of the British government. Not long since Zanzibar was visited by a terrible hurricane, whose destructive fury laid waste its shipping, its houses, and scattered death and desolation over a wide expanse. The affliction was very great, and grievous to be borne. The slave trade of Zanzibar is almost infinitely more cruel than the remorseless elements. Its speedy suppression is demanded by the united cries of Christianity and humanity. It is the undoubted duty of the government of Great Britain to heed this demand, and put an end to the woes which exist through the cupidity of British subjects and the inefficiency of British officials at Zanzibar.

The other great wants of Africa are the abolition of domestic slavery and the destruction of the system of polygamy. To accomplish these great objects will be no easy achievement, nor one, it is believed, which can be speedily brought about. It certainly can be done the more easily and the more speedily after the suppression of the foreign slave trade. Until that be done, it is simply impossible. That having first been brought about, the national characteristic of all African peoples will be found, it is confidently believed, to form an element of vast power in bringing the continent under the sway of civilization. That characteristic is the love of trade. It is another of the singular anomalies of this division of the world, that while it is, upon the whole, the least commercial of all, the people are natural traders. They are universally fond of barter. This may be called the African idiosyncrasy. Taking advantage of it, with his inculcations of religious truth, Dr. Livingstone's labors at the time and afterwards were crowned with magnificent success. Those of his co-laborers who have succeeded have pursued the same plan. Thus throughout a vast expanse have slavery and polygamy passed

away, and the institutions of Christian civilization
been adopted in their stead by a people naturally intelligent, progressive, and brave.

Christianity and modern journalism ought, therefore, to unite in urging commerce to clasp hands with
religion for the purpose of making a common triumph
for trade and civilization over the vast continent
much of which has so long sat in darkness. There,
surely, are the foundations upon which a mighty
commerce may be built; there, beyond question, is a
vast field in which the labors of Christian propagan-
dists have much to engage them, and much to encourage great zeal and self-denial. Journalism and
Christianity thus succeeding in making a firm and
earnest ally of Commerce, cannot help leading the
way, in the good time of Heaven's providence, to
most gratifying triumphs of civilization; so that the
gloom and misery of centuries shall be dispelled, and
even Ethiopia shall soon stretch out her hands unto
GOD.

29

CHAPTER XXIV.

THE LAST JOURNEY, AND THE DEATH OF DR. LIVINGSTONE.

Dr. Livingstone anxiously awaits the Recruits and Supplies sent by Mr. Stanley—
On their arrival sets out Southwestward on his Last Journey—Reaches
Kisera, where Chronic Dysentery seizes him—He refuses to yield; but
pushes on, till Increasing Debility compels him to stop and retrace his
steps—He sinks rapidly, and on May 4th Breathes his Last—His attendants
take Necessary Precautions to Insure the Return of the Corpse to England—
Letter from Mr. Holmwood, Attaché of the British Consulate at Zanzibar.

It will be recollected that Stanley bade Dr. Livingstone farewell on the 14th of March, 1872, at Kwihara,
and that, on his arrival at Zanzibar, he sent back to
Dr. Livingstone the men and means he had expressed
a wish for [see page 299].

From some unexplained cause, this party of recruits,
with their stores, was exceedingly slow in reaching
Dr. Livingstone. According to the account given
Mr. Stanley by Dr. Livingstone's body-servant, Jacob
Wainwright, after the funeral, in London, "The Doctor
expressed great joy, when he at last saw the caravan
of freemen for which he had been anxiously waiting,
before the resumption of his explorations." After
allowing them a few days' rest at Unyanyembe, Dr.
Livingstone and his party started on his last exploring
journey. They traveled southwest by way of Kasa-
gera and Kigandu to Kisera, a district ruled by King
Simba. Here the Doctor had a relapse of his old
malady, the Chronic Dysentery, which so weakened

him that he was compelled to take to riding a donkey. He did not yet regard the attack as dangerous, and accordingly pursued his march, still southwestward, to Mpathwa, and thence into the valley of the Rungwa, where he found many boiling springs; thence he pressed on through Ufipa and Uemba (or Uremba), to Margunga. In the marshes of Uemba (or Uremba) one of their two donkeys died. Traveling along the Moungo, they reached the district called Kawendi, where a lion killed the remaining donkey. Thenceforward, the Doctor, getting daily weaker, had to be borne in a *kitanda* (a native bed resembling a hammock); he still refused to yield, but urged his party on till they came to the head-waters which empty themselves into Lake Bangweolo. Here they made use of Stanley's boat, which they had carried a distance of eleven hundred miles. They crossed the Chambezi, and attempted to push their way along the southern shore to Lake Bangu, and toward the Fountains of Herodotus, reported to be at Katanga (Katanda?), where he hoped to pause and recruit his health. Perceiving, however, how rapidly he was growing weaker, he determined to hasten back to Unyanyembe, and accordingly at last turned his face northward; but on arriving at Kitumbo, he seemed suddenly to realize that his last hour was drawing near, and he tried to stop there, but the chief refused to permit it, and he was forced to proceed farther north toward Kibende. On their arrival at a small village in the district of Mullala, his tent was pitched, and he was placed therein. But, fearing the heat of the sun, he directed that a hut should be built for him "to die in." This was done, and he was carefully removed to it. His last entry in his diary is dated April 27th, 1873, thirteen months and thirteen days after his parting from Mr. Stanley, and in that entry he records his extreme illness and his inability to proceed farther. After this, he seems to have resolutely prepared for the great journey of death.

The boy Majwara states that, during the intervals between the paroxysms of extreme pain, the doctor prayed constantly for his family, and frequently uttered the word "home!" After his being placed in his hut, Dr. Livingstone would permit no one to stay with him except Majwara, and occasionally Susi, though the rest each morning called and greeted him with the customary words "Yambo, bana!" ("Good-morning, master!")

Majwara, on the last morning, made some tea for the Doctor and administered stimulants, which appeared to have no effect. At about midnight of May 1st, Dr. Livingstone quietly breathed his last.

The next morning, the faithful attendants held a consultation as to what was to be done with the remains. Their movements had to be kept very secret, because, if the fact of the death were discovered by the natives, there was reason to fear that their superstitions would lead them to prevent the removal of the corpse.

Fargalla, one of the men sent by Mr. Stanley, then disemboweled the body, and, after leaving the village a safe distance, they hung it in the sun for five days, to dry it thoroughly, after which they packed it carefully in bark.

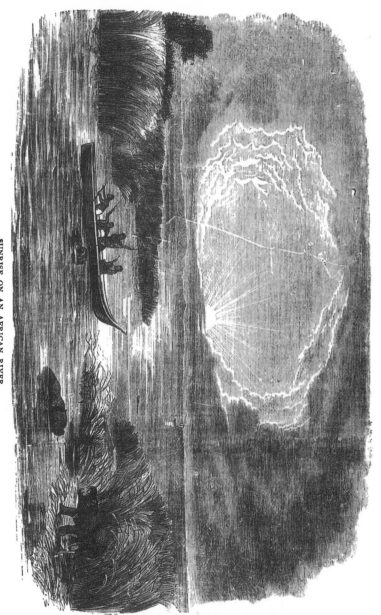

SUNRISE ON AN AFRICAN RIVER.

These steps were taken with the view the better to carry out their determination of sending the body home to England. After the heart and intestines had been carefully removed, a solemn funeral service was held, and they were committed to the earth, Jacob Wainwright officiating as leader in the religious ceremonies.

They then set out on their long journey to Unyanyembe, a journey which consumed six weary months, owing to repeated attempts of natives to bar their march, which necessitated much loss of time in pursuing circuitous routes.

Meanwhile, the fourth Search and Relief Expedition arrived at Zanzibar in February, 1873. This expedition was under the leadership of Lieutenants Murphy and Cameron and Dr. Dillon, and had been sent out by the Royal Geographical Society. Sir Bartle Frere was then at Zanzibar endeavoring to forward the efforts of the Government to suppress the slave trade, in response to the earnest representations of Dr. Livingstone. He rendered the expedition such aid as he could, and it proceeded to Unyanyembe, where it arrived in August. In October, a messenger brought in the sad news of Dr. Livingstone's death. Dr. Dillon, who was sick, with Lieut. Murphy, soon after started to return from their expedition, but at Kasegera Dr. Dillon, under a temporary attack of insanity, committed suicide.

Leaving to the ensuing chapter the notes of the homeward voyage of the party who bore Dr. Livingstone's remains to England, we cannot better close this chapter than by copying an interesting letter from

Mr. Holmwood, the British Vice-Consul at Zanzibar, to Sir Bartle Frere, then the President of the Royal Geographical Society. We have already given the substance of the information, as detailed by Jacob Wainwright, but the letter is interesting enough to justify its insertion, notwithstanding the repetitions and occasional apparent discrepancies.

"ZANZIBAR, March 12, 1874.

"MY DEAR SIR BARTLE—No doubt you will hear from several interested in Dr. Livingstone; but, as I do not feel sure that any one has thoroughly examined the men who came down with his remains, I briefly summarize what I have been able to glean from a careful cross-examination of Majwara, who was always at his side during his last days, and Susi, as well as the Nassick boys, have generally confirmed what he says. I inclose a small sketch-map, merely giving my idea of the locality, and have added a dotted line to show his route during this last journey of his life.

"The party sent by Stanley left Unyanyembe with the Doctor about the end of August, 1872, and marched straight to the south of Lake Tanganyika, through Ufipa, crossing the Rungwa River, where they met with natural springs of boiling water, bubbling up high above the ground. On reaching the Chambezi or Kambezi River, they crossed it about a week's journey from Lake Bemba, also crossing a large feeder; but by Susi's advice Livingstone again turned northward, and recrossed the Kambezi, or Luapula, as he then called it, just before it entered the lake.

"He could not, however, keep close to the north

shore of Lake Bemba, owing to the numerous creeks and streams, which were hidden in forests of high grass and rushes. After making a detour, he again struck the lake, at a village where he got canoes across to an island in the centre, called Matipa. Here the shores on either hand were not visible, and the Doctor was put to great straits by the natives declining to let him use their canoes to cross to the opposite shore. He therefore seized seven canoes by force, and when the natives made a show of resistance he fired his pistol over their heads, after which they ceased to obstruct him. Crossing the lake diagonally, he arrived in a long valley; and the rains having now set in fully, the caravan had to wade rather than walk, constantly crossing blind streams, and, in fact, owing to the high rushes and grass, hardly being able to distinguish at times the land, or rather what was generally dry land, from the lake.

"Dr. Livingstone had been weak and ailing since leaving Unyanyembe; and when passing through the country of Ukabende, at the southwest of the lake, he told Majwara (the boy given him by Stanley, who is now in my service) that he felt unable to go on with his work, but should try and cross the hills to Katanga (Katanda?) and there rest, endeavoring to buy ivory, which in all this country is very cheap (three yards of *merikani* buying a slave or a tusk), and returning to Ujiji through Manuema to recruit and reorganize.

"But as he approached the northern part of Bisa (a very large country), arriving in the province of Ulala, he first had to take to riding a donkey, and then

suffer himself to be carried on a *kitanda* (native bed-
stead), which at first went much against the grain.
During this time he never allowed the boy Majwara
to leave him, and he then told that faithful and honest
fellow that he should never cross the high hills to Katanda. He called for Susi, and asked how far it was
to the Luapula, and on his answering 'three days'
remarked 'he should never see his river again.'

"On arriving at Ilala, the capital of the district,
where Kitambo the Sultan lived, the party were refused permission to stay, and they carried Livingstone
three hours' march back toward Kabende. Here they
erected for him a rude hut and fence, and he would
not allow any to approach him for the remaining days
of his life except Majwara and Susi, except that every
morning they were all desired to come to the door
and say 'Good-morning!'

"During these few days he was in great pain, and
could keep nothing, even for a moment, on his stomach.
He lost his sight so far as hardly to be able to distinguish when a light was kindled, and gradually sank
during the night of the 4th of May, 1873. Only Majwara was present when he died, and he is unable to
say when he ceased to breathe. Susi, hearing that he
was dead, told Jacob Wainwright to make a note in
the Doctor's diary of the things found by him. Wainwright was not quite certain as to the day of the
month; and as Susi told him the Doctor had last written
the day before, and he found this entry to be dated
27th April, he wrote 28th April; but, on comparing
his own diary on arrival at Unyanyembe, he found it
to be the 4th of May; and this is confirmed by Maj-

wara, who says Livingstone was unable to write for the last four or five days of his life. I fancy the spot where Livingstone died is about 11.25 degrees south and 27 degrees east; but, of course, the whole of this is subject to correction, and, although I have spent many hours in finding it all out, the Doctor's diary may show it to be very imperfect.

"I fear you will find this a very unconnected narration, but my apology must be that the Consul-General is not well, and the other assistant absent on duty, and there is much work for me to do. Mr. Arthur Laing has been entrusted with the charge of the remains and diaries, which latter he has been instructed to hand to Lord Derby.

"Trusting that you are in the enjoyment of good health, and with great respect, believe me, dear Sir Bartle, your most obedient servant,

"FREDERICK HOLMWOOD.

"To the Right Hon. Sir BARTLE FRERE, K. C. B., G. C. S. I., etc., President of the Royal Geographical Society."

CHAPTER XXV.

THE CORPSE BORNE TO ENGLAND AND LAID IN WEST-
MINSTER ABBEY.

The body of Dr. Livingstone borne to Unyanyembe by his attendants, and
thence to Zanzibar—The British Consul-General sends it, with the Doctor's
Papers, Books, etc., to England—Arrival at Southampton, and at London—
The People vie in Tributes of Respect—The Funeral—The Grave in Westminster Abbey.

FROM the point where Dr. Livingstone died to Unyanyembe was a distance of upward of one thousand
miles; this the Doctor's faithful attendants traversed
with his remains, frequently having to diverge materially from the road to circumvent hostile demonstrations of parties of natives. Six toilsome months
were consumed in the journey, and the month of
November had opened ere they reached Unyanyembe.
Thence, after a pause, they bore their precious burden
to Zanzibar, where they arrived in February, 1874,
and delivered the corpse and the Doctor's personal
effects (including his Diary, papers, etc.) into the custody of the British Consul-General, who immediately
shipped them, in care of Mr. Arthur Laing, for England. Among those who accompanied the body was
Jacob Wainwright, Dr. Livingstone's body-servant.
At Aden, the steamer *Malwa,* which had been sent
out by the British Government, met them, and the
party were transferred to her.

On the 15th of April, the *Malwa* arrived at Southampton, and at eleven o'clock landed the party, with the corpse, at the Royal Pier, in the presence of a vast concourse of people, estimated at upward of fifty thousand, business having been suspended, and all classes of the people having come to testify their respect for the illustrious dead. The Mayor formally received the remains, and they were borne to the railway station, accompanied by the assembled thousands, while minute guns were fired and the bells tolled. The scene was very impressive. The remains were thence carried to London by rail, and, arriving there at three o'clock, p. m., were taken in charge by the Royal Geographical Society, who had the coffin transferred to a hearse, and taken to their rooms, followed by a numerous line of carriages and a large number of persons afoot. Here the corpse was viewed by Sir William Ferguson in the presence of Drs. Kirk and Loudon, Rev. Dr. Moffat and others, the object being to identify the remains and to remove all possibility of cavil as to their being those of Dr. Livingstone. The result can best be told in Sir William Ferguson's own words, and hence we insert his letter to *The London Lancet:*

"Within the last few months, many have hesitated to believe that Livingstone was dead. Above all, it seemed beyond ordinary probability that his remains would have been brought from Central Africa to the heart of London. That a body was on its way from this all but mythical region could hardly be doubted after the examination at Zanzibar of the remains, but many were skeptical as to this dead frame being that of Livingstone. Happily it was borne in mind by many old friends that he had one condition of body which would mark the identification of his remains, even if years and years had elapsed. If it should be proved on anatomical examination that the remains of an old ununited fracture in his left humerus (arm bone) could be recognized, all doubt on the subject would be settled at once and for ever. It has fallen to my lot to have the honor of being selected to make the crucial examination to this end, and I have accordingly performed that duty. From what I have seen I am much impressed with the ingenious manner in which those who have contrived to secure that the body should be carried through the long distance from where Livingstone died, until it could reach a place where transit was comparatively easy, accomplished their task. The lower limbs were so severed from the trunk that the length of the bulk of package was reduced to a little over four feet. The soft tissues seem to have been removed to a great extent from the bones, and these latter were so disposed that, by doubling and otherwise, the shortening was accomplished. The abdominal viscera were absent, and so were those of the chest, including, of course, heart and lungs. There had been made a large opening in front of the abdomen, and through that the native operators had ingeniously contrived to remove the contents of the chest as well as of the abdomen. The skin over the chest, sternum and ribs had been untouched. Before these points were clearly ascertained some coarse tapes had to be loosened, which set free some rough linen material—a striped colored bit of cotton

Encampment in the Forest.

cloth, such as might have been an attractive material
for the natives among whom Livingstone traveled—a
coarse cotton shirt, which doubtless belonged to the
traveler's scanty wardrobe, and in particular a large
portion of the bark of a tree, which had formed the
principal part of the package—the case thereof no
doubt. The skin of the trunk, from the pelvis to the
crown of the head, had been untouched. Everywhere
was that shriveling which might have been expected
after salting, baking in the sun, and eleven months of
time. The features of the face could not be recognized. The hair on the scalp was plentiful, and much
longer than he wore it when last in England. A
moustache could not be recognized, but whiskers were
in abundance. The forehead was in shape such as
we are familiar with from memory, and from the pictures and busts now extant. The circumference of
the cranium, from the occiput to the brow, was 23⅝
inches, which was recognized by some present to be
in accordance with the measurement when alive.
In particular, the arms attracted attention. They lay
as if placed in ordinary fashion, each down by the
side. The skin and tissues under were on each side
shrunk almost to skeleton bulk, and at a glance to
practiced eyes—there were five, I may say six, professional men present—the state of the left arm was
such as to convince every one present who had examined it during life, that the limb was Livingstone's.
Exactly in the region of the attachment of the deltoid
to the humerus, there were the indications of an
oblique fracture. On moving the arm, there were the
indications of the ununited fracture. A closer inves-

tigation and dissection displayed the false joint which had long ago been so well recognized by those who had examined the arm in former days. The Rev. Dr. Moffat, and in particular Dr. Kirk, late of Zanzibar, and Dr. Loudon, of Hamilton, in Scotland, at once recognized the condition. Having myself been consulted regarding the state of the limb when Livingstone was last in London, I was convinced that the remains of the great traveler lay before us. Thousands of heads with a like large circumference might have been under similar scrutiny; the skeletons of hundreds of thousands might have been so; the humerus in each might have been perfect; if one or both had been broken during life it would have united again in such a manner that a tyro could easily have detected the peculiarity. The condition of ununited fracture in this locality is exceedingly rare. I say this from my personal professional experience, and that such a specimen should have turned up in London from the centre of Africa, excepting in the body of Dr. Livingstone, where it was known by competent authorities to have existed, is beyond human credibility. It must not be supposed by those who are not professionally acquainted with this kind of lesion— which often causes so much interest to the practical surgeon—that a fracture and new joint of the kind now referred to could have been of recent date or made for a purpose. There were in reality all the indications which the experienced pathologist recognizes as infallible, such as the attenuated condition of the two great fragments (common under such circumstances), and the semblance of a new joint, but actually there was a small fragment detached from the others which bore out Livingstone's own view that the bones had been 'crushed into splinters.' Having had ample opportunity of examining the arm during life, and conversing with Livingstone on the subject, and being one of those who entertained hopes that the last reports of Livingstone's death might, like others, prove false, I approached the examination with an anxious feeling regarding this great and most peculiar crucial test. The first glance at the left arm set my mind at rest, and that, with the further examination, made me as positive as to the identity of these remains as that there has been among us in modern times one of the greatest men of the human race—David Livingstone."

On Saturday, the 18th of April, all that was mortal of the great missionary-explorer was consigned to its last resting-place in Westminster Abbey. The funeral procession started at about ten o'clock from the Rooms of the Royal Geographical Society, and was participated in by an immense number of people of all ranks in life. The cortege included the hearse and twelve mourning coaches, and the private carriages of the Queen, the Prince of Wales, the German Ambassador, Baroness Burdett-Coutts, Lady Franklin and many others. The pall-bearers were Mr. Stanley, Jacob Wainwright, Sir Thomas Steele, W. C. Oswell, W. F. Webb, Dr. Kirk, Rev. H. Waller, Mr. Young, Rev. F. Steele and Kalulu (the African boy brought home by Stanley). Among the mourners, we may note the Duke of Sutherland, Lord Houghton (the poet), the Duke of Manchester, the Bishops of Lincoln and Sierra Leone, the Lord Mayor and Corporation of London, Lord Shaftesbury (the philanthropist), Colonel Grant (the explorer), Mr. Moran (the American Secretary of Legation), Sir Bartle Frere, Sir H. Rawlinson, Sir Rutherford Alcock, Rev. Dr. Moffat, Dr. Lyon Playfair, Lord Lawrence, Sir F. Buxton, Hon. Arthur Kinnaird, Admiral Sir William Hall, Sherard Osborn, Codrington and Ommaney, of the British Navy, besides deputations from the various learned societies, and from Glasgow, Edinburgh and Hamilton, together with other men of eminence too numerous to recapitulate. The procession did not enter the Abbey till past one o'clock, and long before that hour every available space in the vicinity of the grave was occupied, and there were persons even in the clerestory.

"Five minutes past one, Dean Stanley, in his full robes, with a purple cap on his head, and the red ribbon of the Order of the Bath, of which he is chaplain, round his neck, is standing at the door of the west nave, attended by the Sub-Dean and Canons, waiting for the body. Now we see the procession slowly filing through the cloisters.

"First come the silver mace-bearers, then the choristers, then the coffin, of brightly polished oak, in which the metal shells have been enclosed. On the brass plate is the inscription,

DAVID LIVINGSTONE,
Born at Blantyre, Lanarkshire, Scotland,
19th March, 1813.
Died at Mullala, Central Africa,
4th May, 1873.

and the lid is covered with wreaths of white camellias and branches of palm."

The solemn and impressive service of the English Church was effectively conducted by Dean Stanley, assisted by the Sub-Dean and Canons; it was choral throughout. The entire effect was grand in its solemn intensity.

The grave is in the centre of the west part of the nave, in close proximity to those of Telford and Stephenson, the engineers, Sir James Outram and General Wade, the soldiers, and other men of eminence in various lines of service. It is in a spot cheered with sunshine, and during the funeral service it was illumined with a ray of sunlight which, passing through the superb stained-glass memorial window erected to the memory of Brunel, the engineer of the Thames Tunnel and the Saltash Viaduct, had a fine effect. The grave is shallow, owing to the fact that the soil is too sandy to admit of digging deep.

The words "Dust to dust, ashes to ashes" having been pronounced and the service closed, the people dispersed slowly and with a solemnity that seemed to betoken a sense of personal loss.

One fact was evident throughout all the doings of the three days, from the time of the landing at Southampton, to the close of the ceremonies in Westminster Abbey—and that was that the deceased explorer-missionary had won the respect, the esteem, nay, the love, of all classes, from the Royal household to the humblest of the people.

Nor are these sentiments confined to the people of the British Empire; all nations and peoples of the Christian world share in them. And in no part of the world are these feelings warmer and stronger

than in the United States. As a partial evidence
of this, we may allude to the immense meeting in
New York on the 23d of April. The spacious Acad-
emy of Music proved far too small to admit the thousands who sought entrance. The warmly eulogistic
addresses of Chief Justice Daly, Rev. Dr. Adams,
Henry Ward Beecher, Dr. I. I. Hayes (the Arctic explorer), the Rev. Dr. Schenck and others, met with
the hearty endorsement of those who were fortunate
enough to gain admittance. And outside of New
York and among those who could not attend the
meeting, the feeling is no less sincere. This universal
sentiment is attributable not so much to Dr. Livingstone's eminent services as an explorer, great as are
their certain results, as to his unwearied philanthropy
and his Christian spirit of self-consecration to the
great work of rescuing the degraded people of Central Africa and of putting an end to the fearful slave
trade. His heart lies buried in the land to whose interests he devoted his best years, and his body in an
honored grave in Westminster Abbey amid England's
most distinguished sons—his soul has found its home
among the "blessed of the Father," with the Lord
whom he loved and served, but he yet lives, a cher-
ished hero, in the memories of the good and true of
all Christian climes.

The British Government and people received more
than they conferred of honor, in their earnest and un-
sparing tributes to his memory.

CHAPTER XXVI.

THE LAST LETTERS OF DR. LIVINGSTONE.

THE following letters to his brother, Mr. John Livingstone, of Listowal, Ontario, Canada, are, with one dated April 9th, 1872, to James Gordon Bennett, Jr., the last of Dr. Livingstone's correspondence:

"MANYUEMA, or Cannibal Country, say 150 miles northwest of Ujiji, April, 1870.—MY DEAR BROTHER: I have not the faintest prospect of being able to send this to the coast for many months to come, but I write to have something in readiness when an opportunity of making up a packet arrives. As soon as I was able to march I went up Tanganyika about fifty or sixty miles, and from south up the Islet Kasange, struck away first northwest, then I passed the beginning of the lake formed by the Lualaba and found myself in the great bend which that lake river makes afterwards, as I saw it coming out of Lake Moreo. I made up to a small Arab party which rendered me most important aid in my illness in Marungu, and we met a lot of Ujijians coming with 18,000 pounds' weight of ivory The ivory was bought in this new field for a mere trifle in beads. After resting a while in the town of the principal Manyuema chief I went west, down a river named Luamo, from 100 to 150 yards broad, and always deep enough to require canoes; but the Ujiji

traders had been obliged to employ their slaves in col
lecting their ivory, and slaves with guns in their hands
are usually limbs of the evil one. The Manyuema
were always in the wrong, wanted to eat them, and always gave the slaves reasons to capture people, goats
and fowls, and carry off as much grain as they needed.
Their head men did not approve of this; they wanted
the ivory only, but the masters and men joined in one
chorus: The Manyuema are bad, bad, bad, very bad.

"When near the confluence of Luamo and Lualaba,
I was coming among people who had suffered very
severely at the hands of the slaves, and they would
not believe that my small party did not belong to the
bloodthirsty strangers. The women were particularly
outspoken, but the worst that was done was to turn
out in force and show us out of the district. Glad
that no collision took place, we returned to the principal town, and with the friendly party which we overtook struck away north, they to buy ivory and I to
get a canoe on the Lualaba, but the rains began, and
travelling, as I found, in Marungu in the wet season
was killing work. The vegetation is indescribably
rank; through the grass—if grass that can be called
which is more than half an inch thick in the stalk, and
twelve feet high—nothing but elephants can walk.
Then large belts of primeval forest stand between
the districts, and into them the sun, though vertical,
cannot penetrate. The rain-water stands in stagnant
pools, and the dead leaves decay in the damp soil and
make the water of the numerous rills and rivulets of
the color of a strong infusion of tea. One feels himself the veriest pigmy before the giant trees. The

roots, high out of the soil, keep you constantly look
ing down, and shot does no harm to guinea fowls on
their tops. The climbing plants prevent you from
leaving the ancient path, and I have heard the soko
or gorilla growling close by without being able to get
a sight of him. Their call to each other is like that
of a tom-cat. The country is mountainous; the light
gray granite of the hills rises through a bed of new
red sandstone, looking like islands in it. Innumerable dells have to be crossed, and the mud of Manyuema is awful. Bad water and perpetual wetting told
on us all by choleraic symptoms and emaciation.

"The news of the chiefs caused a gold fever at
Ujiji, and soon a herd numbering 600 muskets made
up to us, all eager for ivory. I turned back about
seven days, and resolved to remain with the heads of
this party during the rains. Their people are away
and they are as kind to me as I could wish. Rest and
boiling the water I used have restored me.

"After this preamble I may add, that slowly and surely the conviction has crept across my mind that all I can
in honesty and modesty claim is the rediscovery of the
source of the Nile, which had sunk into oblivion like
the circumnavigation of Africa by the Phœnician Admiral of one of the Pharaohs, B. C. about 600. Herodotus did not believe him because he said that in passing around Libya he had the sun on his right hand.
This to us, who have gone round from east to west,
stamps his tale as genuine. He put down the sources
of the Nile and Mountains of the Moon in 10 to 12
degrees south, where I found both them and the water-
shed. Ptolemy, or more probably his predecessors,

had received genuine though oral information from men who had visited this region. This is extremely likely, because the fountains and mountains abound where no theorist would put them. He makes their waters collect into two lacustrine rivers, Tanganyika and Lualaba, extant specimens of those lake and river beds known in the south of Africa as melazzo, and in the north as wadys, both words meaning the same thing—river beds where no water now flows. I am now trying to follow the western arm down, and have seen enough of it to confirm the information which the Greek geographer or others derived from ancient explorers. The eastern arm of Tanganyika, upper and lower, has been much exaggerated in breadth. I carefully watched its steady flow to the north for three months by means of broad masses of aquatic vegetation which, but for this current, would be the means of choking it up, as is the case with Okaro, the Victoria Nyanza. As soon as I shall have ascertained where the western arm joins the eastern I shall retire and pray that the Almighty may lead me safely home. I have no wish to speak dogmatically of what I have done, and I feel a little sorry that I am in a manner compelled to speak disparagingly of the opinions of modern discoverers of the sources of the Nile. The great mistake of Captain Speke was the eager pursuit of a foregone conclusion. When he discovered the Victoria Nyanza, he at once leapt to the conclusion that therein lay the sources of the Nile, the whole lake being 500 miles down the great Nile Valley and so much away from the sources. As soon as Speke and Grant looked toward their Nyanza they turned their backs on the fountains, and in their splendid achievements of following the river down, every step took them farther away from the Caput Nili. Baker came farther up the great valley than any other explorer in modern times, had his face in the right direction, but turned when some 700 miles from the sources. He seemed inclined to make the lower Tanganyika a second source to Speke's. Those two large rivers begin in a lake. I am glad that he has received some of the honors he deserves. Ptolemy's small lake Coloe is a more correct view of Victoria Nyanza than that given nowadays. As to breadth, the native Arabs might be mistaken, but not in saying that they knew three lakes where a huge Victoria Nyanza has been run in.

"No honors seem to have been given the Dutch lady explorer, though her noble perseverance after losing her two aunts by fever awakens my admiration. She had provided so well for both land and water exploration that had she not been, honestly enough no doubt, assured by Speke and Grant that they had already found the sources she sought, she must inevitably by boat or on land have reached the sources. She came a great deal farther up than Nero's centurion. They say exploration was not becoming her sex. Well, considering that 1600 years have elapsed since Ptolemy wrote, and kings, emperors, all the great men of antiquity longed to know the fountains whence flowed the famous river, exploration does not seem to have been very becoming the other sex, either. I do not know anything more about her than what has appeared in newspapers. She possesses indomitable pluck, and no mistake.

"When Sir Roderick Murchison proposed to me the examination of the water-shed of South Central Africa, I indicated the true scientific mode of ascertaining the correct position of the fountains of the Nile. The problem put thus had a charm for my mind. I had no theory on the subject, and was prepared to find the water-shed immediately to the south of Speke's Lake or anywhere else. The dividing line between the drainage south and north was unknown and a fit object for exploration. I recommended Dr. Kirk for the task, and he having declined I ultimately accepted it myself, in the belief that I could in two years pass across the head of Nyassa, examine the water-shed, and in returning begin a benevolent mission on the slope back again to the sea. Had I known all the toil, hunger, hardship and time involved in getting a clear idea of the drainage, I might have preferred a strait waistcoat, the head shaved and a blister on it, to undertaking the task. The water-shed is 800 miles long from west to east. Forward, backward, sideways, I went, in a route which can never all be put down. I had to feel my way, and every step of the way was generally groping in the dark, for who cared where the rivers ran? Native wars were a great hindrance; unsuitable, cowardly attendants an intolerable drag to both body and mind. It is more difficult to get reasonable evidence of the cannibalism of the Manyuema than might be imagined. I have tried ever since I came to see human flesh either cooked or eaten, but in vain. A finger wrapped up in a leaf was all that rewarded my search and offers of payment. This was probably a chance taken by a party which killed a man in revenge. The occurrence of graves frees a district from this imputation—their absence is suspicious, but in the Backwain country a grave is never seen, and the people are not cannibals. Had I believed one-tenth part of the tales told of the Manyuema by the traders and by the tribes in their vicinity, I might not have ventured among them. My mother never frightened me with *bogy*, so I am not subject to *bogyphobia*, in which disease everything horrible is believed if imputed to a black skin. It is epidemic in Jamaica.

"It is no wonder that the Portuguese gained so little knowledge of this country and the drainage into the Nile. Their three visits to Cazembe were simply slaving expeditions. They inquired for ivory and slaves, and heard of nothing else. Gentlemen of good principles at Lisbon will now feel sorry that no higher objects animated their countrymen, but as a nation they had no higher aim in reference to us on the Shire than by thwarting our efforts by murder and arson, till all the people we risked life and fortune to elevate were swept away.

"I felt certain that the water-shed held the solution of the problem, not because it was wished that the water-shed be examined, but because I had already discovered the chief sources of the Zambesi and the southern sources of the Congo. The Nile, I felt persuaded, would not be essentially different. The high flanking ridges of the valleys of these rivers are repeated in those that begin at Katanga and the country of Basango. The theory as to the form of the continent has a more limited application than I thought it had from the observation made in my great journey from Loando to Quillimane. The Lualaba is the central line of drainage of the great Nile Valley. It begins in 10° 12′ south, flows through Lake Bangweola, then through Lake Moreo, to become itself a great lake river, one of the headwaters of the River of Egypt. West of this there are two large rivers of the same name. These two Lualabas united form a large lake, Lake Lincoln. I use the names of the two great and good men, Palmerston and Lincoln, in loving admiration, as if to place my poor garland of love on their tombs. These two rivers rise by two fountains, which by anticipation I named Bartle Frere's (he abolished slavery in Scinde, India) and Young's fountains. About ten miles south of these rise other two fountains ; one is that of the Liamba or Upper Zambesi, the other gives rise to the Kafui. These I named Palmerston and Oswell, which flow into Zambesi. These four fountains are probably the Nile fountains, which were described to Herodotus as unfathomable, and sending one-half of the water to Egypt, the other half to inner Ethiopia. I have only to do this part to finish up the whole discovery, and I have a sore longing to return homewards. I am brought to a stand by my worthless attendants, who, besides deserting, became eager slave-hunters of their own countrymen. They had all been slaves and of the criminal class in Africa, and went with me only to avoid being enslaved again and made to work. Their eager slave-hunting where no danger was incurred was to ingratiate themselves with the Arabs. Assuredly if the freedmen in America turn out well, it will be from having been taught to work, and to like it as we do. My worthies had been petted,

coddled and allowed to live in idleness from mistaken
kindness, and on leaving the school sent me an anony-
mous letter, abusing the master who had fed, clothed
and taught them for years. Had we been treated as
they were, we should have been as useless. I have
travelled with all sorts of Africans—Hottentots, Bechuanas, Makololo, Backwims, and Zambesians of different
tribes—and we soon became attached to each other.
My present lot are exceptions, not fair specimens of
Africans.

"My love to Sarah and the children. I have had no
letters from home for years, except some three years
old. I fear that a large packet, with one for you, I
sent from Ujiji, was destroyed by an Arab Governor,
who sent one of his men to plunder my goods, and
then kept a long box containing two English guns,
medicines, letters and despatches, though I sent it
twice. He does not want evidence of his theft to go
to the coast, and he kept a man who witnessed the
plundering, as well as the packet. All will turn out
right at last, I hope; meantime it is trying.

"Affectionately yours,   DAVID LIVINGSTONE."

The following is from his second letter (headed pri
vate and confidential), dated Lake Bangweola, South
Central Africa, December, 1872:

"MY DEAR BROTHER: * * * I was still determined
not to give in to their villanies, and to work my
way down to Baker for aid. It was then that my good
Samaritan, Stanley, sent by James Gordon Bennett, of
the *New York Herald*, came on the scene, and his

conduct was beyond all praise. I was told that Stanley would make his fortune of me, and if he does he is heartily welcome, for he saved me a wearisome tramp after Baker, and probably saved my life. * * * And if the good Lord above me gives me strength and influence to complete the task in spite of everything, I shall not grudge my hunger and toils. Above all, if He permits me to put a stop to the enormous evils of this inland slave trade I shall bless His name with all my heart. The Nile sources are valuable to me only as a means of opening my mouth with power among men. It is this power I hope to apply to remedy an enormous evil and join my poor little helping hand in the great revolution that in His all-embracing Providence He has been carrying on for ages and is now actively helping forward.

"Affectionately yours,　　DAVID LIVINGSTONE."

The letter to Mr. Bennett is quite long, and, though interesting, contains nothing but what we have given in other words in this book, and hence we do not insert it.

THE MASSACRE OF THE MANYUEMA WOMEN.

CHAPTER XXVII.

LIVINGSTONE'S LAST JOURNAL.

Parting Messages—Metza's People Arrive—Ancient Geography—Tabora—Description of the Country—The Banyamwezi—Causes of Fever—The Population of Unyanyembe—The Mirambo War—Thoughts on Sir Samuel Baker's Policy—Prospects for Missionaries—News of other Travelers—Tidings of his Men—Chuma is Married—Nile or Congo?

[IN the midst of the universal sorrow caused by the death of Dr. Livingstone, a faint hope was indulged that some of his journals might survive the disaster. Through the faithfulness of his native attendants, this hope has been realized beyond the most sanguine expectations. It will be remembered that when Mr. Stanley returned to England, in 1872, Dr. Livingstone entrusted to his care a very large diary, sealed up and consigned to the safe-keeping of his daughter, Miss Agnes Livingstone. After his death, this book was examined, and found to contain a considerable portion of the notes which he had made during his travels previous to the time of Mr. Stanley's meeting him.

The Doctor's custom was always to have metallic note-books in use, in which the day's jottings were recorded. When time and opportunity served, the larger volume was posted up with scrupulous care.

It seems, however, that in the last three or four years of his life, this excellent rule had to give way to the toils of travel and the exhaustion of most distressing illnesses. Whilst in the Manyuema country, he ran out of note-books, ink, and pencils, and had to resort to shifts which at first made it a very debatable point whether the most diligent attempt at deciphering would succeed, after all. Such pocket-books as remained at this period of his travels were utilized, to the last inch of paper. At last pocket-books gave out, and old newspapers, yellow with African damp, were sewn together, and his notes were written across the type, with a substitute for ink made from the juice of a tree.

In comparing this great mass of material with the journal brought to England by Mr. Stanley, one finds that a great deal of most interesting matter can be added. It would seem that in the hurry of writing and copying despatches previous to his companion's departure, the Doctor rapidly entered up as much from his note-books as time and space permitted.

Most fortunately, he still carried the greater part of these original notes till the time of his death, so that they were forthcoming when his effects were subsequently saved.

When the battered tin traveling-case, which was with Livingstone to the last, was opened, in the spring of 1874, not only were these valuable papers disclosed, which have just been mentioned, but it was found, also, that Livingstone had kept a copious journal during his stay at Unyanyembe, in some copy-books, and that when his stock of note-books was replenished, a daily record of his subsequent travels had been made.

It has been already stated that Mr. Stanley parted from the great explorer on the 14th of March, 1872, taking with him the journal entrusted to his care, which had been brought down to that date. The second installment of his notes, found among his effects after his death, commences with a record made on the following day; and in this journal will be found a much more detailed account of his last journey than has been given in the preceding pages.]

15th March.—Writing to send after Mr. Stanley by two of his men, who wait here for the purpose. Copied line of route, observations from Kabuire to Casembe's, the second visit, and on to Lake Bangweolo; then the experiment of weight on watch-key at Nyangwe and Lusize.

16th March.—Sent the men after Mr. Stanley, and two of mine to bring his last words, if any.

[Sunday was kept in the quiet of the Tembe, on the 17th of March. Two days after, his birthday again comes around—that day which seems always to have carried with it such a special solemnity. He has yet time to look back on his marvellous deliverances, and the venture on which he is about to launch forth.]

19th March.—Birthday. My Jesus, my King, my life, my all; I again dedicate my whole self to Thee. Accept me, and grant, O Gracious Father, that ere this year is gone I may finish my task. In Jesus' name I ask it. Amen, so let it be. DAVID LIVINGSTONE.

25th March.—Susi brought a letter back from Mr. Stanley. He had a little fever, but I hope he will go on safely.

26th March.—Rain of Masika chiefly by night. The Masika of 1871 began on 23d of March, and ended 30th of April.

28th March.—Moenyembegu asked for the loan of a "doti." He is starving, and so is the war-party at McFutu; chaining their slaves together to keep them from running away to get food anywhere.

1st April, 1872.—Read Young's "Search after Livingstone;" thankful for many kind words about me. He writes like a gentleman.

2d April.—Making a sounding-line out of lint left by Mr. Stanley.

4th April.—We hear that Dugumbe's men have come to Ujiji with fifty tusks. He went down Lualaba with three canoes a long way and bought much ivory. They were not molested by Monangungo as we were.

My men whom I had sent to look for a book left by accident in a hut some days' journey off, came back stopped by a flood in their track.

8th April.—An Arab called Seyed bin Mohamad Magibbe called. He proposes to go west to the country west of Katanga (Urange).

9th April.—About one hundred and fifty Waganga of Mteza carried a present to Seyed Burghash, Sultan of Zanzibar, consisting of ivory and a young elephant. He spent all the ivory in buying return presents of gunpowder, guns, soap, brandy, gin, etc., and they have stowed it all in this Tembe. This morning they have taken everything out to see if anything is spoilt. They have hundreds of packages.

15th April.—Hung up the sounding-line on poles one fathom apart, and tarred it. Three hundred and seventy-five fathoms of five strands.

Ptolemy's geography of Central Africa seems to say that the science was then (second century A.D.) in a state of decadence from what was known to the ancient Egyptian priests as revealed to Herodotus six hundred years before his day (or say B.C. 440). They seem to have been well aware by the accounts of travelers or

traders that a great number of springs contributed to the
origin of the Nile, but none could be pointed at distinctly as the "Fountains," except those I long to discover, or rather rediscover. Ptolemy seems to have
gathered up the threads of ancient explorations, and
made many springs (six) flow into two lakes situated
east and west of each other—the space above them being
unknown. If the Victoria Lake were large, then it and
the Albert would probably be the lakes which Ptolemy
meant, and it would be pleasant to call them Ptolemy's
sources, rediscovered by the toil and enterprise of our
countrymen, Speke, Grant, and Baker—but unfortunately Ptolemy has inserted the small Lake "Coloe,"
nearly where the Victoria Lake stands, and one cannot
say where his two lakes are. Of Lakes Victoria, Bangweolo, Moero, Kamolondo—Lake Lincoln and Lake
Albert, which two did he mean? The science in his
time was in a state of decadence. Were two lakes not the
relics of a greater number previously known? What
says the most ancient map known of Sethos II.'s time?

16th April.—Went over to visit Sultan bin Ali near
Tabora—country open, plains sloping very gently down
from low, rounded granite hills covered with trees.
Rounded masses of the light gray granite crop out all
over them, but many are hidden by the trees: Tabora
slopes down from some of the same hills that overlook
Kwihara, where I live. Sultan bin Ali is very hospitable. He is of the Bedawee Arabs, and a famous marks-
man with his long Arab gun or matchlock. He is about
sixty-five years of age, black eyed, six feet high and inclined to stoutness, and his long beard is nearly all gray.
He provided two bountiful meals for self and attendants.

Called on Mohamad bin Nassur. He gave the news that came from Dugumbe's underling Nserere, and men now at Ujiji; they went southwest to country called Nombe, it is near Rua, and where copper is smelted. After I left them on account of the massacre at Nyangwe, they bought much ivory, but acting in the usual Arab way, plundering and killing, they aroused the Bakuss' ire, and as they are very numerous, about two hundred were killed. They brought fifty tusks to Ujiji. We dare not pronounce positively on any event in life, but this looks like prompt retribution on the perpetrators of the horrible and senseless massacre of Nyangwe. It was not vengeance by the relations of the murdered ones we saw shot and sunk in the Lualaba, for there is no communication between the people of Nyangwe and the Bakuss or people of Nombe of Lomame—that massacre turned my heart completely against Dugumbe's people. To go with them to Lomame as my slaves were willing to do, was so repugnant I preferred to return that weary four hundred or six hundred miles to Ujiji. I mourned over my being baffled and thwarted all the way, but tried to believe that it was all for the best—this news shows that had I gone with these people to Lomame, I could not have escaped the Bakuss spears, for I could not have run like the routed fugitives. I was prevented from going in order to save me from death. Many escapes from danger I am aware of; some make me shudder, as I think how near to death's door I came. But how many more instances of Providential protecting there may be of which I know nothing! But I thank most sincerely the good Lord of all for His goodness to me

18th April.—I pray the good Lord of all to favor me so as to allow me to discover the ancient fountains of Herodotus, and if there is anything in the underground excavations to confirm the precious old documents, the Scriptures of truth, may He permit me to bring it to light, and give me wisdom to make a proper use of it.

19th April.—A roll of letters and newspapers, apparently, came to-day for Mr. Stanley. The messenger says he passed Mr. Stanley on the way, who said "Take this to the Doctor;" this is erroneous.

20th April.—Opened it on 20th, and found nine New York Heralds of December 1–9, 1871, and one letter for Mr. Stanley, which I shall forward, and one stick of tobacco.

21st April.—Tarred the tent presented by Mr. Stanley.

23d April.—Visited Kwikuru, and saw the chief of all the Banyamwezi (around whose Boma it is), about sixty years old, and partially paralytic. He told me that he had gone as far as Katanga by the same Fipa route I now propose to take, when a little boy following his father, who was a great trader. The Banyamwezi have turned out good porters, and they do most of the carrying work of the trade to and from the East Coast; they are strong and trustworthy. One I saw carried six frasilahs, or two hundred pounds, of ivory from Unyanyembe to the sea-coast.

25th and 26th April.—A touch of fever, from exposure.

27th April.—Better, and thankful. Zahor died of small-pox here, after collecting much ivory at Fipa and Urungu.

The rains seem nearly over, and are succeeded by very cold easterly winds; these cause fever by checking the perspiration, and are well known as eminently febrile. The Arabs put the cause of the fever to the rains drying up. In my experience it is most unhealthy during the rains if one gets wet; the chill is brought on, the bowels cease to act, and fever sets in. Now it is the cold wind that operates, and possibly this is intensified by the malaria of the drying-up surface. A chill from bathing on the 25th in cold water gave me a slight attack.

1st *May*, 1872.—Unyanyembe: bought a cow for eleven dotis of merikano (and two kanike for calf) ; she gives milk, and this makes me independent.

Bought three more cows and calves for milk; they give a good quantity enough for me and mine, and are small short-horns. Finished a letter to the New York Herald, trying to enlist American zeal to stop the East Coast slave-trade; I pray for a blessing on it from the All-Gracious.

[Through a coincidence a singular interest attaches to this entry. The concluding words of the letter he refers to are as follows :

" All I can add in my loneliness is, may Heaven's rich blessing come down on every one, American, English, or Turk, who will help to heal the open sore of the world."

It was felt that nothing could more palpably represent the man, and this quotation has consequently been inscribed upon the tablet erected to his memory near his grave in Westminster Abbey. It was noticed some time after selecting it that Livingstone wrote these words exactly one year before his death, which took place on the 1st of May, 1873.]

3d May.—The entire population of Unyanyembe called Arab is eighty males; many of these are country born, and are known by the paucity of beard and bridgeless noses, as compared with men from Muscat; the Muscatees are more honorable than the mainlanders, and more brave—altogether better looking and better every way.

If we say that the eighty so-called Arabs here have twenty dependants each, 1500 or 1600 is the outside population of Unyanyembe in connection with the Arabs. It is called an ivory-station, that means simply that elephant's tusks are the chief articles of trade. But little ivory comes to market; every Arab who is able sends bands of his people to different parts to trade; the land being free, they cultivate patches of maize, dura, rice, beans, etc., and after one or two seasons, return with what ivory they may have secured. Ujiji is the only mart in the country, and it is chiefly for oil, grain, goats, salt, fish, beef, native produce of all sorts, and is held daily. A few tusks are sometimes brought, but it can scarcely be called an ivory mart for that. It is an institution begun and carried on by the natives in spite of great drawbacks from unjust Arabs. It resembles the markets of Manyuema, but is attended every day by about three hundred people. No dura has been brought lately to Ujiji, because a Belooch man found the son of the chief of Mbwara Island peeping in at his women, and beat the young man, so that on returning home he died. The Mbwara people always brought much grain before that, but since that affair never come.

4th May.—Many palavers about Mirambo's death having taken place and being concealed. Arabs say that he is a brave man, and the war is not near its end. Some northern natives called Bagoye get a keg of powder and a piece of cloth, go and attack a village, then wait a month or so eating the food of the captured place, and come back for stores again; thus the war goes on. Prepared tracing-paper to draw a map for Sir Thomas Maclear. Lewale* invites me to a feast.

7th May.—Went to breakfast with Lewale. He says that the Mirambo war is virtually against himself as a Séyed Majid man. They wish to have him removed, and this would be a benefit.

The Banyamwezi told the Arabs that they did not want them to go to fight, because when one Arab was killed all the rest ran away, and the army got frightened.

"Give us your slaves only, and we will fight," say they.

9th May.—No fight, though it was threatened yesterday; they all like to talk a great deal before striking a blow. They believe that in the multitude of counsellors there is safety.

The Africans' idea seems to be that they are within the power of a power superior to themselves—apart from and invisible; good; but frequently evil and dangerous. This may have been the earliest religious feeling of dependence on a Divine power, without any conscious feeling of its nature. Idols may have come in to give a definite idea of superior power, and the primitive faith or impression obtained by Revelation seems to have mingled with their idolatry without any sense of incongruity. (See Micah in Judges.)†

* Lewale appears to be the title by which the governor of the town is called.
† Judges xviii.

The origin of the primitive faith in Africans and others, seems always to have been a divine influence on their dark minds, which has proved persistent in all ages. One portion of primitive belief—the continued existence of departed spirits—seems to have no connection whatever with dreams, or, as we should say, with "ghost-seeing;" for great agony is felt in prospect of bodily mutilation or burning of the body after death, as that is believed to render return to one's native land impossible. They feel as if it would shut them off from all intercourse with relatives after death. They would lose the power of doing good to those once loved, and evil to those who deserved their revenge. Take the case of the slaves in the yoke, singing songs of hate and revenge against those who sold them into slavery. They thought it right so to harbor hatred, though most of the party had been sold for crimes—adultery, stealing, etc.—which they knew to be sins.

If Baker's expedition should succeed in annexing the valley of the Nile to Egypt, the question arises,—Would not the miserable condition of the natives, when subjected to all the atrocities of the White Nile slave-traders, be worse under Egyptian dominion? The villages would be farmed out to tax-collectors, the women, children, and boys carried off into slavery, and the free thought and feeling of the population placed under the dead weight of Islam. Bad as the situation now is, if Baker leaves it matters will grow worse. It is probable that actual experience will correct the fancies he now puts forth as to the proper mode of dealing with Africans.

10th May.—Hamees Wodin Tagh, my friend, is

reported slain by the Makoa of a large village he went to fight. Other influential Arabs are killed, but full information has not yet arrived.

12*th May.*—The reported death of Hamees Wodin Tagh is contradicted. It was so circumstantial that I gave it credit, though the false reports in this land are one of its most marked characteristics.

Ajala's people, sent to buy ivory in Uganda, were coming back with some ten tusks, and were attacked at Ugalla by robbers, and one free man slain; the rest threw everything down and fled. They came here with their doleful tale to-day.

14*th May.*—People came from Ujiji to-day, and report that many of Mohamad Bogharib's slaves have died of small-pox. Others sent out to get fire-wood have been captured by the Waha. Mohamad's chief slave, Othman, went to see the cause of their losses, and received a spear in the back, the point coming out at his breast.

Lewale off to Mfutu to loiter and not to fight. The Bagoye don't wish Arabs to come near the scene of action, because, say they, "When one Arab is killed all the rest run away, and they frighten us thereby. Stay at McFutu; we will do all the fighting." This is very acceptable advice.

16*th May.*—A man came from Ujiji to say one of the party at Kasongo's reports that a marauding party went thence to the island of Bazula, north of them. They ferried them to an island, and in coming back they were assaulted by the islanders in turn. They speared two in canoes shoving off, and the rest, panic-struck, took to the water, and thirty-five were slain. It was a just punishment, and shows what the Manyuema can do, if aroused, to right their wrongs. No news of Baker's party; but Abed and Hassani are said to be well, and far down the Lualaba. Nassur Masudi is at Kasongo's, probably afraid by the Zula slaughter to go further. Lewale sends off letters to the Sultan to-day. I have no news to send, but am waiting wearily.

18th–19th May.—One of Dugumbe's men came to-day from Ujiji. He confirms the slaughter of Matereka's people, but denies that of Dugumbe's men. They went to Lomame about eleven days west, and found it to be about the size of Luamo; it comes from a lake, and goes to Lualaba, near the Kisingite, a cataract. Dugumbe then sent his people down Lualaba, where much ivory is to be obtained. They secured a great deal of copper—one thousand thick bracelets—on the southwest of Nyanwe, and some ivory, but not so much as they desired.

20th May.—The cattle of the Batusi were captured by the Arabs to prevent them going off with the Baganda; my four amongst them. I sent over for them and they were returned this morning. Thirty-five of Mohamad's slaves died of small-pox.

I wish I had some of the assurance possessed by others, but I am oppressed with the apprehension that after all it may turn out that I have been following the Congo; and who would risk being put into a cannibal pot, and converted into black man for it?

23d May.—There seems but little prospect of Christianity spreading by ordinary means among Mohamadans. Their pride is a great obstacle, and is very industriously nurtured by its votaries. No new invention or increase of power on the part of Christians seems to

32

disturb the self-complacent belief that ultimately all power and dominion in this world will fall into the hands of Moslems. When Mr. Stanley's Arab boy from Jerusalem, told the Arab bin Saleh, that he was a Christian, he was asked, "Why so, don't you know that all the world will soon be Mohamadan? Jerusalem is ours, and in a short time we shall overcome all." Theirs are great expectations!

25th and 26th May.—Cold weather. Lewale sends for all Arabs to make a grand assault, as it is now believed that Mirambo is dead, and only his son, with few people, remain.

28th May.—Many parts of this interior land present most inviting prospects for well-sustained efforts of private benevolence. Karague, for instance, with its intelligent friendly chief Rumainyika (Speke's Rumanika), and Bouganda, with its teeming population, rain, and friendly chief, who could easily be swayed by an energetic prudent missionary. The evangelist must not depend on foreign support other than an occasional supply of beads and calico; coffee is indigenous, and so is sugar-cane. Wheat and rice are cultivated by the Arabs in all this upland region; the only thing a missionary needs in order to secure an abundant supply is to follow the Arab advice as to the proper season for sowing.

It would be a sort of Robinson Crusoe life, but with abundant materials for surrounding oneself with comforts, and improving the improvable among the natives. Clothing would require but small expense; four suits of strong tweed served me comfortably for five years. Woolen clothing is the best; if all wool, it wears long and prevents chills. The temperature here in the beginning of winter ranges from sixty-two to seventy-five degrees, Fahrenheit. In summer it seldom goes eighty-four degrees, as the country generally is from three thousand six hundred to four thousand feet high. Gently undulating plains with outcropping tree-covered granite hills on the ridges and springs in valleys will serve as a description of the country.

31st May.—The so-called Arab war with Mirambo drags its slow length along most wearily. After it is over then we shall get Banyamwezi pagazi in abundance. It is not now known whether Mirambo is alive or not; some say that he died long ago, and his son keeps up his state instead.

In reference to this Nile source I have been kept in perpetual doubt and perplexity. I know too much to be positive. Great Lualaba, or Lualubba, as Manyuema say, may turn out to be the Congo and Nile, a shorter river after all—the fountains flowing north and south seem in favor of its being the Nile. Great westing is in favor of the Congo. It would be comfortable to be positive like Baker. "Every drop from the passing shower to the roaring mountain torrent must fall into Albert Lake, a giant at its birth." How soothing to be positive.

1st June, 1872.—Visited by Jemadar Hamees from Katanga, who gives the following information:

UNYANYEMBE, *Tuesday.*—Hamees bin Jumaadar-sabel, a Beluch, came here from Katanga to-day. He reports that the three Portuguese traders, Jao, Domasiko, and Domasho, came to Katanga from Matiamvo. They bought quantities of ivory and returned; they

were carried in Mashilahs* by slaves. This Hamees
gave them pieces of gold from the rivulet there between
the two copper or malachite hills from which copper is
dug. He says that Tipo Tipo is now at Kantanga, and
has purchased much ivory from Kayomba or Kayombo
in Rua. He offers to guide me thither, going first to
Merere's, where Amran Masudi has now the upper
hand, and Merere offers to pay all the losses he has
caused to Arabs and others. Two letters were sent by
the Portuguese to the East Coast; one is in Amran's
hands. Hamees Wodin Tagh is alive and well. These
Portuguese went nowhere from Katanga, so that they
have not touched the sources of the Nile, for which I
am thankful.

Tipo Tipo has made friends with Merosi, the Mony-
amweze headman at Katanga, by marrying his daughter,
and has formed the plan of assaulting Casembe in conjunction with him, because Casembe put six of Tipo
Tipo's men to death. He will now be digging gold at
Katanga till this man returns with gunpowder.

[Many busy calculations are met with here which are
too involved to be given in detail. At one point we see
a rough conjecture as to the length of the road through
Fipa.]

On looking at the projected route by Merere's I see
that it will be a saving of a large angle into Fipa = 350
into Basango country S.S.W. or S. and by W.; this
comes into latitude 10′ S., and from this W.S.W. 400′ to
longitude of Katanga, skirting Bangweolo S. shore in
12° S. = the whole distance = 750′, say 900′.

* The Portuguese name for palanquin.

[Further on, we see that he reckoned on his work occupying him till 1874.]

If Stanley arrived the 1st of May at Zanzibar: allow = 20 days to get men and settle with them = May 20th, men leave Zanzibar 22d of May = now 1st of June.

On the road may be . . . . 10 days
Still to come 30 days, June . . . . . 30 "
                                        ——
Ought to arrive 10th or 15th of July . 40 "
                                        ——

14th of June = Stanley being away now three months; say he left Zanzibar 24th of May = at Aden 1st of June = Suez 8th of June = near Malta 14th of June.

Stanley's men may arrive in July next. Then engage pagazi half a month = August, five months of this year will remain for journey, the whole of 1873 will be swallowed up in work, but in February or March, 1874, please the Almighty Disposer of events, I shall complete my task and retire.

7th June.—Sultan bin Ali called. He says that the path by Fipa is the best; it has plenty of game, and people are friendly. By going to Amran I should get into the vicinity of Merere, and possibly be detained, as the country is in a state of war. The Beluch would naturally wish to make a good thing of me, as he did of Speke. I gave him a cloth, and arranged the Sungomaze beads, but the box and beads weigh one hundred and forty pounds, or two men's loads. I visited Lewale. Heard of Baker going to Unyoro Water, Lake Albert. Lewale praises the road by Moeneyungo and Merere, and says he will give a guide, but he never went that way.

10th June.—Othman, our guide from Ujiji hither, called to-day, and says positively that the way by Fipa is decidedly the shortest and easiest; there is plenty of game, and the people are all friendly. He reports that Mirambo's headman, Merungwe, was assaulted and killed, and all his food, cattle, and grain used. Mirambo remains alone. He has, it seems, inspired terror in the Arab and Banyamwezi mind by his charms, and he will probably be allowed to retreat north by flight, and the war for a season close; if so, we shall get plenty of Banyamwezi pagazi, and be off, for which I earnestly long and pray.

13th June.—Sangara, one of Mr. Stanley's men, returned from Bagamoio, and reports that my caravan is at Ugogo. He arrived to-day, and reports that Stanley and the American Consul acted like good fellows, and soon got a party of over fifty off, as he heard while at Bagamoio, and he left. The main body, he thinks, are in Ugogo. He came on with the news, but the letters were not delivered to him. I do most fervently thank the good Lord of all for His kindness to me through these gentlemen. The men will come here about the end of this month.

After Sangara came, I went over to Kukuru to see what the Lewale had received, but he was absent at Tabora. A great deal of shouting, firing of guns, and circumgyration by the men who had come from the war just outside the stockade of Nkisiwa (which is surrounded by a hedge of dark euphorbia and stands in a level hollow) was going on as we descended the gentle slope towards it. Two heads had been put up as trophies in the village, and it was asserted that Marukwe, a chief man of Mirambo, had been captured at Uvinza, and his head would soon come too. It actually did come, and was put upon a pole.

I am most unfeignedly thankful that Stanley and Webb have acted nobly.

14th June.—On 22d June Stanley was one hundred days gone : he must be in London now.

Seyed bin Mohamad Margibbe called to say that he was going off towards Katanga to-morrow by way of Amran. I feel inclined to go by way of Fipa rather, though I should much like to visit Merere.

15th June.—Lewale doubts Sangara on account of having brought no letters. Nothing can be believed in this land unless it is in black and white, and but little even then; the most circumstantial details are often mere figments of the brain. The one-half one hears may safely be called false, and the other half doubtful or *not proven.*

Sultan bin Ali doubts Sangara's statements also, but says " Let us wait and see the men arrive, to confirm or reject them." I incline to belief, because he says that he did not see the men, but heard of them at Bagamoio.

16th June.—Mirambo made a sortie against a headman in alliance with the Arabs, and was quite successful, which shows that he is not so much reduced as reports said.

About two hundred Baguha came here, bringing much ivory and palm-oil for sale because there is no market nor goods at Ujiji for the produce. A few people came also from Buganda, bringing four tusks and an invitation to Seyed Burghash to send for two housefuls of ivory which Mteza has collected.

18th June.—Sent over a little quinine to Sultan bin Ali—he is ailing of fever—and a glass of "Moiko" the shameful!

The Ptolemaic map defines people according to their food. The Elephantophagi, the Struthiophagi, the Ichthyophagi, and Anthropophagi. If we followed the same sort of classification our definition would be the drink, thus:—the tribe of stout-guzzlers, the roaring potheen-fuddlers, the whisky-fishoid-drinkers, the vin-ordinaire bibbers, the lager-beer-swillers, and an outlying tribe of the brandy cocktail persuasion.

[How fully he hoped to reach the hill from which he supposed the Nile to flow, is shown in the following words, written at this time:]

I trust in Providence still to help me. I know the four rivers Zambesi, Kafue, Luapula, and Lomame; their fountains must exist in one region.

Great hopes are held that the war which has lasted a full year will now be brought to a close, and Mirambo either be killed or flee. As he is undoubtedly an able man, his flight may involve much trouble and guerilla warfare.

Clear cold weather, and sickly for those who have only thin clothing, and not all covered.

The women work very hard in providing for their husbands' kitchens. The rice is the most easily prepared grain; three women stand around a huge wooden mortar with pestles in their hands, a gallon or so of the unhusked rice—called Mopunga here, and paddy in India—is poured in, and the three heavy pestles worked in exact time; each jerks up her body as she lifts the pestle and strikes it into the mortar with all her might, lightening the labor with some wild ditty the while, though one hears by the strained voice that she is nearly out of breath. When the husks are pretty well loosened, the grain is put into a large plate-shaped basket, and tossed so as to bring the chaff to one side; the vessel is then heaved downwards, and a little horizontal motion given to it which throws the refuse out; the partially cleared grain is now returned to the mortar, again pounded, and cleared of husks, and a semi-circular toss of the vessel sends all the remaining unhusked grain to one side, which is lifted out with the hand, leaving the chief part quite clean; they certainly work hard and well. The maize requires more labor by far; it is first pounded to remove the outer scales from the grain, then steeped for three days in water, then pounded, the scales again separated by the shallow-basket tossings, then pounded fine, and the fine white flour separated by the basket from certain hard, rounded particles, which are cooked as a sort of granular porridge—"Mtyelle."

When Ntaoeka chose to follow us rather than go to the coast, I did not like to have a fine-looking woman among us unattached, and proposed that she should marry one of my three worthies, Chuma, Gardner, or Mabruki; but she smiled at the idea. Chuma was evidently too lazy ever to get a wife; the other two were contemptible in appearance, and she has a good presence and is buxom. Chuma promised reform; "he had been lazy," he admitted, "because he had no wife." Circumstances led to the other women wishing Ntaoeka married, and on my speaking to her again she consented. I have noticed her ever since working hard from morning to night; the first up in the cold mornings, making fire and hot water, pounding, carrying water, wood, sweeping, cooking.

21st June.—No jugglery or sleight-of-hand, as was recommended to Napoleon III., would have any effect in the civilization of the Africans; they have too much good sense for that. Nothing brings them to place thorough confidence in Europeans but a long course of well-doing. They believe readily in the supernatural as effecting any new process or feat of skill, for it is part of their original faith to ascribe everything above human agency to unseen spirits. Goodness or unselfishness impresses their minds more than any kind of skill or power. They say, " You have different hearts from ours; all black men's hearts are bad, but yours are good." The prayer to Jesus for a new heart and right spirit at once commends itself as appropriate. Music has great influence on those who have musical ears, and often leads to conversion.

[Here and there he gives more items of intelligence from the war, which afford a perfect representation of the rumors and contradictions which harass the listener in Africa, especially if he is interested, as Livingstone was, in the re-establishment of peace between the combatants.]

Lewale is off to the war with Mirambo; he is to finish it now! A continuous fusilade along his line of march west will expend much powder, but possibly get the spirits up. If successful, we shall get Banyamwezi pagazi in numbers.

Mirambo is reported to have sent one hundred tusks and one hundred slaves towards the coast to buy gunpowder. If true, the war is still far from being finished; but falsehood is fashionable.

26th June.—Went over to Kwikhuru and engaged

Mohamad bin Seyde to speak to Nkasiwa for pagazi; he wishes to go himself. The people sent to Mirambo to buy gunpowder in Ugogo came to Kitambi; he reported the matter to Nkasiwa that they had come, and gave them pombe. When Lewale heard it, he said, "Why did Kitambi not kill them; he is a partaker in Mirambo's guilt." A large gathering yesterday at McFutu to make an assault on the last stockade in hostility.

[A few notes in another pocket-book are placed under this date. Thus:]

24th June.—The medical education has led me to a continual tendency to suspend the judgment. What a state of blessedness it would have been had I possessed the dead certainty of the homœopathic persuasion, and as soon as I found the Lakes Bangweolo, Moero, and Kamolondo pouring out their waters down the great central valley, bellowed out, "Hurrah! Eureka!" and gone home in firm and honest belief that I had settled it, and no mistake. Instead of that I am even now not at all "cock-sure" that I have not been following down what may after all be the Congo.

25th June.—Send over to Tabora, to try and buy a cow from Basakuma, or northern people, who have brought about one hundred for sale. I got two oxen for a coil of brass wire and seven dotis of cloth.

CHAPTER XXVIII.

RESTING AT UNYANYEMBE.

Letters Arrive at Last—Hippopotamus Hunters—Arab Caution—Dearth of Missionary Enterprise—The Slave-Trade and its Horrors—Moslem Gallantry—Carping Benevolence—African " Craw-Taes "—A Venerable Piece of Artillery —Bin Nasib—An African Cyclone—The Baganda Leave at Last—A New Follower Enlisted—Weary Waiting.

[AND now the long-looked for letters came in by various hands, but with little regularity. It is not here necessary to refer to the withdrawal of the Livingstone Relief Expedition, which took place as soon as Mr. Stanley confronted Lieutenant Dawson on his way inland. Suffice it to say that the various members of this expedition, of which his second son, Mr. Oswell Livingstone, was one, had already quitted Africa for England when these communications reached Unyanyembe.]

27th June, 1872.—Received a letter from Oswell yesterday, dated Bagamoio, 14th May, which awakened thankfulness, anxiety, and deep sorrow.

28th June.—Went over to Kwikuru yesterday to speak about pagazi. Nkasiwa was off at McFutu to help in the great assault on Mirambo, which is hoped to be the last. But Mohamad bin Seyed promised to arrange with the chief on his return. I was told that Nkasiwa has the head of Morukwe in a kirindo or band-box, made of the inner bark of a tree, and when Morukwe's people have recovered they will come and redeem it with ivory and slaves, and bury it in his grave, as they did the head of Ishbosheth in Abner's grave in Hebron.

Dugumbe's man, who went off to Ujiji to bring ivory, returned to-day, having been attacked by robbers of Mirambo. The pagazi threw down all their loads and ran; none were killed, but they lost all.

29th June.—Received a packet from Sheikh bin Nasib containing a letter for him and one " Pall Mall Gazette," one Overland Mail, and four Punches. Provision has been made for my daughter by Her Majesty's Government of three hundred pounds, but I don't understand the matter clearly.

2d July, 1872.—Make a packet for Dr. Kirk and Mr. Webb, of Zanzibar; explain to Kirk, and beg him to investigate and punish, and put blame on right persons. Write Sir Bartle Frere and Agnes: send large packet of astronomical observations and sketch map to Sir Thomas Maclear by a native, Suleiman.

3d July.—Wearisome waiting, this; and yet the men cannot be here before the middle or end of this month. I have been sorely let and hindered in this journey, but it may have been all for the best. I will trust in Him to whom I commit my way.

5th July.—Weary! weary!

7th July.—Waiting wearily here, and hoping that the good and loving Father of all may favor me, and help me to finish my work quickly and well.

At the Loangwa of Zumbo we came to a party of hereditary hippopotamus hunters, called Makombwe or Akombwe. They follow no other occupation, but when their game is getting scanty at one spot they remove to some other part of the Loangwa, Zambesi, or Shire, and build temporary huts on an island, where their women cultivate patches; the flesh of the animals they kill is eagerly exchanged by the more settled people for grain. Their hunting is the bravest thing I ever saw. Each canoe is manned by two men; each man uses a broad, short paddle, and as they guide the canoe slowly down stream to a sleeping hippopotamus not a single ripple is raised on the smooth water; they look as if holding in their breath, and communicate by signs only. As they come near the prey the harpooner in the bow lays down his paddle and rises slowly up, and there he stands erect, motionless, and eager, with the long-handled weapon poised at arm's length above his head, till coming close to the beast he plunges it with all his might in towards the heart. During this exciting feat he has to keep his balance exactly. His neighbor in the stern at once backs his paddle, the harpooner sits down, seizes his paddle, and backs too to escape; the animal, surprised and wounded, seldom returns the attack at this stage of the hunt. The next stage, however, is full of danger.

The barbed blade of the harpoon is secured by a long and very strong rope wound around the handle; it is intended to come out of its socket, and while the iron head is firmly fixed in the animal's body the rope unwinds and the handle floats on the surface. The hunter next goes to the handle and hauls on the rope till he knows that he is right over the beast; when he feels the the line suddenly slacken he is prepared to deliver another harpoon the instant that hippo.'s enormous jaws appear, with a terrible grunt, above the water. The backing by the paddles is again repeated, but hippo. often assaults the canoe, crunches it with his great jaws, or shivers it with a kick by his hind foot. Deprived of their canoe the gallant comrades instantly dive and

swim to the shore under water; they say that the infu-
riated beast looks for them on the surface, and being
below they escape his sight. When caught by many
harpoons the crews of several canoes seize the handles
and drag him hither and thither till, weakened by loss
of blood, he succumbs.

This hunting requires the greatest skill, courage, and
nerve that can be conceived. The Makombwe are certainly a magnificent race of men, hardy and active in
their habits, and well fed, as the result of their brave
exploits; every muscle is well developed, and though
not so tall as some tribes, their figures are compact and
finely proportioned.

8th July.—At noon, wet bulb, 66°; dry, 74°. These
observations are taken from thermometers hung four
feet from the ground on the cool side (south) of the
house, and beneath an earthen roof, with complete protection from wind and radiation. Noon known by the
shadows being nearly perpendicular. To show what is
endured by a traveler, the following register is given of
the heat on a spot, four feet from the ground, protected
from the wind by a reed fence, but exposed to the sun's
rays, slanting a little:

Noon.	Wet Bulb 78°		Dry Bulb	102°
2 P.M	" 77°		"	99°
3 P.M.	" 78°		"	102°
4 P.M.	" 72°		"	88°
	(Agreeable marching now.)			
6 P.M.	" 66°		"	77°

9th July.—War forces have gone out of McFutu and
built a camp. Fear of Mirambo rules them all; each
one is nervously anxious not to die, and in no way

33

ashamed to own it. The Arabs keep out of danger: " Better to sleep in a whole skin" is their motto.

Noon.—Spoke to Singeri about the missionary reported to be coming; he seems to like the idea of being taught, and opening up the country by way of the Nile. I told him that all the Arabs confirmed Mtesa's cruelties, and that his people were more to blame than he; it was guilt before God. In this he agreed fully, but said, " What Arab was killed?" meaning, if they did not suffer, how can they complain?

10th July.—No great difficulty would be encountered in establishing a Christian Mission a hundred miles or so from the East Coast. The permission of the Sultan of Zanzibar would be necessary, because all the tribes of any intelligence claim relationship, or have relations with him. His permission would be readily granted, if respectfully applied for through the English Consul. The Suaheli, with their present apathy on religious matters, would be no obstacle. Care to speak politely, and to show kindness to them, would not be lost labor in the general effect of the Mission on the country, but all discussion on the belief of the Moslems should be avoided; they know little about it.

No objection would be made to teaching the natives of the country to read their own languages in the Roman character. No Arab has ever attempted to teach them the Arabic-Koran ; they are called *guma*, hard, or difficult as to religion. One only of all the native chiefs, Monyumgo, has sent his children to Zanzibar to be taught to read and write the Koran; and he is said to possess an unusual admiration of such civilization as he has seen among the Arabs. To the natives, the chief attention of the Mission should be directed. It would not be desirable, or advisable, to refuse explanation to others; but I have avoided giving offence to intelligent Arabs, who have pressed me, asking if I believed in Mohamad, by saying, "No, I do not; I am a child of Jesus bin Miriam," avoiding anything offensive in my tone, and often adding that Mohamad found their forefathers bowing down to trees and stones, and did good to them by forbidding idolatry, and teaching the worship of the only One God. This they all know, and it pleases them to have it recognized.

It might be good policy to hire a respectable Arab to engage free porters, and conduct the Mission to the country chosen, and obtain permission from the chief to build temporary houses. If this Arab were well paid, it might pave the way for employing others to bring supplies of goods and stores not produced in the country, as tea, coffee, sugar. The first porters had better all go back, save a couple or so, who have behaved especially well. Trust to the people among whom you live for general services, as bringing wood, water, cultivation, reaping, smith's work, carpenter's work, pottery, baskets, etc. Educated free blacks from a distance are to be avoided; they are expensive, and are too much of gentlemen for your work. You may in a few months raise natives who will teach reading to others better than they can, and teach you also much that the liberated never know. A cloth and some beads occasionally will satisfy them, while neither the food, the wages, nor the work will please those who, being brought from a distance, naturally consider themselves missionaries. It seems indispensable that each Mission should raise its own

native agency. A couple of Europeans beginning, and
carrying on a Mission without a staff of foreign attendants, implies coarse country fare, it is true, but this
would be nothing to those who at home amuse themselves with fastings, vigils, etc. A great deal of power
is thus lost in the Church. Fastings and vigils, without a special object in view, are time run to waste.
They are made to minister to a sort of self-gratification,
instead of being turned to account for the good of others.
The forty days of Lent might be annually spent in visiting adjacent tribes, and bearing unavoidable hunger and
thirst with a good grace. Considering the greatness of
the object to be attained, men might go without sugar,
coffee, tea, etc. I went from September, 1866, to December, 1868, without either.

12th July.—When endeavoring to give some account
of the slave-trade of East Africa, it was necessary to
keep far within the truth, in order not to be thought
guilty of exaggeration ; but in sober seriousness, the subject does not admit of exaggeration. The sights I have
seen are so nauseous that I always strive to drive them
from memory; but the slaving scenes come back unbid-
den, and make me start up at dead of night horrified
by their vividness.

The monuments of Egypt show that this curse has
venerable antiquity. Some people say, "If so ancient,
why try to stop an old established usage now?" Well,
some believe that the affliction that befel the most ancient
of all the patriarchs, Job, was small-pox. Why, then,
stop the ravages of this venerable disease in London and
New York by vaccination?

But no one expects any benevolent efforts from those

who cavil and carp at efforts made by governments and peoples to heal the enormous open sore of the world. Some profess that they would rather give "their mite" for the degraded of our own countrymen than to "niggers!" Verily, it is "a mite," and they most often forget, and make a gift of it to themselves. It is almost an axiom that those who do most for the heathen abroad are most liberal for the heathen at home. It is to this class we turn with hope. With others, arguments are useless, and the only answer I care to give is the remark of an English sailor, who, on seeing slave-traders actually at their occupation, said to his companion, "Shiver my timbers, mate! if the devil don't catch these fellows, we might as well have no devil at all."

In conversing with a prince at Johanna, one of the Comoro islands lying off the north end of Madagascar, he took occasion to extol the wisdom of the Arabs in keeping strict watch over their wives. On suggesting that their extreme jealousy made them more like jailers than friends of their wives, he asserted that the jealousy was reasonable, because all women were bad; they could not avoid going astray. And on remarking that this might be the case with Arab women, but certainly did not apply to English women, for though a number were untrustworthy, the majority deserved all the confidence their husbands could place in them, he reiterated that women were universally bad. He did not believe that women ever would be good; and the English allowing their wives to gad about with faces uncovered, only showed their weakness, ignorance, and unwisdom.

15th July.—Reported to-day that twenty wounded men have been brought into McFutu from the field of fighting. About two thousand are said to be engaged on the Arab side, and the side of Mirambo would seem to be strong, but the assailants have the disadvantage of firing against a stockade, and are unprotected, except by ant-hills, bushes, and ditches in the field. I saw the first kites to-day; one had spots of white feathers on the body below, as if it were a young one—probably came from the north.

17th July.—Went over to Sultan bin Ali yesterday. Very kind, as usual; he gave me guavas and a melon—called " matanga." It is reported that one of Mirambo's chief men, Sorura, set sharp sticks in concealed holes, which acted like Bruce's " craw-taes" at Bannockburn, and wounded several, probably the twenty reported. This has induced the Arabs to send for a cannon they have, with which to batter Mirambo at a distance. The gun is borne past us this morning; a brass seven-pounder, dated 1679. Carried by the Portuguese Commander-in-Chief to China, 1679, or one hundred and ninety-three years ago—and now to beat Mirambo, by Arabs who have very little interest in the war.

[Mtesa's people on their way back to Uganda were stuck fast at Unyanyembe the whole of this time; it does not appear at all who the missionary was to whom he refers.]

Lewale sends off the Baganda in a great hurry, after detaining them for six months or more till the war ended, and he now gets pagazi of Banyamwezi for them. This haste (though war is not ended) is probably because Lewale has heard of a missionary through me.

Mirambo fires now from inside the stockade alone.

20th July.—High cold winds prevail. Temperature,

FISH-EAGLE ON A HIPPOPOTAMUS TRAP.

6 A.M., 57°; noon, on the ground, 122°. It may be higher, but I am afraid to risk the thermometer, which is graduated to 140° only.

21st July.—Bought two milch cows (from a Motusi), which, with their calves, were seventeen dotis or thirty-four fathoms. The Baganda are packing up to leave for home. They take a good deal of brandy and gin for Mtesa from the Moslems.

Lewale returns to-day from McFutu on his own private business at Kwikuru. The success of the war is a minor consideration with all. I wish my men would come, and let me off from this weary waiting.

23d July.—The departure of the Baganda is countermanded, for fear of Mirambo capturing their gunpowder.

Lewale interdicts them from going; he says, " You may go, but leave all the gunpowder here, because Mirambo will follow and take it all to fight with us." This is an afterthought, for he hurried them to go off. A few will go and take the news and some goods to Mtesa, and probably a lot of Lewale's goods to trade at Karagwe.

The Baganda are angry, for now their cattle and much of their property are expended here; but they say, " We are strangers, and what can we do but submit?" The Banyamwesi carriers would all have run away on the least appearance of danger. No troops are sent by Seyed Burghash, though they were confidently reported long ago. All trade is at a stand-still.

24th July.—The Bagohe retire from the war. This month is unlucky. I visited Lewale and Nkasiwa, putting a blister on the latter, for paralytic arm, to please him. Lewale says that a general flight from the war has taken place. The excuse is hunger. He confirms the great damage done by a cyclone at Zanzibar to shipping, houses, cocoa-nut palms, mango-trees, and clove-trees, also houses and dhows, five days after Burghash returned. Sofeu volunteers to go with us, because Mohamad Bogharib never gave him anything, and Bwana Mohinna has asked him to go with him. I have accepted his offer, and will explain to Mohamad, when I see him, that this is what he promised me in the way of giving men, but never performed.

27th July.—At dawn a loud rumbling in the east as if of thunder, possibly a slight earthquake; no thunder-clouds visible.

Bin Nassib came last night and visited me before going home to his own house; a tall, brown, polite Arab. He says, that he lately received a packet for Mr. Stanley from the American Consul, sealed in tin, and sent it back; this is the eleventh that came to Stanley. A party of native traders who went with the Baganda were attacked by Mirambo's people, and driven back with the loss of all their goods and one killed. The fugitives returned this morning sorely downcast. A party of twenty-three loads left for Karagwe a few days ago, and the leader alone has returned; he does not know more than that one was killed. Another was slain on this side of McFutu by Mirambo's people yesterday, the country thus is still in a terribly disturbed state. Sheikh bin Nassib says that the Arabs have rooted out fifty-two headmen who where Mirambo's allies.

28th July.—To Nkasiwa; blistered him, as the first relieved the pain and pleased him greatly; hope he may derive benefit.

29th July.—Making flour of rice for the journey. Visited Sheika bin Nassib, who has a severe attack of fever; he cannot avoid going to the war. He bought a donkey with the tusk he stole from Lewale, and it died yesterday ; now Lewale says, "Give me back my tusk;" and the Arab replies, " Give me back my donkey." The father must pay, but his son's character is lost as well as the donkey. Bin Nassib gave me a present of wheaten bread and cakes.

30th July.—Weary waiting this, and the best time for traveling passes over unused. High winds from the east every day bring cold, and, to the thinly-clad Arabs, fever. Bin Omari called; goes to Katanga with another man's goods to trade there.

31st July.—We heard yesterday from Sahib bin Nassib that the caravan of his brother Kisessa was at a spot in Ugogo, twelve days off. My party had gone by another route. Thankful for even this in my wearisome waiting.

CHAPTER XXIX.

THE START FROM UNYANYEMBE.

A Party of Baganda—Boys' Playthings in Africa—Reflections—Arrival of the Men—Fervent Thankfulness—An End of the Weary Waiting—Jacob Wainwright takes Service under the Doctor—Preparations for the Journey—Flagging and Illness—Great Heat—Approaches Lake Tanganyika—The Borders of Fipa—Capes and Islands of Lake Tanganyika—Mountain Climbing—Large Bay.

1st August, 1872.—A LARGE party of Baganda have come to see what is stopping the way to Mtesa, about ten headmen and their followers; but they were told by an Arab in Usui that the war with Mirambo was over. About seventy of them come on here to-morrow, only to be despatched back to fetch all the Baganda in Usui, to aid in fighting Mirambo. It is proposed to take a stockade near the central one, and therein build a battery for the cannon, which seems a wise measure. These arrivals are a poor, slave-looking people, clad in barkcloth, "Mbuzu," and having shields with a boss in the centre, round, and about the size of the ancient Highlanders' targe, but made of reeds. The Baganda already here said that most of the new-comers were slaves, and would be sold for cloths. Went over to apply medicine to Nkasiwa's neck to heal the outside; the inside is benefited somewhat, but the power will probably remain incomplete, as it now is.

3d August.—Visited Salem bin Seff, who is ill of fever. Called on Sultan bin Ali, and home. It is he who effected the flight of all the Baganda pagazi, by giving ten strings of beads to Motusi to go and spread a panic among them by night; all bolted.

4th August.—Wearisome waiting, and the sun is now rainy at mid-day, and will become hotter right on to the hot season in November; but this delay may be all for the best.

5th August.—Visited Nkasiwa, and recommended shampooing the disabled limbs with oil or flour. He says that the pain is removed. More Baganda have come to Kwihara, and will be used for the Mirambo war.

In many parts one is struck by the fact of the children having so few games. Life is a serious business, and amusement is derived from imitating the vocations of the parents—hut-building, making little gardens, bows and arrows, shields and spears. Elsewhere, boys are very ingenious little fellows, and have several games; they also shoot birds with bows, and teach captured linnets to sing. They are expert in making guns and traps for small birds, and in making and using bird-lime. They make play-guns of reed, which go off with a trigger and spring, with a cloud of ashes for smoke. Sometimes they make double-barreled guns of clay, and have cotton-fluff as smoke. The boys shoot locusts with small toy-guns very cleverly.

. . . What is the atonement of Christ? It is Himself; it is the inherent and everlasting mercy of God made apparent to human eyes and ears. The everlasting love was disclosed by our Lord's life and death. It showed that God forgives, because He loves to forgive. He works by smiles if possible; if not, by frowns; pain is only a means of enforcing love.

If we speak of strength, lo! He is strong. The Almighty; the Over Power; the Mind of the Universe. The heart thrills at the idea of His greatness.

. . . All the great among men have been remarkable at once for the grasp and minuteness of their knowledge. Great astronomers seem to know every iota of the Knowable. The Great Duke, when at the head of armies, could give all the particulars to be observed in a cavalry charge, and took care to have food ready for all his troops. Men think that greatness consists in lofty indifference to all trivial things. The Grand Llama, sitting in immovable contemplation of nothing, is a good example of what a human mind would regard as majesty; but the Gospels reveal Jesus, the manifestation of the blessed God over all, as minute in His care of all. He exercises a vigilance more constant, complete, and comprehensive, every hour and every minute, over each of His people, than their utmost self-love could ever attain. His tender love is more exquisite than a mother's heart can feel.

6th August.—I can think of nothing but "when will these men come?" Sixty days was the period named; now it is eighty-four. It may be all for the best, in the good Providence of the Most High.

9th August.—I do most devoutly thank the Lord for His goodness in bringing my men near to this. Three came to-day, and how thankful I am I cannot express. It is well—the men who went with Mr. Stanley came again to me. "Bless the Lord, O my soul, and all that is within me, bless His holy name." Amen.

[At last this trying suspense was put an end to by the arrival of a troop of fifty-seven men and boys, made up of porters hired by Mr. Stanley on the coast, and some more Nassick pupils, sent from Bombay to join Lieutenant Dawson. We find the names of John and Jacob Wainwright amongst the latter on Mr. Stanley's list.

Before we incorporate these new recruits on the muster-roll of Dr. Livingstone's servants, it seems right to point to five names which alone represented at this time the list of his original followers; these were Susi, Chuma, and Amoda, who joined him in 1864, on the Zambesi; that is, eight years previously; and Mabruki and Gardner, Nassick boys, hired in 1866. We shall see that the new-comers by degrees became accustomed to the hardships of travel, and shared with the old servants all the danger of the last heroic march home. Nor must we forget that it was to the intelligence and superior education of Jacob Wainwright (whom we now meet with for the first time) that we were indebted for the earliest account of the eventful eighteen months during which he was attached to the party.

And now all is pounding, packing, bargaining, weighing, and disputing among the porters. Amidst the inseparable difficulties of an African start, one thankful heart gathers comfort and courage :]

15th August.—The men came yesterday (14th), having been seventy-four days from Bagamoio. Most thankful to the Giver of all good I am. I have to give them a rest of a few days, and then start.

16th August.—An earthquake, "Kiti-ki-sha!" about 7 P.M., shook me in my katanda with quick vibrations. They gradually became fainter; it lasted some fifty seconds, and was observed by many.

17th August.—Preparing things.

18th August.---Fando to be avoided as extortionate. Went to bid adieu to Sultan bin Ali, and left goods with him for the return journey, and many cartridges full and empty, nails for boat, two iron pillars, etc.

19th August.—Waiting for pagazi. Sultan bin Ali called; is going off to McFutu.

20th August.—Weighed all the loads again, and gave an equal load of fifty pounds to each, and half loads to the Nassickers. Mabruki Speke is left at Taborah with Sultan bin Ali. He has long been sick, and is unable to go with us.

21st August.—Gave people an ox, and to a discarded wife a cloth, to avoid exposure by her husband stripping her. She is somebody's child!

22d August.—Sunday. All ready, but ten pagazi lacking.

23d August.—Cannot get pagazi. Most are sent off to the war.

[At last the start took place. It is necessary to mention that Dr. Livingstone's plan in all his travels was to make one short stage the first day, and generally late in the afternoon. This, although nothing in point of distance, acted like the drill-sergeant's "Attention!" The next morning every one was ready for the road, clear of the town, and unencumbered with parting words.]

25th August.—Started and went one hour to village of Manga or Yuba by a granite ridge; the weather clear, and a fine breeze from the east refreshes. It is important to give short marches at first. Marched one and one-quarter hour.

26th August.—Two Nassickers lost a cow out of ten head of cattle. Marched to Borna of Mayonda. Sent back five men to look after the cow. Cow not found; she was our best milker.

27th August.—Started for Ebulua and Kasekera of

Mamba. Cross torrent, now dry, and througn forest to village of Ebulua; thence to village of Kasekera, three and one-half hours. Direction, S. by W.

28th August.—Reached Mayole village in two hours and rested; S. and by W. Water is scarce in front. Through flat forest to a marshy-looking piece of water, where we camp, after a march of one and one-half hour; still S. by W.

29th August.—On through level forest without water. Trees present a dry, wintry aspect; grass dry, but some flowers shoot out, and fresh grass where the old growth has been burnt off.

30th August.—Engaging pagazi and rest.

Pass Kisari's village, one and one-half mile distant, and on to Penta or Phinta to sleep, through perfectly flat forest. Three hours, S. by W.

1st September, 1872.—The same flat forest to Chikulu, S. and by W., four hours and twenty-five minutes. Bought food and served out rations to the men for ten days, as water is scarce, and but little food can be obtained at the villages. The country is very dry and wintry-looking, but flowers shoot out.

2d September. The people are preparing their ten days' food. Two pagazi ran away with twenty-four dotis of the men's calico. Sent after them, but with small hopes of capturing them.

3d September.—Unsuccessful search.

4th September.—Leave Chikulu's, and pass a large puff-adder in the way. A single blow on the head killed it, so that it did not stir. About three feet long, and as thick as a man's arm, a short tail, and flat broad head. The men say that this is a very good sign for

34

our journey, though it would have been a bad sign, and suffering and death, had one trodden on it. Come to Liwane; large tree and waters. S.S.W. four and one-half hours.

5th September.—A long hot tramp to Manyara's. He is a kind old man. Many of the men very tired and sick. S.S.W. five and three-quarter hours.

6th September.—Rest the caravan, as we shall have to make forced marches on account of tsetse fly.

7th September.—Obliged to remain, as several are ill with fever.

8th September.—On to N'gombo nullah. Very hot and people ill.

9th September.—Telekeza* at broad part of the nullah, then went on two hours and passed the night in the forest.

10th September.—On to Mweras, and spent one night there by a pool in the forest. Village two miles off.

11th September.—On eight and a half hours to Telekeza. Sun very hot, and marching fatiguing to all.

We found that an old path from Mwaro has water, and must go early to-morrow morning, and so avoid the roundabout by Morefu. We shall thus save two days, which in this hot weather is much for us. We hear that Simba has gone to fight with Fipa. Two Bany-amwezi volunteer.

12th September.—We went by this water till 2 P.M., then made a march, and to-morrow get to villages. Got a buffalo and remain overnight. Water is in hæmatite. I engaged four pagazi here.

---

* Mid-day halt.

15th September.—On to near range of hills. Much large game here. Ill.

16th September.—Climbed over range about two hundred feet high; then on westward to stockaded villages of Kamirambo. His land begins at the M'toni.

17th September.—To Metambo River; one and a quarter broad, and marshy. Here begins the land of Merera. Through forest with many strychnus trees, three and a quarter hours, and arrive at Merera's.

18th September.—Remain at Merera's to prepare food. [There is a significant entry here; the old enemy was upon him. It would seem that his peculiar liability during these travels to one prostrating form of disease was now redoubled. The men speak of few periods of even comparative health from this date.]

19th September.—Ditto, ditto, because I am ill with bowels, having eaten nothing for eight days. Simba wants us to pass by his village, and not by the straight path.

20th September.—Went to Simba's; three and a half hours. About northwest. Simba sent a handsome present of food, a goat, eggs, and a fowl, beans, split rice, dura, and sesame. I gave him three dotis of superior cloth.

21st September.—Rest here, as the complaint does not yield to medicine or time; but I begin to eat now, which is a favorable symptom. The Banyamwezi women are in general very coarse, not a beautiful woman amongst them, as is so common among the Batusi; squat, thickset figures, and features too; a race of pagazi. They are generally respectful in deportment, but not very generous; they have learned the Arab adage, "nothing for nothing," and are keen slave-traders.

22d September.—Preparing food, and one man pretends inability to walk; send for some pagazi to carry loads of those who carry him.

23d September.—The pagazi, after demanding enormous pay, walked off. We went on along rocky banks of a stream, and, crossing it, camped, because the next water is far off.

24th September.—Recovering and thankful, but weak; cross broad, sedgy stream, and so on to Boma Misonghi, W. and by S.

25th September.—Got a buffalo and M'jure, and remain to eat them. I am getting better slowly. The M'jure, or water-hog, was all eaten by hyenas during the night; but the buffalo is safe.

26th September.—Through forest, along the side of a sedgy valley. Cross its head water, which has rust of iron in it, then W. and by S. The forest has very much tsetse. Zebras calling loudly, and Senegal long claw in our camp at dawn, with its cry, "O-o-o-o-o-o-o-o-o-o."

27th September.—On at dawn. No water expected, but we crossed three abundant supplies before we came to hill of our camp. Much game about here. Getting well again; thanks. About W. three and three-quarter hours. No people, or marks of them. Flowers sprouting in expectation of rains; much land burned off, but grass short yet.

28th September.—At two hills with mushroom-topped trees on west side. Crossed a good stream, twelve feet broad and knee deep. Buffaloes grazing. Many of the men sick.

29th September.—Through much bamboo and low hills to M'pokwa ruins and river. The latter in a deep rent, in alluvial soil. Very hot, and many sick in consequence. Course W.

30th September.—Away among low tree-covered hills of granite and sandstone. Found that Bangala had assaulted the village to which we went a few days ago, and all were fugitives. Our people found plenty of Batatas* in the deserted gardens. A great help, for we all were hungry.

1st October, 1872, *Friday.*—On, through much deserted cultivation in rich damp soil. We saw a few people, but all are in terror.

2d October.—Obtained M'tama in abundance for brass wire, and remained to grind it. The people have been without any for some days, and now rejoice in plenty.

3d October.—Southwards, and down a steep descent into a rich valley, with much green maize in ear; people friendly; but it was but one hour's march, so went on through hilly country S.W. Men firing off ammunition, had to be punished. We crossed the Katuma River, in the bottom of a valley; it is twelve feet broad, and knee deep; camped in a forest. The weather disagreeably hot and sultry.

4th October.—Over the same hilly country; the grass is burnt off, but the stalks are disagreeable. Came to a fine valley, with a large herd of zebras feeding quietly. We went only an hour and a half to-day, as one sick man is carried, and it is hot and trying for all.

5th October.—Up and down mountains; very sore on legs and lungs. Trying to save donkey's strength, I climbed and descended, and as soon as I mounted, off he

---

* Sweet potatoes.

set as hard as he could run, and he felt not the bridle; the saddle was loose, but I stuck on till we reached water in a bamboo hollow with spring.

6th October.—Traveled W. and by S. two and three-quarter hours. Short marches, on account of carrying one sick man.

7th October.—Over fine park-like country, with large belts of bamboo, and fine, broad, shady trees. Trees large and open. Large game evidently abounds, and waters generally are not far apart.

8th October.—Came on early, as sun is hot, and in two hours saw the Tanganyika from a gentle hill. All are very tired, and in coming to a stockade we were refused admittance, because Malongwana had attacked them lately, and we might seize them when in this stronghold. Very true; so we sit outside, in the shade of a single palm (Borassus).

9th October.—Rest, because all are tired, and several sick. This heat makes me useless, and constrains me to lie like a log. Inwardly I feel tired, too.

10th October.—People very tired, and it being moreover Sunday, we rest. Give each a keta of beads.

11th October.—Reach Kalema district after two and three-quarter hours over black mud, all deeply cracked, and many deep torrents now dry. Kalema is a stockade. We see Tanganyika, but a range of low hills intervenes. A rumor of war to-morrow.

12th October.—We wait till 2 P.M., and then make a forced march towards Fipa. The people cultivate but little, for fear of enemies; so we can buy few provisions. We left a broad valley, with a sand river in it, where we have been two days, and climbed a range of hills parallel to Tanganyika, of mica schist and gneiss, tilted away from the lake. Course S.W. to brink of Tanganyika water.

13*th October.*—Our course went along the top of a range of hills lying parallel with the lake. A great part of yesterday was on the same range. It is a thousand feet above the water, and is covered with trees rather scraggy. At sunset the red glare on the surface made the water look like a sea of reddish gold; it seemed so near that many went off to drink, but were three or four hours in doing so. One cannot see the other side, on account of the smokes in the air; but this morning three capes jut out, and the last, bearing S.E. from our camp, seems to go near the other side. Very hot weather. To the town of Fipa to-morrow. Course about S. Though we suffer much from the heat by traveling at this season, we escape a vast number of running and often muddy rills, also muddy paths which would soon knock the donkey up. Tipo Tipo is reported to be carrying it with a high hand in Nsama's country, Itawa, insisting that all the ivory must be brought as his tribute—the conqueror of Nsama. Our drum is the greatest object of curiosity we have to the Banyamwezi. A very great deal of cotton is cultivated all along the shores of Lake Tanganyika; it is manufactured into coarse cloth, which is the general clothing of all.

14*th October.*—Crossed two deep gullies with sluggish water in them, and one surrounding an old stockade. Camp on a knoll, overlooking modern stockade and Tanganyika very pleasantly. Saw two beautiful sultanas with azure blue necks. Mukembe land is ruled by chief Kariaria; village, Mokaria. Mount M'Pumbwe

goes into the Lake. N'Tambwe Mount; village, Kafu-
mfwe. Kapufi is the chief of Fipa.

Noon, and about fifty feet above lake; clouded over.
Temperature 91°, noon; 94°, 3 P.M.

15th October.—Rest, and kill an ox. The dry heat
is distressing, and all feel it sorely. I am right glad of
the rest, but keep on as constantly as I can. By giving
dura and maize to the donkeys, and riding on alternate
days, they hold on; but I feel the sun more than if
walking. The chief Kariaria is civil.

16th October.—Leave Mokaia and go south. We
crossed several bays of Tanganyika, the path winding
considerably. The people set fire to our camp as soon
as we started.

17th October.—Leave a bay of Tanganyika, and go
on to Mpimbwe; two lions growled savagely as we
passed. Game is swarming here, but my men cannot
shoot except to make a noise. We climbed up a pass
at the east end of Mpimbwe mountain, at a rounded
mass of it found water.

18th October.—Went on about south among mountains all day till we came down, by a little westing,
to the lake again, where there were some large villages,
well stockaded, with a deep gully half round them. Ill
with my old complaint again.

19th October.—Remained to prepare food and rest
the people. Two islets, Nkoma and Kalenge, are here,
the latter in front of us.

20th October.—Started at 2 P.M. Went on and passed
a large arm of Tanganyika, having a bar of hills on its
outer border Country swarming with large game.
Course east, and then south.

"The Main Stream came up to Susi's Mouth."

21st October.—Mokassa, a Moganda boy, has a swelling of the ankle, which prevents his walking. We went one hour to find wood to make a litter for him. The bomas round the villages are plastered with mud, so as to intercept balls or arrows. The trees are all cut down for these stockades, and the flats are cut up with deep gullies. There is an arm of Tanganyika here called Kafungia.

I sent a doti to the headman of the village, where we made a litter, to ask for a guide to take us straight south instead of going east to Fipa, which is four days off, and out of our course. Tipo Tipo is said to be at Morero, west of Tanganyika.

22d October.—Turned back westwards, and went through the hills down to some large islets in the lake, and camped in villages destroyed by Simba.

23d October.—First east, and then passed two deep bays, at one of which we put up, as they had food to sell. The sides of the Tanganyika Lake are a succession of rounded bays, answering to the valleys which trend down to the shore between the numerous ranges of hills. In Lake Nyassa they seem made by the prevailing winds. We only get about one hour and a half south and by east. Rain probably fell last night, for the opposite shore is visible to-day. The mountain range of Banda slopes down as it goes south. This is the district of Motoshi.

24th October.—There are many rounded bays in mountainous Fipa. We rested two hours in a deep shady dell, and then came along a very slippery mountain-side to a village in a stockade. It is very hot to-day, and the first thunderstorm away in the east. The name of this village is Linde.

25th October.—The coast runs south-south-east to a cape. We went up southeast, then over a high, steep hill to turn to south again, then down into a valley of Tanganyika, over another stony side, and down to a dell with a village in it.

26th October.—Over hills and mountains again, past two deep bays, and on to a large bay with a prominent islet on the south side of it, called Kitanda, from the chief's name.

27th October.—Remained to buy food, which is very dear. We slaughtered a tired cow to exchange for provisions.

28th October.—Left Kitanda, and came around the cape, going south. The cape furthest north bore north-north-west. We came to three villages and some large spreading trees, where we were invited by the headman to remain, as the next stage along the shore is long. Morilo islet is on the other or western side, at the crossing-place.

The chief Mosirwa, or Kasamane, paid us a visit, and is preparing a present of food. Molilo or Morilo islet is the crossing-place of Banyamwezi when bound for Casembe's country, and is near to the Lofuko River, on the western shore of the lake. The lake is about twelve or fifteen miles broad, at latitude 7° 52′ south. It takes about three hours to cross at Morilo.

29th October.—Crossed the Thembwa Rivulet, twenty feet broad and knee deep, and sleep on its eastern bank. Fine cold water over stony bottom. The mountains now close in on Tanganyika, so there is no path but one, over which luggage cannot be carried. The stage after this is six hours up hill before we come to water.

This forced me to stop after only a short crooked march of two and a quarter hours. We are now on the confines of Fipa. The next march takes us into Burungu.

30*th October.*—The highest parts of the mountains are from five hundred feet to seven hundred feet higher than the passes, say from thirteen hundred feet to fifteen hundred feet above the lake. A very rough march to-day. We arrive at a village on the lake shore. Kirila islet is about a quarter of a mile from the shore. Thunder all the morning, and a few drops of rain fell. It will ease the men's feet when it does fall. They call out earnestly for it, "Come, come with hail!" and prepare their huts for it.

31*st October.*—Through a long pass, after we had climbed over Winelao. Came to an islet one and a half mile long, called Kapessa, and then into a long pass.

Going south, we came to a very large arm of the lake, with a village at the end of it in a stockade. This arm is seven or eight miles long, and about two broad.

CHAPTER XXX.

THE MARCH TOWARDS BANGWEOLO.

False Guides—Difficult Traveling—He leaves the Lake—The Kasonso Family—
A Hospitable Chief—The River Lofu—Famine—Ill—Arrives at Chama's
Town—A Difficulty—An Immense Snake—Account of Casembe's Death—
Chungu—Reaches the River Lopopsi—Misled and Baffled—Arrives at Chi-
tunkue's—Terrible Marching—The Doctor is borne through the Flooded
Country.

1st November, 1872.—WE hear that an eruption of
Babemba, on the Baulungu, destroyed all the food.
We tried to buy food here, but everything is hidden in
the mountains, so we have to wait to-day till they fetch
it. If in time, we shall make an afternoon's march.
Raining to-day. The River Mulu from Chingolao gave
us much trouble in crossing, from being filled with
vegetation; it goes into Tanganyika. Our course south
and east.

2d November.—Deceived by a guide, who probably
feared his countrymen in front. Went round a stony
cape, and then to a land-locked harbor, three miles long
by two broad. Here was a stockade, where our guide
absconded. They told us that if we continued our
march we should not get water for four hours, so we
rested, having marched four and and a quarter hours.

3d November.—We marched this morning to a village
where food was reported. The people of Liemba village
having a cow or two, and some sheep and goats, eagerly
advised us to go on to the next village, as being just
behind a hill, and well provisioned. Four very rough
hills were the penalty of our credulity, taking four

hours of incessant toil in these mountain fastnesses.
They hide their food, and the paths are the most difficult that can be found, in order to wear out their enemies. To-day we got to the River Luazi, having
marched five and a half hours, and sighting Tanganyika near us twice.

4th November.—All very tired. We tried to get food,
but it is very dear, and difficult to bargain for.

6th November.—Pass a deep narrow bay and climb a
steep mountain. After a few hours' climb we look down
on the lake, with its many bays. A sleepy glare floats
over it. Further on we came on a ledge of rocks, and
looked sheer down five hundred feet or six hundred
feet into its dark green waters.

7th November, Sunday.—Remained, but the headman forbade his people to sell us food. We keep quiet
except to invite him to a parley, which he refuses, and
makes loud lullilooing in defiance, as if he were inclined to fighting. At last, seeing that we took no
notice of him, he sent us a present; I returned three
times its value.

8th November.—The large donkey is very ill, and
unable to climb the high mountain in our front. I left
men to coax him on, and they did it well. I then sent
some to find a path out from the Lake mountains, for
they will kill us all; others were despatched to buy
food, but the lake folks are poor except in fish.

The sun makes the soil so hot that the radiation is
as if it came from a furnace. It burns the feet of the
people, and knocks them up. Subcutaneous inflammation is frequent in the legs, and makes some of my most
hardy men useless. We have been compelled to slow-

ness very much against my will. I too was ill, and became better only by marching on foot. Riding exposes one to the bad influence of the sun, while by walking the perspiration modifies beneficially the excessive heat.

9th November.—We got very little food, and kill a calf to fill our mouths a little. A path east seems to lead out from these mountains of Tanganyika. We went on east this morning in highland open forest, then descended by a long slope to a valley in which there is water. The highlands are of a purple color from the new leaves coming out. The donkey began to eat, to my great joy. Men sent off to search for a village return empty-handed, and we must halt. I am ill and losing much blood.

10th November.—Out from the Lake mountains, and along high ridges of sandstone and dolomite. Our guide volunteered to take the men on to a place where food can be bought—a very acceptable offer. The donkey is recovering; it was distinctly the effects of tsetse, for the eyes and all the mouth and nostrils swelled. Another died at Kwihara with every sympton of tsetse poison fully developed.

11th November.—Over gently undulating country, with many old garden sand watch-houses, some of great height, we reached the River Kalambo, which I know as falling into Tanganyika. The Kalambo is shallow, and say twenty yards wide, but it spreads out a good deal.

[Their journey of the 12th and 13th led them over low ranges of sandstone and hæmatite, and past several strongly stockaded villages. They struck the Halocheche River, a rapid stream fifteen yards wide and

thigh deep, on its way to the Lake, and arrived at
Zombe's town, which is built in such a manner that the
river runs through it, whilst a stiff palisade surrounds
it. He says:]

It was entirely surrounded by M'toka's camp, and a
constant fight maintained at the point where the line
of stakes was weakened by the river running through.
He killed four of the enemy, and then Chitimbwa and
Kasonso coming to help him, the siege was raised.

M'toka compelled some Malongwana to join him, and
plundered many villages; he has been a great scourge.
The siege lasted three months, till the two brothers of
Zombe, before-mentioned, came, and then a complete
rout ensued. It is two months since this rout, so we
have been prevented by a kind Providence from coming
soon enough. He was impudent and extortionate before,
and much more now that he has been emboldened by
success in plundering.

16th November.—After waiting some time for the men,
I sent men back yesterday to look after the sick donkey;
they arrived, but the donkey died this morning. Its
death was evidently caused by tsetse bite and bad usage
by one of the men, who kept it forty-eight hours without water. The rain, no doubt, helped to a fatal end;
it is a great loss to me.

17th November.—We went on along the bottom of a
high ridge that flanks the lake on the west, and then
turned up south-east to a village hung on the edge of a
deep chasm in which flows the Aeezy.

18th November.—We were soon overwhelmed in a
pouring rain, and had to climb up the slippery red path
which is parallel and near to Mbette's. Our march

35

took us about S. W. to Kampamba's, the son of Kasonso, who is dead.

19th November.—I visited Kampamba. He is still as agreeable as he was before when he went with us to Liemba. He has a good-sized village.

20th, 21st, and 23d November.—The men turn to stringing beads for future use, and to all except defaulters I give a present of two dotis, and a handful of beads each. I have diminished the loads considerably, which pleases them much. We have now three and a half loads of calico, and one hundred and twenty bags of beads. Several go idle, but have to do any odd work, such as helping the sick or anything they are ordered to do.

24th November.—Left Kampamba's to day, and cross a meadow S. E. of the village in which the River Muanani rises. It flows into the Kapondosi and so on to the lake.

We came at last to Kasonso's successor's village on the River Molulwe. It goes to the Lofu. The chief here gave a sheep—a welcome present, for I was out of flesh for four days. Kampamba is stingy as compared with his father.

25th November.—We came in an hour's march to a rivulet called the Casembe—the departed Kasonso lived here. The stream is very deep and flows slowly to the Lofu. Our path lay through much pollarded forest, troublesome to walk in, as the stumps send out leafy shoots.

26th November.—Started at daybreak. Passed two villages of people come out to cultivate this very fertile soil, which they manure by burning branches of trees. The Rivulet Loela flows here.

27th November.—As it is Sunday we stay here at N'dari's village, for we shall be in an uninhabited track to-morrow, beyond the Lofu.

28th November.—We came to the River Lofu in a mile. It is sixty feet across and very deep. We made a bridge, and cut the banks down, so that the donkey and cattle could pass over. It took us two hours, during which time we hauled them all across with a rope. We came to another village with a river which must be crossed—no stockade here, and the chief allowed us to camp in his town.

29th November.—Crossed the Loozi in two branches, and climbed up the gentle ascent of Malembe to the village of Chiwe, whom I formerly called Chibwe, being misled by the Yao tongue. Ilamba is the name of the rill at his place. The Loozi's two branches were waist deep. The first was crossed by a natural bridge of a fig-tree growing across. It runs into the Lofu, which river rises in Isunga country at a mountain called Kwitette. The Chambeze rises east of this, and at the same place as Louzua.

[The road lay through the same country among low hills, for several miles, till they came, on the 1st December, to a rivulet called Lovu Katanta.

Passing on with heavy rain pouring down, they found themselves in the Wemba country, the low, tree-covered hills exhibiting here and there "fine-grained schist and igneous rocks of red, white, and green color."]

3d December, 1872.—No food to be got, on account of M'toka's and Tipo Tipo's raids.

A stupid or perverse guide took us away to-day N. W. or W.N.W. The villagers refused to lead us to

Chipwite's, where food was to be had; he is S.W., one and one-half day off. The guide had us at his mercy, for he said, "If you go S.W. you will be five days without food or people." We crossed the Kanomba, fifteen yards wide, and knee deep. Here our guide disappeared, and so did the path. We crossed the Lampussi twice; it is forty yards wide, and knee deep; our course is W.N.W. for about four and a half hours today. We camped, and sent men to search for a village that has food.

4th December.—Waiting for the return of our men in a green wooded valley on the Lampussi River. Those who were sent yesterday return without anything.

5th December.—My men returned about 5 P.M. with two of Kafimbe's men, bringing a present of food to me. A little was bought, and we go on to-morrow to sleep two nights on the way, and so to Kafimbe, who is a brother of Nsama's, and fights him.

6th December.—We cross the Lampussi again, and up to a mountain, along which we go, and then down to some ruins. This took us five hours, and then with two and one-quarter more hours we reach Sintila.

7th December.—Off at 6.15 A.M. Our course lay along between two ranges of low hills, then, where they ended, we went by a good-sized stream, thirty yards or so across, and then down into a valley to Kafimbe's.

8th December.—I visited Kafimbe. He is an intelligent and pleasant young man, who has been attacked several times by Kitandula, the successor of Nsama of Itawa, and compelled to shift from Motononga to this rivulet, Motosi, which flows into the Kisi, and thence into Lake Moero.

9th December.—Send off men to a distance for food, and wait, of course. Here there is none, for either love or money.

10th December.—Left Kafimbe's. He gave us three men to take us into Chama's village, and came a mile along the road with us. Our road took us, by a winding course, from one little deserted village to another.

11th December.—Being far from water, we went two hours across a plain dotted with villages, to a muddy rivulet called the Mukubwe (it runs to Moero), where we found the village of a nephew of Nsama. This young fellow was very liberal in gifts of food, and in return I gave him two cloths.

12th December.—Marenza sent a present of dura flour and a fowl, and asked for a little butter as a charm. He seems unwilling to give us a guide, though told by Kafimbe to do so. We went on half an hour to the River Mokoe, which is thirty yards wide, and carries off much water into Malunda, and so to Lake Moero.

[The note made on the following day is written with a feeble hand, and scarce one penciled word tallies with its neighbor in form or distinctness; in fact, it is seen at a glance what exertion it cost him to write at all. He says no more than " Ill" in one place, but this is the evident explanation; yet with the same painstaking determination of old, the three rivers which they crossed have their names recorded, and the hours of marching, and the direction, are all entered in his pocket-book.]

13th December.—Westward about by south, and crossed a river, Mokobwe, thirty-five yards. Ill; and after going S.W. camped in a deserted village, S.W., traveling five hours. River Mekanda, 2d. Menomba, 3, where we camp.

14th December.—Guides turned N. W., to take us to a son of Nsama. After going a mile along the bank of the Menomba, Susi broke through and ran south, till he got a S. by W. path, which we followed, and came to a village having plenty of food. Crossed the Lupere, which runs into the Makobwe.

A leech crawling towards me in the village this morning, elicited the Bemba idea that they fall from the clouds or sky—"mulu." It is called here "Mosunda a maluze," or leech of the rivers; "Luba" is the Zanzibar name. In one place I counted nineteen leeches in our path, in about a mile; rain had fallen, and their appearance out of their hiding-places suddenly after heavy rain, may have given rise to the idea of their fall with it, as fishes do, and the thunder frog is supposed to do. Always too cloudy and rainy for observations of stars.

15th December.—The country is now level. There are many deserted villages; few birds. Cross the River Lithabo, running fast to the S.W. Reached village of Chipala, on the Rivulet Chikatula, which goes to Moipanza. The Lithabo goes to Kalongwesi by a S.W. course.

16th December.—Off at 6 A.M. across the Chikatula, and in three-quarters of an hour crossed the Lopanza. The Lolela was before us in half an hour, both streams perennial; and embowered in tall umbrageous trees that love wet; both flow to the Kalongwesi.

We came to quite a group of villages having food, and remain, as we got only driblets in the last two camps.

At noon we got to the village of Kasiane, which is close to two rivulets, named Lopanza and Lolela. The headman, a relative of Nsama, brought me a large present of flour of dura, and I gave him two fathoms of calico.

17th December.—It looked rainy, but we waited half an hour, and then went on one hour and a half, when it set in, and forced us to seek shelter in a village. The district is called Kisinga, and flanks the Kalongweze.

18th December.—We reached the Kalongwese River on the right bank. The donkey sends a foot every now and then through the roof of cavities made apparently by ants, and sinks down eighteen inches or more and nearly falls. These covered hollows are right in the paths.

19th December.—So cloudy and wet that no observations can be taken for latitude and longitude at this real geographical point. The Kalongwese is sixty or eighty yards wide and four yards deep, about a mile above the confluence of the Luena. We crossed it in very small canoes, and swamped one twice, but no one was lost. Marched S. about one and a quarter hour.

20th December.—Shut in by heavy clouds. Wait to see if it will clear up. Went on at 7.15, drizzling as we came near the Mozumba or chief's stockade.

A wet bed last night, for it was in the canoe that was upset. It was so rainy that there was no drying it.

21st December.—Arrived at Chama's. Chama's brother tried to mislead us yesterday, in hopes of making us wander hopelessly and helplessly. Failing in this, he ran before us to the chief's stockade, and made all the women flee, which they did, leaving their chickens damless. We gave him two handsome cloths, one for himself and one for Chama, and said we wanted food only, and would buy it. They are accustomed to the bullying of half-castes, who take what they like for nothing. They are alarmed at our behaviour to-day, so we took quiet possession of the stockade, as the place that they put us in was on the open defenceless plain. Seventeen human skulls ornament the stockade.

22d December.—We crossed a rivulet at Chama's village ten yards wide and thigh deep, and afterwards in an hour and a half came to the sedgy stream which we could barely cross. We hauled a cow across bodily. Went on mainly south, and through much bracken.

23d December.—Off at 6 A.M., and in an hour and a quarter came to three large villages by three rills called Misangwa; went on to other villages south, and a stockade.

24th December.—Passed the Lopopussi running west to the Lofubu about seven yards wide, it flows fast over rocks with heavy aquatic plants. The people are not afraid of us here as they were so distressingly elsewhere; we hope to buy food here.

25th December, Christmas Day.—I thank the good Lord for the good gift of His Son Christ Jesus our Lord. Slaughtered an ox, and gave a fundo and a half to each of the party. This is our great day, so we rest. It is cold and wet, day and night. The headman is gracious and generous, which is very pleasant compared with awe, awe, and refusing to sell or stop to speak, or show the way.

The White Nile, carrying forward its large quasi-tidal wave, presents a mass of water to the Blue Nile, which acts as a buffer to its rapid flood. The White Nile being at a considerable height when the Blue rushes down its steep slopes, presents its brother Nile with a soft cushion, into which it plunges, and is restrained by the *vis inertiæ* of the more slowly moving river, and, both united, pass on to form the great inundation of the year in Lower Egypt. The Blue River brings down the heavier portion of the Nile deposit, while the White River comes down with the black, finely divided matter from thousands of square miles of forest in Manyuema, which probably gave the Nile its name, and is in fact the real fertilizing ingredient in the mud that is annually left. Some of the rivers in Manyuema, as the Luia and Machila, are of inky blackness, and make the whole main stream of a very Nilotic hue. An acquaintance with these dark, flowing rivers, and scores of rills of water tinged as dark as strong tea, was all my reward for plunging through the terrible Manyuema mud or " glaur."

26th December.—Along among the usual low, tree-covered hills of red, and yellow, and green schists—paths wet and slippery. Came to the Lofubu, fifteen yards broad and very deep, water clear, flowing north-west to join Luena or Kisaki, as Lopopussi goes west too into Lofubu it becomes large, as we saw. We crossed by a bridge, and the donkey swam with men on each side of him. We came to three villages on the other side, with many iron furnaces. Wet and drizzling weather made us stop soon.

27th December.—Leave the villages on the Lofubu. A cascade comes down on our left. The country undulating deeply; the hills, rising at times three hundred to four hundred feet, are covered with stunted wood. We cross one rivulet running to the Lofubu, and camp by a blacksmith's rill in the jungle.

I killed a Naia Hadje snake seven feet long here; he reared up before me, and turned to fight. No observations have been possible through most of this month. People assert that the new moon will bring drier weather. We are evidently ascending, as we come near the Chambeze.

29th, or 1st January, 1873.—I am wrong two days.

29th December.—We went on southwards, three and one-quarter hours to a river, the Luongo, running strongly west and south to the Luapulu; then, after one hour crossed it, twelve yards wide and waist deep. We met a man with four of his kindred stripping off bark to make bark-cloth; he gives me the above information about the Luongo.

1st January, 1873 (30*th*.)—Came on at 6 A.M., very cold. The rains have ceased for a time. Arrive at the village of the man who met us yesterday. As we have been unable to buy food, I camp here.

2d January.—Thursday—Wednesday was the 1st, I was two days wrong.

3d January.—The villagers very anxious to take us to the west to Chikumbi's, but I refused to follow them, and we made our course to the Luongo. Went in the forest south without a path for one and a half hour, then through a flat forest. We camped in the forest at the Situngula Rivulet. A damp climate this—lichens on all the trees, even on those of two inches diameter. Our last cow died of injuries received in crossing the Lofubu. People buy it for food, so it is not an entire loss.

4th January.—March south one hour to the Lopoposi or Lopopozi stream of twenty-five or thirty feet, and

now breast deep, flowing fast southwards to join the
Chambeze. Camped at Ketebe's at 2 P.M., on the Rivulet Kizima after very heavy rain.

6th January.—Ketebe or Kapesha very civil and
generous. He sent three men to guide us to his elder
brother Chungu. The men drum and sing harshly for
him continually. I gave him half a pound of powder,
and he lay on his back rolling and clapping his hands,
and all his men lulliloed; then he turned on his front,
and did the same. The men are very timid—no wonder, the Arab slaves do as they choose with them. The
women burst out through the stockade in terror when
my men broke into a chorus as they were watching my
tent.

7th January.—A cold, rainy day keeps us in a poor
village very unwillingly. 3 P.M., on to the Rivulet Kamalopa, which runs to Kamolozzi and into Kapopozi.

8th January.—Detained by heavy continuous rains
in the village Moenje. We are near Lake Bangweolo
and in a damp region. Got off in the afternoon in a
drizzle; crossed a rill six feet wide, but now very deep;
it is called the Kamalopa. Came on through flat forest
as usual S.W. and S.

[His men speak of the march from this point as one
continual plunge in and out of morass, and through
rivers which were only distinguishable from the surrounding waters by their deep currents and the necessity
for using canoes. To a man reduced in strength and
chronically affected with dysenteric symptoms ever
likely to be aggravated by exposure, the effect may be
well conceived! It is probable that had Dr. Livingstone
been at the head of a hundred picked Europeans, every

man would have been down within the next fortnight. As it is, we cannot help thinking of his company of followers, who must have been well led and under the most thorough control to endure these marches at all, for nothing cows the African so much as rain. The next day's journey may be taken as a specimen of the hardships every one had to endure:—]

9th January.—Mosumba of Chungu. After an hour we crossed the rivulet and sponge of Nkulumuna, one hundred feet of rivulet and two hundred yards of flood, besides some two hundred yards of sponge full and running off; we then, after another hour, crossed the large rivulet Lopopozi by a bridge which was forty-five feet long, and showed the deep water; then one hundred yards of flood thigh deep, and two hundred or three hundred yards of sponge. After this we crossed two rills, called Linkanda, and their sponges, the rills in flood ten or twelve feet broad and thigh deep. After crossing the last we came near the Mosumba, and received a message to build our sheds in the forest, which we did.

Chungu knows what a nuisance a Safari (caravan) makes itself. Cloudy day, and at noon heavy rain from N.W. The headman, on receiving two cloths, said he would converse about our food and show it to-morrow. No observations can be made, from clouds and rain.

10th January.—Mosumba of Chungu. Rest to-day, and get an insight into the ford; cold, rainy weather. When we prepared to visit Chungu, we received a message that he had gone to his plantations to get millet. He then sent for us at 1 P.M. to come, but on reaching the stockade we heard a great uproar, and found it being

shut from terror. We spoke to the inmates, but in vain,
so we returned. Chungu says that we should put his
head on a pole, like Casembe's! We shall go on without him to-morrow. The terror guns have inspired is
extreme.

11*th January.*—Chungu sent a goat and big basket
of flour, and excused his fears because guns had routed
Casembe and his head was put on a pole; it was his
young men that raised the noise. We remain to buy
food, as there is scarcity at Mombo, in front. Cold and
rainy weather, never saw the like; but this is among
the sponges of the Nile, and near the northern shores of
Bangweolo.

12*th January.*—A dry day enabled us to move forward an hour to rivulet and sponge, but by ascending it
we came to its head and walked over dry shod, then one
hour to another broad rivulet—Pinda, sluggish, and
having one hundred yards of sponge on each side.

13*th January.*—Storm-stayed by rain and cold at the
village on the Rivulet Kalambosi, near the Chambeze.
Sent back for food.

14*th January.*—Went on dry S.E., and then S. two
hours to River Mozinga, and marched parallel to it
till we came to the confluence of Kasie. Mosinga,
twenty-five feet, waist deep. The villagers are much
afraid of us. After four and a half hours we were
brought up by the deep rivulet Mpanda, to be crossed
to-morrow in canoes. The people are Babisi, who have
fled from the west, and are busy catching fish in basket
traps.

15*th January.*—Found that Chungu had let us go
astray towards the Lake, and into an angle formed by

the Mpande and Lopopussi, and the Lake-full of rivulets which are crossed with canoes. Chisupa, a headman on the other side of the Mpanda, sent a present and denounced Chungu for heartlessness. We explained to one man our change of route and went first N.E., then E. to the Monsinga, which we forded again at a deep place full of holes and rust-of-iron water, in which we floundered over 300 yards; the whole march about east for six hours.

16*th January.*—Away northeast and north to get out of the many rivulets near the lake back to the River Lopopussi, which now looms large, and must be crossed in canoes. We have to wait in a village till these are brought, and have only got one and three-quarter hour nearly north.

We were treated scurvily by Chungu. He knew that we were near the Chambeze, but hid the knowledge and himself too. It is terror of guns.

17*th January.*—We are troubled for want of canoes, but have to treat gently with the owners, otherwise they would all run away, as they have around Chungu's, in the belief that we should return to punish their silly headman. By waiting patiently yesterday, we drew about twenty canoes towards us this morning, but all too small for the donkey, so we had to turn away back northwest to the bridge above Chungu's. If we had tried to swim the donkey across alongside a canoe it would have been terribly strained, as the Lopopussi is here quite two miles wide and full of rushes, except in the main stream.

18*th January.*—We lost a week by going to Chungu (a worthless terrified headman), and came back to the ford of Lopopussi, which we crossed, only from believing him to be an influential man who would explain the country to us. We came up the Lopopussi three hours yesterday, after spending two hours in going down to examine the canoes.

19th January.—After prayers we went on to a fine village, and on from it to the Mononse.

20th January.—Tried to observe lunars in vain; clouded over all, thick and muggy. Came on, disappointed, and along the Lovu one and one-half mile. Crossed it by a felled tree lying over it. Marched about two and one-half hours; very unsatisfactory progress.

[In answer to a question as to whether Dr. Livingstone could possibly manage to wade so much, Susi says that he was carried across these sponges and the rivulets on the shoulders of Chowpere or Chumah.]

21st January.—We went on two and one-half hours, and were brought up by the River Malalanzi, which is about fifteen feet wide, waist deep, and has three hundred yards or more of sponge. Guides refused to come, as Chitunkue, their headman, did not own them. We started alone; a man came after us and tried to mislead us, in vain.

22d January.—We pushed on through many deserted gardens and villages, the man evidently sent to lead us astray from our S.E. course; he turned back when he saw that we refused his artifice. Crossed another rivulet, possibly the Lofu, now broad and deep, and then came to another, of several deep streams but sponge, not more than fifty feet in all. Here we remained, having traveled in fine, drizzling rain all the morning. Population all gone, from the war of Chitoka with this Chitunkue.

It is trying beyond measure to be baffled by the natives, lying and misleading us wherever they can. They fear us very greatly, and with a terror that would gratify an anthropologist's heart. Their unfriendliness is made more trying, by our being totally unable to observe for our position. It is either densely clouded, or continually raining day and night. The country is covered with brackens, and rivulets occur at least one every hour of the march. These are deep, and have a broad selvage of sponge.

23d January.—We have to send back to villages of Chitunkue to buy food. It was not reported to me that the country in front was depopulated for three days, so I send a day back. I don't know where we are, and the people are deceitful in their statements; unaccountably so, though we deal fairly and kindly. Rain, rain, rain as if it never tired on this water-shed. The showers show little in the gauge, but keep everything and every place wet and sloppy.

Our people return, with a wretched present from Chitunkue; bad flour and a fowl, evidently meant to be rejected. He sent also an exorbitant demand for gunpowder, and payment of guides. I refused his present, and must plod on without guides, and this is very difficult, from the numerous streams.

24th January.—Went on E. and N.E., to avoid the deep part of a large river, which requires two canoes; but the men sent by the chief would certainly hide them. Went one and three-quarter hour's journey to a large stream, through drizzling rain, at least three hundred yards of deep water, amongst sedges and sponges of one hundred yards. We plunged in elephants' footprints, one and one-half hour, then came on one hour to a small rivulet ten feet broad, but waist deep, bridge covered and broken down. Carrying me across one of the broad, deep, sedgy rivers, is really a very difficult task. One we crossed was at least two thousand feet ıbroad, or more than three hundred yards. The first part, the main stream, came up to Susi's mouth, and wetted my seat and legs. One held up my pistol behind, then one after another took a turn, and when he sank into a deep elephant's foot-print, he required two to lift him, so as to gain a footing on the level, which was over waist deep. Others went on, and bent down the grass to insure some footing on the side of the elephants' path. Every ten or twelve paces brought us to a clear stream, flowing fast in its own channel, while over all a strong current came bodily through all the rushes and aquatic plants. Susi had the first spell, then Farijala; then a tall, stout, Arab-looking man; then Amoda; then Chanda; then Wade Sale; and each time I was lifted off bodily, and put on another pair of stout, willing shoulders, and fifty yards put them out of breath; no wonder! It was sore on the women folk of our party. It took us full an hour and a half for all to cross over, and several came over turn to help me and their friends. The water was cold, and so was the wind. We had to hasten on the building of sheds after crossing the second rivulet, as rain threatened us. After 4 P.M. it came on a pouring cold rain, when we were all under cover. We are anxious about food. The lake is near, but we are not sure of provisions, as there have been changes of population. Our progress is distressingly slow. Wet, wet, wet; sloppy weather, truly, and no

36

observations, except that the land near the lake being very level, the rivers spread out into broad friths and sponges. The streams are so numerous that there has been a scarcity of names.

25th January.—Kept in by rain. Rivulets and sponges again, and through flat forest. One and a half hour more, and then to the River Loou, a large stream with bridge destroyed. Sent to make repairs before we go over it, and then passed. The river is deep, and flows fast to the S.W., having about two hundred yards of safe flood flowing in long grass—clear water. The men built their huts, and had their camp ready by 3 P.M. A good day's work, not hindered by rain. The country all depopulated, so we can buy nothing.

26th January.—I arranged to go to our next River Luena, and ascend it till we found it small enough for crossing, as it has much "Tinga-tinga," or yielding, spongy soil; but another plan was formed by night, and we were requested to go down the Loou. Not wishing to appear overbearing, I consented until we were, after two hours' southing, brought up by several miles of Tinga-tinga. The people in a fishing village ran away from us, and we had to wait for some sick ones. A man came near us, but positively refused to guide us to Matipa, or anywhere else.

The sick people compelled us to make an early halt.

28th January.—A dreary, wet morning, and no food that we know of near. We killed our last calf but one last night, to give each a mouthful. At 9.30 we were allowed by the rain to march S.E. for two hours to a rivulet ten feet broad only, but waist deep, and one hundred and fifty yards of flood, all deep, too. Camped by a broad prairie or Bouga.

THE LAST MILE OF DR. LIVINGSTONE'S TRAVELS.

29th January.—We tramped one and one-quarter hour to a broad sponge, having at least three hundred yards of flood, and clear water flowing S.W., but no usual stream. All was stream flowing through the rushes, knee and thigh deep. On still with the same, repeated again and again till we came to broad branching sponges, at which I resolved to send out scouts S., S.E., and S.W. The music of the singing birds, the music of the turtle doves, the screaming of the frankolin proclaim man to be near.

30th *January.*—Remain waiting for the scouts. Manuasera returned at dark, having gone about eight hours south, and seen the lake and two islets. Smoke now appeared in the distance, so he turned, and the rest went on to buy food where the smoke was.

CHAPTER XXXI.

1st February, 1873.—WAITING for the scouts. They return unsuccessful—forced to do so by hunger. They did not come across a single soul.

2d February.—March smartly back to our camp of 28th ult. The people bear their hunger well. They collect mushrooms and plants, and often get lost in this flat, featureless country.

3d February.—Return march to our bridge on the Lofu, five hours. In going we went astray, and took six hours to do the work of five. On the Luena.

5th February.—Arrived at Chitunkue's, crossing two broad deep brooks, and on to the Malalenzi, now swollen. We are now at Chitunkue's mercy.

We find the chief more civil than we expected. He said each chief had his own land and his own peculiarities. He was not responsible for others. We were told that we had been near to Matipa and other chiefs; he would give us guides if we give him a cloth and some powder.

He is a fine, jolly-looking man, of a European cast of countenance, and very sensible and friendly. I gave him two cloths, for which he seemed thankful, and promised good guides to Matipa's. We have lost half a month by this wandering, but it was all owing to the unfriendliness of some and the fears of all. I begged for a more northerly path, where the water is low. It is impossible to describe the amount of water near the lake. Rivulets without number. They are so deep as to damp all ardor.

7th February.—This chief showed his leanings by demanding prepayment for his guides. This being a preparatory step to their desertion, I resisted, and sent men to demand what he meant by his words; he denied all, and said that his people lied, not he. We take this for what it is worth. He gives two guides to-morrow morning, and visits us this afternoon.

8th February.—The chief dawdles, although he promised great things yesterday. He places the blame on his people, who did not prepare food on account of the rain. Time is of no value to them. We have to remain over to-day. It is most trying to have to wait on frivolous pretences. I have endured such vexatious delays. The guides came at last with quantities of food which they intend to bargain with my people on the way.

9th February.—Slept in a most unwholesome, ruined village. Rank vegetation had run over all, and the soil smelled offensively. By a rocky passage we crossed the Mofiri, or great Tinga-tinga, a water running strongly, waist and breast deep, above thirty feet broad here, but very much broader below. After this we passed the River Methonua.

10th February.—Back again to our old camp on the Lovu or Lofu by the bridge.

11th February.—Our guides took us across country, where we saw tracks of buffaloes. A drizzly night was followed by a morning of cold, wet fog, but in three hours we reached our old camp. We camped on a deep bridged stream, called the Kiachibwe.

12th February.—We crossed the Kasoso, which joins the Mokisya, a river we afterwards crossed; it flows N. W., then over the Mofungwe.

13th February.—In four hours we came within sight of the Luena and Lake, and saw plenty of elephants and other game, but very shy. The forest trees are larger. The guides are more at a loss than we are, as they always go in canoes in the flat rivers and rivulets. Went E., then S.E. round to S.

14th February.—The water stands so high in the paths that I cannot walk dry shod, and I found in the large bougas or prairies in front, that it lay knee deep, so I sent on two men to go to the first villages of Matipa for large canoes to navigate the lake, or give us a guide to go east to the Chambeze, to go round on foot.

[We cannot but believe Livingstone saw great danger in these constant recurrences of his old disorder; we find a trace of it in the solemn reflections which he wrote in his pocket-book, immediately under the above words :]

If the good Lord gives me favor, and permits me to finish my work, I shall thank and bless Him, though it has cost me untold toil, pain, and travel; this trip has made my hair all gray.

15th Februrary, Sunday.—Service. Killed our last goat while waiting for messengers to return from Matipa's. Evening; the messenger came back, having been foiled by deep tinga-tinga and bouga. They say that

Matipa is on Chirube islet, a good man too, but far off from this.

16*th February*.—Sent men to Chirube, with a request to Matipa to convey us west if he has canoes; but, if not, to tell us truly, and we will go east and cross the Chambeze where it is small.

17*th February*.—The men will return to-morrow, but they have to go all the way out to the islet of Chirube to Matipa's.

18*th February*.—We wait, hungry and cold, for the return of the men who have gone to Matipa, and hope the good Lord will grant us influence with this man.

Our men have returned to-day, having obeyed the native who told them to sleep instead of going to Matipa. They bought food, and then believed that the islet Chirube was too far off, and returned with a most lame story. We shall make the best of it by going N.W., to be near the islets and buy food, till we can communicate with Matipa. If he fails us by fair means, we must seize canoes and go by force. The men say fear of me makes them act very cowardly. I have gone amongst the whole population kindly and fairly, but I fear I must now act rigidly, for when they hear that we have submitted to injustice, they at once conclude that we are fair game for all, and they go to lengths in dealing falsely that they would never otherwise attempt. It is, I can declare, not my nature, nor has it been my practice, to go as if "my back were up."

19*th February*.—A cold wet morning keeps us in this uncomfortable spot. When it clears up we go to an old stockade, to be near an islet to buy food. The people, knowing our need, are extortionate. We went on at 9

A.M., over an extensive water-covered plain. I was carried three miles to a canoe, and then in it we went westward, in branches of the Luena, very deep and flowing W. for three hours. I was carried three miles to a canoe, and we were then near enough to hear Bangweolo bellowing. The water on the plain is four, five, and seven feet deep. Camped in an old village of Matipa's, where, in the west, we see the Luena enter Lake Bangweolo. A large party in canoes came with food as soon as we reached our new quarters; they had heard that we were in search of Matipa. All are eager for calico, though they have only raw cassava to offer. They are clothed in bark-cloth and skins. Without canoes no movement can be made in any direction, for it is water everywhere, water above and water below.

20th February.—I sent a request to a friendly man to give me men, and a large canoe to go myself to Matipa; he says that he will let me know to-day if he can. Heavy rain by night and drizzling by day. No definite answer yet, but we are getting food, and Matipa will soon hear of us as he did when we came and returned back for food. I engaged another man to send a canoe to Matipa, and I showed him his payment, but retain it here till he comes back.

21st February.—The men engaged refuse to go to Matipa's; they have no honor. It is so wet we can do nothing. Another man spoken to about going, says that they can run the risk of being killed by some hostile people on another island between this and Matipa's.

22d February.—I was ill all yesterday, but escape fever by hemorrhage. A man turned up at 9 A.M., to carry our message to Matipa; Susi and Chumah went with him. The good Lord go with them, and lend me influence and grant me help.

26th February.—Susi returned this morning, with good news from Matipa, who declares his willingness to carry us to Kabende for the five bundles of brass wire I offered. It is not on Chirube, but amid the swamps of the mainland on the lake's north side.

27th February.—Waiting for other canoes to be sent by Matipa. His men say that there is but one large river on the south side of Lake Bangweolo, and called Luomba.

Matipa's men not having come, it is said they are employed bringing the carcass of an elephant to him. I propose to go near to him to-morrow, some in canoes and some on foot.

1st March, 1873.—Embarked women and goods in canoes, and went three hours S.E. to Bangweolo. Stopped on an island, where people were drying fish over fires. Heavy rain wetted us all as we came near the islet. We went over flooded prairie four feet deep, and covered with rushes, and two varieties of lotus, or sacred lily. Three canoes are behind. The men are great cowards. I took possession of all the paddles and punting poles, as the men showed an inclination to move off from our islet. The water in the country is prodigiously large; plains extending further than the eye can reach, have four or five feet of clear water, and the lake and adjacent lands for twenty or thirty miles are level. We are on a miserable, dirty, fishy island, called Motovinza. We are surrounded by scores of miles of rushes, an open sward, and many lotus plants.

3d March.—Matipa paid off the men who brought us

here. He says that five Sangos or coils (which brought
us here) will do to take us to Kabende, and I sincerely
hope that they will. His canoes are off, bringing the
meat of an elephant. I visited Matipa at noon. He is
an old man, slow of tongue, and self-possessed; he recommended our crossing to the south bank of the lake
to his brother, who has plenty of cattle, and to go along
that side where there are few rivers and plenty to eat.
Kabende's land was lately overrun by Banyamwezi, who
now inhabit that country, but as yet have no food to sell.
I am rather in a difficulty, as I fear I must give the five
coils for a much shorter task; but it is best not to appear
unfair, although I will be the loser. He sent a man to
catch a Sampa for me, it is the largest fish in the lake,
and he promised to have men ready to take my men
over to-morrow.

4th March.—Sent canoes off to bring our men over to
the island of Matipa. They brought ten, but the donkey
could not come as far through the " tinga-tinga" as they,
so they took it back for fear that it should perish. I
spoke to Matipa this morning to send more canoes, and
he consented. We move outside, as the town swarms
with mice, and is very closely built and disagreeable.

5th March.—Time runs on quickly. The real name
of this island is Masumbo, and the position may be probably long. 31° 3'; lat. 10° 11' S. Men not arrived yet.
Matipa very slow.

6th March.—Building a camp outside the town for
quiet and cleanliness, and no mice to run over us at
night. This islet is some twenty or thirty feet above
the general flat country and adjacent water.

At 3 P.M., we moved up to the highest part of the

island, where we can see around us, and have the fresh breeze from the lake. Rainy as we went up, as usual.

7th March.—We expect our men to-day. I tremble for the donkey! Camp sweet and clean; but it, too, has mosquitoes, from which a curtain protects me completely—a great luxury, but unknown to the Arabs, to whom I have spoken about it. Abed was overjoyed by one I made for him; others are used to their bites, as was the man who said that he would get used to a nail through the heel of his shoe. The men came at 3 P.M., but eight had to remain, the canoes being too small. The donkey had to be tied down, as he rolled about on his legs and would have forced his way out. Chanza is near Kabinga, and his last chief is coming to visit me in a day or two.

8th March.—I press Matipa to get a fleet of canoes equal to our number, but he complains of their being stolen by rebel subjects. He tells me his brother Kabinga, would have been here some days ago, but for having lost a son, who was killed by an elephant. Kabinga is on the other side of the Chambeze. A party of male and female drummers and dancers is sure to turn up at every village; the first here had a leader that used such violent antics perspiration ran off his whole frame. I gave a few strings of beads, and the performance is repeated to-day by another lot, but I rebel and allow them to dance unheeded. We got a sheep for a wonder, for a doti; fowls and fish alone could be bought, but Kabinga has plenty of cattle.

The Luena goes into Bangweolo at Molandangao. The eight men came from Motovinza this afternoon, and now all our party is united. The donkey shows many sores inflicted by the careless people, who think that force alone can be used to inferior animals.

11*th March.*—Matipa says, " Wait; Kabinga is coming, and he has canoes." Time is of no value to him. His wife is making him pombe, and will drown all his cares; but mine increase and plague me.

Better news comes; the son of Kabinga is to be here to-night, and we shall concoct plans together.

12*th March.*—The news was false; no one came from Kabinga. The men strung beads to-day, and I wrote part of my despatch for Earl Granville.

13*th March.*—I went to Matipa, and proposed to begin the embarkation of my men at once, as they are many, and the canoes are only sufficient to take a few at a time. He has sent off a big canoe to reap his millet; when it returns, he will send us over to see for ourselves where we can go. I explained the danger of setting my men astray.

14*th March.*—Rains have ceased for a few days. Went down to Matipa, and tried to take his likeness, for the sake of the curious hat he wears.

16*th March, Sunday.*—Service. I spoke sharply to Matipa for his duplicity. He promises everything, and does nothing; he has, in fact, no power over his people. Matipa says that a large canoe will come to-morrow, and next day men will go to Kabinga to reconnoitre. There may be a hitch there which we did not take into account; Kabinga's son, killed by an elephant, may have raised complications; blame may be attached to Matipa, and in their dark minds it may appear all important to settle the affair before having communication with him. Ill all day with my old complaint.

17th March.—The delay is most trying. So many detentions have occurred they ought to have made me of a patient spirit.

As I thought, Matipa told us to-day that it is reported he has some Arabs with him who will attack all the Lake people forthwith, ʲand he is anxious that we shall go over to show them that we are peaceful.

18th March.—Sent off men to reconnoitre at Kabinga's, and to make a camp there. Matipa is acting the villain, and my men are afraid of him; they are all cowards, and say that they are afraid of me, but this is only an excuse for their cowardice.

19th March.—Thanks to the Almighty Preserver of men for sparing me thus far on the journey of life. Can I hope for ultimate success? So many obstacles have arisen. Let not Satan prevail over me, Oh! my good Lord Jesus!*

8 A.M. Got about twenty people off to canoes. Matipa not friendly. They go over to Kabinga, on S.W. side of the Chambeze, and thence we go overland. 9 A.M. Men came back, and reported Matipa false again; only one canoe had come. I made a demonstration by taking quiet possession of his village and house; fired a pistol through the roof, and called my men, ten being left to guard the camp; Matipa fled to another village. The people sent off at once and brought three canoes, so at 11 A.M. my men embarked quietly. They go across the Chambeze, and build a camp on its left bank.

20th March.—Matipa sent two large baskets of flour (cassava), a sheep, and a cock. He hoped that we should remain with him till the water of the over-flood

---

* This was written on his last birthday.—ED.

dried, and help him to fight his enemies; but I explained our delays, and our desire to complete our work and meet Baker.

21st March.—I gave Matipa a coil of thick brass wire, and his wife a string of large neck-beads, and explained my hurry to be off. He is now all fair, and promises largely; he has been much frightened by our warlike demonstration.

22d March.—Susi not returned from Kabinga. I hope that he is getting canoes, and men also, to transport us all at one voyage. It is flood as far as the eye can reach. One does not know where land ends and lake begins.

23d March.—Men returned at noon. Kabinga is mourning for his son, and keeps in seclusion.

24th March.—The people took the canoes away, but in fear sent for them. I got four, and started with all our goods, first giving a present, that no blame should follow me. We punted six hours to a little islet without a tree, and no sooner did we land than a pitiless pelting rain came on. We turned up a canoe, to get shelter. We shall reach the Chambeze to-morrow. The loads are all soaked, and with the cold it is bitterly uncomfortable. No grass, but we made a bed of the loads, and a blanket fortunately put into a bag.

25th March.—Nothing earthly will make me give up my work in despair. I encourage myself in my Lord my God, and go forward.

We got off from our miserably small islet of ten yards at 7 A.M., a grassy sea on all sides, with a few islets in the far distance. The flood extends out in slightly depressed arms of the lake for twenty or thirty

miles, and far too broad to be seen across. Lukutu
flows from east to west to the Chambeze, as does the Lubanseusi also. After another six hours' punting over
the same wearisome prairie, or bouga, we heard the
merry voices of children. It was a large village, on a
flat, which seems flooded at times, but much cassava is
planted on mounds. We got a dry spot for the tent.
The people offered us huts. We had, as usual, a smart
shower all the way to Kasenga, where we slept. We
passed the islet Luangwa.

26th March.—We started at 7.30, and got into a large
stream out of the Chambeze, called Mabziwa. One
canoe sank in it, and we lost a slave-girl of Amoda.
We lost the donkey's saddle too. After this mishap,
we crossed the Lubanseusi near its confluence with the
Chambeze. We crossed the Chambeze. It is about
four hundred yards wide, with a quick, clear current of
two knots, and three fathoms deep. The volume of
water is enormous. We punted five hours, and then
camped.

27th March.—I sent canoes and men back to Matipa's
to bring all the men that remained. Kabinga keeps his
distance from us, and food is scarce. At noon he sent
a man to salute me in his name.

28th March.—Making a pad for a donkey, to serve
instead of a saddle. Kabinga attempts to sell a sheep at
an exorbitant price, and says that he is weeping over his
dead child.

29th March.—I bought a sheep for one hundred
strings of beads. I wished to begin the exchange by
being generous, and told his messenger so ; then a small
quantity of maize was brought, and I grumbled at the

37

meanness of the present. The man said that Kabinga would send more when he had collected it.

30th March, Sunday.—Men returned, but the large canoe having been broken by the donkey, we have to go back and pay for it, and take away about twenty men now left. Matipa kept all the payment from his own people, and so left us in the lurch.

31st March.—I sent the men back to Matipa's for all our party. Made stirrups of thick brass wire fourfold. Sent Kabinga a cloth and a message, but he is evidently a niggard, like Matipa. Seven of our men returned, having got a canoe from one of Matipa's men. Kabinga, it seems, was pleased with the cloth, and says that he will ask for maize from his people, and buy it for me. He will send a canoe to carry me over the next river.

3d April, 1873.—The men at last have come from Matipa's.

4th April.—Sent over to Kabinga to buy a cow, and got a fat one for two dotis and a half, to give the party a feast, ere we start.

[The next entry is made in a new pocket-book, numbered XVII. For the first few days pen and ink were used; afterward a well-worn stump of pencil, stuck into a steel pen-holder and attached to a piece of bamboo, served his purpose.]

5th April.—March from Kabinga's on the Chambeze, our luggage in canoes, and men on land. We punted on flood six feet deep, with many ant-hills all about, covered with trees. Course south-south-east, for five miles, across the River Lobingela.

6th April.—Leave in the same way, but men where sent from Kabinga to steal the canoes which we paid his brother Mateysa handsomely for. A stupid drummer, beating the alarm in the distance, called us inland. We found the main body of our people had gone on, and so by this our party got separated,* and we pulled and punted six or seven hours southwest in great difficulty, as the fishermen we saw refused to show us where the deep water lay. The whole country south of the lake was covered with water, thickly dotted over with lotus-leaves and rushes. It is quite impossible at present to tell where land ends and lake begins; it is all water, water everywhere, which seems to be kept from flowing quickly off by the narrow bed of the· Luapula, which has perpendicular banks, worn deep down in new red sandstone. It is the Nile apparently enacting its inundations, even at its sources.

Near sunset we saw two fishermen paddling quickly off from an ant-hill, where we found a hut, plenty of fish, and some fire-wood. There we spent the night, and watched by turns, lest thieves should come and haul away our canoes and goods. Heavy rain. One canoe sank, wetting everything in her. We did not touch the fish, and I cannot conjecture who has inspired fear in all the inhabitants.

7th April.—Went on southwest, and saw two men, who guided us to the River Muanakazi, which forms a connecting link between the River Lotingila and the Lolotikila, about the southern borders of the flood. Men were hunting, and we passed near large herds of antelopes, which made a rushing, plunging sound as they ran and sprang away among the waters. A lion

---

* Dr. Livingstone's object was to keep the land-party marching parallel to him while he kept nearer to the lake in a canoe.—ED.

had wandered into this world of water and ant-hills, and roared night and morning, as if very much disgusted; we could sympathize with him! Near to the Muana-kazi, at a broad bank in shallow water near the river, we had to unload and haul. Our guides left us, well pleased with the payment we had given them. The natives beating a drum on our east made us believe them to be our party, and some thought that they heard two shots. This misled us, and we went toward the sound through papyrus, tall rushes, arums, and grass, till tired out, and took refuge on an ant-hill for the night. Lion roaring. We were lost in stiff, grassy prairies, from three to four feet deep in water, for five hours. We fired a gun in the stillness of the night, but received no answer; so on the 8th we sent a small canoe at day-break to ask for information and guides from the village where the drums had been beaten. Two men came, and they thought likewise that our party was south-east; but in that direction the water was about fifteen inches in spots, and three feet in others, which caused constant dragging of the large canoe all day, and at last we unloaded at another branch of the Muanakazi with a village of friendly people. We slept there.

All hands at the large canoe could move her only a few feet. Putting all their strength to her, she stopped at every haul with a jerk, as if in a bank of adhesive plaster.

9th April.—After two hours' threading the very winding, deep channel of this southern branch of the Muanakazi, we came to where our land-party had crossed it and gone to Gandochite, a chief on the Lolo-tikila. My men were all done up, so I hired a man to call some of his friends to take the loads; but he was stopped by his relations in the way, saying, " You ought to have one of the traveler's own people with you." He returned, but did not tell us plainly or truly till this morning.

[The recent heavy exertions, coupled with constant exposure and extreme anxiety and annoyance no doubt brought on the severe attack which is noticed, as we see in the words of the next few days.]

10*th April.*—I am pale, bloodless, and weak, from bleeding profusely ever since the 31st of March last; an artery gives off a copious stream, and takes away my strength. Oh, how I long to be permitted by the Over Power to finish my work!

12*th April.*—Cross the Muanakazi. Great loss of blood made me so weak I could hardly walk, but tottered along nearly two hours, and then lay down quite done. Cooked coffee—our last—and went on ; but in an hour I was compelled to lie down. Very unwilling to be carried; but, on being pressed, I allowed the men to help me along by relays to Chinama, where there is much cultivation. We camped in a garden of dura.

13*th April.*—Found that we had slept on the right bank of the Lolotikila, a sluggish, marshy-looking river. Fish and other food abundant, and the people civil and reasonable. They usually partake largely of the character of the chief, and this one, Gondochite, is polite. The sky is clearing. It is the dry season well begun.

We were four hours in being ferried over the Loitikila, or Lolotikila, in four small canoes, and then two hours southwest down its left bank to another river, where our camp has been formed. I sent over a present to the headman, and a man returned with the information that he was ill at another village, but his wife would send canoes to-morrow to transport us over, and set us on our way to Muanazambamba, southwest, and over Lolotikila again.

15th April.—Cross Lolotikila again by canoes, and went southwest an hour. I being very weak, had to be carried part of the way. Am glad of resting; blood flowed copiously last night. A woman, the wife of the chief, gave a present of a goat and maize.

16th April.—Went southwest two and a half hours, and crossed the Lombatwa River, of one hundred yards in width, rush deep, and flowing fast in aquatic vegetation, papyrus, etc., into the Loitikila. In all, about three hours southwest.

17th April.—A tremendous rain, after dark, burst all our now rotten tents to shreds. Went on, at 6.35 A.M., for three hours; and I, who was suffering severely all night, had to rest. We got water near the surface by digging in yellow sand. Three hills now appear in the distance. Our course, southwest three hours and three-quarters to a village on the Kazya River.

18th April.—On leaving the village on the Kazya, we forded it, and found it seventy yards broad, waist to breast deep all over. A large weir spanned it, and we went on the lower side of that. I was forced to stop at a village, after traveling southwest for two hours; very ill all night, but remembered that the bleeding and most other ailments in this land are forms of fever. Took two-scruple doses of quinine, and stopped it quite.

19th April.—A fine bracing south-east breeze kept me on the donkey across a broad sponge and over flats of white sandy soil, and much cultivation, for an hour and a half, when we stopped at a large village on the right bank of   ,* and men went over to the chief Muanzambamba to ask canoes to cross to-morrow. I am excessively weak, and but for the donkey, could not move a hundred yards. It is not all pleasure, this exploration. No observations now, owing to great weakness: I can scarcely hold a pencil, and my stick is a burden. Tent gone; the men build a good hut for me and the luggage. Southwest one hour and a half.

20th April, Sunday.—Service. Cross over the sponge Moenda for food, and to be near the headman of these parts, Muanzambamba. I am excessively weak. Village on Moenda sponge. 7 A.M.—Cross Lokulu in a canoe. The river is about thirty yards broad, very deep, and flowing in marshes two knots from south-south-east to north-north-west, into Lake.

---

* He leaves room for a name which perhaps in his exhausted state he forgot to ascertain.

CHAPTER XXXII.

LAST ILLNESS AND DEATH OF DR. LIVINGSTONE.

Dr. Livingstone Rapidly Sinking—Last Entries in his Diary—Great Agony—
Carried across Rivers and through Flood—Kalunganjovu's Kindness—Arrives
at Chitambo's, in great Pain—The Last Night—Livingstone Expires in the act
of Praying—Council of the Men—The Chief Discovers that his Guest is Dead
Noble Conduct of Chitambo—The Preparation of the Corpse—Honor shown
to Dr. Livingstone—Interment of the Heart at Chitambo's—An Inscription
and Memorial Sign—Posts left to Denote the Spot.

[WE have now arrived at the last words written in
Dr. Livingstone's diary; a copy of the two pages in his
pocket-book which contains them is, by the help of
photography, set before the reader. It is evident that
he was unable to do more than make the shortest
memoranda, and to mark on the map which he was
making the streams which enter the lake as he crossed
them. From the 22d to the 27th of April he had not
strength to write down anything but the several dates.
Fortunately, Susi and Chuma give a very clear and circumstantial account of every incident which occurred
on these days, and we shall therefore add what they
say, after each of the Doctor's entries. He writes:]

21st April.—Tried to ride, but was forced to lie down,
and they carried me back to vil. exhausted.

[The men explain this entry thus: This morning the
Doctor tried if he were strong enough to ride on the
donkey, but he had only gone a short distance when he
fell to the ground, utterly exhausted and faint. Susi
immediately undid his belt and pistol, and picked up

his cap, which had dropped off, while Chuma threw down his gun, and ran to stop the men on ahead. When he got back, the Doctor said, "Chuma, I have lost so much blood, there is no more strength left in my legs; you must carry me." He was then assisted gently to his shoulders, and, holding the man's head to steady himself, was borne back to the village, and placed in the hut he had so recently left. It was necessary to let the chief Muanzambamba know what had happened, and for this purpose Dr. Livingstone despatched a messenger. He was directed to ask him to supply a guide for the next day, as he trusted then to have recovered so far as to be able to march. The answer was, "Stay as long as you wish, and when you want guides to Kalunganjovu's you shall have them."]

22d April.—Carried on kitanda over Buga southwest two and a quarter.*

[Instead of rallying, his strength was becoming less and less; and in order to carry him, his servants made a kitanda of wood, consisting of two side-pieces of seven feet in length crossed with rails three feet long, and about four inches apart, the whole lashed strongly together. This frame-work was covered with grass, and a blanket laid on it. Slung from a pole, and born between two strong men, it made a tolerable palanquin, and on this the exhausted traveler was conveyed to the next village through a flooded grass plain. To render the kitanda more comfortable, another blanket was suspended across the pole, so as to hang down on either side, and allow the air to pass under while the sun's rays were fended off from the sick man. The

* Two hours and a quarter in a south-westerly direction.

start was deferred this morning until the dew was off the heads of the long grass sufficiently to insure his being kept tolerably dry.

The excruciating pains of his dysenteric malady caused him the greatest exhaustion as they marched, and they were glad enough to reach another village in two hours and a quarter, having traveled southwest from the last point. Here another hut was built. The villagers fled at their approach; indeed the noise made by the drums sounding the alarm had been caught by the Doctor some time before, and he exclaimed with thankfulness on hearing it, "Ah, now we are near!"]

23d April.—(No entry except the date.)

[They advanced another hour and a half through the same expanse of flooded, treeless waste, passing numbers of small fish-weirs set in such a manner as to catch the fish on their way back to the Lake, but seeing nothing of the owners, who had either hidden themselves or taken to flight on the approach of the caravan. Another village afforded them a night's shelter, but it seems not to be known by any particular name.]

24th April.—(No entry except the date.)

[But one hour's march was accomplished to-day, and again they halted among some huts. His great prostration made progress exceedingly painful, and frequently, when it was necessary to stop the bearers of the kitanda, Chuma had to support the Doctor from falling.]

25th April.—(No entry except the date.)

[In an hour's course southwest they arrived at a village in which they found a few people. While his servants were busy completing the hut for the night's encampment, the Doctor, who was lying in a shady place on the kitanda, ordered them to fetch one of the villagers. The chief of the place had disappeared, but the rest of his people seemed quite at their ease, and drew near to hear what was going to be said. They were asked whether they knew of a hill on which four rivers took their rise. The spokesman answered that they had no knowledge of it; they themselves, said he, were not travelers, and all those who used to go on trading expeditions were now dead. In former years Malenga's town, Kutchinyama, was the assembling place of the Wabisa traders, but these had been swept off by the Mazitu. Such as survived had to exist as best they could among the swamps and inundated districts around the Lake. Whenever an expedition was organized to go to the coast, or in any other direction travelers met at Malenga's town to talk over the route to be taken; then would have been the time, said they, to get information about every part. Dr. Livingstone was here obliged to dismiss them, and explained that he was too ill to continue talking, but he begged them to bring as much food as they could for sale to Kalunganjovu's.]

26th April.—(No entry except the date.)

[They proceeded as far as Kalunganjovu's town, the chief himself coming to meet them on the way, dressed in Arab costume and wearing a red fez. While waiting here, Susi was instructed to count over the bags of beads, and on reporting that twelve still remained in stock, Dr. Livingstone told him to buy two large tusks if an opportunity occurred, as he might run short of goods by the time they got to Ujiji, and could then exchange them with the Arabs there for cloth, to spend on their way to Zanzibar.

588 EXPLORATIONS IN AFRICA.

To-day, *April 27th*, 1873, he seems to have been
almost dying. No entry at all was made in his diary
after that which follows, and it must have taxed him to
the utmost to write.

"Knocked up quite, and remain—recover—sent to
buy milch goats. We are on the banks of the Molilamo."

[They are the last words that David Livingstone
wrote. From this point we have to trust entirely to the
narrative of the men. They explain the above sentence
as follows: Salimane, Amisi, Hamsani, and Laede, accompanied by a guide, were sent off to endeavor, if possible, to buy some milch goats on the upper part of the
Molilamo. (The name Molilamo is allowed to stand, but
in Dr. Livingstone's map we find it Lulimala, and the
men confirm this pronunciation.) They could not, however, succeed; it was always the same story—the Mazitu
had taken everything. The chief, nevertheless, sent a
substantial present of a kid and three baskets of ground-
nuts, and the people were willing enough to exchange
food for beads. Thinking he could eat some mapira
corn pounded up with ground-nuts, the doctor gave instructions to the two women, M'sozi and M'toweka, to
prepare it for him, but he was not able to take it when
they brought it to him.]

28th April.—Men were now dispatched in an opposite direction, that is, to visit the villages on the right
bank of the Molilamo as it flows to the Lake; unfortunately, they met with no better result, and returned
empty handed.

On *April 29th*, Kalunganjovu and most of his people
came early to the village. The chief wished to assist

20th April 1873 = S. service
cross over <strike>Sranble</strike> Moenda
for food & to be near the
head men of these parts
Muanza-bamba - I am
excessively weak
vil on <strike>R</strike> Molenda 7 Attl. ^sponge

25.88 } 66°
26.12 } clouds
25.70 } high

cross Lukolu in a canoe
R. is about 30 yds broad
very deep and flowing
in marshes - 2 knots
from SSE to N N W'
into Lake
_____

21st tried to ride but was
forced to be down and
they carried me back to
vil. exhausted
_____

22d carried in Kitanda.
over Buga S W   2¼

FAC-SIMILE OF THE LAST ENTRIES IN

23 ?   ♂   .1 ½
24   ♂   1.
25 ᵐᵉ ♂   1
26 `to   2 ½

─────────────

to Kalunga Mofu s
total   33   ⇒ 8 ¼

─────────────

27 knocked up quite
and remain = remain
sent to buy milch
goats we are on the
banks of R Mohilamo

DR. LIVINGSTONE'S NOTE-BOOK.

his guest to the utmost, and stated tnat as he could not be sure that a sufficient number of canoes would be forthcoming unless he took charge of matters himself, he should accompany the caravan to the crossing-place, which was about an hour's march from the spot. " Everything should be done for his friend," he said.

They were ready to set out. On Susi's going to the hut, Dr. Livingstone told him that he was quite unable to walk to the door to reach the kitanda, and he wished the men to break down one side of the little house, as the entrance was too narrow to admit it, and in this manner to bring it to him where he was; this was done, and he was gently placed upon it, and borne out of the village.

Their course was in the direction of the stream, and they followed it till they came to a reach where the current was uninterrupted by the numerous little islands which stood partly in the river, and partly in the flood on the upper waters. Kalunganjovu was seated on a knoll, and actively superintended the embarkation, while Dr. Livingstone told his bearers to take him to a tree at a little distance off, that he might rest in the shade till most of the men were on the other side. A good deal of care was required, for the river, by no means a large one in ordinary times, spread its waters in all directions, so that a false step, or a stumble in any unseen hole, would have drenched the invalid and the bed also on which he was carried.

A good deal of care was required for the difficult task of conveying the Doctor across, for the canoes were not wide enough to allow the kitanda to be deposited in the bottom of either of them. Hitherto, Livingstone had

38

always been able to sit in the various canoes they had used, but now he had no power to do so. Taking his bed off the kitanda, they laid it in the bottom of the strongest canoe, and tried to lift him; but he could not bear the pain of a hand being passed under his back. Beckoning to Chuma, in a faint voice he asked him to stoop down over him as low as possible, so that he might clasp his hands together behind his head, directing him at the same time how to avoid putting any pressure on the lumbar region of the back; in this way he was deposited in the bottom of the canoe, and quickly ferried across the Molilamo. The same precautions were used on the other side; the kitanda was brought close to the canoe, so as to prevent any unnecessary pain in disembarking.

Susi now hurried on ahead to reach Chitambo's village, and superintend the building of another house. For the first mile or two they had to carry the Doctor through swamps and plashes, glad to reach something like a dry plain at last.

It would seem that his strength was here at its very lowest ebb. Chuma, one of his bearers on these, the last weary miles the great traveler was destined to accomplish, says, that they were every now and then implored to stop and place their burden on the ground. So great were the pangs of his disease during this day that he could make no attempt to stand, and if lifted for a few yards a drowsiness came over him, which alarmed them all excessively. This was specially the case at one spot where a tree stood in the path. Here one of his attendants was called to him, and, on stooping down, he found him unable to speak from faintness. They replaced him in the kitanda, and made the best of their way on the journey. Some distance farther on great thirst oppressed him; he asked them if they had any water, but, unfortunately, for once, not a drop was to be procured. Hastening on for fear of getting too far separated from the party in advance, to their great comfort they now saw Farijala approaching with some, which Susi had thoughtfully sent off from Chitambo's village. Still wending their way on, it seemed as if they would not complete their task, for again at a clearing the sick man entreated them to place him on the ground, and to let him stay where he was. Fortunately at this moment some of the outlying huts of the village came in sight, and they tried to rally him by telling him that he would quickly be in the house that the others had gone to build; but they were obliged, as it was, to allow him to remain for an hour in the native gardens outside the town.

On reaching their companions, it was found that the work was not quite finished, and it became necessary, therefore, to lay him under the broad eaves of a native hut till things were ready.

Chitambo's village at this time was almost empty When the crops are growing, it is the custom to erect little temporary houses in the fields, and the inhabitants, leaving their more substantial huts, pass the time in watching their crops, which are scarcely more safe by day than by night; thus it was that the men found plenty of room and shelter ready to their hand. Many of the people approached the spot where he lay whose praises had reached them in previous years, and in silent wonder they stood around him, resting on their bows. Slight drizzling showers were falling, and as soon as possible his house was made ready, and banked around with earth.

Inside, the bed was raised from the floor by sticks and grass, occupying a position across and near to the bay-shaped end of the hut; in the bay itself bales and boxes were deposited, one of the latter doing duty for a table, on which the medicine-chest and sundry other things were placed. A fire was lighted outside, nearly opposite the door, while the boy, Majwara, slept just within, to attend to his master's wants in the night.

On *April 30th*, 1873, Chitambo came early to pay a visit of courtesy, and was shown into the Doctor's presence; but the Doctor was obliged to send him away, telling him to come again on the morrow, when he hoped to have more strength to talk to him, and he was not again disturbed. In the afternoon he asked Susi to bring his watch to the bedside, and explained to him the position in which to hold his hand, that it might lie in the palm while he slowly turned the key.

So the hours stole on till night-fall. Some of the men silently took to their huts, while others, whose duty it was to keep watch, sat around the fires, all feeling that the end could not be far off. About 11 P.M., Susi, whose hut was close by, was told to go to his master. At the time there were loud shouts in the distance, and, on entering, Dr. Livingstone said, "Are our men making that noise?" "No," replied Susi; "I can hear, from the cries, that the people are scaring away a buffalo from their dura fields." A few minutes afterward he said, slowly, and evidently wandering, "Is this Luapula?" Susi told him they were in Chitambo's village, near the Molilamo, when he was silent for a while.

Again, speaking to Susi, in Suaheli this time, he said, "How many days is it to the Luapula?" "I think it is three days, master," replied Susi.

A few seconds after, as if in great pain, he half sighed, half said, "Oh dear, dear!" and then doze ff again.

It was about an hour later that Susi heard Majwara again outside the door, " Bwana wants you, Susi." The Doctor wished him to boil some water, and for this purpose he went to the fire outside, and soon returned with the copper kettle full. Calling him close, he asked him to bring his medicine-chest, and to hold the candle near him, for the man noticed he could hardly see. With great difficulty the Doctor selected the calomel, which he told him to place by his side; then, directing him to pour a little water into a cup, and to put another empty one by it, he said, in a low, feeble voice, " All right; you can go out now." These were the last words he was ever heard to speak.

It must have been about 4 A.M. when Susi heard Majwara's step once more. " Come to Bwana; I am afraid; I don't know if he is alive." The lad's evident alarm made Susi run to arouse Chuma, Chowpere, Matthew, and Muanuasere, and the six men went immediately to the hut.

Passing inside, they looked toward the bed. Dr. Livingstone was not lying on it, but appeared to be engaged in prayer, and they instinctively drew backward for the instant. Pointing to him, Majwara said, " When I lay down he was just as he is now, and it is because I find that he does not move that I fear he is dead." They asked the lad how long he had slept?

Majwara said he could not tell, but he was sure that it was some considerable time; the men drew nearer.

A candle, stuck by its own wax to the top of the box, shed a light sufficient for them to see his form. Dr. Livingstone was kneeling by the side of his bed, his body stretched forward, his head buried in his hands upon the pillow. For a minute they watched him; he did not stir, there was no sign of breathing; then one of them, Matthew, advanced softly to him, and placed his hands to his cheeks. It was sufficient; life had been extinct some time, and the body was almost cold; *Livingstone was dead.*

His sad-hearted servants raised him tenderly up, and laid him full length on the bed; then, carefully covering him, they went out into the damp night air to consult together. It was not long before the cocks crew; and it is from this circumstance—coupled with the fact that Susi spoke to him some time shortly before midnight—that we are able to state with tolerable accuracy that he expired early on the 1st of May.

It has been thought best to give the narrative of these closing hours as nearly as possible in the words of the two men who attended him constantly, both here and in the many illnesses of like character which he endured in his last six years' wanderings; in fact, from the first moment of the news arriving in England, it was felt to be indispensable that they should come home to state what occurred.

The men have much to consider as they cower around the watch-fire, and little time for deliberation. They are at their farthest point from home, and their leader has fallen at their head; we shall see presently how they faced their difficulties.

Several inquiries will naturally arise, on reading this distressing history ; the first, perhaps, will be with regard to the entire absence of everything like a parting word to those immediately about him, or a farewell line to his family and friends at home. It must be very evident to the reader that Livingstone entertained very grave forebodings about his health during the last two years of his life, but it is not clear that he realized the near approach of death when his malady suddenly passed into a more dangerous stage.

It may be said, " Why did he not take some precautions or give some strict injunctions to his men to preserve his note-books and maps at all hazards, in the event of his decease ?" Did not his great ruling passion suggest some such precaution ?

Fair questions, but, reader, you have all—every word written, spoken, or implied.

Is there, then, no explanation ? Yes ; we think past experience affords it, and it is among the peculiar features of death by malarial poisoning.

In eight deaths on the Zambesi and Shire districts, not a single parting word or direction in any instance was uttered. Neither hope nor courage give way as death approaches. In most cases, a comatose state of exhaustion supervenes, which, if it be not quickly arrested by active measures, passes into complete insensibility; this is almost invariably the closing scene.

In Dr. Livingstone's case, we find some departure from the ordinary symptoms. The great loss of blood may have had a bearing on the case. He was alive to the conviction that malarial poison is the basis of every disorder in Tropical Africa, and he did not doubt but that he was fully under its influence while suffering so severely. A man of less endurance in all probability would have perished in the first week of the terrible approach to the lake, through the flooded country and under the continual downpour that he describes. It tried every constitution, saturated every man with fever-poison, and destroyed several. The greater vitality in his iron system very likely staved off for a few days the last state of coma to which we refer; but there is quite sufficient to show us that only a thin margin lay between the heavy drowsiness of the last few days before reaching Chitambo's and the final and usual symptom that brings on unconsciousness and inability to speak.

He hoped to recover as he had so often done before; and this in a measure accounts for the absence of anything like a dying statement. It may be that at the last a flash of conviction for a moment lighted up the mind; if so, what greater consolation can those have who mourn his loss, than the account that the men give of what they saw when they entered the hut? Livingstone had not merely turned himself, he had risen to pray; he still rested on his knees, his hands were clasped under his head; when they approached him, he seemed to live. He had not fallen to right or left when he rendered up his spirit to God. Death required no change of limb or position; there was merely the gentle settling forward of the frame unstrung by pain, for the Traveler's perfect rest had come.

Before daylight the men were quietly told in each hut what had happened, and that they were to assemble. Susi and Chuma wished every body to be present while the boxes were opened, so that, in case money or valuables were in them, all might be responsible. Jacob

Wainwright (who could write, they knew) was asked to make some notes which should serve as an inventory, and then the boxes were brought out from the hut.

Before he left England in 1865, Dr. Livingstone had arranged that his traveling equipment should be as compact as possible. An old friend gave him some exceedingly well-made tin boxes, two of which lasted out the whole of his travels. In these his papers and instruments were safe from wet and from white ants, which have to be guarded against more than anything else. Besides the articles mentioned below, a number of letters and dispatches in various stages were likewise inclosed, and one can never sufficiently extol the good feeling which after his death invested all these writings with something like a sacred care in the estimation of all his men. It was the Doctor's custom to carry a small metallic note-book in his pocket; a quantity of these have come to hand, filled from end to end; and as the men preserved every one that they found, we have almost a daily entry to fall back upon. Nor was less care shown for his rifles, sextants, his Bible and Church-service, and the medicine chest.

Jacob's entry is as follows, and it was thoughtfully made at the back end of the same note-book that was in use by the Doctor when he died. It runs as follows:

" 11 o'clock night, 28th April.

" In the chest was found about a shilling and a half, and in other chest his hat, one watch, and two small boxes of measuring instrments, and in each box there was one. One compass, three other kind of measuring instruments. Four other kind of measuring instruments. And in another chest three drachmas and half half scrople."

A word is necessary concerning the first part of this. It will be observed that Dr. Livingstone made his last note on the 27th of April. Jacob, referring to it as the only indication of the day of the month, and fancying, moreover, that it was written on the preceding day, wrote down "28th April." Had he observed that the few words opposite the 27th in the pocket-book related to the stay at Kalunganjovu's village, and not to any portion of the time at Chitambo's the error would have been avoided. Again, with respect to the time. It was about 11 o'clock P.M, when Susi last saw his master alive, and therefore this time is noted; but both he and Chuma feel quite sure, from what Majwara said, that death did not take place till some hours after.

It was not without some alarm that the men realized their more immediate difficulties; none could see better than they what complications might arise in an hour.

They knew the superstitious horror connected with the dead prevalent in the tribes around them, for the departed spirits of men are universally believed to have vengeance and mischief at heart as their ruling idea in the land beyond the grave. All rites turn on this belief. The religion of the African is a weary attempt to propitiate those who show themselves to be still able to haunt and destroy, as war comes on or an accident happens.

On this account it is not to be wondered at that chief and people make common cause against those who wander through their territory, and have the misfortune to lose one of their party by death. Such occurrences are looked on as most serious offences, and the men regarded their position with no small apprehension.

Calling the whole party together, Susi and Chuma placed the state of affairs before them, and asked what should be done. They received a reply from those whom Mr. Stanley had engaged for Dr. Livingstone, which was hearty and unanimous. "You," said they, "are old men in traveling and in hardships; you must act as our chiefs, and we will promise to obey whatever you order us to do." From this moment we may look on Susi and Chuma as the captains of the caravan. To their knowledge of the country, of the tribes through which they were to pass, but, above all, to the sense of discipline and cohesion which was maintained throughout their safe return to Zanzibar at the head of their men must, under God's good guidance, be mainly attributed.

All agreed that Chitambo must be kept in ignorance of Dr. Livingstone's decease, or otherwise a fine so heavy would be inflicted upon them as compensation for damage done that their means would be crippled, and they could hardly expect to pay their way to the coast. It was decided that, come what might, the body must be borne to Zanzibar. It was also arranged to take it secretly, if possible, to a hut at some distance off, where the necessary preparations could be carried out, and for this purpose some men were now dispatched with axes to cut wood, while others went to collect grass. Chuma set off to see Chitambo, and said that they wanted to build a place outside the village, if he would allow it, for they did not like living among the huts. His consent was willingly given.

Later on in the day two of the men went to the people to buy food, and divulged the secret; the chief was at once informed of what had happened, and started for the spot on which the new buildings were being set up. Appealing to Chuma, he said, "Why did you not tell me the truth? I know that your master died last night. You were afraid to let me know, but do not fear any longer. I, too, have traveled, and more than once have been to Bwani (the coast), before the country on the road was destroyed by the Mazitu. I know that you have no bad motives in coming to our land, and death often happens to travelers in their journeys." Reassured by this speech, they told him of their intention to prepare the body, and to take it with them. He, however, said it would be far better to bury it there, for they were undertaking an impossible task; but they held to their resolution. The corpse was conveyed to the new hut the same day on the kitanda, carefully covered with cloth and a blanket.

2d May, 1873.—The next morning Susi paid a visit to Chitambo, making him a handsome present, and receiving in return a kind welcome. It is only right to add that the men speak on all occasions with gratitude of Chitambo's conduct throughout, and say that he is a fine, generous fellow. Following out his suggestion, it was agreed that all honors should be shown to the dead, and the customary mourning was arranged forthwith.

At the proper time, Chitambo, leading his people, and accompanied by his wives, came to the new settlement. He was clad in a broad red cloth, which covered the shoulders, while the wrapping of native cotton cloth, worn round the waist, fell as low as his ankles. All carried bows, arrows, and spears, but no guns were seen. Two drummers joined in the loud wailing lamentation, which so indelibly impresses itself on the memories of people who have heard it in the East, while the band of servants fired volley after volley in the air, according to the strict rule of Portuguese and Arabs on such occasions.

As yet, nothing had been done to the corpse.

A separate hut was now built, about ninety feet from the principal one. It was constructed in such a manner that it should be open to the air at the top, and sufficiently strong to defy the attempts of any wild beast to break through it. Firmly driven boughs and saplings were planted side by side, and bound together, so as to make a regular stockade. Close to this building the men constructed their huts, and, finally, the whole settlement had another high stockade carried completely around it.

Arrangements were made the same day to treat the corpse on the following morning. One of the men, Safene, while in Kalunganjovu's district, bought a large quantity of salt; this was purchased of him for sixteen strings of beads; there was, besides, some brandy in the Doctor's stores, and with these few materials they hoped to succeed in their object.

Farijala was appointed to the necessary task. He had picked up some knowledge of the method pursued in making *post-mortem* examinations while a servant to a doctor at Zanzibar, and at his request Carras, one of the Nassick boys, was told off to assist him. Previous to this, however, early on May 3d, a special mourner arrived. He came with the anklets which are worn on these occasions, composed of rows of hollow seed-vessels filled with rattling pebbles, and in low, monotonous chant sang, while he danced, what, translated into English, would read:

> " To-day the Englishman is dead,
> Who has different hair from ours;
> Come round to see the Englishman. "

His task over, the mourner and his son, who accompanied him in the ceremony, retired with a suitable present of beads.

The emaciated remains of the deceased traveler were soon afterward taken to the place prepared. Over the heads of Farijala and Carras, Susi, Chuma, and Muanuasere held a thick blanket as a kind of screen, under which the men performed their duties. Tofike and John Wainwright were present. Jacob Wainwright had been asked to bring his Prayer-book with him, and stood apart against the wall of the inclosure.

In reading about the lingering sufferings of Dr. Livingstone as described by himself, and subsequently by these faithful fellows, one is quite prepared to understand their explanation, and to see why it was possible to defer these operations so long after death; they say that his frame was little more than skin and bone. Through an incision carefully made, the viscera were removed, and a quantity of salt was placed in the trunk. All noticed one very significant circumstance in the autopsy. A clot of coagulated blood, as large as a man's hand, lay in the left side,* while Farijala pointed to the state of the lungs, which they described as dried up, and covered with black-and-white patches.

The heart, with the other parts removed, were placed

---

* It has been suggested by one who attended Dr. Livingstone professionally in several dangerous illnesses in Africa, that the ultimate cause of death was acute splenitis.

in a tin box, which had formerly contained flour, and decently and reverently buried in a hole dug some four feet deep on the spot where they stood. Jacob then read the English Church Burial Service, in the presence of all. The body was then left fully exposed to the sun. No other means were taken to preserve it, beyond placing some brandy in the mouth and some in the hair; nor can one imagine for an instant that any other process would have been available either for Europeans or natives, considering the rude appliances at their disposal. The men kept watch day and night to see that no harm came to their sacred charge. Once a day the position of the body was changed, but at no other time was any one allowed to approach it.

No molestation of any kind took place during the fourteen days exposure. At the end of this period preparations were made for retracing their steps. The corpse, tolerably dried, was wrapped round in some calico, the legs being bent inward at the knees to shorten the package. The next thing was to plan something in which to carry it, and in the absence of planking or tools, an admirable substitute was found by stripping from a myonga tree enough of the bark in one piece to form a cylinder, and in it their master was laid. Over this case a piece of sail-cloth was sewn, and the whole package was lashed securely to a pole, so as to be carried by two men.

Jacob Wainwright was asked to carve an inscription on the large mvula-tree which stands by the place where the body rested, stating the name of Dr. Livingstone, and the date of his death ; and, before leaving, the men gave strict injunctions to Chitambo to keep the grass cleared away, so as to save it from the bush-fires which annually sweep over the country and destroy so many trees, Besides this, they erected close to the spot two high, thick posts, with an equally strong cross-piece, like a lintel and door posts in form, which they painted thoroughly with the tar that was intended for the boat; this sign they think will remain for a long time, from the solidity of the timber. Before parting with Chitambo, they gave him a large tin biscuit-box and some newspapers, which would serve as evidence to all future travelers that a white man had been at this village.

The chief promised to do all he could to keep both the tree and the timber sign-posts from being touched, but added that he hoped the English would not be long in coming to see him, because there was always the risk of an invasion of Mazitu, when he would have to fly, and the tree might be cut down for a canoe by some one, and then all trace would be lost. All was now ready for starting.

CHAPTER XXXIII.

THE BODY BROUGHT HOME.

THE homeward march was then begun. Throughout its length we shall content ourselves with giving the approximate number of days occupied in traveling and halting. Although the memories of both men are excellent—standing the severest test by the light of Dr. Livingstone's journals, or " set on" at any passage of his travels—still they kept no precise record of the time spent at villages where they were detained by sickness, and so the exactness of a diary can no longer be sustained.

They found, on the first day's journey, that some other precautions were necessary to enable the bearers of the mournful burden to keep to their task. Sending to Chitambo's village, they brought thence the cask of tar which they had deposited with the chief, and gave a thick coating to the canvas outside. This answered all purposes ; they left the remainder at the next village, with orders to send it back to headquarters, and then continued their course through Ilala, led by their guides in the direction of the Luapulu.

A moment's inspection of the map will explain the line of country traversed. Susi and Chuma had traveled with Dr. Livingstone in the neighborhood of the north-west shores of Bangweolo in previous years. The last fatal road from the north might be struck by a march in a due northeast direction, if they could but hold out so far without any serious misfortune; but, in order to do this, they must first strike northward so as to reach the Luapulu, and then crossing it at some part not necessarily far from its exit from the lake, they could at once lay their course for the south end of Tanganyika.

There were, however, serious indications among them First one and then the other dropped out of the file, and by the time they reached a town belonging to Chitambo's brother—and on the third day only since they set out —half their number were sick. It was impossible to go on. A few hours more, and all seemed affected. The symptoms were intense pain in the limbs and face, great prostration, and, in the bad cases, inability to move. The men attributed it to the continual wading through water before the Doctor's death. They think that ill-ness had been waiting for some further slight provoca-tion, and that the day's previous tramp, which was almost entirely through plashy bougas, or swamps, turned the scale against them.

Susi was suffering very much. The disease settled in one leg, and then quickly shifted to the other. Songolo nearly died. Kaniki and Behati, two of the women, expired in a few days, and all looked at its worst. It took them a good month to rally sufficiently to resume their journey. Fortunately, in this interval, the rains entirely ceased, and the natives day by day brought an abundance of food to the sick men. From them they heard that the districts they were now in were notoriously unhealthy, and that many an Arab had fallen out from the caravan march, to leave his bones in these wastes. One day five of the party made an excursion to the westward, and on their return reported a large deep river flowing into the Luapula on the left bank. Unfortunately no notice was taken of its name, for it would be of considerable geographical interest.

At last they were ready to start again, and came to one of the border villages in Ilala the same night; but the next day several fell ill for the second time, Susi being quite unable to move.

Muanamazungu, at whose place these relapses occurred, was fully aware of everything that had taken place at Chitambo's, and showed the men the greatest kindness. Not a day passed without his bringing them some present or other, but there was a great disinclination among the people to listen to any details connected with Dr. Livingstone's death. Some return for their kindness was made by Farijala shooting three buffaloes near the town; meat and good-will go together all over Africa, and the liberal sportsman scores points at many a turn. A cow was purchased here for some brass bracelets and calico, and on the twentieth day all were sufficiently strong on their legs to push forward.

The broad waters of the long-looked for Luapula soon appeared in sight. Putting themselves under a guide,

they were conducted to the village of Chisalamalama,
who willingly offered them canoes for the passage across
the next day.*

As one listens to the report that the men give of this
mighty river, he instinctively bends his eyes on a dark
burden laid in the canoe! How ardently would he have
scanned it whose body thus passes across these waters,
and whose spirit, in its last hours' sojourn in this world,
wandered in thought and imagination to its stream!

It would seem that the Luapula at this point is double
the width of the Zambesi at Shupanga. This gives a
breadth of fully four miles. A man could not be seen
on the opposite bank; trees looked small; a gun could
be heard, but no shouting would ever reach a person
across the river—such is the description given by those
who were well able to compare the Luapula with the
Zambesi. Taking to the canoes, they were able to use
the "m'phondo," or punting-pole, for a distance through
reeds, then came clear, deep water for some four hundred yards, again a broad, reedy expanse, followed by
another deep part, succeeded in turn by another current
not so broad as those previously paddled across, and
then, as on the starting side, gradually shoaling water,
abounding in reeds. Two islands lay just above the
crossing-place. Using pole and paddle alternately, the
passage took them fully two hours across this enormous
torrent, which carries off the waters of Bangweolo
toward the north.

---

* The men consider it five days' march "only carrying a gun" from the
Molilamo to the bank of the Luapula—this in rough reckoning, at the rate of
native traveling, would give a distance of say one hundred and twenty to one
hundred and fifty miles.

ARRIVAL AT ILALA—APRIL 29TH, 1873.

A sad mishap befell the donkey the first night of camping beyond the Luapula, and this faithful and sorely-tried servant was doomed to end his career at this spot!

According to custom, a special stable was built for him close to the men. In the middle of the night a great disturbance, coupled with the shouting of Amoda, aroused the camp. The men rushed out, and found the stable broken down, and the donkey gone. Snatching some logs, they set fire to the grass, as it was pitch dark, and by the light saw a lion close to the body of the poor animal, which was quite dead. Those who had caught up their guns on the first alarm fired a volley, and the lion made off. It was evident that the donkey had been seized by the nose, and instantly killed. At daylight the spoor showed that the guns had taken effect. The lion's blood lay in a broad track (for he was apparently injured in the back, and could only drag himself along); but the foot-prints of a second lion were too plain to make it advisable to track him far in the thick cover he had reached, and so the search was abandoned. The body of the donkey was left behind; but two canoes remained near the village, and it is most probable that it went to make a feast at Chisalamalama's.

Traveling through incessant swamp and water, they were fain to make their next stopping-place in a spot where an enormous ant-hill spread itself out—a small island in the waters. A fire was lighted, and by employing hoes, most of them dug something like a form to sleep in on the hard earth.

Thankful to leave such a place, their guide led them next day to the village of Kawinga, whom they describe as a tall man, of singularly light color, and the owner of a gun, a unique weapon in these parts, but one already made useless by wear and tear. The next village, N'kossu's, was much more important. The people, called Kawende, formerly owned plenty of cattle, but now they are reduced; the Banyamwezi have put them under the harrow, and but few herds remain. It is a somewhat singular fact that the hump quite disappears in the lake breed; the cows would pass for respectable short-horns.

A present was made to the caravan of a cow; but it seems that the rule, "First catch your hare," is in full force in N'kossu's pastures. The animals are exceedingly wild, and a hunt has to be set on foot whenever beef is wanted; it was so in this case. Safene and Muanuasere, with their guns, essayed to settle the difficulty. The latter, an old hunter, was not likely to do much harm; but Safene, firing wildly at the cow, hit one of the villagers, and smashed the bone of the poor fellow's thigh. Although it was clearly an accident, such things do not readily settle themselves down on this assumption in Africa. The chief, however, behaved very well. He told them a fine would have to be paid on the return of the wounded man's father, and it had better be handed to him, for by law the blame would fall on him, as the entertainer of the man who had brought about the injury. He admitted that he had ordered all his people to stand clear of the spot where the disaster occurred, but he supposed that in this instance his orders had not been heard. They had not sufficient goods in any case to respond to the demand. The process adopted to set the broken limb is a sample of native surgery which must not be passed over.

First of all, a hole was dug, say two feet deep and four in length, in such a manner that the patient could sit in it with his legs out before him. A large leaf was then bound round the fractured thigh, and earth thrown in so that the patient was buried up to the chest. The next act was to cover the earth which lay over the man's legs with a thick layer of mud; then plenty of sticks and grass were collected, and a fire lighted on the top directly over the fracture. To prevent the smoke smothering the sufferer, they held a tall mat as a screen before his face, and the operation went on. After some time the heat reached the limbs under-ground. Bellowing with fear, and covered with perspiration, the man implored them to let him out. The authorities concluding that he had been under treatment a sufficient time, quickly burrowed down and lifted him from the hole. He was now held perfectly fast, while two strong men stretched the wounded limb with all their might! Splints duly prepared were afterward bound round it, and we must hope that in due time benefit accrued; but as the ball had passed through the limb, we must have our doubts on the subject. The villagers told Chuma that after the Banyamwezi engagements they constantly treated bad gunshot-wounds in this way with perfect success.

Leaving N'kossu's they rested one night at another village belonging to him, and then made for the territory of the Wa Ussi. Here they met with a surly welcome, and were told they must pass on. No doubt the intelligence that they were carrying their master's body had a great deal to do with it, for the news seemed to spread with the greatest rapidity in all directions. Three times they camped in the forest, and, for a wonder, began to find some dry ground. The path lay in the direct line of Chawende's town, parallel to the north shore of the lake, and at no great distance from it.

Some time previously a solitary Unyamwesi had attached himself to the party at Chitankooi's, where he had been left sick by a passing caravan of traders; this man now assured them the country before them was well known to him.

Approaching Chawende's, according to native etiquette, Amoda and Sabouri went on in front to inform the chief, and to ask leave to enter his town. As they did not come back, Muanuasere and Chuma set off after them, to ascertain the reason of the delay. No better success seemed to attend this second venture; so, shouldering their burdens, all went forward in the track of the four messengers.

In the mean time Chuma and Muanuasere met Amoda and Sabouri coming back toward them with five men. They reported that they had entered the town, but found it a very large stockaded place; moreover, two other villages of equal size were close to it. Much pombe-drinking was going on. On approaching the chief, Amoda had rested his gun against the principal hut innocently enough. Chawende's son, drunk and quarrelsome, made this a cause of offence, and, swaggering up, he insolently asked them how they dared to do such a thing. Chawende interfered, and for the moment prevented further trouble; in fact, he himself seems to have been inclined to grant the favor which was asked; however, there was danger brewing, and the men retired.

When the main body met them returning, tired with
their fruitless errand, a consultation took place. Wood
there was none.   To scatter about and find materials
with which to build shelter for the night would only
offer a great temptation to these drunken, excited people
to plunder the baggage.   It was resolved to make for
the town.

When they reached the gate of the stockade they were
flatly refused admittance, those inside telling them to
go down to the river and camp on the bank.   They
replied that this was impossible; that they were tired,
it was very late, and nothing could be found there to
give them shelter.   Meeting with no different answer,
Safene said, "Why stand talking to them? let us get
in somehow or other;" and, suiting the action to the
word, they pushed the men back who stood in the gate-
way.   Safene got through, and Muanuasere climbed
over the top of the stockade, followed by Chuma, who
instantly opened the gate wide and let his companions
through.   Hostilities might still have been averted had
better counsel prevailed.

The men began to look about for huts in which to
deposit their things, when the same drunken fellow
drew a bow and fired at Muanuasere.   The man called
out to the others to seize him, which was done in an
instant.   A loud cry now burst forth that the chief's
son was in danger, and one of the people hurling a
spear, wounded Sabouri slightly in the thigh· this was
the signal for a general scrimmage.

Chawende's men fled from the town; the drums beat
the assembly in all directions, and an immense number
flocked to the spot from the two neighboring villages,

armed with their bows, arrows, and spears. An assault
instantly began from the outside. N'chise was shot with
an arrow in the shoulder through the palisade, and
N'taru in the finger. Things were becoming desperate.
Putting the body of Dr. Livingstone and all their goods
and chattels in one hut, they charged out of the town,
and fired on the assailants, killing two and wounding
several others. Fearing that they would only gather together in the other remaining villages and renew the attack at night, the men carried these quickly one by one,
and subsequently burned six others, which were built on
the same side of the river ; then crossing over, they fired
on the canoes which were speeding toward the deep water
of Bangweolo, through the channel of the Lopopussi,
with disastrous results to the fugitive people.

Returning to the town, all was made safe for the
night. By the fortunes of war, sheep, goats, fowls, and
an immense quantity of food fell into their hands, and
they remained for a week to recruit. Once or twice
they found men approaching at night to throw fire on
the roofs of the huts from outside; but, with this exception, they were not interfered with. On the last day
but one, a man approached and called to them, at the
top of his voice, not to set fire to the chief's town (it
was his that they occupied) ; for the bad son had
brought all this upon them ; he added that the old man
had been overruled, and they were sorry enough for his
bad conduct.

Listening to the account given of this occurrence,
one cannot but lament the loss of life, and the whole
circumstances of the fight. While, on the one hand,
we may imagine that the loss of a cool, conciliatory,

brave leader was here felt in a grave degree, we must also see that it was known far and wide that this very loss was now a great weakness to his followers. There is no surer sign of mischief in Africa than these trumpery charges of bewitching houses by placing things on them; some such overstrained accusation is generally set in the front rank when other difficulties are to come; drunkenness is pretty much the same thing in all parts of the world, and gathers misery around it as easily in an African village as in an English city. Had the cortege submitted to extortion and insult, they felt that their night by the river would have been a precarious one, even if they had been in a humor to sleep in a swamp when a town was at hand. These things gave occasion to them to resort to force. The desperate nature of their whole enterprise in starting for Zanzibar perhaps had accumulated its own stock of determination, and now it found vent under evil provocation. If there is room for any other feeling than regret, it lies in the fact that, on mature consideration and in sober moments, the people who suffered cast the real blame on the right shoulders.

For the next three days after leaving Chawende's, they were still in the same inundated fringe of bouga which surrounds the Lake, and on each occasion had to camp at night-fall wherever a resting place could be found in the jungle, reaching Chama's village on the fourth day. A delay of forty-eight hours was necessary, as Susi's wife fell ill; and for the next few marches she was carried in a kitanda. They met an Unyamwezi man here, who had come from Kumba-kumba's town in the Wa Ussi district. He related to them how on

two occasions the Wanyamwezi had tried to carry Chawende's town by assault, but had been repulsed both
times. It would seem that, with the strong footing
these invaders have in the country, armed as they are
besides with the much-dreaded guns, it can only be a
matter of time before the whole rule, such as it is, passes
into the hands of the new-comers.

The next night was spent in the open air, before coming to the scattered huts of Ngumbu's, where a motley
group of stragglers, for the most part Wabisa, were
busy felling the trees and clearing the land for cultivation. However, the little community gave them a welcome, in spite of the wide-spread report of the fighting
at Chawende's and dancing and drumming were kept
up till morning.

One more night was passed in the plain, and they
reached a tributary of the Lopopussi River, called the
M'Pamba ; it is a considerable stream, and takes one up
to the chest in crossing. They now drew near to Chiwaie's town, which they describe as a very strong place,
fortified with a stockade and ditch. Shortly before
reaching it some villagers tried to pick a quarrel with
them for carrying flags. It was their invariable custom
to make the drummer-boy, Majwara, march at their
head, while the union-jack and the red colors of Zanzibar were carried in a foremost place in the line. Fortunately a chief of some importance came up and stopped
the discussion, or there might have been more mischief,
for the men were in no temper to lower their flag, knowing their own strength pretty well by this time. Making
their settlement close to Chiwaie's, they met with much
kindness, and were visited by crowds of the inhabitants.

Three days' journey brought them to Chiwaie's uncle's village; sleeping two nights in the jungle, they made Chungu's, and in another day's march found themselves, to their great delight, at Kapesha's. They knew their road from this point, for on the southern route with Dr. Livingstone they had stopped here, and could therefore take up the path that leads to Tanganyika. Hitherto their course had been easterly, with a little northing; but now they turned their backs to the lake, which they had held on the right hand since crossing the Luapula, and struck almost north.

From Kapesha's to Lake Bangweolo is a three days' march, as the crow flies, for a man carrying a burden. They saw a large quantity of iron and copper wire being made here by a party of Unyamwezi. The process is as follows: A heavy piece of iron, with a funnel-shaped hole in it, is firmly fixed in the fork of a tree. A fine rod is then thrust into it, and a line attached to the first few inches which can be coaxed through. A number of men haul on this line, singing and dancing in tune, and thus it is drawn through the first drill; it is subsequently passed through others to render it still finer, and excellent wire is the result. Leaving Kapesha, they went through many of the villages already enumerated in Dr. Livingstone's diary. Chama's people came to see them as they passed by him, and, after some mutterings and growlings, Kasonga gave them leave to buy food at his town. Reaching Chama's headquarters, they camped outside, and received a civil message, telling them to convey his orders to the people on the banks of the Kalongwese, that the travelers must be ferried safely across. They found great fear and misery prevailing in the neighborhood, from the constant raids made by Kumba-kumba's men.

Leaving the Kalongwese behind them, they made for M'sama's son's town, meeting four men on the way who were going from Kumba-kumba to Chama to beat up recruits for an attack on the Katanga people. The request was sure to be met with alarm and refusal, but it served very well to act the part taken by the wolf in the fable. A grievance would immediately be made of it, and Chama "eaten up" in due course for daring to gainsay the stronger man. Such is too frequently the course of native oppression. At last Kumba-kumba's town came in sight. Already the large district of Itawa has tacitly allowed itself to be put under the harrow by this ruffianly Zanzibar Arab. Black-mail is levied in all directions, and the petty chiefs, although really under tribute to Nsama, are sagacious enough to keep in with the powers that be. Kumba-kumba showed the men a storehouse full of elephants' tusks. A small detachment was sent off to try and gain tidings of one of the Nassick boys, who had mysteriously disappeared a day or two previously on the march. At the time no great apprehensions were felt, but as he did not turn up, the grass was set on fire in order that he might see the smoke if he had wandered, and guns were fired. Some think he purposely went off rather than carry a load any further; while others fear he may have been killed. Certain it is that after a five days' search in all directions no tidings could be gained either here or at Chama's, and nothing more was heard of him.

Numbers of slaves were collected here. On one occasion they saw five gangs bound neck to neck by chains, and working in the gardens outside the towns.

The talk was still about the break-up of Casembe's power, for it will be recollected that Kumba-kumba and Pemba-motu had killed him a short time before; but by far the most interesting news that reached them was that a party of Englishmen, headed by Dr. Livingstone's son, on their way to relieve his father, had been seen at Bagamoio some months previously.

The chief showed them every kindness during their five days' rest, and was most anxious that no mishap should by any chance occur to their principal charge. He warned them to beware of hyenas, at night more especially, as the quarter in which they had camped had no stockade around it as yet.

Marching was now much easier, and the men quickly found they had crossed the water-shed. The Lovu ran in front of them on its way to Tanganyika. The Kalongwese, we have seen, flows to Lake Moero in the opposite direction. More to their purpose it was, perhaps, to find the terror of Kumba-kumba dying away as they traveled in a northeasterly direction, and came among the Mwambi. As yet no invasion had taken place. A young chief, Chungu, did all he could for them, for when the Doctor explored these regions before, Chungu had been much impressed with him; and now, throwing off all the native superstition, he looked on the arrival of the dead body as a cause of real sorrow.

Asoumani had some luck in hunting, and a fine buffalo was killed near the town. According to native game laws (which in some respects are exceedingly strict in Africa), Chungu had a right to a fore-leg—had it been an elephant, the tusk next the ground would have

40

been his, past all doubt—in this instance, however, the men sent in a plea that theirs was no ordinary case, and that hunger had laws of its own; they begged to be allowed to keep the whole carcass, and Chungu not only listened to their story, but willingly waived his claim to the chief's share.

It is to be hoped that these sons of Tafuna, the head and father of the Amambwi a lungu, may hold their own. They seem a superior race, and this man is described as a worthy leader. His brothers, Kasonso, Chitimbwa, Sombe, and their sister Mombo, are all notorious for their reverence for Tafuna. In their villages an abundance of colored homespun cloth speaks for their industry; while from the numbers of dogs and elephant-spears no further testimony is needed to show that the character they bear as great hunters is well deserved.

The steep descent to the lake now lay before them, and they came to Kasakalawe's. Here it was that the Doctor had passed weary months of illness on his first approach to Tanganyika in previous years. The village contained but few of its old inhabitants, but those few received them hospitably enough, and mourned the loss of him who had been so well appreciated when alive. So they journeyed on day by day till the southern end of the lake was rounded.

The previous experience of the difficult route along the heights bordering on Tanganyika made them determine to give the lake a wide berth this time, and for this purpose they held well to the eastward, passing a number of small deserted villages, in one of which they camped nearly every night. It was necessary to go through the Fipa country, but they learned from one

man and another that the chief, Kafoofi, was very
anxious that the body should not be brought near to
his town; indeed, a guide was purposely thrown in
their way who led them past by a considerable detour.
Kafoofi stands well with the coast Arabs. One, Ngom-
besassi by name, was at the time living with him, accompanied by his retinue of slaves. He had collected·
a very large quantity of ivory further in the interior,
but dared not approach nearer at present to Unyanyembe with it, to risk the chance of meeting one of Mirambo's hordes.

This road across the plains seems incomparably the
best. No difficulty whatever was experienced, and one
cannot but lament the toil and weariness which Dr.
Livingstone endured while holding a course close to
Tanganyika; although one must bear in mind that by
no other means at the time could he complete his survey
of this great inland sea, or acquaint us with its harbors,
its bays, and the rivers which find their way into it on
the east. These are details which will prove of value
when small vessels come to navigate it in the future.

The chief feature after leaving this point was a three
days' march over Lambalamfipa, an abrupt mountain
range, which crosses the country east and west, and
attains, it would seem, an altitude of some four thousand feet. Looking down on the plain from its highest
passes a vast lake appears to stretch away in front
toward the north, but an descending this resolves itself
into a glittering plain, for the most part covered with
saline incrustations. The path lay directly across this.
The difficulties they anticipated had no real existence,
for small villages were found, and water was not scarce,

although brackish. The first demand for toll was made near here, but the headman allowed them to pass for fourteen strings of beads. Susi says that this plain literally swarms with herds of game of all kinds; giraffe and zebra were particularly abundant, and lions reveled in such good quarters. The settlements they came to belonged chiefly to elephant hunters. Farijala and Muanuasere did well with the buffalo, and plenty of beef came into camp.

They gained some particulars concerning a salt-water lake on their right, at no very considerable distance. It was reported to them to be smaller than Tanganyika, and goes by the name Bahari ya Muarooli—the sea of Muarooli—for such is the name of the paramount chief who lives on its shore, and, if we mistake not, the very Merere, or his successor, about whom Dr. Livingstone from time to time showed such interest. They now approached the Likwa River, which flows to this inland sea; they describe it as a stream running breast-high, with brackish water; little satisfaction was got by drinking from it.

Just as they came to the Likwa, a long string of men was seen on the opposite side filing down to the water, and being uncertain of their intentions, precautions were quickly taken to insure the safety of the baggage. Dividing themselves into three parties, the first detachment went across to meet the strangers, carrying the Arab flag in front. Chuma headed another band at a little distance in the rear of these, while Susi and a few more crouched in the jungle, with the body concealed in a roughly-made hut. Their fears, however, were needless; it turned out to be a caravan bound for Fipa to

HIPPOPOTAMUS IN HIS LAIR.

hunt elephants and buy ivory and slaves. The new
arrivals told them that they had come straight through
Unyanyembe from Bagamoio, on the coast, and that the
Doctor's death had already been reported there by
natives of Fipa.

With no small satisfaction the men learned from the
outwardbound caravan that the previous story was a

true one, and they were assured that Dr. Livingstone's
son, with two Englishmen and a quantity of goods, had
already reached Unyanyembe.

The country here showed all the appearance of a salt-
pan; indeed, a quantity of very good salt was collected
by one of the men, who thought he could turn an honest
bunch of beads with it at Unyanyembe.

Petty tolls were levied on them. Kampama's deputy
required four dotis, and an additional tax of six was
paid to the chief of the Kanongo when his town was
reached.

The Lungwa River bowls away here toward Tanganyika. It is a quick, tumbling stream, leaping among
the rocks and boulders, and in its deeper pools it affords
cool delight to schools of hippopotami. The men, who
had hardly tasted good water since crossing Lambalamfipa, are loud in its praise. Muanuasere improved relations with the people at the next town by opportunely
killing another buffalo, and all took a three days' rest.
Yet another caravan met them, bound likewise for the
interior, and adding further particulars about the Englishmen at Unyanyembe. This quickened the pace
till they found at one stage they were melting two days
of the previous outward journey into one.

Arriving at Baula, Jacob Wainwright, the scribe of
the party, was commissioned to write an account of the
distressing circumstances of the Doctor's death, and
Chuma, taking three men with him, pressed on to deliver it to the English party in person. The rest of the
cortege followed them through the jungle to Chilunda's
village. On the outskirts they came across a number of
Wagogo hunting elephants with dogs and spears; but

THE AFRICAN ELEPHANT.

although they were well treated by them, and received
presents of honey and food, they thought it better to
keep these men in ignorance of the charge.

The Manyara River was crossed, on its way to Tanganyika, before they got to Chikooloo. Leaving this
village behind them, they advanced to the Ugunda district, now ruled by Kalimangombi, the son of Mbereke,
the former chief, and so on to Kasekera, which, it will
be remembered, is not far from Unyanyembe.

20*th October*, 1873.—We will here run on ahead with
Chuma on his way to communicate with the new arrivals. He reached the Arab settlement without let or
hinderance. Lieutenant Cameron was quickly put in
possession of the main facts of Dr. Livingstone's death
by reading Jacob's letter, and Chuma was questioned

concerning it in the presence of Dr. Dillon and Lieutenant Murphy. It was a disappointment to find that
the reported arrival of Mr. Oswell Livingstone was entirely erroneous; but Lieutenant Cameron showed the
wayworn men every kindness. Chuma rested one day
before setting out to relieve his comrades, to whom he
had arranged to make his way as soon as possible.
Lieutenant Cameron expressed a fear that it would not
be safe for him to carry the cloth he was willing to furnish them with, if he had not a stronger convoy, as he
himself had suffered too sorely from terrified bearers on
his way thither; but the young fellows were pretty well
acquainted with native marauders by this time, and set
off without apprehension.

And now the greater part of their task is over. The
weather-beaten company wind their way into the old
well-known settlement of Kwihara. A host of Arabs
and their attendant slaves meet them, as they sorrow-
fully take their charge to the same tembe in which the
"weary waiting" was endured before, and then they
submit to the systematic questioning which the native
traveler is so well able to sustain.

News in abundance was offered in return. The porters
of the Livingstone East Coast Aid Expedition had plenty
to relate to the porters sent by Mr. Stanley. Mirambo's
war dragged on its length, and matters had changed
very little since they were there before, either for better
or for worse. They found the English officers extremely
short of goods; but Lieutenant Cameron, no doubt
with the object of his expedition full in view, very properly felt it a first duty to relieve the wants of the party
that had performed this herculean feat of bringing the

THE TEMPORARY VILLAGE IN WHICH DR. LIVINGSTONE'S BODY WAS PREPARED.

633

body of the traveler he had been sent to relieve, together with every article belonging to him at the time of his death, as far as this main road to the coast.

In talking to the men about their intentions, Lieutenant Cameron had serious doubts whether the risk of taking the body of Dr. Livingstone through the Ugogo country ought to be run. It very naturally occurred to him that Dr. Livingstone might have felt a wish during life to be buried in the same land in which the remains of his wife lay—it will be remembered that the grave of Mrs. Livingstone is at Shupanga, on the Zambesi. All this was put before the men; but they steadily adhered to their first conviction, that it was right, at all risks, to attempt to bear their master home, and therefore they were no longer urged to bury him at Kwihara.

To the new-comers it was of great interest to examine the boxes which the men had conveyed from Bangweolo. As we have seen, they had carefully packed up everything at Chitambo's—books, instruments, clothes, and all which would bear special interest in time to come, from having been associated with Livingstone in his last hours.

It cannot be conceded for a moment that these poor fellows would have been right in forbidding this examination, when we consider the relative position in which natives and English officers must always stand to each other; but it is a source of regret to relate that the chief part of Livingstone's instruments were taken out of the packages and appropriated for future purposes. The instruments with which all his observations had been made throughout a series of discoveries extending over seven years—aneroid barometers, compasses, thermometers, the sextant, and other things—have gone on a new series of travels, to incur innumerable risks of loss, while one only of his thermometers comes to hand.

We could well have wished these instruments safe in England with the small remnant of Livingstone's personal property, which was allowed to be shipped from Zanzibar.

The Doctor had deposited four bales of cloth as a reserve stock with the Arabs, and these were immediately forthcoming for the march down.

Lieutenant Cameron gave the men to understand that it was agreed Lieutenant Murphy should return to Zanzibar, and asked that if they could attach his party to their march; if so, the men who acted as carriers should receive six dollars a man for their services. This was agreed to. Susi had arranged that they should avoid the main path of the Wagogo; inasmuch as, if difficulty was to be encountered anywhere, it would arise among these lawless, pugnacious people.

By making a ten days' detour at "Jua Singa," and traveling by a path well known to one of their party, through the jungle of Poli ya vengi, they hoped to keep out of harm's way, and to be able to make the cloth hold out with which they were supplied. At length the start was effected, and Dr. Dillon likewise quitted the expedition, to return to the coast. It was necessary to stop, after the first day's march, for a long halt; for one of the women was unable to travel, they found, and progress was delayed till she could resume the journey. There seem to have been some serious misunderstanding between the leaders of Dr. Living-

stone's party and Lieutenant Murphy soon after setting
out, which turned mainly on the subject of beginning
of the day's march. The former, trained in the old
discipline of their master, laid stress on the necessity of
very early rising, to avoid the heat of the day, and perhaps pointed out more bluntly than pleasantly, that if
the Englishmen wanted to improve their health, they
had better do so too. However, to a certain extent,
difficulty was avoided by the two companies pleasing
themselves.

Making an early start, the body was carried to Kasekera by Susi's party, where, from an evident disinclination to receive it into the village, an encampment was
made outside. A consultation now became necessary.
There was no disguising the fact that if they kept along
the main road intelligence would precede them concerning that in which they were engaged, stirring up certain
hostility, and jeopardizing the most precious charge they
had. A plan was quickly hit upon. Unobserved, the
men removed the corpse of the deceased explorer from
the package in which it had hitherto been conveyed,
and buried the bark case in the hut in the thicket
around the village in which they had placed it. The
object now was to throw the villagers off their guard,
by making believe that they had relinquished the attempt to carry the body to Zanzibar. They feigned
that they had abandoned their task, having changed
their minds, and that it must be sent back to Unyanyembe, to be buried there. In the mean time the corpse
of necessity had to be concealed in the smallest space
possible, if they were actually to convey it secretly for
the future; this was quickly managed.

Susi and Chuma went into the wood and stripped off a fresh length of bark from an n'gombe-tree; in this the remains conveniently prepared as to length, were placed, the whole being surrounded with calico in such a manner as to appear like an ordinary traveling bale, which was then deposited with the rest of the goods. They next proceeded to gather a fagot of mapira-stalks, cutting them in lengths of six feet or so, and swathing them round with cloth, to imitate a dead body about to be buried. This done, a paper, folded as to represent a letter, was duly placed in a cleft stick, according to the native letter-carrier's custom, and six trustworthy men were told off ostensibly to go with the corpse to Unyanyembe. With due solemnity the men set out. The villagers were only too thankful to see it, and no one suspected the ruse. It was near sundown. The bearers of the package held on their way till fairly beyond all chance of detection, and then began to dispose of their load. The mapira-sticks were thrown, one by one, far away into the jungle, and when all were disposed of, the wrappings were cunningly got rid of in the same way. Going further on, first one man, and then another sprung clear from the path into the long grass, to leave no trace of footsteps, and the whole party returned by different ways to their companions, who had been anxiously awaiting them during the night. No one could detect the real nature of the ordinary-looking bale, which henceforth was guarded with no relaxed vigilance, and eventually disclosed the bark coffin and wrappings containing Dr. Livingstone's body, on the arrival at Bagamoio. And now, devoid of fear, the people of Kasekera asked them all to come and take up their quarters in the town—a privilege which was denied them so long as it was known that they had the remains of the dead with them.

But a dreadful event was about to recall to their minds how many fall victims to African disease.

Dr. Dillon now came on to Kasekera, suffering much from dysentery; a few hours more, and he shot himself in his tent with a rifle. The malaria imbibed during their stay at Unyanyembe laid upon him the severest form of fever, accompanied by delirum, under which he at length succumbed in one of its violent paroxysms. His remains are interred at Kasekera.

We must follow Susi's troop through a not altogether eventless journey to the sea. Some days afterward, as they wended their way through a rocky place, a little girl in their train, named Losi, met her death in a shocking way. It appears that the poor child was carrying a water-jar on her head in the file of people, when an enormous snake dashed across the path, deliberately struck her in the thigh, and made for a hole in the jungle close at hand. This work of a moment was sufficient, for the poor girl fell mortally wounded. She was carried forward, and all means at hand were applied, but in less than ten minutes the last symptom (foaming at the mouth) set in, and she ceased to breathe.

Here is a well-authenticated instance which goes far to prove the truth of an assertion made to travelers in many parts of Africa. The natives protest that one species of snake will deliberately chase and overtake his victim with lightning speed, and so dreadfully dangerous is it, both from the activity of its poison and its vicious propensities, that it is perilous to approach its quarters. Most singular to relate, an Arab came to some of the men after their arrival at Zanzibar, and told them that he had just come by the Unyanyembe road, and that, while passing the identical spot where this disaster occurred, one of the men was attacked by the same snake, with precisely the same results; in fact, when looking for a place in which to bury him they saw the grave of Losi, and the two lie side by side.

This snake was doubtless a mamba; it is much to be desired that specimens should be procured for purposes of comparison. In Southern Africa so great is the dread it inspires that the Kaffirs will break up a kraal and forsake the place, if a mamba takes up his quarters in the vicinity, and, from what we have seen above, with no undue caution.

Susi, to whom this snake is known in the Shupanga tongue as "bubu," describes it as about twelve feet long, dark in color, of a dirty blue under the belly, with red markings, like the wattles of a cock, on the head. The Arabs go so far as to say that it is known to oppose the passage of a caravan at times. Twisting its tail around a branch, it will strike one man after another in the head with fatal certainty. Their remedy is to fill a pot with boiling water, which is put on the head and carried under the tree. The snake dashes his head into this, and is killed; the story is given for what it is worth.

It would seem that at Ujiji the natives, as in other places, can not bear to have snakes killed. "chatu," a species of python, is common, and, from being highly favored, becomes so tame as to enter houses at night. A little meal is placed on the stool, which the uncanny visitor laps up, and then takes its departure; the men significantly say they never saw it with their own eyes. Another species utters a cry, much like the crowing of a young cock ; this is well authenticated. Yet another black variety has a spine like a black-thorn at the end of the tail, and its bite is extremely deadly.

At the same time it must be added that, considering the enormous number of reptiles in Africa, it rarely occurs that any one is bitten, and a few months' residence suffices to dispel the dread which most travelers feel at the outset.

February, 1874.—No further incident occurred worthy of special notice. At last the coast-town of Bagamoio came in sight, and before many hours were over, a British cruiser conveyed the acting consul, Captain Prideaux, from Zanzibar to the spot which the cortege had reached. Arrangements were quickly made for transporting the remains of Dr. Livingstone to the island, some thirty miles distant, and then it became perhaps rather too painfully plain to the men that their task was finished.

One word on a subject which will commend itself to most before we close this eventful history.

We saw what a train of Indian sepoys, Johanna men, Nassick boys, and Shupanga canoe-men accompanied Dr. Livingstone when he started from Zanzibar in 1866 fto enter upon his last discoveries; of all these, five only could answer to the roll-call as they handed over the dead body of their leader to his countrymen on the shore whither they had returned, and this after eight years' desperate service.

Once more we repeat the names of these men. Susi and James Chuma have been sufficiently prominent throughout—hardly so, perhaps, has Amoda, their com-

rade ever since the Zambesi days of 1864 ; then we have
Abram and Mabruki, each with service to show from
the time he left the Nassick College with the Doctor in
1865. Nor must we forget Ntoaeka and Halima, the
two native girls of whom we have heard such a good
character ; they cast in their lot with the wanderers in
Manyuema. It does seem strange to hear the men say
that no sooner did they arrive at their journey's end
than they were so far frowned out of notice, that not so
much as a passage to the island was offered them when
their burden was borne away. We must hope that it is
not too late—even for the sake of consistency—to put it
on record that *whoever* assisted Livingstone, whether
white or black, has not been overlooked. Surely those
those with whom he spent his last years must not pass
away into Africa again unrewarded, and be lost to sight.

Yes, a very great deal is owing to these five men, and
we say it emphatically. If the world has had gratified
a reasonable wish in learning all that concerns the last
days on earth of a truly noble man and his wonderful
enterprise, the means of doing so could never have been
placed at our disposal but for the ready willingness
which made Susi and Chuma determine, if possible, to
render an account to some of those whom they had
known as their master's old companions. If the geographer finds before him new facts, new discoveries, new
theories, as Livingstone alone could record them, it is
right and proper that he should feel the part these men
have played in furnishing him with such valuable matter. For we repeat that nothing but such leadership
and staunchness as that which organized the march home
from Ilala, and distinguished it throughout, could have

brought Livingstone's bones to England, or his last notes and maps to the outer world. To none does the feat seem so marvelous as to those who know Africa, and the difficulties which must have beset both the first and the last in the enterprise. Thus in his death, not less than in his life, David Livingstone bore testimony to that good-will and kindliness which exists in the heart of the African.

THE END.

OTHER COOPER SQUARE PRESS TITLES OF INTEREST

**IN SEARCH OF
ROBINSON CRUSOE**
Daisuke Takahashi
312 pp., 24 b/w photos
0-8154-1200-2
$24.95 cloth

THE NORTH POLE
Robert E. Peary
Foreword by
Theodore Roosevelt
New introduction by
Robert M. Bryce
472 pp.,
110 b/w illustrations
0-8154-1138-3
$22.95

MY ATTAINMENT OF THE POLE
Dr. Frederick A. Cook
New introduction by
Robert M. Bryce
664 pp.,
52 b/w illustrations
0-8154-1137-5
$22.95

ARCTIC EXPERIENCES
Aboard the Doomed *Polaris*
Expedition and Six Months
Adrift on an Ice-Floe
Captain George E. Tyson
New introduction by
Edward E. Leslie
504 pp.,
78 b/w illustrations
0-8154-1189-8
$24.95 cl.

A NEGRO EXPLORER
AT THE NORTH POLE
Matthew A. Henson
Preface by
Booker T. Washington
Foreword by
Robert E. Peary
New introduction by
Robert M. Bryce
264 pp.,
6 b/w photos, 1 map
0-8154-1125-1
$15.95

THE *KARLUK'S* LAST VOYAGE
An Epic of Death and
Survival in the Arctic
Captain Robert A. Bartlett
New introduction by
Edward E. Leslie
378 pp.,
23 b/w photos, 3 maps
0-8154-1124-3
$18.95

THE VOYAGE OF THE *DISCOVERY*
Scott's First Antarctic
Expedition, 1901–1904
Volumes I & II
Captain Robert F. Scott
Preface by Fridtjof Nansen
New introduction by
Ross MacPhee
Volume I
782 pp.,
187 b/w illustrations,
2 maps
0-8154-1079-4
$35.00 cloth
Volume II
628 pp.,
139 b/w illustrations,
1 map
0-8154-1151-0
$35.00 cloth

THE SOUTH POLE
An Account of the Norwegian
Antarctic Expedition in the
***Fram*, 1910–1912**
Captain Roald Amundsen
Foreword by
Fridtjof Nansen
New introduction by
Roland Huntford
896 pp., 136 b/w photos,
20 maps & charts
0-8154-1127-8
$29.95

THE GREAT WHITE SOUTH
Traveling with Robert F. Scott's
Doomed South Pole Expedition
Herbert G. Ponting
New introduction by
Roland Huntford
518 pp.,
175 b/w illustrations
3 maps & diagrams
0-8154-1161-8
$18.95

EDGE OF THE WORLD:
ROSS ISLAND, ANTARCTICA
A Personal and Historical
Narrative of Exploration,
Adventure, Tragedy, and Survival
Charles Neider
with a new introduction
536 pp., 45 b/w photos,
15 maps
0-8154-1154-5
$19.95

ANTARCTICA
Firsthand Accounts of
Exploration and Endurance
Edited by Charles Neider
468 pp.
0-8154-1023-9
$18.95

EDGE OF THE JUNGLE
William Beebe
New introduction by
Robert Finch
334 pp., 1 b/w photo
0-8154-1160-X
$17.95

AFRICAN GAME TRAILS
An Account of the African
Wanderings of an American
Hunter-Naturalist
Theodore Roosevelt
New introduction by
H. W. Brands
616 pp.,
210 b/w photos and maps
0-8154-1132-4
$22.95

AFRICA EXPLORED
Europeans in the Dark Continent,
1769–1889
Christopher Hibbert
344 pp., 54 b/w
illustrations, 16 maps
0-8154-1193-6
$18.95

STANLEY
The Making of an
African Explorer
Frank McLynn
424 pp., 19 b/w photos &
illustrations
0-8154-1167-7
$18.95

THROUGH THE
BRAZILIAN WILDERNESS
Theodore Roosevelt
New introduction by
H. W. Brands
448 pp.,
9 b/w photos,
3 maps
0-8154-1095-6
$19.95

THE DESERT AND THE SOWN
The Syrian Adventures of the
Female Lawrence of Arabia
Gertrude Bell
New introduction by
Rosemary O'Brien
380 pp., 162 b/w photos
0-8154-1135-9
$19.95

MAN AGAINST NATURE
Firsthand Accounts of
Adventure and Exploration
Edited by Charles Neider
512 pp.
0-8154-1040-9
$18.95